FIRE
AND
LIGHT

James
MacGregor
Burns

FIRE
AND
LIGHT

*How the Enlightenment
Transformed Our World*

THOMAS DUNNE BOOKS
ST. MARTIN'S GRIFFIN
NEW YORK

THOMAS DUNNE BOOKS.
An imprint of St. Martin's Press.

FIRE AND LIGHT. Copyright © 2013 by James MacGregor Burns. All rights reserved. Printed in the United States of America. For information, address St. Martin's Press, 175 Fifth Avenue, New York, N.Y. 10010.

www.thomasdunnebooks.com
www.stmartins.com

The Library of Congress has cataloged the hardcover edition as follows:

Burns, James MacGregor.
　Fire and light : how the enlightenment transformed our world / James MacGregor Burns.—First edition.
　　　p. cm.
　Includes bibliographical references and index.
　　ISBN 978-1-250-02489-3 (hardcover)
　　ISBN 978-1-250-02490-9 (e-book)
　1. Enlightenment—Influence.　2. Enlightenment—France.　3. Enlightenment—Great Britain.　4. Enlightenment—United States.　I. Title.
　　B802.B87 2013
　　940.2'5—dc23

2013023486

ISBN 978-1-250-05392-3 (trade paperback)

St. Martin's Griffin books may be purchased for educational, business, or promotional use. For information on bulk purchases, please contact the Macmillan Corporate and Premium Sales Department at 1-800-221-7945, extension 5442, or write specialmarkets@macmillan.com.

First St. Martin's Griffin Edition: November 2014

10　9　8　7　6　5　4　3　2　1

For

Milton Djuric

and

Susan Dunn

Contents

FIRE
AND
LIGHT

Introduction

Enlightenment as Revolution

For hundreds of years European minds were locked in orthodoxy. Save for scattered rebellions against the Catholic Church and the emperors and kings it anointed, most Europeans had no prospects other than the "life after life" in heaven promised to true believers. With church and state united in their determination to uphold their centuries-old authority, the laboring people were exploited by nobility and clergy, as a Czech layman wrote, "stripped of everything, downtrodden, oppressed, beaten, robbed," and forced by hunger and misery from their land.

At the close of this era, historian Johan Huizinga wrote, "a sombre melancholy weighs on people's souls." Their unhappiness sounded in chronicles or poems. Huizinga recalled a French court ballad:

> *Time of mourning and of temptation,*
> *Age of tears, of envy and of torment,*
> *Time of languor and of damnation,*
> *Age of decline nigh to the end . . .*

Then, like a thunderbolt, Martin Luther's nailing of his *Theses* to a church door in Wittenberg in 1517 shattered the old order. It was, Luther taught, not the pope and his clerical legions who were the source of divine knowledge but a book, the Bible, as read and understood by believers. This radical insight opened the Western mind to new and even revolutionary ideas, both sectarian and secular.

What would happen in a West liberated from orthodoxy? Chaos, warned the Holy See—without a single authority, humankind would dissolve into warring states and factions. The church fathers were right. The Reformation swiftly ignited an age of ceaseless strife as Catholics and Protestants battled for preeminence. By the early seventeenth century, Europe collapsed into a ferocious and engulfing civil war of all against all. Protestant leaders proved as authoritarian and brutal as Catholic princes and cardinals. A great fear dominated ruler and ruled alike—a fear of anarchy in a time of searing religious and political hatreds. Rulers had to deal not only with rival powers but with violence that erupted among their subjects—peasant revolts, urban riots. Even the nobles that surrounded them were a danger. Uneasy was the head that held the crown. Far uneasier were the people who suffered invasions, famine, plagues, persecution.

Yet, amid the devastation, Europe was intellectually alive. A torrent of fresh ideas and intense disputes erupted when the restraints that had bound men's minds for so long were smashed. With the authority of the Catholic Church broken, every phenomenon—from the stars in the heavens above to the bedrock beneath the earth, from the inward lives and spirits of human beings to their blossoming into political communities—was seen in a new light, exposed to a fresh examination, to discussion and debate, as people were encouraged to think for themselves.

It was the beginning of a wondrous era of enlightenment, a time of transforming leadership across the widest fields of action, of creative, revolutionary thought about human nature and liberty and equality and happiness, of ideas that thrilled readers of books and newspapers and echoed on the lips of the illiterate, ideas that brought conflict to courts and parliaments and clashes to city streets and remote villages.

The Enlightenment project would range over three centuries and migrate from the Old World to the New and then around the globe; it would be vast, all-encompassing, cutting across collective life and action, empowering some leaders, destroying others, mobilizing poets and industrialists, factory workers and university students and people's armies. The ideas of the Enlightenment and the leadership and action they inspired would transform the world.

* * *

Change was at the very root of this new era, and knowledge and freedom were change's twinned preconditions and outcomes. Together enlightenment and liberation raised men and women into a condition of possibility, the opportunity to better themselves and their world. And "as the human mind becomes more enlightened" over time, declared the French economist Turgot in 1750, "the whole human race . . . goes on advancing, although at a slow pace, towards greater perfection." Revolutionaries and innovators were inspired to push beyond the status quo in politics and government, science and technology, in entrepreneurship and the arts, in philosophy, in every field of human endeavor.

The human mind was where revolution originated. Breaking from a universe in which God was the final answer to any question, Enlightenment philosophers moved attention to human beings as the measure of all things. Now, as Alexander Pope put it, "[the] proper study of Mankind is Man," especially the human mind and its potentialities. The old philosophy held that the mind was furnished top-to-bottom by God. And mental submission to clerics was imperative, especially among the lower orders, when the alternative was an eternity of hellfire.

But Enlightenment savants condemned these shackles on the human mind. They tested received ideas by the new, unflinching standards of empiricism. Science, previously erected on stilts of axioms and premises, was stripped to the ground. As the founder of the New Science, Francis Bacon, insisted, "Man, being the servant and interpreter of Nature, can do and understand so much and so much only as he has observed in fact or in thought of the course of nature." Only from close observation and careful experiment could the grandest theories be built—the "conclusions of human reason," the general laws that governed nature, such as Isaac Newton's explanation of gravity. The empirical assault on dogma was the method not only of the natural sciences but of such emerging disciplines as sociology, anthropology, and political economy that studied human life in all its complexities. For over a decade, Adam Smith analyzed financial data from all sources to create his groundbreaking account of the new capitalist economy in *The Wealth of Nations*.

That fresh spirit of empiricism transformed the Enlightenment's understanding of the nature of thought itself. John Locke rejected the "received doctrine" that men had "native ideas" stamped "upon their minds in their very first being." Instead he described the mind of an infant as like a "white paper, void of all characters, without any new ideas." The mind was all potential, like wax, according to Locke, to be shaped and vitalized by experience and education. In fact, "the difference to be found in the Manners and Abilities of Men, is owing more to their *Education* than to anything else." Great care, therefore, "is to be had of the forming Children's *Minds*," not least because enlightenment was critical to their preparation to live in rational and virtuous freedom, the highest condition of human life.

The tool for liberation, the mind's crowning glory, was its power to *reason*. The "motto of enlightenment," according to Immanuel Kant, was "Have courage to use your own reason!" By reasoning, the mind exposed false-hoods and discovered truths and gave birth to far-reaching ideas from an intake of humble facts. Reason equipped men and women to live freely, enabled them to make their own way, to think and act for themselves, even the lower orders of servants and shoemakers, peasants and pieceworkers. And when people began to think for themselves, an English friend of Jean-Jacques Rousseau cautioned ironically in 1792, "when they have carried their temerity of free-thinking perhaps so far as to suspect that nations may exist without monks or tyrants, it is already too late to burn libraries or philosophers."

* * *

If enlightenment empowered the human mind for new worlds of liberty and self-government, why should it not enable a community to govern it-self, free of monks and tyrants? Enlightenment philosophers knew men *needed* government—that without it, in an anarchic "state of nature," it was every man for himself, making life, in Thomas Hobbes's vivid phrase, "soli-tary, poore, nasty, brutish, and short." But the regimes of that age, whether absolute monarchies or parliamentary governments under aristocratic con-trol, answered neither to their subjects' wants and needs nor to their dig-nity as human beings. A new doctrine of natural rights—to life, liberty, and property, in Locke's influential formulation—established those values, which belonged to all people by birth, as the bedrock of individual free-dom. How were they to be secured under conditions that kept most of the populace voiceless and in subjection?

It became a cornerstone of Enlightenment thought that governments were not, as Locke put it, born of "the *Ordinance of God* and *Divine Institu-tion*" and descended from "*Adam*'s Monarchical Power," but were the work of men in a time and place and as such could be changed by men. In the Declaration of Independence, Thomas Jefferson contended that inasmuch as government derived its "just powers from the consent of the governed," the people had the right to abolish it when it violated its compact with them, as when a ruler, in Locke's example, "sets up his own Arbitrary Will in place of the Laws." Such a tyrant was the true rebel, an aggressor in a war against his own people. His abuses of power led to "the *Dissolution of the Government.*"

Governments, as Locke well knew, did not simply dissolve. Many power-ful factors were behind the great revolutionary movements of the era: al-ways the struggle for political power; typically, severe economic and social crises; and, too often, searing religious conflict. But in the upheavals that transformed Britain, America, and France in these centuries, the ideas of the Enlightenment were at the center of the action, as both inspiration and end. With them, leaders and their activist followers justified rebellions, explained motives, and fashioned visions for change based on the values they risked their lives and liberties to achieve. The American colonies in the years before 1776 were a hotbed of debates over representation, self-determination, natural rights, and, above all, liberty, the most cherished value in the war for independence. In 1787, with the French government on the verge of fiscal collapse, King Louis XVI himself tried on the robes of Enlightenment philosophy. His controller general declared that the royal principle of "as the king wills, so wills the law" would be amended to "as the people's happiness wills, so wills the king." The king's people were not persuaded and two years later sent deputies to the Estates-General who were genuine men of enlightenment, authors of tracts that challenged royal policies, advocates of legal and economic reforms, members of learned academies, and sometimes philosophes themselves. To their own surprise, they became revolutionaries, too, and, "with all the force of a conversion experience," in historian Timothy Tackett's words, began to think that "a new political order and a new system of social values could actually be realized."

This sweeping ambition could not have been conceived without the Enlightenment and the possibilities it created for transformation. The institutions American revolutionaries established in 1789 and the settlement forged by British statesmen a century earlier after the Glorious Revolution that enshrined the liberties of citizens were no less achievements of Enlightenment thought, the work of leaders who took seriously the intellectual currents of their time and were responding to the rising aspirations of their people.

And their accomplishments stood the test of time. Even the French Revolution, with stages that appeared to fulfill Enlightenment expectations and others that perverted them, remains at the core of French identity and a touchstone of its politics. Still, it was an Enlightenment imperative that, in the words of Jefferson, "laws and institutions" advance "hand in hand with progress of the human mind." As people became more enlightened and their "manners and opinions change with the change of circumstances," their political order must "keep pace with the times."

The greatest change of circumstances, which both confirmed and challenged the Enlightenment, was the Industrial Revolution that began to sweep the West in the eighteenth century. The power of enlightened science and technology, as well as the Enlightenment's celebration of social mobility through individual achievement and ambition, created what historian Joel Mokyr called the "enlightened economy," a new economic order that especially empowered the middle classes. They would dominate politics and society in the nineteenth century. Liberalism was their ideology, championing individualism and personal liberty and free enterprise.

Yet progress in the Industrial Revolution left behind another new class— impoverished workers laboring in often subhuman conditions in factories, fields, and mines, while living with their starveling and sick families in overgrown cities and squalid factory towns. Philosophy came to speak for these working men, women, and children only slowly, at first through Utopian thinkers and radical journalists; it was not until 1867, when Karl Marx published *Das Kapital,* a monument to the Enlightenment's critical method and empiricism, that Adam Smith's *The Wealth of Nations* was answered by an equally compelling study that centered on the exploitation of labor by rampant capitalism.

Meanwhile, barred in Britain, France, and the United States from forming "combinations," workers searched for their own answers. They realized that among the inequalities confronting them was that of knowledge; ignorance was a tool of capitalist domination. In response, workers sought to enlighten themselves. They opened lending libraries and newsrooms and met together in reading groups. They devoured working-class journals as well as Voltaire's essays and Thomas Paine's *Age of Reason.* They absorbed the ideas of contemporary thinker-activists like Louis Blanc, a French apostle of organized labor, and Englishman William Cobbett with his plainspoken depiction of the "two classes of men" the industrial economy had created, "*masters,* and *abject dependants.*"

At stake for laborers was the full dignity of human beings promised by Enlightenment precepts. They wanted to be treated as men and women capable of reason and of freedom, not as wage slaves or beasts of burden; they wanted to join together in order to fight for their common interests and to have a voice in choosing those who governed them.

Enlightenment was their pathway, the tenacious faith that self-improvement would lead ultimately, through enlightened activism, to improvement in their conditions. And that persistent drive for betterment gradually spread its transforming power until few corners of the earth remained untouched. The nineteenth-century wars of liberation against Spanish rule that spread across Latin America were led by enlightened generals, including Simón Bolívar, who followed Locke and Montesquieu and others but, equally, embraced the Enlightenment injunction to think for oneself. In the twentieth century, anticolonial campaigns in Asia and Africa drew on Enlightenment ideas imported by the Westerners that native peoples now sought to evict. Proclaiming Vietnam's separation from French rule in 1945, Ho Chi Minh's Declaration of Independence opened with Jefferson's "immortal statement" on human equality and inalienable rights. In South Africa, the anti-apartheid movement appealed to the principles of majority rule and equal rights while its leaders, notably Nelson Mandela, spoke eloquently of a "rainbow nation" of toleration and respect for white minority rights.

The last four centuries have demonstrated that once the flame of Enlightenment has been lit, however much it might be repressed or distorted, it cannot be extinguished. Enlightenment remains the most powerful tool for challenging authority and liberating the human mind, an inspiration to leaders and followers worldwide, a method for effective change, and a framework of values by which that change can be measured. For these same reasons, the Enlightenment remains a target for authorities of all colorations, who regard ignorance—and in modern propaganda terms, minds force-fed with falsehoods—as the bulwarks of their power, apart from brutal force. But in an age of quicksilver networks of mutual enlightenment that continually widen through newer and newer social media, ignorance is a wasting resource.

Even so, as demonstrated by the overthrow of despots in Tunisia, Egypt, Yemen, and Libya in the remarkable Arab Spring launched late in 2010, revolution may put people on the path to freedom and self-government, but many urgent questions about means and ends remain. English, American, and French revolutionaries faced them centuries ago, but they are no less vital and controversial today, not only in nations struggling to invent a new civil society but in regimes long-established on enlightened principles. The latter, too, face, as they ought to, constant critical examination of their dedication to those principles. What should a people expect from government? Who should lead and how are leaders to be chosen? How should leadership be made accountable, how should its powers be limited, and how can the rights of all citizens be protected? How can people be readied to play an enlightened role in exercising their freedom and governing themselves? How far should tolerance extend for those of differing religious or political views or ethnicities or classes? In what ways should government promote the great Enlightenment values of freedom and equality for all of its people? Are freedom and equality complementary or clashing values?

So long as the potential for human betterment—the philosophers' "perfectibility of man"—persists, Enlightenment will be a living, vital work in progress, a continuing condition of possibility. Its transformative power has always been in the crucial binding of means and ends. It has never been limited to pondering purely abstract ideas nor has it been a guide for the merely pragmatic. To consider a principled outcome has been to consider the method to achieve it. For men and women, Enlightenment is both the destination and the road. It means that people think for themselves and act in their own interests, with reason as their tool and enlightened values to live by and strive for. They become interpreters of their world and shapers of it. "Know then thyself," Alexander Pope urged when declaring the proper study of mankind. In the age of the Enlightenment, to seek self-knowledge is to discover humanity.

1

The Revolution in Ideas

A century after Martin Luther unleashed the Reformation in Wittenberg, strife between Catholics and Protestants was reaching a terrible climax. The Thirty Years' War engulfed Europe in brutal and chaotic conflict. Mercenary armies of competing emperors and popes, princes, dukes, and archbishops roamed Europe, pillaging towns and villages and slaughtering civilians. They destroyed food stocks and spread plague. Some regions lost more than half of their population. And even as the frenzy of all-against-all conflict gripped the continent, bloody civil war mounted in England that would end in a king's execution and rule by Protestant zealots. Many Europeans despaired that the Apocalypse was at hand.

It was in this world of violence and fear that the first, frail lamps of the Enlightenment were lit. The early philosophers witnessed the devastation, testimony to the desperate need for new thinking, for a revolution in ideas about humankind. The question was simple and stark: How could people be secure in their lives, empowered to make choices conducive to their peace and liberty and happiness?

But those early philosophers were scarcely secure in their own lives or free to publish their writings. Apart from the deadly hazards of war, they faced persecution for their ideas. It could come from Catholics or Protestants or, in Benedict de Spinoza's case, his fellow Jews. It might appear as the wrath of kings or of generals or the fury of a mob intent on lynching. Exile, freely chosen or not, could swiftly become dangerous as political winds shifted and sympathetic rulers changed their minds. The Catholic Inquisition condemned heretics like Galileo Galilei, while the church's *Index Liborum Prohibitorum* condemned their works. Censorship operated throughout Europe; any petty dukedom might have its own list of banned books. And it took a brave printer to publish an author whose writings had been denounced publicly as blasphemous and dangerous. The massed attacks of priests and preachers, of traditionalist academics and government officials, meant that some of the most challenging works of philosophers were suppressed or hidden and unpublished in their lifetimes. This left their ideas to the mercies of fate or to loyal, tenacious followers willing to risk their own liberties and lives to bring them to the public.

In its early years, for the Enlightenment to take root and thrive, its leadership and its ideas had to *survive*.

THE STATE OF NATURE

Few men of the Enlightenment were as disputatious as Britain's Thomas Hobbes. He provoked controversies in matters ranging from God's responsibility for the sins of man to fine points of Greek and Latin grammar to mathematics, including his attempt to square the circle. Like so many of the great intellectuals of the age, he was a polymath, putting his stamp on nearly all the cutting-edge issues, with an intellectual leadership characterized as much by the enemies he provoked as by the followers he won. Unlike other Enlightenment philosophers—and here was a prime source of controversy—Hobbes had a remarkably grim view of human nature, one that saw men plunged into a violent anarchy, redeemed only by their power to reason and thus create for themselves safety in civil society. Hobbes indirectly offered reason an exceptional tribute by suggesting it could rescue men from utterly desperate conditions.

Hobbes's difficult early years fed his combativeness, as well as his bleak view of what men were and how they lived. Born in 1588, in the reign of Queen Elizabeth I, he was brought up in an impoverished home ruled by his father, a poorly educated, quarrelsome curate who was given more to bouts with alcohol than churchly duties. Excommunicated after slandering another clergyman and facing new charges for brawling in a churchyard, Thomas Hobbes Sr. fled into obscurity. Happily, young Hobbes had a prosperous uncle, a glover able to put his young nephew through Oxford. Hobbes entered the university at the tender age of fourteen.

Shy and sickly, he had to compete with classmates two or three years older, in classes usually taught in Latin. He was no grind, absorbed more by catching jackdaws at his window than by attending dull classes, but he was presentable enough on graduation to be sought out by members of the Cavendish clan, a wealthy and powerful family with grand estates at Chatsworth and Hardwick. Hobbes was hired to tutor William Cavendish, heir to the first earl of Devonshire and only two years his junior, and he remained closely tied to the family for the rest of his long life, eventually tutoring William's son and heir, serving as an agent in their political intrigues and a propagandist for their causes, becoming virtually a member of the aristocratic family.

The Cavendishes were bulwarks of the monarchy and its Church of England, created after Henry VIII's rejection of papal authority. For a long time, Hobbes echoed their devotion, but he was motivated not by doctrinal faith, or piety, or self-interest. In an age when the old foundations of authority were being dismantled, he proposed a new, even sterner justification of power: the preservation of order against man's instinct for selfishness and violence.

Aristotle and two millennia of pagan and Christian followers had held that "the polis belongs to the class of things that exist by nature, and that man is by nature an animal intended to live in a polis." But for Hobbes, men were not naturally social creatures. The human being was an animal driven selfishly by appetites, by passions, above all by "a perpetuall and restlesse desire of Power after power, that ceaseth onely in Death," devoted to assuring "for ever, the way of his future desire." Not naturally social creatures, men sought their own selfish ends at any cost. Their original state was lawless, a "War of every man against every man," violent disorder, total insecurity, and fear. Far from "contented," human lives in that state could be nothing but "solitary, poore, nasty, brutish, and short."

Hobbes's terrifying portrait of the "state of nature" did not rely on the doctrine of original sin, nor was its alternative the city of God. He considered himself a scientist, and, like many of the Enlightenment's most innovative thinkers, his "natural philosophy" aimed at a unified body of scientific thought, from fundamental principles of matter and motion to geometry, mechanics, physics, to moral and civil philosophy. Hobbes refused to acknowledge theology as a science and ridiculed churchmen who offered authoritative views about God, describing them as a "Confederacy of Deceivers" who endeavored to control men "by dark, and erroneous Doctrines, to extinguish in them the Light, both of Nature, and of the Gospell." In his own doctrine, "the good," the summit of ethics classical and Christian, was nothing more than "the common name for all things that are desired" and these were "relative to person, place, and time."

But while Hobbes showed that men were powerfully inclined to pursue immediate goals, he also believed that they were capable of acting on long-term interests. In the Enlightenment, the highest quality of human beings was not their resemblance to God but their capacity to reason. For Hobbes, reason was what distinguished men from beasts; it gave humans the power to control and guide the passions. It also distinguished civil society from the chaos of the natural state. Men were motivated to join together in a social compact by fear and the desire for self-preservation. They reasoned that by sacrificing an anarchic freedom, they would gain the safety of laws.

Hobbes imagined that civil society was conventional, the product of an agreement among men to submit to government. But given his gloomy view of human nature, how could government achieve its main end, "the procuration of *the safety of the people*"? As he warned, "Covenants, without the Sword, are but Words, and of no strength to secure a man at all." Obedience to the laws, if not given freely, must be coerced. Or as philosopher Alan Ryan summarized it: "The sovereign in effect says to us, 'If you submit, I will not kill you.'"

Hobbes was no democrat. To allow men a voice in their own government was to invite conflict, factionalism, and perhaps a relapse to the anarchy of nature. For similar reasons, he objected to any group or allegiance that might stand between sovereign and citizen and dilute the latter's submission to the former. He was suspicious of aristocracies and universities and guilds—even those of beggars—that might challenge the authority of the sovereign.

As for the church, it should be under the complete control of the sovereign power; otherwise it would establish "*Supremacy* against the *Soveraignty, Canons* against *Lawes,* and a *Ghostly Authority* against the *Civill.*" In Hobbes's commonwealth, it was not private belief that counted but conformity in conduct, a willingness, as political scientist Patricia Springborg put it, "to profess what is commanded" by the sovereign as "commander of the faithful." Conscience was free, a personal matter, but speech was public and subject to control. "The tongue of man," Hobbes warned, "is a trumpet of warre, and sedition."

So dire was the state of nature, he reckoned, that men would sacrifice everything except their lives to escape it. His was a profoundly pessimistic view of men, medieval in its gloom, lacking the faith in human progress that would drive and inspire other Enlightenment leaders. But the medieval church and its philosophers had at least offered the possibility of grace and ultimate salvation. For Hobbes, there was only the eternal struggle against the darkness and disorder that were the work not of the devil but of men themselves, written in their nature. Yet his justification of civil society and his account of its formation by the consent of the governed became cornerstones of Enlightenment thought, adopted by such diverse thinkers as

Spinoza and Locke and Rousseau as well as American and French revolutionaries.

* * *

Through the Cavendishes, Hobbes had met Francis Bacon, whose proposal of a new empirical science to replace the arid abstractions of medieval scholasticism gave the Enlightenment its characteristic methods of inquiry and reason. Born in 1561, Bacon was well connected in the courts of Elizabeth I and James I and held an array of offices before reaching the pinnacle as lord chancellor in 1618, about the time Hobbes met him and, according to biographer John Aubrey, served as his secretary. Bacon was a lord, a courtier, a statesman, a polymath, yet he had the revolutionary idea that the search for truth began with the humble station of a *fact*. For millennia scientists and philosophers had trod in the path of Aristotle, beginning with their conclusion, the assertion of a "truth," and then seeking proofs for it. "In the manner of spiders," Bacon wrote, they spun "webs from their own entrails." Science and philosophy had been left to the "blindness of traditions, the swirling bluster of arguments, or the turbulent waves of chance"—to everything but "experience marshalled and well-grounded" in fact. Fact was reason's raw material, from which the scientist or philosopher could reach more and more general truths, ascending "the proper ladder by successive, uninterrupted or unbroken steps, from particulars to lower axioms, then to middle ones, each higher than the last." Ultimately, they would arrive at what Bacon considered the grand prize, knowledge of the laws that govern the physical world. And knowledge was power: "the sovereignty of Man lieth hid in knowledge . . . which kings with their treasure cannot buy, nor with their force command."

This powerful man did not disdain the gritty work of gathering facts. Indeed, according to a story Hobbes told Aubrey, Bacon died of it. Traveling in a coach through snow one day in March 1626, Bacon suddenly was struck by the question whether "flesh might not be preserved in snow, as in Salt." Stopping the coach, he went to a poor woman's house nearby and bought a hen. After the woman gutted it, Bacon stuffed the bird with snow. The outcome of the test is not known, nor has a connection between this experiment, the chill the snow gave him, and Bacon's subsequent illness been proven. The fact, at least as attested by Hobbes, is that the father of the modern scientific method died two or three days later.

Following Bacon, Hobbes built his own general ideas up from observations and experience, including, doubtless, his own profound fears of violence, dissolution, and death. The battles of the Reformation continued to rage, and in Protestant England, they grew ever more intense, with the threat of aggression by Catholic Spain, the nearly successful attempt in 1605 by Catholic extremists to blow up the king and Parliament, and the rising tensions between Crown and Commons, a power struggle embittered by sectarianism. All this threatened to destabilize Hobbes's world. In 1640, as Parliament undertook to examine "the prerogative of the king," Hobbes felt "a disorder comming on" and feared that, owing to his own defense of monarchical power, anti-royalist enemies would persecute him. He found haven in France, where, for a decade, while England exploded into a civil war that climaxed with the beheading of Charles I in 1649, Hobbes enjoyed his most creative period, culminating with the publication of his masterwork, *Leviathan,* in 1651. A special vellum copy of the book was presented to the late king's heir, Charles II, also in French exile.

But Hobbes was nothing if not a realist. *Leviathan*'s description of the religious establishment as a "Kingdome of Darknesse" that seduced men "by abuse of Scripture" made him enemies in Charles's Anglican circles, as well as among the powerful French clergy, who reportedly sought his arrest. In 1652, Hobbes returned to England, where the old royalist soon enough made peace with Oliver Cromwell's Puritan Commonwealth. And why not? Cromwell met the two critical conditions of a sovereign— he had the power to protect the people, as Charles over in France did not, and he had the consent of the people, which, even if gained through force and fear, was valid. Even monarchists owed the Commonwealth obedience.

The consistency of Hobbes's stance failed, of course, to impress the royal court and its clerics after Charles II was restored to the throne in 1660. Though he had come safely back into the Cavendish fold, Hobbes was denounced from the pulpit as an atheist and denied membership in the Royal Society for the Improvement of Natural Knowledge, created by the king after the Restoration. The Royal Society would become one of Europe's greatest vehicles of enlightenment, a place for leading scientists to discuss experimental results and new hypotheses. But so soon after the Civil War and Restoration, even members sympathetic to Hobbes were inclined to be cautious. They may have respected his ideas, but they feared his notoriety, while Aristotelians and religious conservatives rejected him on principle. Hobbes, naturally, gave as good as—or better than—he got, jeering at the Royal Society's cult of laborious experimentation, the waste of "the expense of machines of difficult manufacture, just so you could get as far as Hobbes had already progressed." Why, he asked arrogantly, continuing in the third person, "did you not use the principles he established?"

Hobbes continued to write, argue, and criticize well into his final years. He was ninety when a crisis erupted that was all too reminiscent of the prelude to the Civil War. In 1678, after Charles's heir apparent, his brother James, announced his conversion to Catholicism, a "Popish Plot" was alleged—a scheme by the pope and the king of France to have Charles murdered and James raised to the throne. It was all nonsense, but James's opponents demanded that he be excluded from the succession. William Cavendish, the vehemently anti-Catholic grandson of the William who was Hobbes's first student, asked the old tutor whether, if a "Successour to a Crown, be for some reason or other which is notorious, incapable to protect the people," the king was not obliged to eliminate him from the succession "upon the request of his subjects?" The prospect of uncertainty in the succession returned Hobbes to his deepest, most recurrent nightmare. In his last word on politics—echoing his warning in *Leviathan* three decades earlier—he told William that the king's dying would mean a dissolution of the sovereign power, with the people becoming "a multitude of lawless men relapsed into a condition of war of every man against man."

In the warm Cavendish embrace, Hobbes was safe from such a fate. A few months later, he was "suddainly striken with a dead Palsie," a stroke, and within a week he was dead, at age ninety-one. It was, by the standards of his time, a peaceful death. There was "nothing remarkable or extraordinary" in his passing, wrote a Cavendish secretary, disappointing those who were sure that God would exercise his wrath against the freethinker on his deathbed.

THE TRIUMPH OF REASON

Bene vixit, bene qui latuit—to live well is to live concealed—was the motto René Descartes adopted for himself. Though he would become a master of enlightenment, even literally, as a tireless student of optics, much of his life remained in shadows. He dissembled to friend and foe alike—conduct he raised to a philosophical issue, contending that it was a "good thing to demonstrate the freedom of the will" by evading "a clearly perceived truth." He insisted on his Catholic orthodoxy even as his writings undermined the church's authority. Not even his closest friends knew until much later that

Descartes, who never married, had a daughter by a serving maid, and that the girl's death at the age of five caused him "the greatest sorrow" of his life.

After her death, Descartes packed up his belongings and moved on, as he would so often. His astonishing itinerancy gave the impression of a man on the run—he moved at least thirty-five times before his death in 1650 at the age of fifty-four, through a great arc of his native France, Holland, Germany, Italy, and finally Scandinavia. Sometimes, he gave out his new address to no one, as though he meant to disappear.

In his origins, Descartes seemed eminently respectable. His father was a physician and councillor in the parlement of Brittany, while on his mother's side was a host of merchants and officials. But that first household broke up a year after his birth with his mother's death. Farmed out to a grandmother, he would see his father only rarely. At ten, he was sent to board at the Jesuit college in La Flèche, whose curriculum was decidedly old school—mainly Greek and Latin classics Christianized. Year after year the boys studied Catholicism's favorite pagan, Aristotle, whose philosophy was used to demonstrate such things as the existence of God and the soul's immortality, as well as serving as the ground for Christian moral philosophy.

The Counter-Reformation, the Catholic Church's ferocious response to the Protestant revolution, was in full swing. Orthodoxy and obedience to authority were the orders of the day, not only by external show but in the recesses of the soul. Students were not allowed to forget their original sinfulness, which could be overcome by a disciplined *self*-reformation, the self-control needed to bring themselves in total accord with the doctrines of the faith. The aim was to create a militant caste of Catholic theological warriors.

But Descartes left La Flèche at age eighteen and drifted, suffering from the melancholia that would afflict him the rest of his life. After two years of legal studies at Poitiers, he enlisted in an actual army—the Protestant Dutch army, allied with France against Spain. He later described the travel and experiences of these years as liberating him from the confines of his Jesuit education, from the "many errors which may obscure our natural light and make us less capable of heeding reason." Still, the idleness of army life among uneducated soldiers frustrated him.

What shook Descartes from his aimlessness was a chance meeting in late 1618 with a Dutch mathematician, Isaac Beeckman. Descartes had displayed a gift for mathematics at La Flèche, but Beeckman reignited his interest in the subject, opening his eyes to the possibility that arithmetic and geometry could become the basis for a mechanics that might reach all phenomena, from optics to falling bodies to the sounds of music. After working for several months on mathematical and mechanical problems under the older man's guidance, Descartes resumed his waywardness, traveling through war-torn Europe to join a Catholic army in Bavaria. But in the search for a *mathesis universalis,* Descartes had glimpsed his true vocation.

. . .

One night in the winter of 1619, Descartes dreamt three dreams that motivated his enlightenment. The first was a nightmare of phantoms and howling winds, the second a thunderclap that woke him. The third featured an encyclopedia, a book of poetry where he found the question, *Quod vitae sectabor iter?*—What path in life shall I follow?—and verses a stranger gave him that began, *est et non*: it is and is not. The first two dreams Descartes interpreted as a rebuke for his past life, while the third pointed forward— the encyclopedia suggested universal knowledge; *est et non* the black-white opposition of truth and error.

The last dream confirmed the path Descartes had already begun to follow—broadening the mechanical studies he had undertaken with Beeckman to the pursuit of a unified knowledge that encompassed all the sciences and offered the same certainty as mathematics. The quest for incontrovertible truths would become an obsession, a search for "clear and distinct" ideas that would act as building blocks for greater, more complex truths. The way to such ideas was inward, through intuition, which in turn fed the constructive work of *reason*. The first criterion and test of truth, Descartes emphasized, was the individual mind.

Despite this breakthrough, the following years found Descartes again wandering obscurely through Europe, as though he had lost the thread of his thought. It was only in 1625, when he settled in Paris, that he began to consolidate the insights of 1619, publishing *Rules for the Direction of the Mind* in 1629. For the first time, he was living among peers in a city that, despite censorship, was a hotbed of ideas, especially among the caste known as "libertines"—skeptics and freethinkers out to shatter the intellectual chains of the past. They were the first generation of the Enlightenment in France.

Though he profited from collaboration with Parisian thinkers, Descartes left the city abruptly in the winter of 1628 for the Netherlands, where, he said, he could work without distraction. That work was staggering in its ambition, a complete body of philosophy to be called *Le Monde*—and that was only the first part, which ranged from algebra to cosmology to the nature of fire and light; in fact, the work's subtitle was to be *Traité de la Lumière*. Another work, *L'Homme*, was to extend the study to the human body and mind. What united these disparate phenomena was Descartes' dismissal of the multitude of Aristotelian principles used to explain nature—the active "forms" and inert "prime matter," the four elements of earth, air, fire, water, the four qualities of dry, cold, hot, moist. His mechanistic account was more economical, recognizing only a single essence shared by all phenomena—extension, the property of occupying space, which included size, shape, and motion. The physical world was made up of particles in motion, change explicable in terms of the laws of motion. Applied to the human body, as Descartes did in *L'Homme,* his theory explained how the functions of "this machine" followed "entirely from the disposition of the organs—no more nor less than do the movements of a clock or other automaton, from the arrangement of its counterweights and wheels." He demonstrated how the machine could "sneeze, yawn, cough, and make the movements necessary to reject the various excrements."

The human body as a kind of self-regulating hydraulic contraption—was there nothing more to be said for man? The machine-model encompassed not only heartbeats and digestion but also the senses, imagination, memory, and "common sense." Everything that remained and that was not mechanical belonged to the "rational soul," with which Descartes promised to conclude *Le Monde*. But before he could do so, a mighty event shook him to the core.

⁘

The Inquisition in Rome had fired a blast at mathematician and astronomer Galileo Galilei in 1616, forbidding him to teach or defend heliocentrism, the Copernican theory that Earth revolved around the sun. Invoking its authority "to control petulant minds," the church relied on a scrap of scripture and the views of a second-century Egyptian astronomer to insist that Earth stood where God had put it, at the universe's still center, around which all other celestial bodies turned. In 1633, the Inquisition struck again, now condemning Galileo for violating the earlier edict, forcing him to recant and making clear that heliocentrism could not be discussed even as a hypothesis.

Though Galileo did not share the fate of another heretical cosmological speculator, Giordano Bruno, whom the Inquisition burned at the stake in 1600, Descartes was appalled and frightened by the condemnation. His own cosmology in *Le Monde* was Copernican and "so closely interwoven in every part of my treatise that I could not remove it without rendering the whole work defective." Yet he was unwilling, "for anything in the world," to maintain these ideas against the Inquisition, which left him little choice but to suppress his masterpiece and "forfeit almost all my work of the last four years in order to give my obedience to the Church."

The man who had jotted the motto in an early notebook, "The fear of God is the beginning of wisdom," had written little of theology. Where scholasticism mingled or blurred the natural and supernatural, Descartes had drawn a bright line between them. God in his mechanistic philosophy was transcendent, independent of the world, and therefore beyond human understanding. Even so, Descartes had claimed in 1630 to have proof of God's existence as certain as "any proposition of geometry; but I do not know whether I would be able to make everyone understand it the way I can," and therefore he thought it wiser "not to treat of this matter at all than to treat of it imperfectly." Galileo's trial, though, clarified the stakes of "imperfect" philosophy; Descartes knew that he had to get it right.

It was paradoxical that one of the most radical thinkers in Western philosophy, who was doing so much to prove that every part of the world could be subject to human reason, should be so determined to embed an abstract, unknowable God fully into his physics. It was no less paradoxical and startling that he should begin a new search for truth not with a profession of faith but by rejecting "as if absolutely false everything in which I could imagine the least doubt"—the evidence of the senses, the proofs of reason, even God—"in order to see if I was left believing anything that was entirely indubitable." He noticed "immediately" that he himself, the one with this thought that all was false, necessarily was something.

Cogito ergo sum—I think, therefore I am—no skepticism could shake the certainty of his own existence.

Descartes' faith in subjective intuition as the foundation of knowledge had been evident since his dreams of 1619. But the stark rejection of any authority except the mind, with all certainty built up from the new *cogito,* was revolutionary. Just as Copernicus had replaced Earth with the sun at the center of the cosmos, so with the *cogito,* as the authority of God yielded to the thought of man, an idea that would become a first principle of the Enlightenment.

But did Descartes believe it? He immediately followed his discovery of the *cogito* with a proof of God's existence. His mind was able to imagine a being more perfect than himself, Descartes wrote, only because the idea had been implanted by a more perfect being: "that is—to explain myself in one word—by God."

Certainty about God was second only to certainty about self. But the circularity of his logic, with its dubious premise, pointed to Descartes' difficulties in finding a meaningful role for God. Earlier, he had described reason as constituted by the "clear and distinct" ideas that were basic to knowledge. Now, reason was an inborn power given to men by God. Before, clear and distinct ideas took their truth-value from self-conviction, from intuition. Now, they became entangled in Descartes' struggle to drag God back from the edge of irrelevance. As biographer Stephen Gaukroger noted, "Descartes must use the doctrine of clear and distinct ideas to prove the existence of God, and then use God to provide a divine guarantee for these clear and distinct ideas."

Descartes' God remained ultimately unknowable to human beings, with their finite "rational souls," faint reflections of the "uncreated and independent thinking substance" that was God. But he increasingly pushed divine authority to the fore, as the ultimate guarantor of both individual minds and the whole of creation. Even as he proved the power of radical doubt, he tried to lay new foundations for the doctrines of faith. Even as he pioneered a new route to human self-determination via the *cogito*, he fell back into medieval terms to defend God against his own revolutionary insights. He had taken scholasticism to task for its faulty reasoning and reliance on empty "qualities" and "essences." Didn't his own version of God fit this bill? His straining efforts to salvage divine authority had the paradoxical effect of shoving God deeper into the shadows of a world penetrated by the light of reason.

. . .

Despite—or because of—his claims to orthodoxy, Descartes' radical metaphysics made him the most controversial philosopher at a time when the devastating Thirty Years' War was elevating sectarian bitterness to new heights. Protestants saw him as a new-style Catholic apologist, while Catholics condemned him as a heretic, undermining the church's traditional teachings and authority. He faced the fury of that "troop of theologians, followers of scholastic philosophy," he wrote in 1647, who "seem to have formed a league in an attempt to crush me by their slanders." At the same time, Descartes was gaining passionate followers drawn by his stance as what historian of the Enlightenment Peter Gay called, "the bold, persistent, skeptic who liberates himself" from traditional philosophy "to stand forth as a model to his fellow men." Yet as schools of Cartesians formed, first in the Netherlands and France, they divided over interpretations of the master's philosophy. At times they pressed their new and controversial faith so fervently as to draw the attention of church or public authorities. Descartes found himself dragged into quarrels incited or exacerbated by his followers. The fire grew so hot on the continent that, even as Thomas Hobbes was fleeing England for France, Descartes thought of moving across the Channel, where he imagined that he would be well received by the Catholic-leaning Charles I.

Not only conservatives inveighed against Descartes. Even disciples were puzzled by and divided over, for instance, Descartes' dualism—what became notorious as the "mind-body problem"—with doctrinal hairs split as finely as in any of the theological controversies that wracked Christianity. How could the insubstantial mind or soul be joined with the purely material body in what Descartes called "true substantial union"? There were perhaps as many answers to that question as there were Cartesians and anti-Cartesians. But none was simpler than Thomas Hobbes's: abolish dualism. "A thinking thing is something corporeal," Hobbes wrote flatly in response to Descartes' *Meditations* in 1641; understanding of the proposition "I am thinking" depended "on our inability to separate thought from the matter that is thinking."

To Descartes, this was absurd—how could inert matter think? As for his proof of God's existence through man's imagination of a more perfect being, Hobbes was no less dismissive: "We do not have an idea of God," therefore the whole of Descartes' argument collapses. Descartes replied: "We do have an idea of God," therefore the whole of Hobbes's objection collapses. Perhaps unsurprisingly, at a time when intellectual disputes could escalate to mortal combat, a real enmity arose between the two radicals. They were jealous men, prickly over the priority of their ideas. To Hobbes, Descartes' great failing was that he was not a Hobbesian. He ought to have stuck to geometry, Hobbes said—"his head did not lye for Philosophy." Descartes feared both being overshadowed by Hobbes and seeing his own carefully calibrated materialism tainted by association with Hobbes's infamous ideas. They quarreled when they met in 1648 and never saw each other again.

At least the conflict between Hobbes and Descartes pointed forward to struggles that would clarify the meaning and direction of the Enlightenment, as would the conflict after Descartes' death between Cartesians who defended his method of intuition and rationalism as the path to truth and the champions of Newtonian empiricism. But Descartes' decision to apply his philosophy to transubstantiation, the Catholic belief that consecrated bread and wine was transformed into the body and blood of Christ, proved an embarrassment to his cause. He had long steered clear of doctrinal issues, but now he was eager, as he wrote to the head of the Jesuits in France, to address "a topic where it is notoriously difficult to reconcile philosophy with theology." The new materialism, along with Protestant disdain, had made the nature of transubstantiation controversial—Descartes to the rescue! But his subtle and complex explanation, characteristically dividing the bread and wine into their divine and material elements, did not satisfy the orthodox, who rejected his methods while doubting his motives and sincerity—as did a disgusted Hobbes, who claimed to know it "was absolutely against his opinion and donne meerly to putt a compliment on the Jesuites."

Ultimately, Descartes' Christian apologetics, with their medieval taint, would be forgotten, while his Copernican revolution that put human beings and their thinking power at the center of philosophy and science, as well as his example of skepticism, gave decisive impetus to the Enlightenment. He served as a starting point even for those philosophers who would eventually turn away from his thought, such as the British school of empiricists. But Descartes' meddling in the transubstantiation controversy drew him into a complex battle involving Catholics and Protestants, assorted heretics, and Cartesians that came to threaten the unity of the Netherlands. It ended with Descartes being summoned in 1643 to the town council of Utrecht on charges of slandering a Protestant clergyman, a firebrand who accused him of being a Jesuit spy. Threatened with expulsion and the burning of his books, Descartes was saved only by the intervention of friends in high places.

Nevertheless, Cartesianism had become a European sensation. Even those who could make neither head nor tail of it cheered it as the vanguard of enlightenment or condemned it as, in the words of the authorities at the University of Angers, a new heresy "injurious to Faith, the Sovereign, and the State." Louis XIV agreed, banning its teaching in French universities. The transubstantiation controversy gave the Inquisition its excuse to put Descartes' works on its *Index Liborum Prohibitorum* in 1663, with the proviso *donec corrigantur*—until they are corrected.

By then Descartes was beyond correcting. He had died in Sweden in 1650 sheltered by a young queen who had acquired a liking for his philosophy. His material remains proved nearly as itinerant as the man himself. Buried temporarily in Sweden, his body was returned to France in 1667—the royal court forbade a funeral sermon at the reburial—and over the next century and a half his bones were repeatedly exhumed, moved, and reburied. Perhaps fittingly for this dualist, at some point his skull disappeared. Later, in 1821, a skull labeled Descartes'—literally, carved across its forehead—was bought at auction in Sweden and eventually put on display in Paris's Museum of Natural History. A French newspaper called it *la précieuse relique*.

THE FREEDOM OF THOUGHT

In the thick of the battle over Cartesianism in the Netherlands was a young man who made his living grinding lenses for spectacles, telescopes, and microscopes. A descendant of Marranos, Spanish Jews who had been forcibly converted to Christianity, he was excommunicated in 1656 at age twenty-four by the leaders of Amsterdam's Jewish community for questioning the Bible's authority, doubting that Jews were God's chosen people, and other "abominable heresies."

Baruch Spinoza, who after his expulsion changed his name to Benedict, was guilty as charged. For years, he had been making it clear that he would think for himself, and with that liberation of mind Spinoza pioneered a radical path to enlightenment and freedom for all. Born in 1632, the son of a prosperous merchant and leader of the community, he had studied at its school for boys, learning Hebrew prayers, poring over Torah and Jewish philosophers. A rabbi there, seeing Spinoza's ardor for knowledge, introduced him to secular literature, classical and medieval. But far from confirming him in the Jewish faith, as the rabbi had expected, these studies opened new worlds beyond its confines. Spinoza went on to study with Franciscus van den Enden, a respected teacher of Latin but also an ex-Jesuit, religious skeptic, and political radical. After his father's death in 1654, the young scholar came to live with Van den Enden and even courted his daughter, the only romance recorded in his book of life. He was then a merchant, too, running his late father's business, but what ignited his intellect were *ideas*, the search for truth, for what he had already identified as the highest knowledge, "the union that the mind has with the whole of Nature." From that vague thread, Spinoza would determinedly weave a whole fabric of thought more radical than any philosopher of the Enlightenment. But first he needed an alternative to his lost Jewish faith. He found it in René Descartes.

It did not take long for Spinoza to master Descartes' thought and then to begin teaching it to a student from the University of Leiden, a Cartesian center. Spinoza's text was the *Principles of Philosophy*, a late work that brought together Descartes' ideas in textbook form—Descartes had hoped it would displace the Aristotelian tomes that monopolized university curricula. Spinoza was preparing an exposition of the *Principles,* urged on by friends who admired the lucidity of his explanations of Descartes' thought. He even, according to one friend, "superseded Descartes with his distinct and probable ideas." The result was Descartes' absorption into Spinoza's own emerging "geometric" style of reasoning. Like Descartes, Spinoza set philosophical certainty as his goal; the problem, as Spinoza saw it, was that Descartes hadn't gone far enough. Spinoza would use mathematics as the model, but with greater rigor. Borrowing from Euclid, he began with definitions, axioms, postulates—his version of clear and distinct ideas that were indubitably true—and used them to demonstrate a mounting series of propositions, each incontrovertible because built solely of such elements. It made for forbidding reading, a severity of order that Descartes could scarcely have envisioned. It was the master on the disciple's terms.

* * *

Spinoza was not the kind of man to remain anyone's follower for long. Among the errors he found in Descartes, the most consequential inevitably involved religion. His anxiety to remain orthodox had led Descartes to violate his own enlightened principles and thrown him off the path to truth, Spinoza thought. To accommodate free will and the immortal soul, the Frenchman had invented a realm separate from nature—"a dominion within a dominion," Spinoza called it, as though "man disturbs, rather than follows, the order of nature." Even more absurd, in Spinoza's eyes, was Descartes' attempt to solve the mind-body dilemma that came of that separation. Locating the "seat of the soul" in the brain's pineal gland, Descartes hypothesized that the insubstantial mind communicated with the material body via "animal spirits," tiny particles that traveled back and forth between mind and body. To Spinoza, this was an example of the foolishness and falsehood that religion led even men of genius to adopt.

As his confrontation with Amsterdam's Jewish leadership had shown, Spinoza was not for compromise. He passionately believed that religion was the greatest impediment to enlightenment, worse than ignorance because it imposed falsehoods on people, handed down by theologians and ministers and typically backed by governments whose censorship denied dissenters the freedom "to say what we think." Moreover, he held religion to account for the wars that had been racking Europe for decades, for "spreading contention among men and in fostering the bitterest hatred."

His proposal was revolutionary—to make a "straightforward study" of religion, using the natural light of reason, in order "to free our minds from the prejudices of theologians and to avoid the hasty acceptance of human fabrications as divine teachings." In what would become the *Theological-Political Treatise*, Spinoza subjected the Bible to unprecedented scrutiny, examining it not as a divine artifact but as an historical document. It was a part of nature, he insisted, to be studied as all other phenomena were, with rational inquiry. In Spinoza's light, the Bible appeared as an often-indiscriminate mass of superstitions, fictions, and well-intentioned but dubious claims of knowledge of God's mind. The book did not teach knowledge but obedience to authority. Miracles, for instance, were vivid stories made to strengthen people's faith and so to secure their submission. As events they were impossibilities—"Nothing happens in nature that does not follow from her laws." Impossible, too, was an anthropomorphic God, a God "in the likeness of man" that had "mind, heart, emotions, and even body and breath," a God that was interested in human affairs, that had made the world for man or had a plan for the world or man.

To those who nevertheless maintained that the Bible was God's word, Spinoza replied in the *Treatise* that "instead of God's Word, they are beginning to worship likenesses and images, that is, paper and ink." No one before Spinoza had so rigorously examined scripture as just that—paper and ink—and his example of biblical criticism would become a powerful weapon in the Enlightenment's long struggle to come to terms with religion.

* * *

Though Spinoza followed progress in science closely and won praise from leading scientists of the day for the excellence of his microscopes and telescopes, he would not be found dissecting rabbits and eels and live dogs as Descartes had done. Descartes was foremost a man of science who sought a unified and certain explanation of the phenomenal world through the acquisition, organization, and exposition of knowledge. Spinoza was above all a moral philosopher, consumed by the search for truth about human life, human relationships, human communities, and by the faith that the truth would set men free. The critical method and high-intensity reasoning were his tools.

After error and falsehood were swept from the Bible, then, what truth remained? Spinoza found this one: "To love God above all, and one's neighbor as oneself"—so simple that even the "most sluggish mind" might grasp it by "the natural light that is common to all, and not any supernatural light, nor any eternal authority." The Bible itself was unnecessary—a person who knew God by the natural light and pursued "a true way of life, is altogether blessed."

Spinoza was no atheist, but the God he enjoined people to know resembled no divinity in the Western tradition, and indeed seemed scarcely knowable. It had a body, but that body was all of nature; its substance was the substance of the world—"Except God, no substance can be or be conceived." Spinoza's God indeed was identical with nature, both in its active, generative aspect (*natura naturans*) and in its passive, receptive form (*natura naturata*) as both cause and effect, both creator and creation. Even in creation, though, God did not act with free will or a purpose but strictly according to the laws of its nature—"Things could have been produced by God in no other way, and in no other order than they have been produced."

As Spinoza piled up his geometric propositions, as they rose to dizzying heights of abstraction, his God must have bewildered even the most unorthodox and sophisticated readers. Was this a God for the new age, with theology as natural philosophy? Was Spinoza conflating the search for the truth of God with the work of mathematicians and geometers, cosmologists and botanists, who day by day were dispelling the obscurities of the Middle Ages with new beams of enlightenment?

And what place was there in Spinoza's faith for human beings? The God of Judaism and Christianity had a special relationship with men and women. They were singled out from the rest of creation—as sinners to suffer but also to know God's love and reach salvation. Even Descartes had bent his system to acknowledge an immortal soul, distinct from bodies. But Spinoza afforded human beings no such privilege. While he distinguished minds from bodies, they were equally wholly inside nature, determined like the rest of creation and like God by infinite chains of causality which could not be altered or broken because "the laws and rules of nature, according to which all things happen, and change from one form to another, are always and everywhere the same." Any hope or promise otherwise was a man-made illusion—there was no escape from nature.

Such was the hard reality of human existence, yet for Spinoza, it was no cause for despair—rather, it opened new and less delusive paths to self-realization. Enlightenment was the key—the use of reason to fulfill the injunction that Descartes had planted as the root for modern thought: Know thyself. Spinoza identified the passions, sensual life, as the great obstacles to self-knowledge, agents of passivity and "Bondage." To control them rather than be controlled by them was a rational discipline, liberating men to mount the stages of knowledge. Unlike Descartes, Spinoza put no limit on the reach of human understanding. Reason had the potential to grasp everything that was in nature, including, crucially, one's own place in it—that is, one's relationship to God. The coming to terms with the realities of existence was the road to truth. If we understand that we are "part of the whole of nature, whose order we follow," then "we can want nothing except what is necessary, nor absolutely be satisfied with anything except what is true." Spinoza described the ultimate of truth, of understanding "things under a species of eternity," as "the intellectual love of God," a state of blessedness and liberation. No philosopher would make so intoxicating a claim for enlightenment, nor make enlightenment so central to human salvation.

. . .

After his excommunication in 1656, Spinoza lived in Amsterdam four more years, apart from the Jewish community. Following Descartes, as a preliminary to a great, systematic work, he began an explanation of his methods, but abandoned it before he left Amsterdam in 1661 for the small village of Rijnsburg. This was scarcely a hermitage. The village was famed for its tolerance; not long before it had been the center of the Dutch "Collegiant" movement. Dissenting from the dogmatics and hierarchies of the established churches, Collegiants met on Sundays for their own unstructured, preacherless but intellectually intense meetings. In Amsterdam, Spinoza had befriended a number of Collegiants and may even have attended their gatherings. Rijnsburg, moreover, was near Leiden with its university, which Spinoza had attended for a time and where he still had friends. In fact, he was hard-pressed by the stream of visitors to the village, some from afar. It testified to the liveliness and strength of the informal networks that linked intellectuals across Europe that Spinoza, who had as yet published nothing, was already renowned as a thinker, worthy of a pilgrimage by a leading disseminator of information among European scientists, Henry Oldenburg, a German who had recently helped to found the Royal Society in London and served as its first secretary.

Spinoza was embarked on an array of projects, including the analysis of Descartes' *Principles*, which he published in 1663 as the first and last work that appeared under his name in his lifetime. He was drafting a *Short Treatise*, another attempt to clarify his philosophical methods, and in 1662, he began the masterwork that would expound his entire system of thought, the *Ethics*. The next year he left Rijnsburg for Voorburg, another small village but quieter, near The Hague.

The theological turmoil of these years had their counterpart in Dutch politics. A decade earlier, Johan de Witt, a graduate of Leiden, had become "Grand Pensionary of Holland," which, despite the peculiar title, meant that he was, in effect, ruler of the Netherlands. A lawyer whose real passion was mathematics, De Witt was the most powerful liberal in Europe, devoted to fashioning a secular republic that assured free thought and religious toleration. Not surprisingly, though he successfully wound down a damaging war with England and restored the nation's finances, he aroused an equally determined opposition among royalist supporters of the House of Orange and from the Dutch Reformed Church.

Spinoza greatly admired De Witt, though not without reservation, and in 1665, when renewed warfare with England emboldened the opposition to demand the transfer of power to the Prince of Orange, Spinoza decided to come to his defense. Putting aside the *Ethics*—by now he had nearly a complete draft—he undertook the painstaking examination of the Bible that would form the backbone of his "natural history of religion." But the *Theological-Political Treatise*, as the title indicated, also contained Spinoza's political science, which he had already begun to outline in the *Ethics*, and to which he would return in the later *Treatise on Politics*.

Spinoza started, as he had learned to do from his studies of Hobbes, in the lawless state of nature where men's lives, whipped along by appetites and passions, were better fitted for animals. To get what he wanted, "natural" man would press "by any means, by force, deceit, entreaty," taking "as his enemy anyone who tries to hinder him." Nothing was prohibited except "those things that no one desires and no one can do." But self-interest would teach natural man that he could find greater security—from attack or in fulfilling needs—in a commonwealth, where he would have the protection of laws. In exchange, the commonwealth would require the complete surrender of his "sovereign natural right" and submission to the principle that what the government "decides to be just and good must be regarded as having been so decided by every citizen."

So far, Spinoza was closely tracking Hobbes, but as with Descartes he was no mere follower. The breach came over the best form of government, with Spinoza rejecting Hobbesian absolutism, pointing out that coercive rule would rapidly lose legitimacy—and risk dissolution—when people became convinced that it was acting against their interests. Hobbes made no provision for legitimate dissent, Spinoza noted, yet independent thought— "freedom of judgment"—was impossible to suppress entirely. A commonwealth based on nothing but apathy and servility "may more properly be called a desert."

Spinoza had a more optimistic view of men removed from their natural condition and therefore of politics than Hobbes, imagining a state whose true purpose was liberty, a state that would promote the lofty values of his moral philosophy, "a truly human existence," powered by reason, "the true virtue and life of the mind." The best state in that case was one that few men of Spinoza's time even dreamt of—*democracy,* because it approached "most closely to that freedom which nature grants to every man." Government by the people encouraged—required—free thought and speech, and, as philosopher Henry Allison wrote, "more than any other form of government has a vested interest in the rationality of its subjects." But Spinoza understood that most men, though capable of it, did not live by reason. What if a majority passed laws that were valid but unjust? Well, the citizen had "no right to decide what is fair or unfair, moral or immoral," and no matter how unjust the laws, "he is bound to carry them out." But was that not to sacrifice free judgment? And if self-interest was the basis of the state, why, as Allison asked, "should rational subjects obey laws that they know to be counter to their true self-interest?"

Spinoza created an unsatisfactory syllogism that linked greater rationality to greater freedom and therefore to greater obedience to the sovereign and its laws. If that didn't work, the rational man would realize that obedience, however irksome or painful, would be the lesser of two evils—the other being the dissolution of the political order, a return to the state of nature. That would make Spinoza's democracy a modest advance over Hobbes's coercive absolutism since reason, rather than brute force, would bring complete submission to the majority's commands. As it did in Spinoza, this dilemma of effective and just government would reflect conflicting strains in Enlightenment thought about human nature, one more optimistic, the other more pessimistic. Reconciliation of the twin imperatives of democratic government—majority rule and the protection of minority rights—would bedevil philosophers and statesmen for centuries, not least the authors of the American Constitution.

◆ ◆ ◆

Spinoza's *Theological-Political Treatise* appeared after five years of intensive labor, in 1670, and, though it was published anonymously, his authorship quickly became notorious for the *Treatise*'s unprecedented, uncompromising assault on religion. Howls of outrage burst from Calvinists, Cartesians, and Collegiants alike. To the Synod of South Holland, it was "as vile and blasphemous a book as the world has ever seen." The synod at The Hague condemned it as "idolatry and superstition." Spinoza himself was denounced as a monster, satanic, even as the Anti-Christ. A flood of refutations poured from the presses, even as the heavy machinery of censorship swung into motion. As for Thomas Hobbes, he was amazed by—perhaps a bit envious of—Spinoza's courage, saying that the *Treatise* "cut through him a barre's length, for he durst not write so boldly."

And what of its intended beneficiary, the Grand Pensionary? His enemies tried to bind Johan de Witt to "the fallen Jew Spinoza"—even claiming that he had read the *Treatise* in manuscript and approved it—but, though he checked the attempt to ban the book, De Witt kept his distance from Spinoza, reportedly letting him know that "his excellency did not want to see him pass his threshold." De Witt would have frowned on much of the book, in any case. His liberalism, great in comparison with other European leaders, shone meagerly against Spinoza's blasts of radical Enlightenment. De Witt's toleration did not go so far as to deny a privileged position for the Dutch Reformed Church, the religious establishment Spinoza abhorred. And De Witt was no democrat. His power base was the oligarchy that had long dominated commercial and political life at The Hague. Majority rule would have had no attraction for him—the continual agitation of royalists and clergy had long since turned the majority of the Dutch bitterly against him.

The depth of that hatred was revealed in the summer of 1672, the "disaster year" in Dutch history, as the Netherlands faced French and German invasion as well as the prospect of a new war with England. The whole country was *radeloos, redeloos en reddeloos*—desperate, irrational, and past recovery—and the Dutch blamed De Witt for their plight. When the Orange Prince William III was named to the vacant executive position of stadtholder, De Witt resigned. Two weeks later, he went to the prison at The Hague to see his brother, Cornelis, who had been arrested on trumped-up charges and then acquitted but not yet released. A mob enraged by the acquittal broke into the prison and killed both men, and then hung them by their feet from a scaffold and tore their bodies to pieces.

Spinoza was so horrified and outraged by the grisly murders that he prepared to go to the site and leave a placard that read, *Ultimi Barbarorum*—You are the worst barbarians. He might have shared the fate of the brothers had his landlord not locked the door to keep him in. But for all the rage that continued to be directed his way in the Netherlands, regard for Spinoza abroad, colored perhaps with curiosity, only grew. In 1673, the elector palatine tendered him a professorship at the University of Heidelberg, and that same year, he was promised a French pension—if he dedicated a book to Louis XIV. He declined both offers, but his contact with the French at Utrecht, which their army occupied, led to Spinoza's own confrontation with a mob when he returned to his house at The Hague. Suspicious that he was a spy or traitor, the crowd worked itself up to a state of threatening to smash into the house and murder him. Bravely he went out the door and managed to calm the mob with assurances that he was a loyal republican with the welfare of his country at heart.

But two years later, in 1675, when word spread that he would publish the completed *Ethics,* the old calumnies were heard again, along with rumors that the new work was more dangerous than the *Treatise,* that Spinoza would try to prove that there was no God. Ominously, theologians lodged complaints with the government, which was controlled by Orangists determined to crack down on republicans. Courageous though he was, Spinoza had had enough of vitriolic controversy; he abandoned his plan to publish the *Ethics.*

By then, his health was in decline, lungs irreparably harmed by years of inhaling glass dust from the lenses he was grinding. He took his illness with customary stoicism for the most part, like the free man who, in his description, "thinks of nothing less than of death, and his wisdom is a meditation on life, not on death."

He died in February 1676, only forty-four years old. Soon after, a friend sent his writing desk, crammed with unpublished manuscripts including the *Ethics,* to Amsterdam, where other friends prepared them for publication. Editions of his work, in Dutch and Latin and under his own name, appeared the next year.

THE LIGHT OF EXPERIENCE

John Locke, the most consequential of Enlightenment philosophers, was a latecomer to the vocation. Born the same year as Spinoza, 1632, he was nearly forty before he attempted a systematic work and in his late fifties before any of his major treatises were delivered to the presses. A slow worker, his thoughts gestating for decades, Locke filled large notebooks with ideas and citations, writing draft after draft with such extensive changes that they scarcely seemed the same work.

Locke's hesitation to publish had yet another source—an aversion to controversy, worsened by his habit of escalating "trifling quarrels" into bitter, long-lived tempests. Hypersensitivity to criticism ill-served the man who talked of his "unmedleing temper" and claimed to desire nothing more than "to passe silently through this world," yet who was meddling in—actually overturning—received opinion in almost every way that counted.

The gradual tug of Locke's thought was in ever more radical directions. It was this evolution, endpoint uncertain, that most accounted for his late appearance in print. Grandson of a rich merchant, son of a man who defied Charles I, a scion of the landed gentry, Locke was a conventionally minded, not very distinctive scholar at Westminster and Oxford. Though impatient with the Aristotelian curriculum, complaining that it was "perplex'd with obscure Terms and stuff'd with useless Questions," Locke himself, in his teaching at Oxford and early writings, was a model of scholastic form and substance. He was no less conservative in his opinions, boasting that "there is no one who can have a greater respect and veneration for authority than I" and welcoming the restoration of Charles II as a reestablishment of "the *happiest state*" and "the *purest church*."

It was experience that changed John Locke's mind, as he haltingly emerged from Oxford's ivory tower. A "Bachelor of Medicine," he had his first sustained encounter with the Enlightenment in the form of Robert Boyle, experimentalist extraordinaire who would become known as the father of modern chemistry. Boyle gave new direction to Locke's medical studies at Oxford. Locke for instance put to use Boyle's air pump to reconsider inherited notions about respiration. He also helped Boyle collect data, though an attempt to take a barometer into a lead mine to measure the pressure underground was frustrated by miners who disbelieved Locke's explanation of his purpose—and by women who in their fear took Locke and a friend for "Conjurers."

Boyle also gave Locke an important push by inspiring him with his own fascination with the new natural philosophy. He opened his library to the young man and Locke plunged in with pleasure. He was particularly struck by the physics of Descartes, whose methods differed so radically from the Aristotelianism he had been fed at Oxford. Though he "very often differed in opinion" from Descartes, he told a friend that it was the Frenchman's work that first gave him "a relish of philosophical studies."

Locke's life of study and contemplation was transformed when in 1667 he entered the great world as companion to an aristocrat immersed in high-level power struggles. His patron and friend, Anthony Ashley Cooper, a baron and later first Earl of Shaftesbury, was one of the most accomplished and turbulent politicians of the day, serving as chancellor of the exchequer and lord chancellor.

Locke plunged into the turmoil of parliamentary life in London despite the heavy smog that aggravated his asthma and would shorten his life. Besides serving as Ashley's secretary and advisor, he held the small offices of Secretary of Presentations, which involved him in ecclesiastical matters, and Secretary and Treasurer of the Council of Trade. He was a minor participant in—but the closest observer of—a conflict that began to intensify rapidly in the early 1680s until it threatened again to plunge the "happiest state" into civil war. Ashley was an early leader of the Whig faction of aristocrats and leading citizens opposed to the succession of Charles II's brother James, heir apparent and open Catholic. When Ashley and his fellow Whigs failed to obtain a parliamentary act excluding James from the succession on religious grounds, they turned to planning for insurrection, laying a succession of plots. Not one of them thrived, but Ashley felt enough heat from the government that he escaped to Holland in 1682, where he died soon after. Locke was so closely identified with Ashley and associated with other plotters that a year later he, too, departed for exile in Holland.

* * *

Exile stimulated Locke to bring to fruition the many works he had been preparing for decades. His distinctiveness as a thinker blossomed on the other side of the Channel. Like most other philosophers of the Enlightenment, he gave a central place to the glowing idea of reason, but his account of it was more qualified, better grounded in empiricism. Though Descartes helped introduce him to the power of rational thought, the Englishman was alive to its limitations, that it would approach the truth only when combined with experience, which included the crucial factor of education. Experience "*must teach me,* what Reason cannot." In experience, Locke wrote, "all our Knowledge is founded; and from that it ultimately derives it self" and "*supplies our Understandings with all the materials of thinking.*" But even with all those materials, the mathematical certainty about the whole world that Descartes sought was impossible. "Our Business here is not to know all things, but those which concern our Conduct," Locke concluded. "If we can find out those Measures . . . we need not be troubled, that some other things escape our Knowledge."

Here was Locke's pragmatic, "common-sense" philosophy in a nutshell, whose spirit of modesty and accessibility would give the Enlightenment a new breadth of reach and influence. In France, it would challenge Cartesianism and win over such philosophes as Jean le Rond d'Alembert. In Locke's thought, d'Alembert wrote admiringly, "the principles of metaphysics . . . are the same for the philosophers as for the general run of the people."

This reasonableness of temper and empiricism in method were, in fact, Britain's distinctive contributions to the Enlightenment's search for truth. English empiricism had roots in Francis Bacon's championing of induction and was taken further by the experimental work of Locke's mentor Boyle. The towering figure in this British scientific tradition was Isaac Newton, who pronounced in his greatest work, the 1687 *Principia, "hypotheses non fingo"*—"I feign no hypotheses"—meaning that his physics would be based not on metaphysics but on observation and experimentation. And like Locke, Newton acknowledged that not all phenomena were explicable by mechanical science. He did not *know,* he said, the cause of gravity; "it is enough that gravity really exists and acts according to the laws we have set forth and is sufficient to explain all the motions of the heavenly bodies and of our sea."

Locke became well acquainted with Newton after his return from Holland in 1689, and the two thinkers worked in occasional and informal tandem. The question of their influence on one another has been much debated. Probably the *Principia* helped confirm Locke in his long-held methodological conclusions—delightful confirmation, with all the wonders Newton was able to expose by applying those methods. Both were admirers of Descartes and both turned away from him in a common direction. Of course, to the imagination, Newton was the greater figure, a man who had puzzled out two of nature's grandest mysteries, gravity and light, whom William Wordsworth would portray as "voyaging through strange seas of Thought, alone." Alexander Pope's verse memorialized him as a demiurge, a divine emanation:

> Nature, and Nature's Laws lay hid in Night,
> God said, Let Newton be! and All was Light.

But for d'Alembert, Locke was Newton's equal, the creator of metaphysics—philosophy—just as Newton had created physics.

* * *

Locke's methodological empiricism was closely related to his thoughts about human nature, especially the mind. His most radical contribution was his dismissal of innate ideas—of right and wrong, of good and evil, of original sin or the existence of God. He saw them as impositions by "Dictators of Principles" and "Teachers of unquestionable Truths," who demanded that men suspend their own "Reason and Judgment" and accept as "an innate principle" anything the authorities decided would make them more easily governed.

Descartes had discovered the foundation of knowledge in the total skepticism that led to the *cogito*. For Locke, it began in the mind of a newborn child, a tabula rasa—"white Paper, or Wax, to be moulded and fashioned as one pleases." The mind had inherent capacities or potentials, including for reason. "We are born to be, if we please, rational creatures," although "it is use and exercise only that makes us so."

Locke's model was of a radical equality—all human beings born with equally unfurnished but equally potential-laden minds. "Ancient savage *Americans*," he wrote, were alike to any European in "natural Endowments and Provisions." Day laborer and country gentleman differed not in their "natural parts" but in the "different scope" of their lives, the range of education and experience responsible for "furnishing their heads with ideas." Locke asserted that "of all the Men we meet with, Nine Parts of Ten are what they are, Good or Evil, useful or not, by their Education," including all aspects of environment and experience. Education was decisive though not final—the human mind never entirely lost its plasticity as it responded to new ideas and experiences. The laborer could, even as a grown man, obtain enlightenment, though the overcoming of lifelong habits might be difficult. Meanwhile, the gentleman of "freer fortune and education" might, if he neglected his understanding, descend to "brutish stupidity."

No single idea of the Enlightenment was so laden and sweeping as this. If people could transform their minds, they could change their lives, and together with others they could change their communities and beyond. Against the fixity and fatalism that underlay the authority of state and church, Locke put this potential, this humble seed, in the human mind with world-altering possibilities. For centuries, people were understood—and understood themselves—to be born corrupt, damaged by sin, torn between dueling impulses toward good and evil, and threatened with eternal damnation. Locke wiped the slate clean; he gave people the possibility of starting the world anew.

His idea of mind forever altered the way education was thought of, including the hated scholastic "cramming" of his own experience. But though it followed from Locke that every child, equal at birth, knowing nothing of rank or station, should have a right to education, it would be more than a century before the principle of universal education began tentatively to take hold against the resistance of the "Teachers of unquestionable Truths." The shaping of the human mind became at the same time more important and more complex, as well as more contested. Even Locke's greatest admirers, like Voltaire, seemed to miss the point, doubtful that education really could be beneficial to the low-born, those Voltaire called the canaille, or pack of dogs.

* * *

That there were vast disparities even within the same society, differences that in some cases created human beings others scarcely recognized as such, was indisputable. But what if one rejected the conventional thought that such inequalities were inevitable—natural—because people were born unequal, with sometimes radically different mental furniture? Could any political order allow men and women to realize the possibilities glimpsed in Locke's thinking about natural human equality?

Just as he was less pessimistic about human nature, so the men and women in Locke's state of nature were less brutish than Hobbes or even Spinoza portrayed. Indeed, these natural humans might live reasonably together in a "State of Peace, Good Will, Mutual Assistance, and Preservation," though war could break out at any moment. Locke described it like this: "In the beginning all the World was *America*."

Why, then, should people join together in a civil society? After all, governments were also known to wage war, sometimes against their own citizens. But in Locke's state of nature, the insecurity and fear that would drive people together centered directly not on life or liberty, but on property, or what he also called "estates." Property, for Locke, was more than a means of subsistence; it was the product of labor, which was the "unquestionable Property of the Labourer" and which, by taking and transforming something from nature, "annexes" it, thereby excluding "the common right of other Men." Civil society, then, was created "for the Regulating and Preserving of Property." Of course, in Locke's imagined "America," property was little more than what people were able to produce for their own consumption, suggesting a rough and enduring equality. But in real civil society—in Locke's England, for example—property was not distributed equally, especially with the "*Invention of Money*." Was the natural right to property unlimited, protecting any amount of all types of property, including those that had no meaningful relation at all to a person's own labor?

The ambiguities of Locke's various remarks on the issue have led many to see him as, for better or worse, the first great apologist for capitalism, for the unlimited accumulation of wealth secured by nearly absolute property rights, for the virtual identification of property with life and liberty. Others, noting Locke's comments on the communal origins of property—as a grant from God to all men collectively—and what he called his bold affirmation of the "Rule of Propriety," that "every Man should have as much as he could make use of," claim him as a proto-socialist, or at least a redistributionist who would ensure that everyone had a stake in society.

The challenge in evaluating Locke's views on property was to reconcile them with the egalitarian thrust of his theories of mind and, even more, with the faith in individual freedom so powerful that his entire body of work might be seen as a multifaceted brief for human liberty. His dismissal of innate ideas liberated men from inherited burdens, while the blank page of the mind offered wide opportunities for self-realization. A foe of fanaticism, Locke challenged the coercion of established churches. "Whatsoever may be doubtful in religion, yet this at least is certain, that no religion which I believe not to be true, can be either true or profitable for me," he wrote in *A Letter Concerning Toleration*. ". . . The care of each man's soul, and of the things of heaven, which neither does belong to the commonwealth nor can be subjected to it, is left entirely to every man's self." Toleration, he held, should be extended to the different Protestant sects, as well as to pagans and Muslims and Jews. But Locke himself tolerated some intolerance—toward Catholics with their allegiance to Rome and toward atheists because they had no religion to be tolerated!

But more than religious liberty or liberty through property was to be written into the Lockean state. By denying that kings were divinely authorized or were sovereign, that government was their property, or that people's rights depended on their grace and favor, Locke struck blows at the pillars of absolutism. In their place he envisioned a civic order founded on the consent of the governed, in which the people, possessed of inalienable natural rights to "Lives, Liberties, and Estates," were sovereign and government was responsible to them for action or inaction. That meant, contrary to Hobbes, that the people retained the right and power to dissolve their government and create a new one.

Such principles would secure a government of laws that in turn allowed people to live in freedom. For Locke, liberty was not a merely negative value, defined by an absence of infringement by government or other people. As a natural right possessed by all, it obliged government to create conditions for its enjoyment and enlargement, though what that meant in practice would be debated for centuries. Still, liberty was a means, not an end. The greatest good, Locke thought, was *happiness*. "The businesse of men" was "to be happy in this world by the enjoyment of the things of nature subservient to life health ease and pleasure and by the comfortable hopes of an other life when this is ended." Locke doubted that men could reach such an equable state in this life, beset as they were by "a constant succession of *uneasinesses.*" Moreover, there was no single road to happiness, no authority to prescribe it. True to the individualism that pervaded Locke's philosophy, each person had to find his or her own way. But the "highest perfection" of human nature lay in the effort, in the "careful and constant pursuit of true and solid happiness."

• • •

Locke's Dutch exile ended after James II, who had succeeded his brother Charles in 1684, was toppled from the throne five years later by an invasion from the Netherlands commanded by William III, the same Prince of Orange who had displaced Johan de Witt in The Hague two decades before.

The Glorious Revolution, as it came to be called, was a Whig triumph. Attempted invasions in earlier years, with little more than tacit Dutch support, had failed miserably. In one case, an English spy made note of "John Locke, previously the secretary to Lord Shaftesbury," aboard an invasion ship at the port of Amsterdam. Whigs had courted and cajoled Dutch leaders, with a delegation of senior aristocrats from across the Channel finally persuading William to save England from "Popery and Slavery."

After his takeover, William summoned a Convention to resolve constitutional issues raised by the events—in his words, to "lay the foundations of a firm security for your religion, laws, and your liberty." The questions included the status and power of the king. After the struggle with James and remembering the war provoked by James's father, Charles I, the Convention was determined to settle this once and for all and did so on a Whig principle: the king was not sovereign but a constitutional monarch, elected not by God but by the British people.

Locke was invited to share the spoils of victory, reportedly offered the position of envoy to Austria or Prussia. He turned down the flattering proposal with a list of reasons, but he didn't mention that he was then seeing to the publication, at last, of his major works. In 1689 and 1690, he published the *Letter Concerning Toleration,* the *Two Treatises of Government* that contained his political science, and *An Essay Concerning Human Understanding.* A few years later came another masterpiece, *Some Thoughts Concerning Education,* and *The Reasonableness of Christianity.*

It was a great, late harvest, a testament to his own evolution through experience and a fitting end to a century when the intellectual life of Europe had been utterly transformed. But the practical implications of the revolution in ideas had scarcely been tested. That would be the work of the next century.

2

Rule Britannia?

The Glorious Revolution—it turned out—was something less than glorious. It was not even, leading Tories and Whigs would both agree, a revolution—not a rising of the English people against intolerable tyranny, but the abdication of one king and his replacement by another. The balance of powers at the top of government shifted. The king lost sovereign power and became a limited, constitutional monarch whose authority remained to be clarified. Old aristocratic Tories, champions of James II, lost their grip while new ones, triumphant Whigs, competed for place. The year 1689 resembled, more than anything, a reshuffle of elites, far above the heads of the people.

That was how England's rulers meant it to be. Even for the Whigs who accomplished it, revolution was an alarming term, reminiscent of the upheaval and violence that had attended the rebellion against Charles I and the triumph of Cromwell. Now the aim was not a revolutionary new order but stability, after two brutal centuries of religious violence, civil wars, coups and failed coups, and horrendous slaughters. Chaos and upheaval would now rarely spill beyond the political battlegrounds of Westminster and the royal palaces in London and Windsor. The 1689 Act of Toleration defused strife among Protestant sects, though it excluded unitarians, Catholics, and atheists from what John Locke called "the establishment of equal liberty."

Locke would be credited with the revolution's intellectual leadership, his *Two Treatises of Government* seen as its most effective apologia, but the "settlement" of 1689 was hardly the enactment of Enlightenment principles espoused by radical Whigs like Locke. Though Whig moderates extolled its perfection of liberty, it seemed designed to deny the most unsettling of Locke's doctrines, principles that were, as one clergyman declared from the pulpit, "fit for nothing, but to ruin kingdoms and commonwealths"—above

39

all, Locke's transforming idea that government was established and maintained by the consent of the governed, in which all men had an equal voice. "*Who shall be Judge* whether the Prince or Legislative act contrary to their Trust?" he had asked, and answered, "*The People shall be Judge.*"

The 1689 settlement was careful to deny the people that power. Its Declaration of Rights, despite the resounding promise to restore the "antient rights and Liberties" of Englishmen, was mainly a forceful statement of *Parliament's* rights against the Crown. Indeed, the keystone of the settlement was Parliament's assumption of the sovereignty that had before belonged to monarchs, in a fatal blow to the divine right of kings, who now were, in theory, subject to Parliament's control. And Parliament in turn was—in theory—accountable to the people.

Kings, though, retained formidable independent authority, not least the power to summon and dissolve Parliament and to make and break ministries. The "Royal Closet"—the room in which they granted audiences to ministers—became a prime jostling ground for rivalrous politicians. Moreover, a "Patriot King," still possessed of the symbolism if not the reality of sovereignty, could portray himself as standing above the petty and self-interested contentions of political factions to represent England's true interests.

As for those politicians, most parliamentary leaders were aristocrats with hereditary seats in the House of Lords. Members of the "people's House"—the Commons—were elected by a narrow sliver of propertied Englishmen from constituencies often dominated by those same aristocrats. They bore no real responsibility to the people. As an influential commentator described it in 1700, elected MPs had the "Power absolute to consent or dissent, without ever acquainting those that sent" them to the Commons.

In defining the English Enlightenment, John Locke had sought to elevate the dignity of all men, ascribing to each natural rights and a claim to freedom, the powers of reason, and the capacity to learn—to gain enlightenment. But English government after the Glorious Revolution remained nearly feudal, with aristocratic factions, as well as the Crown, battling for preeminence, each claiming to speak for England, while ordinary English people stood by like mute beasts in the shadow of power. How would they emerge into the light and gain their voice and their vote?

THE WIDENING GAP

England in the eighteenth century was a place of extraordinary economic and demographic dynamism. Inventors and other innovators spearheaded industrial change, especially in textiles, coal, and iron. There were water wheel improvements, innovative steam pumps, and new processes for "puddling and rolling" wrought iron. Largely due to improved hygiene and better nutrition, population was soaring across the island—from a total of around five million in 1730 to above six million in 1750 to almost eight million by 1790. Industrial centers and port cities expanded rapidly. Birmingham was the first provincial city to reach a population of fifty thousand, in 1780. Liverpool, with its trade in grain and slaves, and Glasgow, marketing tobacco and linen, both grew apace.

London was the biggest and busiest city in England—and in all of Europe. Its population was well over half a million in the 1770s and swelling rapidly as people streamed in from Scotland, Wales, and Ireland, from the Home Counties, from abroad. The Irish settled into a "Little Dublin," while other neighborhoods filled with thousands of Jews who had fled Spain and Portugal and eastern Europe, and with French Huguenots escaping religious persecution. Several thousands of blacks had settled in London from the West Indies or, later, the American South; some were slaves, many others free servants.

The city was the world's greatest trading center. At the docks a wilderness of slender masts lined the Thames. The sailing vessels disgorged tea, china, muslin, cotton yarn, pepper and spices from the East Indies, sugar, rum, coffee, cocoa from the West Indies, rice, tobacco, cotton, corn, skins, indigo from North America, fruit and gums from Africa, hemp, linen, iron and tallow from the Baltics. London handled the bulk of the nation's imports and also dominated internal traffic, especially produce. While most roads were execrable, they were improving. An agrarian writer noted that getting to London from the country had once taken four or five days: "But now! a country fellow one hundred miles from London jumps on to a coach-box in the morning and for eight or ten shillings gets to town by night."

For anyone with enough shillings London was a pleasure garden, abounding in markets, parks, chocolate and coffee houses, taverns and brandy shops. Fleet Street and Drury Lane were known for sparkling theater, Russell Street in Covent Garden for bustling bookshops, dim alleys for warrens of prostitutes. To the rich, London offered fashions in large, well-lighted shops on Bond Street, art salesrooms in Pall Mall, perfumes, millinery, furs, and parasols in the great squares of the West End.

*   *   *

The old rich, living off their ancestral lands, flocked to London in their fine carriages and reopened their town houses for the "season." Some remained to take their seats in Parliament, where they were heavily overrepresented in both Houses. They were mainly of Tory heritage, descendants of the High Church conservatives who had opposed the Glorious Revolution sponsored by their political enemies, the Whigs. Some would remain loyal to King James II and the Jacobite cause until the final defeat of "Bonnie Prince Charlie," James's grandson, at the Battle of Culloden in 1746. Tories were critical of the centralization of power in Parliament and the toleration of nonconforming Protestants. Especially under Anne, Mary's younger sister who succeeded as queen in 1702, party combat between Whigs and Tories was so furious and engrossing that Joseph Addison, the Whig essayist, wrote that children "no sooner begin to speak, but Whig and Tory are the first words they learn." They "contract all the virulence and passion of party before they come to the use of their reason."

The two parties alternated in power until the fatal illness of childless Queen Anne in 1714 again raised the dangerous issue of succession. In a devastating miscalculation, Tory leaders played for a Stuart restoration—and lost. The Whigs successfully championed the importation of the Elector of Hanover, Anne's closest living Protestant relative, both great-grandchildren of James I. He became George I, and the Whigs grew so dominant in the new regime that the Tory party virtually disappeared. Yet Whig rule was scarcely enlightened by the ideals of 1689, and as the Whigs themselves fractured, party labels grew vague and almost meaningless, while politics descended into factional brawls on loosely defined "Country" and "Court" platforms.

As so often, disorderly politics led to the assumption of power by a strongman. The first was Robert Walpole, who became principal minister in 1724. As leader of the Court faction, made up mainly of loyalist Whigs, Walpole showed genius in controlling a fragmented House of Commons. He was, acknowledged a Whig dissident, the Earl of Chesterfield, the "best parliament-man, and the ablest manager of Parliament, that I believe ever lived." Walpole served under two King Georges, I and II, before falling in 1742 in a dispute over his conduct of England's role in a continental war.

A second strongman emerged a decade and a half later, propelled into power by renewed hostilities in Europe. William Pitt was called by a reluctant George II in 1757 to lead a new cabinet. Pitt was an anti-Hanoverian Whig who claimed to speak not for a party but as a "patriot," for the nation. He was a formidable-looking man with a long nose and haughty stare. Through sheer force of conviction and assuredness—his qualities of leadership—the "Great Commoner" dominated the government as he plotted grand strategy against France and its Spanish and Austrian allies.

The Seven Years' War, 1756–63, later dubbed by Winston Churchill as the "First World War," was fought in Europe, America, and on the seas between, at enormous cost in men and money, but ending in British victory. Conquering Canada, driving France out of most of its colonies, and seizing Manila and Havana from the Spanish, the British, according to historian Linda Colley, "assumed for themselves the reputation of being the most aggressive, the most affluent and the most swiftly expanding power in the world." Hail Brittannia!

But if war empowered Pitt, negotiations over restoring peace disabled him, as bitter disputes broke out over his conduct and intentions. No one followed him as a model leader. Nor had the political system changed. After his resignation in 1761, the British reverted to weak parliamentary rule with continually shifting ministries. The factions re-fought their old battles, played over the heads of the small electorate and of the vast majority with no vote at all.

· · ·

And then there were the kings, God's anointed. The three Hanoverian Georges of the eighteenth century were so unremarkable as persons—dull, duller, dullest, a wag said—that their monarchies were often pictured as governmentally weak, even *fainéant*. The first two Georges were almost subservient to their Whig sponsors and more preoccupied with using British power to advance their Hanoverian interests than with the governance of England. By pointed contrast, George III declared on his accession in 1760, "Born and educated in this Country, I glory in the name of *Briton*." He identified himself as a Patriot King—virtuous, dutiful, and steadfastly devoted to the interests of England above faction or party.

Bulky of body and fleshly of jowl, he hardly looked the part of a sovereign majesty. Comfortably married, he had no mistresses to pique the press and the public. Even his coronation, featuring royal barges on the Thames and a cavalcade of carriages and the Guard, was judged less than a triumph. Later a cartoon showed a court official trying to awaken him from a deep sleep on a couch. He was not concerned enough, though, to make pretensions. He traveled, people noted, in a plain carriage escorted by a few light horse.

But George III did not need to demonstrate his authority. It existed. He had to respect the limits placed on royal power after the Glorious

Revolution—Parliament's control of the king's purse was a particular rub—but, as he confided to the French ambassador in 1763, "his fixed plan was to establish his authority without breaking the law."

To do so, he behaved much like a party politician with exceptional resources. Not sharing the pro-Whig prejudices of his predecessors, George III was drawn instinctively to Tory conservatism. He took seriously his role at the head of the nobility, using his patronage not only to reward friends but to uphold rank and precedent. Hostile to factions as he was—he wished to "put an end to those unhappy distinctions of party called Whigs and Tories"—he took for granted government by aristocratic oligarchies, by "Gentlemen of landed property." He used his prerogative to elevate favorites to high office—he made the Earl of Bute, who had been a surrogate father for him in childhood, his chief minister in 1761, despite Bute's own protests of his "ignorance in business." As readily, he brought down ministers—usually Whig—whose policies displeased him.

Unlike so-called Enlightened despots on the continent, George III scorned schemes of modernization and reform. He did not share the Enlightenment—and Whiggish—view of history as an inexorable march of progress. Though he delighted in gadgets and new technologies and paid the occasional royal visit to a pin factory or new canal, his true interests were rural and agricultural. The industrialization that was sweeping the country during his reign left "Farmer George" cold. Yet evidences of that transformation were all about him in the king's capital.

* * *

London's economic expansion had long been fueled by banks, insurance companies, the Royal Exchange, and the Bank of England, but its undergirding was the "laboring masses": coal heavers, drovers, bellows menders, knife grinders, rag pickers, and, among the more skilled, carpenters, apothecaries, clothiers, brewers, ironmongers, confectioners, chandlers, hatters. "At every level," according to historian Roy Porter, "labour had its own ranking of honour: the actress Mrs. Charke admitted that when down on her luck she had hawked sausages, but indignantly refuted the aspersion that she had sold flowers."

People struggled to maintain human dignity in circumstances that threatened their existence. Wages, even for skilled workers, were meager. While the government's first minister earned £3,000 a year and James Boswell's father gave his son an annual London allowance of £200, a printer or journeyman tailor might earn £1 a week and textile workers less than half that.

A footman's annual pay of £8 was little more than the £5 his master paid for his livery. Women and children labored for their survival. Historian Dorothy Marshall described "dirty, bedraggled women, eking out a pitiable existence by crying their wares." Washerwomen worked incredibly long hours for a pittance. "Sifting ashes and cinders was another ill-paid employment that absorbed much female labour of the lowest kind." Children as young as four were for hire as chimney sweeps, sent up to extinguish fires and sometimes having fires set beneath them if they hesitated.

If London was a pleasure garden for some, it was a hellhole for countless numbers of the poor and a forerunner of the teeming, devastated cities that began to spot the globe over the next two centuries. Destitute families crowded one room in ramshackle dwellings looking out on narrow, filthy alleys. Sanitation was primitive, with cesspools lodged in basements. Parasites bred and black rats roamed. Life was shorter in the slums. Every year, thousands died from consumption and smallpox. Children especially suffered from rickets and worms. People also starved: a magistrate told Samuel Johnson that Johnson had "under-rated the number" when he had computed that twenty every week—more than a thousand a year—died of hunger in hovels like these. Outdoors, the streets were haunted by undernourished, stunted, abandoned children. Youths organized street gangs, dividing up their territories, shoplifting, picking pockets, terrorizing residents and each other. Streetwalkers numbered in the tens of thousands. For decades, poor Londoners were under the sway of a "gin madness"; in his 1751 *Enquiry into the Causes of the Late Increase of Robbers,* novelist and magistrate Henry Fielding estimated that for more than a hundred thousand people, "that poison called *Gin*" was their principal sustenance.

*   *   *

Conditions were little better in King George's beloved countryside. His enthusiasm for agricultural efficiencies did little to improve the lot of rural people, except perhaps the tenants who farmed his own vast estates. Much was made of the bucolic life in the countryside—the fellowship of farm communities, the "independence of the yeoman," the children's games and the dances on the village common. But the vaunted independence of farmworkers was largely mythical—they were the victims of harsh landowners and overseers, unpredictable markets, ravaging diseases, weather conditions, far-off wars and revolutions. Whole families would labor at piecework in "workshops" that were also their bedrooms, cramped spaces filled with charcoal fumes. Out in the fields people worked from daybreak to sunset—sixteen hours in summer—on an unnourishing diet of barley bread, potatoes, and tea. Wages fell behind the cost of living as too many hands chased too few jobs, and with recurrent bad harvests, more and more farm families dropped into destitution, while young people migrated to the cities.

When harvests failed or prices fell, farmers fought back against middlemen and profiteers, amid sporadic rioting. Some outbreaks were more colorful than lethal, as at Nottingham's Goose Fair, when whole cheeses were rolled down the streets in protest against high prices. Other incidents suggested a measure of solidarity among the hard-pressed. In Honiton in 1766, lace-workers seized corn from farmers they thought was being withheld in order to drive prices up, sold it in the market at a popular price, and returned the money to the farmers. But all too often poor farmers were pitched against impoverished buyers, as in Halifax, where weavers assaulted corn sellers. In Ireland a "mob" bought up all the corn in the market to prevent it from being shipped out in a Dutch vessel waiting in the quay.

In London, too, workers periodically rose in protest. Silk weavers in Spitalfields, the East End, rioted in 1719 and again in 1720 against the importation of calico, which fed a growing fashion for the cheap printed material. In 1768, workers from a variety of trades—watermen, glass grinders, tailors, coopers, coal heavers—protested low wages. Some of these actions had a short-term effect—the second wave of Spitalfields protests in 1720, which included attacks on women dressed in calico, induced Parliament to ban the wearing of all calicoes. But other protests were brutally repressed—seven coal heavers were hanged in 1768 before a crowd of fifty thousand. And in the anti-Irish riots of 1736, protesters targeted workers who were no better—and perhaps worse—off than themselves.

The potential strength of the working poor lay in converting their hardships and grievances into massed political action, but the riots of the eighteenth century were episodic and ephemeral events, with few lasting effects and no enduring leadership or organization. In London and other cities, workers formed clubs so they could share in primitive social insurance arrangements and even formed "combinations" to challenge their employers, but these, too, rarely lasted. Where such combinations overcame repression, historian Paul Langford wrote, "as in the London tailoring trade, or in the royal dockyards, it was a tribute to the determination of well-established industrial groups. In most of the new industries the manufacturer swept all before him." Despite sporadic attempts, no citywide or industry-wide trade unions could form to unify urban labor.

For some workers, the most unifying force of all was anti-Catholicism, which inevitably led to a broader disunity among the poor. "Anti-Papist" riots erupted in the Scottish Lowlands in 1778 and in parts of London two years later when Protestant militants thronged to Westminster to present a petition for repeal of a bill that had granted relief to Catholics. When the Commons refused to debate the question, the demagogic Lord George Gordon spouted bitter harangues that aroused tens of thousands of protesters. The cry was simple and ancient: "No Popery." Violence swept London as mobs attacked Catholic chapels and homes, as well as Newgate, the Clink, and Fleet prisons and that citadel of the Establishment, the Bank of England. Creating their own street leadership, the rioters held London at their mercy for almost a week. The bigots, along with pickpockets and released inmates, had had their moment. But it ended with hundreds of protesters shot down by the army—an episode that illuminated all that was divisive and self-destructive among the poor.

. . .

The central thrust of the Enlightenment was contained in its very name— the pursuit of knowledge and understanding. Its philosophers held that it was available to all men, in adequate, if not equal, measure, and working-class Britons, left uneducated by their rulers, were enlightening themselves, through reading and participation in voluntary clubs and societies. It had a transforming effect.

With the "increase of reading," testified Thomas Preston, a radical "Patriot and Shoemaker," "the charm of *Ignorance* which had so long lulled my mind into a *comparative* indifference at the people's wrongs, was now beginning to disappear." There was as yet no press aimed at the working class and its concerns in the 1780s, but people found ideas and inspiration in all kinds of sources. If books and newspapers were too expensive to be bought, they could be borrowed or rented from the growing number of libraries or read in newsrooms. Francis Place, whose radical career would extend into the era of the Reform Act, was a teenaged apprentice in the leather trade when he borrowed a copy of *Aristotle's Compleat Master Piece*. The book made him doubt the authority of religion; though he struggled to keep his faith, finally "reason was too strong for superstition."

The spread of reading was abetted by a thriving print culture. London had been the cradle of printing since 1485, when William Caxton had set up his press in Westminster. The city boasted hundreds of printers and booksellers, but London had no monopoly: by 1740, there were four hundred printing outlets in two hundred towns. By the 1770s, nine London dailies and fifty provincial papers were selling twelve million copies a year. To Samuel Johnson, this proliferation of print, the "boundless liberty" of the press, was the glory of the English Enlightenment, perpetuating "new sentiments to the public without danger of suffering either ridicule or censure." A Bristol clergyman huffed in 1768 that "every man in this Enlightened age" had been "fully instructed by those genteel and easy conveyances of knowledge, newspapers and magazines," and presumed to have the "liberty of making a philosophy (and I might add indeed a religion) for himself."

Perhaps the most influential of publications—certainly the most quoted—were the *Tatler* and the *Spectator,* founded by Joseph Addison and Richard Steele in the early years of the century. The first issue of the *Spectator* borrowed its goal of enlightenment from Horace—"After smoke, the light." Though both periodicals were short-lived, their devotion to bringing "Philosophy out of Closets and Libraries, Schools and Colleges, to dwell in Clubs and Assemblies, at Tea-Tables and in Coffee-Houses," to "enliven Morality with Wit, and to temper Wit with Morality," became a model to legions of successors in the United States as much as in Britain. Appearing in midcentury, *The Female Spectator,* said to be the first magazine written by and about women, offered articles on love, family, female education, and health, including such warnings as that excessive tea drinking could cause hysteria.

Easier to produce were pamphlets, typically pointed, caustic, personal, sometimes urbane, usually aimed at political figures and their vagaries. A doctor complained about trying to keep up with the endless pamphlets, periodicals, books, "the new play—the new poem—the last novel." You would, he said, "hang your heavy head, and roll your bloodshot eyes over thousands of pages weekly."

And those books, books by the thousands: from twenty-one thousand titles published in the 1710s to fifty-six thousand in the century's last decade. Some individual sales were remarkable. Samuel Richardson's novel *Pamela,* published in 1740, went through five editions in twelve months. And while Daniel Defoe's *Robinson Crusoe,* appearing in 1719, had a print run of five thousand in its first year, three decades later, Henry Fielding's *Amelia* sold that many in one week.

Closely entwined with London's burgeoning print culture was its network of clubs and societies rooted in the city's hundreds of coffeehouses, whose main draw was the presence of newspapers. "All Englishmen are great newsmongers," a visiting Frenchman noted. "Workmen habitually begin the day by going to coffee-rooms in order to read the latest news. I have often seen shoeblacks and other persons of that class club together to purchase a farthing paper." Coffeehouses and taverns, too, offered rooms for private groups that sponsored debates and lectures or simply discussions of the issues of the day. At the Robin Hood, workmen paid a small sum for a pint of beer and the chance to have their say—with a five-minute limit—on any topic, including religion and politics.

The most famous of all the clubs met at the Turk's Head tavern. Known simply as The Club, it was founded in 1764 by Samuel Johnson and Joshua Reynolds and included among its members the stalwart Whig Edmund Burke, the great Shakespearean actor David Garrick, and the poet and playwright Oliver Goldsmith. James Boswell sat in when he was in London, making notes of the table talk. Johnson dominated—indeed, Reynolds had conceived of the club as a way of relieving his old friend's loneliness and melancholy.

Johnson has come down in history as a man of far-reaching talents—poet, biographer, journalist, dictionary-maker, scholar, social critic, philosopher—and, especially through Boswell's *Life* of him, as an epic talker with an annihilating wit and brutal candor. Born in 1709 in provincial Lichfield, Johnson epitomized Georgian London in its vigorous combat over ideas and principles, its bitter political factions, its raking, penetrating journalism, its literary genius. He embodied the vital cross-pressures between intellectual dynamism and experimentation and the claims of authority. In an age of change, of Enlightenment, Johnson, as much as any man, stood between the old and the new.

He was a parcel of contradictions—a monarchist who rebuked errant kings, a philosopher who luxuriated in day-to-day political strife, a religious man tormented by doubt and contemptuous of "enthusiasm," a scorner of the "rabble" who sympathized with American Indians and West Indies slaves, a blatant English nationalist and cosmopolitan European thinker, a believer in social order and stability who had broken the trammels of class hierarchy, rising from humble provincial origins to become the arbiter of letters in the great capital. Even so, he was never far from Grub Street, scraping a living by his pen until he received a state pension in his later years.

Politically, Johnson was no party man, but had strong Tory leanings that were drawn not from solidarity with the rich and powerful—he never forgot his background of privation and striving—but from realism, even pessimism, about human nature and society. He disdained the Whig "prejudice" for innovation, for constitutional abstractions. His idea of government had more of Hobbes than of Locke. "Were not the law to interpose," he wrote, "even honest and beneficent men might often . . . fill the country with violence." Given the "instability of human virtue," government was the necessary "coercive power" that might "restrain the exorbitancies of passion, and check the career of natural desires." Enlightenment was, at best, a partial, fragile thing, not leading inexorably to sunny uplands, but dimly illuminating the gloom.

For all of his ferocity in debate, Johnson was capable of great personal kindness and of friendship toward political foes like Burke. But his embrace of John Wilkes was unexpected. Wilkes, radical journalist and populist agitator, as well as prevaricator and occasional embezzler, pushed harder than anyone of the time to bridge the widening gap between Parliament and the street—by bringing the street into Parliament. Wilkes's cause was Lockean—parliamentary reform that would lead to popular rule with the enfranchisement of all Englishmen, including the poor. Elected to the Commons during the Seven Years' War, Wilkes was arrested in 1763 for libeling the king in his journal, the *North Briton*. Parliament expelled him and, despite repeated reelection by his London constituency, kept him out for years. His campaign for his seat in 1768 became a national sensation as supporters rioted to cries of "Wilkes and Liberty!"

To Johnson, Wilkes threatened anarchy; politics, he warned, must aim for "not absolute, but comparative good." Defending Parliament's right to exclude Wilkes, he denounced the "plebian grossness, and savage indecency" of Wilkes's "despicable faction."

James Boswell thrilled to the prospect of bringing together two men who had exchanged vituperations for years, eager to see how his hero Johnson would react to Wilkes's provocations. By the time he succeeded in arranging a dinner party in 1776, Wilkes had been allowed to resume his seat in Parliament; he was also lord mayor of London. And there was new tinder for the expected fire: Wilkes was defending the right of Americans to reject their colonial masters in England, while Johnson was violently opposed. But in the event, there was no fire and little light. Over a good dinner, Johnson succumbed to Wilkes's charm and conviviality as they made small talk, discussed poetry, and teamed up to tease Boswell for his Scottish chauvinism. Politics was scarcely mentioned; Johnson left full of satisfaction with a man he had described as a criminal and seditionist.

As for Wilkes, his passion for reconciling England's rulers with the people they ruled would fade. During the Gordon riots, the "people's hero" was in charge of the soldiers who were defending the Bank of England against the mob.

IMPERIAL RULERSHIP

The chasm between the lives of the British governing aristocracy and of the English people they governed was so wide that the aristocrats were unable to see across it. During the eighteenth century, after centuries of exploration and colonization, these landed aristocrats came to rule over about one-fourth of the world's population. This gap was even wider. The fact that some rich young landowner could in effect buy a seat in Parliament, accept a sinecure in the Foreign Office, then hold authority over millions of people he knew little about and would never visit, seemed grotesque on the face of it.

Yet these "empire-builders" on the whole were highly successful in attaining their goals, political, military, economic, despite their ignorance and badly flawed machinery of rule, and even though communication overseas was chancy and impossibly slow, taking weeks for London's instructions to reach Quebec or Boston, months to reach Delhi or Bombay.

What motivated the colossal efforts that imperial Britain and other European states made to accumulate colonies? It was said that England built its empire in a fit of absentmindedness. This was not true. British leaders were highly present-minded, but with diverse goals varying from place to place and time to time.

Enlightenment ideas had inspired much of the early exploration that led to Europe's colonization of the globe—the thirst for knowledge of the earth and seas, of nature in its wild diversity, of human beings in alien cultures. That remained true in the 1700s wherever new frontiers were explored. On his voyages into the Pacific—called by historian Tim Blanning the "Enlightenment's 'New World'"—Captain James Cook sailed with a large complement of scientists and artists to study and depict what they encountered. A naturalist on Cook's second voyage in 1772 testified to Cook's acute attention to the "smallest characteristics" of the peoples he met—"their physical diversity, their temperament, their customs, their mode of life and dress, their form of government, their religion, their ideas of science and works of art, in short everything was collected by Cook for his contemporaries and for posterity."

But whatever the initial thrill of discovery may have been, or the continuing gains in knowledge and understanding, practical men were quick to evaluate the usefulness of what had been found. British rulers saw their overseas possessions variously as bulwarks of imperial power, as checks on rival states, and as supply houses that would make their island less dependent on foreign sources. Distant colonies also served as remote dumping grounds for convicts sentenced to "transportation," as well as for beggars and paupers likely to commit "Crimes and Debaucheries."

Transcending all these motives, though, was Britain's avid appetite for commerce. After all, Cook's explorations eventually drew the wide Pacific into the global network of trade. Colonies were investments, producing raw materials for mother country industries to convert into goods. In the West Indies, first tobacco and then sugar enriched British planters. As British housewives imported ever-increasing quantities of sugar for their jams and biscuits, it became Britain's biggest import. Sugar, though, was a labor-intensive crop, creating a huge demand for an abject workforce: African slaves. The trade in slaves was another source of immense wealth for Englishmen. As early as the 1660s, slaves outnumbered whites in the British West Indies.

On the other side of the globe, the East India Company had served as the agent for the British government in India since the seventeenth century, treating with the ruling Mughal dynasty while thriving on profits from silk and tea, jewels and pepper, and jousting with the French and other rivals.

As the company reached the zenith of its power in the mid-eighteenth century, the Mughal Empire was crumbling into regional successor-states, so the British merchants became the effective rulers of much of the subcontinent. Yet with this power came intensifying corruption as company employees hastened to plunder their new dominions. At the same time, the company was spending vast sums on military operations to maintain its grip on its Indian possessions. Alarmed, political leaders in London sought to rein in their Indian agents. But such was the East India Company's influence in Parliament—numbers of rich company men had returned to buy seats in the Commons—that its Indian monopoly was only dented, not broken.

Were there no higher British stakes in India than profit? The colonists understood little more of the Indians they lived among than did the British government and people far away. Educated Indians bristled at British hauteur and discrimination. "The better classes of the natives of India," according to an Indian petition to Parliament, "are placed under the sway of the Honourable East India Company, in a state of political degradation which is absolutely without a parallel in their former history." They were simply "shut out." It was not only India. Reflecting more broadly on the impact of the European encounter with native peoples, Captain Cook wrote, "we introduce among them wants and perhaps disease which they never before knew and which serve only to disturb that happy tranquility which they and their forefathers enjoyed. If anyone denies the truth of this assertion, let him tell me what the natives of the whole extent of America have gained by the commerce they have had with Europeans."

Rudyard Kipling's bromidic "East is East, and West is West, and never the twain shall meet," was condemned early on as politically incorrect, but the poet did not exaggerate. There was no enlightenment for either side or even much creative conflict in the eighteenth century between Imperial Britain and the alien cultures it invaded. The essential relationship was that between the exploiter and the exploited. Colonies like India on the whole and over the long run were good investments for British bankers and merchants, and British rule in these places aimed to maximize their profits.

＊　＊　＊

It was one thing to try to deal with Asians or Africans. It should have been much easier to manage American colonials. These people were mainly of sound British stock. They were generally Protestant. They read the same British newspapers and pamphlets that Londoners did. Their leaders had been brought up on John Locke and other Enlightenment thinkers. And they had been closely allied with the British in the Seven Years' War, which led to the eviction of the French from northern America.

Moreover, the American colonies consisted of a small, vulnerable population stretched along hundreds of miles of coasts and rivers while Britain had become a world power following its gains in the Seven Years' War, now rivaling other imperial domains—the Ottoman, Persian, Chinese. Its rise had not happened by chance. Crucial had been experienced leadership—not flamboyant, of course, but sensible, flexible, accommodating.

Still, the Seven Years' War brought British irritations with the Americans to a head. The joint military effort had not always been smooth. British who served in North America returned home with a contemptuous view of their partners. Some Americans, they complained, were more interested in profiteering than in providing their share of men and money against the French. "Within parliament about forty to fifty MPs had personal knowledge of or a direct interest in the American colonies," according to historian H. T. Dickinson, "but very few of these men showed any great sympathy with the colonies."

The cardinal issue was *money*. The British leadership wished above all that the colonies support themselves. Running an empire was costly. The Seven Years' War had been ruinously expensive. In 1763 the British national debt stood at an astronomical £132 million. Shouldn't the colonies, as beneficiaries of the war, pay their fair share? In 1765, on the urging of the chief minister, George Grenville, Parliament passed a Stamp Act, requiring Americans to pay duties on bills of sale, legal papers, newspapers, playing cards, and more, just as British taxpayers did. Grenville insisted that the revenue raised by the tax would be spent in America for the benefit of Americans. The colonists brushed that aside; their objection was to the tax itself. Unlike previous taxes levied on them by their own representatives, the stamp duty was imposed by a legislature in which they had no representation.

Reaction was swift and fierce: colonial assemblies rejected the Stamp Act's legality, merchants organized boycotts of British goods, riots shook Boston, New York, and other port cities. "Taxation without representation is tyranny," became the American watchword. Taken aback by the vehemence of the American response, London repealed the act, at the same time reaffirming categorically that Parliament's laws were binding upon its colonial subjects "in all cases whatsoever."

London awaited expressions of gratitude for the Stamp Act repeal. There were none. The British leadership was astonished and indignant. But Americans had other financial grievances, as well as powerful feelings beyond money. Increasingly they were talking about some right of self-government. They were not yet demanding full independence, it was true, and indeed their appeals often attested their loyalty to the king.

Sentiments among English politicians hardened as *their* grievances mounted. Americans violated British trade laws. They resisted colonial governors appointed by the Crown. They refused to pay customs—they smuggled! Their assemblies were tumultuous and sometimes insurrectionary. Some colonies, evidently lacking the most basic loyalty to the mother country, traded and conspired with Britain's mortal enemies, especially France. Hard-liners who saw nothing but selfishness in the American rejection of taxes were eager to teach their rebellious cousins a lesson, and strangely, the East India Company gave them their chance.

To help relieve the company's staggering financial burdens, the government in 1773 exempted it from import duties on Indian tea brought to England and then reexported to America. Americans would have cheaper tea and the company would sell off its stock of seventeen million pounds of tea.

But once again, British leaders seemed to misjudge the American reaction. Import duties on tea had been quietly collected in America for years. But now that Parliament had lifted duties in Britain for the company's benefit, they became a flashpoint. Colonial merchants were outraged: They would be undersold, and perhaps put out of business, by the company. More dangerously, the affair reignited the incendiary charges of parliamentary tyranny.

Then the crisis. Three of the company's first tea ships to reach Boston were boarded by dozens of men dressed as Indians who dumped three hundred chests of tea into the harbor. As news of the Boston Tea Party reached London, the clamor for "coercion" reached a furious pitch. For British leaders, it was a time to choose: either to make the claims of British supremacy in the colonies stick, or to abandon them. In the late spring of 1774, Parliament passed the Coercive Acts. Most notably, the legislation closed the port of Boston until compensation had been paid to the East India Company; altered the Massachusetts charter to provide for its colonial council to be appointed by London, not elected; banned town meetings that were held without royal consent; and, threateningly, ordered the construction of barracks and compulsory quartering of troops in Boston. Lord North, a rare chief minister who had the trust both of George III and of the House of Commons, was confident that his show of force would isolate the Massachusetts extremists and rally loyalists in the colonies. America must bow to the authority of Parliament.

The American response came little more than a month after the Coercive Acts crossed the Atlantic. In September 1774, the first Continental Congress, with fifty-five delegates from twelve of the thirteen colonies, met in Philadelphia to plan coordinated defiance.

⋆ ⋆ ⋆

Through much of the eighteenth century, fragmentation in Parliament meant that opposition to the ruling government was itself split and ineffective. Strongmen like Walpole and Pitt had thrived on strategies of divide and conquer. As transatlantic tensions mounted in the 1770s, opponents of Lord North's coercion flailed ineffectually against his policies. Like much of the British public, the Whig faction led by Lord Rockingham was outraged by the Boston Tea Party. What especially shocked these grandees was the wanton destruction of private property. But when North's coercion only stiffened American spines, the eloquent spokesman for the Rockinghamites, Edmund Burke, demanded conciliation—the restoration of "the former unsuspecting confidence of the colonies in the mother country." To win back the Americans, Burke was ready to give them substantial autonomy within the empire, including the right of consent to parliamentary supremacy.

William Pitt, now Earl of Chatham, could claim to have been one of the original "Friends of America" for siding with the colonists in opposition to taxation without representation in 1766. Now, leading his own band of followers, Pitt proposed a set of conciliations that exceeded Burke's, including recognition of the Continental Congress as a representative body within the empire and the surrender of Parliament's power to tax the colonies. These were far-reaching concessions that would have been unthinkable a decade earlier. But they came too late. While they would place limits on Parliament's supremacy, neither Burke nor Pitt doubted Britain's ultimate right to rule as intrinsic to its imperial mission. Pitt, who had done so much to extend the empire with his leadership during the Seven Years' War, described Britain as "the conducting head, the animating heart, the inspiring soul, which gave life to all the rest." But the Coercive Acts had radicalized Americans—they were moving beyond resistance to revolution.

Two old Whigs like Burke and Pitt might have remembered the teachings of John Locke that justified their own Glorious Revolution. Locke acknowledged that people would rebel only after "a long train of Abuses, Prevarications, and Artifices." But when a government was guilty of "using Force upon the People without Authority," it put itself in "a state of War with the People," and "the People have a right to remove it by force." Blinded by their devotion to empire, Burke and Pitt could not see that a war with the American people had already begun, and they could accept neither American independence nor the measures the government took to end it.

. . .

If North's opponents were more than a few steps behind the Americans, they were also, they feared, too far ahead of the English public. In 1783, when the American war had ended in British defeat, North would claim that his policies had had "almost universal approbation" outside the precincts of Westminster. Yet in 1775, North was to be found worrying to the king that "the cause of Great Britain is not yet sufficiently popular." There was broad support for parliamentary supremacy—hadn't the English struggled for that principle in the previous century?—as well as for empire as a source of power, money, and glory. And there was plenty of resentment toward the Americans—for their refusal to pay taxes ordinary Englishmen were subject to, for their ingratitude and disloyalty.

But at the same time the American crisis polarized the British people, inciting widespread agitation, a press war, and countless petitions and addresses to the king and Parliament. Apart from the endless debates over coercion versus conciliation, most telling were those British who saw the American cause in the mirror of their own, who were stirred by American claims to their rights, whose repression was echoed in the coercion of the colonists.

Foremost among them were the religious Dissenters—the Congregationalists, Quakers, Presbyterians, Baptists—who despite toleration acts still did not enjoy Locke's "equal liberty." To them, America, which had been settled by Dissenters, remained "a Sanctuary to oppressed Protestants in all Parts of the World." Richard Price, a leading nonconformist minister, saw the American Revolution as a "new opening in human affairs," of "free communities under governments which have no religious tests or establishments!"

To radicals like John Wilkes, who praised the Declaration of Independence on the floor of the Commons as a "wise and political measure," the issue was full and equal political rights; they saw kindred spirits in the American revolutionaries. A toast at a "festivity of Liberty" in July 1775 hailed the Americans who were "nobly contending for our rights with their own." The Constitutional Society, founded in 1771, raised money for the relief of the widows and children "of our BELOVED American Fellow Subjects, who, FAITHFUL to the character of Englishmen, preferring Death to Slavery, were, for that Reason only inhumanly murdered by the KING's troops at or near Lexington and Concord." Radicals blamed the corruption of an unrepresentative Parliament for the American disaster—with a free House of Commons, elected by all the people, they claimed, relations between Britain and the colonies would never have come to such a pass. The "vile incendiaries of the war," wrote Thomas Day, a leader of the Society for Constitutional Information, had hastened "the progress of venality and the diminution of the people's influence." With England "doomed to experience every ill it had endeavoured to inflict" on the colonies, it was up to "the free and uncorrupted part of the nation to unite for the assertion of their long-neglected rights, in the most dangerous crisis that ever threatened their destruction."

In fact, models for that unity were also American. The radicals admired—and envied—the networks of associations and "correspondence committees" Americans had created to spread ideas and coordinate action throughout the thirteen colonies. The Americans had a crucial advantage, though, in wresting their rights from their rulers: They waged their campaign against an enemy whose stronghold was an ocean away, while English radicals had to fight their way to freedom from the very heart of the oppressor's citadel.

THE SCOTTISH ENLIGHTENMENT

The people of Scotland knew what it was to live in the shadow of power. For centuries, they had contended with their richer and more powerful neighbors to the south. They had maintained a separate throne, nobility, and legislature, an independent church, their own schools and language. But after the Glorious Revolution overthrew the last Stuart king—James II of England (James VII of Scotland)—followed by a series of disastrous harvests in the 1690s, the Scots were in desperate straits. Continental wars disrupted trade with France, their main commercial partner, while British policy blocked access to markets in England and its colonies.

The initiative for the 1707 Act of Union was in fact Scottish. English Whigs were anxious to forestall a Stuart comeback in the north that would undo their 1689 settlement, but it was the Scots who made the boldest bet: submission to British overlordship in exchange for integration into its commercial empire. Scotland would now become a province of Great Britain, with modest representation in Parliament—based on a franchise even more undemocratic than England's own, with a mere twenty-five persons electing the MP from the city of Edinburgh. But Scotland retained its own religious and legal establishments, as well as control of education. And, baffled by the convolutions of Scottish politics, London left much of its internal government to the natives.

Still, the economic gains of union were painfully slow to appear. Hostility to the unified crown amid continuing privation and high taxes exploded in the Jacobite rebellions of 1715 and 1745. Gradually, though, Scotland revived. Benefiting from imperial commerce and subsidies from the British Treasury, the Scots proved aggressive and resourceful traders. They profited mightily from the Seven Years' War, finding rich markets in England and America. So obvious were the benefits of union by the time of the American crisis that the Scots were the most loyalist of all British subjects, a stance that led to widespread anti-Scottish feeling in the colonies.

But the Scots managed a balance that proved impossible across the Atlantic. Union did not extinguish their national identity. They knew that many Englishmen saw Scotland as a vast "howling Wilderness, a Place of wild Folks that live in the Mountains," as Daniel Defoe described the attitude. After he toured Scotland in 1773, Samuel Johnson noted appreciatively that Scotland's progress since 1707 had in much of the country been "rapid and uniform," but he also encountered appalling destitution in the remote Highlands and Hebrides; he found people for whom, if to their "daily burden of distress any additional weight be added, nothing remains but to despair and die." His traveling companion, James Boswell, recorded Johnson "persevering in the old jokes" at Scottish barbarity, while southern condescension and prejudice enraged David Hume. "Am I, or are you, an Englishman?" he asked a friend. "Will they allow us to be so? Do they not treat with Derision our Pretensions to that Name?" But marginalization within greater Britain mingled so powerfully with the exposure to the wider world brought by union as to create a unique blend of introspection and cosmopolitanism. That outlook contributed to a distinctly Scottish Enlightenment whose originality and impact challenged its southern rival.

· · ·

To a remarkable degree, Scotland's renaissance was the result of what historian Eric Richards termed an "alliance for improvement" between its rising economic and intellectual elites. Union weakened the grip of the Calvinist Church of Scotland and, with increasing toleration, new doors for inquiry opened. While Cambridge and Oxford remained under the stifling scholastic control of the Church of England's Anglican establishment, the pulse of ideas in the university cities of Edinburgh and Glasgow quickened. Intellectual leaders were accorded high status and fame. Hume, an outspoken atheist, liked to tell of the time he stumbled into a deep bog while taking a short cut. An old woman of Edinburgh came by and offered a helping hand up, but recognizing him, she insisted that he first recite not only the Lord's Prayer but the Apostolic Creed.

Undergirding the Scottish Enlightenment was a national school system of "commodious" parish schoolhouses and salaried teachers. By 1750, literacy was over 70 percent. But the glory of Scotland in the eighteenth century was its universities, which became world centers of learning, drawing students from all over Europe and America. Indeed, by the end of the century, it was the fashion for English aristocrats to go north for "Scotch knowledge." Glasgow and Edinburgh came to be known as the "twin cities" of the Scottish Enlightenment, but they were hardly identical twins. Glasgow was a big commercial city, thriving especially on its tobacco trade with the American colonies. Its "tobacco lords"—typically sea captains and traders—made up a new elite that rivaled local aristocrats with ancient lineages. They underwrote the university and supported the city's host of booksellers and presses and its school for the Art of Design.

Edinburgh, Scotland's old capital, was more literary, more intellectual, attracting, Arthur Herman wrote, "outsiders as diverse as Adam Smith, Benjamin Franklin, and the young Robert Burns" with "its close-knit community of scholars and thinkers, who were willing to take up new ideas while putting old ones to the test of discussion and criticism." Scots boasted that only London and Paris could compare with Edinburgh in intellectual creativity.

It was easy to play up the differences and even the rivalry between Glasgow and Edinburgh, but their scholars moved back and forth freely between them—the post coach took only a day and a half—and the two universities were more collegial than competitive, collaborating out of their respective strengths.

* * *

Scotland's perch on the edge of Britain and Europe gave its intellectual leaders a prime vantage from which to view the Enlightenment's main currents. The country's long experience of political turmoil, its skepticism about the glories of the Glorious Revolution, its constitutional union with England and absorption into the empire, its buoyant commercial growth, all encouraged Scottish thinkers to reexamine old assumptions and to give the ideas of the Enlightenment a fresh and distinctive turn.

Francis Hutcheson, for example, was steeped in Locke. Born in 1694 in County Down in Ulster, where the Scots Presbyterian community felt itself besieged not only by Irish Catholics but by the Anglican officials who ruled Ulster, Hutcheson earned a master's in theology in Glasgow before recrossing the Irish Sea to Dublin, where he helped establish a Presbyterian Academy. It was there that he found his direction, much influenced by the work of another English philosopher, Anthony Ashley Cooper, the third Earl of Shaftesbury. A grandson and namesake of Locke's great patron, the first earl, and a student of the philosopher as a child, Shaftesbury had rejected his master's teachings, to hold that people were born with innate ideas, including an instinct for sociability, a need for fellowship. Shaftesbury's family motto was "love, serve."

From Shaftesbury's insight, Hutcheson developed his belief that all human beings were bestowed by God with an inborn moral sensibility, a basic conception of the nature of right and wrong grounded in their natural inclination to pursue happiness. The pursuit of happiness became a keystone to Hutcheson's thought. Locke, too, had written of happiness, as "the enjoyment of the things of nature subservient to life, health, ease, and pleasure, and by the comfortable hopes of another life when this is ended." He would, he wrote, "faithfully pursue that happiness I propose to myself," partaking of "all innocent diversions and delights," as far as they contributed to his well-being and improvement. But here again Hutcheson departed from Locke, breaking with the individualistic emphasis on the happiness of the solitary self.

Hutcheson's idea of happiness was essentially social. It combined self-interest and altruism as complementary moral qualities—as "two Forces impelling the same Body to Motion." Or as Shaftesbury's pupil Alexander Pope put it,

> *Thus God and Nature link'd the gen'ral frame*
> *And bade Self-love and Social be the same.*

Hutcheson was convinced people had an innate "delight in the Good of others" and "Desire of publick Good" that bound their pursuits of happiness to the happiness of all. They were inclined to do good to others—to increase their happiness—because doing so increased their own. The good was what advanced happiness; the bad—whether it was misery in ourselves or causing or witnessing it in others—went against the inclinations because it caused pain. The moral test, then, of all social institutions, including government, was their contribution to "the *greatest happiness* for the *greatest numbers*."

In fashioning an alternative Enlightenment, Hutcheson did not overthrow all of Locke. He agreed that the social contract was the basis of society, though he founded it not in self-interested fear but as an expression of natural inclinations, subscribed to by all in their freedom and equality. Slavery was an abomination, the negation of happiness, injurious to both master and slave. Political and civil liberties were essential to the pursuit of happiness, and the people possessed a right of resistance when power threatened the common good.

The philosopher of happiness was, by all accounts, a happy man, and he spread it to others. Over the opposition of traditionalists in the Church of

Scotland, he returned to Glasgow in 1730 to lecture on religion, morals, and government five days a week and on the excellence of Christianity on Sundays. He advocated curricular reforms, pressing Enlightenment teachings against Presbyterian inflexibility. He was beloved by colleagues and a popular lecturer, though perhaps not entirely for the quality of his thought: He was one of the first professors in Europe to break with the practice of lecturing in Latin—he used English, a boon to less prepared students. In Glasgow, he came to be considered the founder of the Scottish Enlightenment; he wrote to a friend that among the orthodox he was "called new light."

. . .

Between David Hume and Francis Hutcheson, who met in 1739, there was little meeting of minds. That could have surprised neither man. If Hutcheson was the epitome of Enlightenment philosophy at its most optimistic, his fellow Scot and younger contemporary drank deeply of its skepticism and empiricism. Both men believed in the innateness of moral sentiments, but while Hutcheson saw this as a gift from God, Hume's view of human nature was strictly secular, derived, as he claimed, from the "science of man" based on "experience and observation."

Samuel Johnson provided an even more striking contrast. He and Hume had met just once or twice, but Johnson nurtured a special loathing for the philosopher who flaunted what he was never able to suppress in himself. No article of faith—religious, economic, cultural, political—escaped Hume's raking scrutiny.

Johnson knew the skeptical mind all too well. "There is no rational principle by which a man can be contented," he once remarked to Boswell, "but a trust in the mercy of God." Johnson could not trust. He had been tormented with doubt about himself and God all his life. It was everything he could do to keep his terrors—of damnation, annihilation, hell, the abyss, nothingness—at bay, while he sought, as Boswell put it, "more and more evidence for spirit." Johnson told his young friend, "Every thing which Hume has advanced against Christianity had passed through my mind long before he wrote" and would still pass through his mind, to his deathbed. But the cause of such agony in Johnson brought Hume, to every appearance, intellectual pleasure, as well as fame and notoriety.

The source of Hume's intensest pleasure was reading. "From my earliest Infancy," he wrote in an autobiographical note, "I found alwise a strong Inclination to Books & Letters." Many of his observations of men and society were drawn from the tomes and tracts of philosophy and history, politics and literature, that he devoured at the university in Edinburgh, where he began his studies at age twelve, then during several years of lonely reading and writing in France, before he returned to his native land. Disappointed by the "endless Disputes" in the works of "Philosophers or Critics," Hume "found a certain Boldness of Temper, growing in me, which was not enclin'd to submit to any Authority in these Subjects, but led me to seek out some new Medium, by which Truth might be establisht."

The first fruit of Hume's search, *A Treatise of Human Nature,* published when he was in his late twenties, did not lack boldness. In the aftermath of Hutcheson, Hume gave the Enlightenment another powerful twist. He overthrew the reliance of Enlightenment thinkers on reason as the instrument for the pursuit of true knowledge, as the check on human passions, as the source of moral judgment and virtue. He turned Enlightenment doctrine on its head: "Reason is, and ought to be only the slave of the passions." Indeed, passions of "ambition, avarice, self-love, vanity, friendship, generosity, public spirit" were "the source of all the actions and enterprizes, which have ever been observed among mankind."

But if passions were so powerful, how preserve some degree of order? Hume agreed with Hutcheson that people had an instinct for benevolence—a sympathy for others—that was a foundation for moral judgment. But Hume saw it as one passion among many, and believed that self-interest, not benevolence, motivated action. Following Locke, he observed that men were creatures of their environment. Potentially harmful passions and the destructive pursuit of self-interest could be restrained by education and by law. Most of human life was governed by custom and habits, and principles of justice also were customary, artificial constructs created for and tested by their usefulness to society. Hume once told Hutcheson, citing Horace, that utility was the mother of justice and equity.

The job of the philosopher, as Hume saw it, was to study men and societies, to observe their behaviors, to see how they organized themselves, and how, over time, their institutions changed, all according to the principles of utility. Hume disdained abstract ideas and a priori reasoning. The doctrine of natural rights was a fiction, if sometimes a useful one. And history gave no evidence that governments had their origin and legitimacy in the consent of the governed. Conquest, usurpation—*these* were how governments were formed, and as they evolved through time, they gained legitimacy by proving useful to their subjects.

British government in the eighteenth century was one such useful regime, he allowed. Its limited, constitutional monarchy gave the English "the most entire system of liberty, that ever was known amongst mankind." But little irritated Hume more than Whig panegyrics to that liberty, their boast that the Glorious Revolution had restored and secured it for all time. He pointed out that the 1689 constitution was scarcely an Enlightenment pinnacle, merely the latest in its line, the product of changing political and social conditions. He delighted in puncturing English chauvinism and complacency by pointing out the virtues of France's "civilized" absolute monarchy—there was, he suggested, less difference between French "slavery" and English liberty than "vulgar Whigs" liked to imagine.

But, as he turned his skeptical eye on liberty, Hume worried that the English did not really understand how good they had it. By making "liberty" into an abstraction and forgetting that in usefulness "a regard for liberty" ought "commonly to be subordinate to a reverence for established government," they risked losing it. The "Abuse of Liberty" by the mob in the Wilkes riots appalled him. "They roar Liberty," he wrote to a friend in France, "tho' they have apparently more Liberty than any People in the World"—"a great deal more," he could not resist adding, "than they deserve." The passions of political ideologues, with their commitments to the authority of fixed ideas, were as dangerous as those of religious fanatics, yet "no party, in the present age, can well support itself, without a philosophical or speculative system of principles, annexed to its political or practical one . . . to protect and cover that scheme of actions, which it pursues."

Among those dangerous principles was that of empire. Hume was almost alone among Scottish intellectual leaders to declare support for the American colonists and among the first in Britain to call for American independence. "I am an American in my Principles," he wrote. In fact, he was indifferent to many of the Enlightenment ideals animating the colonists, especially natural rights. But he admired the "spirit of independency" that flourished among people who had "sought for freedom amidst those savage desarts." Hume feared that to crush that spirit, Britain would have to wage a brutal, financially ruinous war. Success would lead to even worse, a greater Britain that was unrecognizable—an aggressively commercial, corrupt, and oppressive empire. Better to let the Americans go, Hume concluded, "to govern or misgovern themselves as they think proper: The Affair is of no Consequence, or of little Consequence to us."

* * *

More slowly and regretfully, a close friend of Hume's, Adam Smith, came to the conclusion that the American enterprise would end badly for the

British. Unlike Hume, Smith hoped for success, indeed, for constitutional *union* with America, on the example of his own Scotland in 1707, a plan that would "certainly tend most to the prosperity, to the splendour, and to the duration of the empire." But if "the complete submission of America" could not be achieved by treaty, as appeared certain in 1778, when Smith was writing a memorandum of advice to the government, it could be brought about only "by Conquest," which would mean military rule of the colonies, with Americans "for more than a century to come . . . at all times ready to take up arms in order to overturn it."

Smith described himself writing as a "solitary philosopher," but by 1778, he was one of the most famous and admired men in Britain. He was born in 1723 in Fife, son of a lawyer and civil servant who died before he was born. His mother encouraged his bookish pursuits, sending him to one of the best secondary schools in Scotland, the Burgh School in Kirkcaldy, Fife. Smith continued his studies at the university in Glasgow with "the never to be forgotten Dr Hutcheson," whose enlightened teachings had aroused in Smith a zeal for liberty and a curiosity about what he later described as "the immense and connected system" of the universe, with "co-existent parts" that, "exactly fitted to one another," promoted "the prosperity and happiness" of all. Smith spent a year of study at Oxford and later two years traveling the continent, where he compared political and economic conditions with those back home and came under the sway of French "physiocrats" whose commitment to laissez-faire grew from their pioneering attempt to discern what one physiocrat called "the essential principles of the economic order," which they saw in Enlightenment terms, as included among "the sovereign laws of nature." As a lecturer in jurisprudence at Glasgow, Smith had begun to think deeply about the relationships between law and property, property and commerce, and commerce and government. For over a decade, he labored on a treatise in political economy, struggling to marry theory with observation, talking business with Glasgow's merchants and gathering data on industry, agriculture, and trade.

Finally, in 1776, the year of the Declaration of Independence and of his friend David Hume's death, Smith published *The Wealth of Nations*. It was a massive, closely detailed book that became an instant popular success and was appreciated in the highest circles of government. The very next year, some of Smith's tax recommendations appeared in the British budget.

The impact of *The Wealth of Nations* owed much to its originality. Never before had the economic life of society been described so comprehensively, so systematically. In true Enlightenment style, Smith looked back in time to the history of economic development, described and critiqued the economy of the present day, and looked forward with proposals for its further growth. To a remarkable degree, *The Wealth of Nations* laid out the lineaments of the "enlightened economy," as historian Joel Mokyr would call it, the modern market system that was beginning to envelop Britain and would soon penetrate much of western Europe and eventually the world: the importance of saving and investment in providing the capital to buy machinery and raw goods and to hire labor; the specialization of invention, production, and labor that would make for greater efficiency and profit; and the crucial role of free trade in stimulating productive forces, in contrast to "mercantilist" interventions and manipulations by government, as was British policy in its empire, especially in America. Smith devoted a substantial portion of his book to outlining the strong role governments must play in healthy and growing economies, providing not only defense but justice, public works, and schools, funded by progressive taxes, with all paying "in proportion to their respective abilities; that is, in proportion to the revenue they respectively enjoy under the protection of the state."

But *The Wealth of Nations* was above all a plea for economic liberty: not only the end of restrictions on trade, but also the elimination of anti-competitive practices in industry and the lifting of onerous burdens on apprentices, among others. "All systems either of preference or restraint, therefore, being thus completely taken away, the obvious and simple system of natural liberty establishes itself of its own accord."

Smith was, though, in the tradition of the Scottish Enlightenment, as much moral philosopher and psychologist as economist. He followed Hutcheson and Hume in allowing that human beings had an innate inclination to benevolence or sympathy and that this served as a basis for moral judgment. But like Hume, he argued that benevolence was not the key motive for *action*. Self-interest was. He defended laissez-faire as rooted in the human "desire of bettering our condition," and believed that the "invisible hand" of the free market would ensure that as a man was liberated to pursue his own interests and better his own condition, he would promote the common good of society "more effectually than when he really intends to promote it." Best of all, capitalism would produce a "universal opulence," and the rich, after selecting "from the heap what is most precious and agreeable," would be led by the "invisible hand" to make "nearly the same distribution of the necessaries of life, which would have been made, had the earth been divided into equal portions among all its inhabitants." In a very different way, then, the market society, which rewarded "selfishness and rapacity," could produce "the greatest good for the greatest numbers."

Yet Smith was realist enough to see how it might not. Indeed, no philosopher before Marx offered a more harrowing vision of workingmen under advanced capitalism. As labor became more specialized, workers would be reduced to repetitious drudgery, making them "as stupid and as ignorant as it is possible for a human creature to become," incapable of any "generous, noble, or tender sentiment," utterly unfit for self-government.

How reconcile Smith's account of "mental mutilation, deformity, and wretchedness" with his idea that society should serve human liberty, happiness, and virtue? He never really brought the enlightened economy into alignment with the Enlightenment. Education, he wrote, merely deserved "the most serious attention of government," to persuade men to think philosophically about their condition. They were to understand that in a society devoted to the production of wealth, "opulence" was not the highest value, that happiness was a state of mind. It was enough for them to believe that "the beggar, who suns himself by the side of the highway, possesses that security which kings are fighting for."

It was a mark of the richness and originality of Scotland's intellectual leadership that Smith's work embodied, without resolving, the tension between its two strongest threads—Hutcheson's glowing optimism and drive for comprehensive and systematic understanding and Hume's hard-headed realism and relativism. The power of their ideas, as the influence of the Scots spread near and far, helped to set the terms of the debate over the meanings and course of enlightenment—and to mobilize political leadership that sought to change the world.

3

Revolutionary Americans

Londoners sailing into Boston Harbor in the 1760s, expecting to find a sleepy provincial town of some sixteen thousand souls, would discover a modern port city with a lively citizenry. After disembarking on the Long Wharf, they would view a panorama familiar on the Thames—dozens of wharves, forests of masts, shipyards peopled by caulkers and spinners and sailmakers.

Heading into town, careful to avoid hogs that scavenged the streets, the visitors would pass taverns, printshops, a bookstore, timbered houses along with some fine brick ones, and a plethora of churches, most of them Congregational. If they turned left on Treamount Street they would come to Boston's pride—the Common, where children played and cows grazed and occasionally His Majesty's troops bivouacked.

On the Common the travelers might catch sight of a curious, even ominous structure—a two-story "manufactory" where recently scores of workers, most of them poor women and children, had spun linen from flax. Opened in 1752 by the Society for Encouraging Industry and the Employment of the Poor, this had been colonial Boston's boldest experiment in coping with poverty. It was not a charitable enterprise. Merchants and civic leaders hoped to reduce the public expense of poor relief and make a profit from the cheap labor. But within a few years the project collapsed: impoverished women and children, accustomed to piecework at home, proved reluctant to enter the forbidding confines of a factory.

The Boston elite boasted to visitors of their lawns and gardens and gazebos near the town center, but most people lived in semidarkness, in smoky rooms lighted by a few candles. In winter, warmth came mainly from one fire in the kitchen. There was no real plumbing; most people relied on slop jars, outhouses, and open sewers in the middle of the street.

The Londoners probably would have heard of Boston's most noted leader, Thomas Hutchinson, who had knitted together enough judicial, legislative, and administrative authority to be virtually the boss of the city. He was, among other titles, the chief justice and royal lieutenant-governor, and his relatives also held important public offices in Massachusetts. John Adams thought this "amazing ascendancy of one Family" a "Foundation sufficient on which to erect a Tyranny." Hutchinson would strike the Londoners, though, not as a flinty emissary from the Crown but as a friendly son of Boston, devoutly but tolerantly religious, responding to both Anglican and Congregational teachings.

The visitors could hardly imagine that this quiet, circumspect official was becoming the most hated man in Boston.

• • •

In Boston, Hutchinson, along with a succession of governors and other officials, presided over a social and economic hierarchy as set and stable as England's. Those at the top of the pyramid were Hutchinson's stoutest supporters—merchants and shipowners, importers and exporters, leading physicians and attorneys, and men of inherited wealth. At the next level below were the lesser merchants and shopkeepers, master craftsmen, perhaps sea captains. The next level down included a diversity of apprentices, bound laborers, and hired servants, most tied in tightly with families that had "contracted out" for them. Apprentices provided a pool of semiskilled labor that sometimes enabled them to rise a bit in the class system.

Farthest down in the pyramid lay black slaves. Not only in the American South but in northern port cities slavery had persisted more than a century. After vanquishing Pequot Indians, Massachusetts had sent hundreds of captured women and children to the West Indies in exchange for blacks. While slaves made up only a small percentage of Boston's population, they glaringly challenged the conception of all humanity as children of God proclaimed every Sunday in Boston's churches.

Young professionals—teachers, ministers, writers, but especially lawyers—were rising to oppose the Hutchinson establishment and its supporters. The most conspicuous of these—for his strong convictions and towering ambition—was the attorney John Adams. Unimposing in appearance, given to agonizing self-scrutiny, sensitive to the motivations and ambitions of others because he knew his own, Adams showed a precocious understanding of politics and psychology and of their impact on leadership.

Adams's later fame would overcloud the role of other young leaders in Boston, but they were equally influential at the time. His cousin Samuel Adams, the son of a Boston artisan, early on learned the arts of town meeting and caucus politics; hence he understood the crucial role of followers in leading the leaders. The fiery James Otis, son of a powerful country politician, rose out of the populist melee in Boston to lead the fight against the Hutchinson establishment. Viewed as a near-saint by his friends and as a demagogic hothead by foes, Otis built close ties to impoverished laborers who rewarded him with votes at election time. John Hancock was an anomaly: a wealthy merchant who enjoyed tussling with his foes in the Hutchinson circle.

To single out these leaders is to play down the crucial role of a host of rising activists throughout Massachusetts. These men and women constituted a vital collegial leadership as protest against British control mounted. Most of them have been lost to history. Some are remembered only as leaders of crowds.

But together with growing numbers of others in the colonies, the diverse people of Boston were finding common ground in a rising American Enlightenment.

AN AMERICAN ENLIGHTENMENT

Hungry for ideas after a long diet of religious orthodoxy, an ocean away from the heart of the Enlightenment's intellectual ferment in Europe, readers across the American colonies were, by the mid-eighteenth century, ardent consumers of ideas from the Old World. Societies for debate and discussion formed in cities and towns, while the mails linked networks of far-flung correspondents galvanized by the new ideas of the time.

In New England, where Puritans established free schools for boys from fear that ignorance bred sin and irreligion and so would provoke God's wrath, male literacy was almost universal, while two-thirds of men in the colonies as a whole were literate. The appetite for the secular written word, especially from abroad, was vast and intense, reflected by the growth in the numbers of master printers, increasing across the colonies from nine in 1720 to forty-two in 1760, nearly doubling in Boston and leaping from one to nine in Philadelphia. Newspapers spread far and wide, though their foreign coverage often amounted to little more than months-old circulars from the royal court in London as well as those in Berlin and Naples, and even the Sublime Porte in Istanbul, or essays and poems plundered from English magazines.

Printers struggled to keep up with demand for imported books, especially for popular works like Locke's *Essay Concerning Human Understanding* and *Two Treatises of Government* or Voltaire's *English Letters* and *Age of Louis XIV.* Newspapers sometimes filled the gap, reprinting whole chapters of Montesquieu's *Spirit of the Laws.* Historian Henry May noted that it was impossible for colonial readers to keep up with the latest in European thought because of the considerable time lag before books were published in America. Inevitably, many of the more radical works of the Enlightenment's second phase, such as Rousseau's *Social Contract* and Hume's *Natural History of Religion,* did not reach Americans until later in the century.

For many years the most characteristic voice of the Enlightenment in America was Joseph Addison's *Spectator* from London, the model for Franklin and many other publishers. Moderate in tone, urbane but not too sophisticated, progressive but unrevolutionary, Addison appealed to a provincial readership of the earnest, the self-made, the striving on both sides of the Atlantic. In the colonies, there were few true men of letters, few who lived on private wealth or literary earnings or royal or aristocratic patronage. The American Enlightenment was at its roots democratic; the enlightened and the enlighteners were, in historian Donald H. Meyer's term, part-time literati while also full-time lawyers, doctors, clergymen, tradesmen, artisans, or farmers. They were, Meyer contended, "closer to the common life and its day-to-day concerns" than their European counterparts, and therefore their Enlightenment was characterized by the drive for useful knowledge, knowledge they understood would benefit their communities.

. . .

Even so, Americans remained importers of ideas, with little as yet to teach their European teachers. Ben Franklin himself, the most famous American, was known abroad more for his experiments in electricity than for the enlightened principles he brought down to earth in his witty essays and wise aphorisms. In science as in everything, Franklin was no theorist but an empiricist seeking to find uses for his ideas.

It was Franklin, more than anyone, who gave the American Enlightenment its distinctiveness and made Philadelphia its capital. But he was born in Boston, the son of Josiah Franklin, a maker of soap and candles and a deacon in the church whose fondest hope had been that his precocious son would join the ministry. As a boy Ben Franklin devoured everything in his father's small library—mostly books of "polemic Divinity," he would recall in his *Autobiography,* a landmark of the age of Enlightenment, chronicling the growth of one man's mind and ideas. In those years, Boston remained the theocratic province of Puritanism, with its fierce moral code fed by a dread vision of human sinfulness. Salvation was reserved for an elect while the rest of God's children were abandoned to hellfire. Yet from an early age, Ben was putting together his own, less orthodox, library. "All the little Money that came into my Hands was ever laid out in Books," ranging from the collected works of John Bunyan to "R. Burton's Historical Collections; they were small Chapmen's books, and cheap, 40 or 50 in all."

Josiah sent his eight-year-old son to Boston's Latin School to prepare for theological studies at Harvard. But it was soon obvious that Ben, with his wide-ranging and skeptical curiosity and irreverent wit, was not clerical material. In 1718, when Ben was twelve, Josiah insisted that he apprentice with his older son, James, who had returned from England the year before with a press to set up as a printer in Boston. Ben reluctantly signed the indentures committing him to a nine-year apprenticeship.

The work was mostly drudgery. Printers assembled lead type by hand, "word for word and line by line," as Arthur Schlesinger Sr. wrote, "and then with muscular power worked the pages through the press." But there was a huge perk. "I now had Access to better Books," Franklin remembered, borrowed from apprentices of booksellers. "Often I sat up in my Room reading the greatest Part of the Night, when the Book was borrow'd in the Evening & to be return'd early in the Morning lest it should be miss'd or wanted."

Like so many of the self-taught readers who would model themselves after him, Franklin consumed books almost indiscriminately—from works of science and natural philosophy to deistic tracts that challenged Christianity with a new religion founded not on faith but on reason to the daring works of political philosophy by Locke and Montesquieu. Already, though, Franklin was demonstrating what would become his signal contribution to an American Enlightenment, a devotion to the propagation of *useful* knowledge, knowledge that drove action—change, progress—in people's lives and in the world. Later, he would borrow from Locke the revolutionary idea that the human mind began as a blank slate, to be shaped by education and experience. Franklin proposed an academy whose scholars' minds would be furnished with everything that was "*most useful,*" ranging from arithmetic and accounts to "the Advantages of *Liberty*" to histories of "the invention of arts, rise of manufactures, progress of trade," which would lead to the study of mechanics, "that art by which weak men perform such wonders, labour is saved, manufactures expedited, etc."

Ben would memorialize brother James as a cruel tyrant, but he gained much that was useful from him, and not only the mechanics of the printing business. James had brought home from England new books and maga-zines filled with stimulating ideas, such as Addison's *Spectator,* whose style Ben strove to imitate. James was also a fiercely combative printer, described by Walter Isaacson, Ben's biographer, as "the first great fighter for an inde-pendent press in America," risking his weekly newspaper, the *New England Courant,* by defying censorship to take on the Puritan establishment.

Franklin abandoned his apprenticeship with James when he was seven-teen and escaped to Philadelphia, where he quickly fell in with a printer who shared his love for philosophical debate. After a further apprenticeship in London, Franklin returned to Philadelphia and became editor of the *Pennsylvania Gazette* in 1729, soon transforming it into one of the most influential newspapers in the colonies.

Philadelphia became Franklin's fief as his singular vision transformed the city into the capital of the American Enlightenment. He embraced the core faith of the Old World Enlightenment in human reason, with its skep-ticism toward received ideas and the path it offered to new truths. But for him, reason was no ivory-tower preserve, the arid production of dusty-voiced intellectuals. It thrived in the streets, among the shops, in coffee shops and taverns. It was down-to-earth, democratic. Reasoning was a so-cial activity, a shared process of mutual enlightenment. In the earliest ex-pression of the characteristically American marketplace of ideas, Franklin wrote, in his "Apology for Printers," that "Printers are educated in the Be-lief, that when Men differ in Opinion, both Sides ought equally to have the Advantage of being heard by the Publick; and that when Truth and Error have fair Play, the former is always an overmatch for the latter."

Franklin's vehicle for change in Philadelphia was the "Junto" he formed in 1727 with eleven fellow artisans, including a glazier, a shoemaker, a scrivener, and a clerk. For decades these men met for discussions of phi-losophy and politics, science and business and gossip, and together they gave the Philadelphia Enlightenment their own stamp—heterogeneous, secular, tolerant, pragmatic. Together they founded institutions that fleshed out Franklin's vision of a communicative Enlightenment, most notably America's first subscription library, to which Franklin donated many books from his own collection, and what would become the American Philosophical Society, described by Isaacson as an "intercolonial Junto," dedicated to "Promoting Useful Knowledge Among the British Plantations in America."

Franklin put his educational ideas to work with the College of Philadelphia, opened in 1751. In 1765, the College added America's first medical school. Franklin also raised money for the city's first hospital. He directed medical students, who would make Philadelphia the center of American medicine, to the University of Edinburgh for training. This connection was secured by Franklin's sympathy for the "common-sense" principles of the Scottish Enlightenment and his friendship with its luminaries, including David Hume—an illustration of Franklin's leadership in the translation of the Enlightenment from Old World to New. Hume in fact paid Franklin the compliment that, as he wrote, "America has sent us many good things, Gold, Silver, Sugar, Tobacco, Indigo &c.: But you are the first Philosopher, and indeed the first Great Man of Letters for whom we are beholden to her."

* * *

When John Adams arrived in Philadelphia in the late summer of 1774 as a delegate to the First Continental Congress, he was overawed by its wealth and sophistication. The brilliant lawyer and scholar, who had never before ventured out of New England, felt like a provincial in Ben Franklin's city.

"Dirty, dusty, and fatigued," Adams and his fellow Massachusetts delegates were met by a welcoming committee that included Benjamin Rush, physician and friend of Franklin. The doctor found Adams's dress and manner plain and "his conversation cold and reserved." Perhaps it was the uncertainty of meeting fellow activists for the first time. No one was sure where others stood on the crucial issues facing the Congress, which had been called in response to Parliament's imposition of the Coercive Acts; no one knew where the Congress might lead, though it seemed likely to determine the fate of America one way or another. Its convocation alone was potentially treasonable. Adams knew that he had "passed the Rubicon; swim or sink, live or die, survive or perish with my country, was my unalterable determination." Invited to the City Tavern, "the most genteel one in America," and soon tucking into a supper "as elegant as ever was laid upon a Table," Adams finally relaxed, enjoying a long evening of convivial political conversation.

Benjamin Franklin himself was in London in 1774, pursuing fruitless negotiations for compromise with the British. Franklin's had long been a conciliatory voice in the escalating hostilities between Crown and colonies, even condemning the Tea Party as a reckless provocation, but now, with a rising tide of anti-Americanism in Britain, he fell under suspicion of treason. His mission had reached a low point in January of that year when he was summoned by the Privy Council to a room aptly called the "Cockpit" and, to the cheers and jeers of a packed crowd, subjected to what one spectator called "a torrent of virulent abuse" and Franklin himself likened to "bull baiting." The American maintained a dignified silence, though in the following days he expected to be arrested.

Back in Franklin's Philadelphia, as the Continental Congress convened in Carpenter Hall, dignified silence was not an option. But when Americans spoke to British power, what would they say?

CREATING THE REVOLUTION

In the Puritan stronghold of Boston, new ideas and inventions, products of Enlightenment philosophy and science, were not infrequently regarded as challenges to the authority of God. One such, Ben Franklin's lightning rod, drew a blast from his old hometown in 1755, when a Boston preacher condemned him for interfering with Providence. Lightning was an expression of God's wrath, the minister reasoned; rob the Lord of his thunder, drive it underground, and it would trigger earthquakes like the one that had shaken Boston not long before.

Such "Opposition from the Superstitions," a recent college graduate sighed knowingly, was what "all other usefull Discoveries, have met with in all Ages of the World." Like Franklin, this young man, John Adams, had attended Boston's Latin School. Unlike Franklin, Adams had gone on to Harvard, though only at his father's insistence. The son would have been content to work on the family farm in Braintree and indulge his precocious fondness for "the Society of females." But his father—farmer and shoemaker, Puritan deacon and town selectman—was filled with an "Admiration of Learning" and insisted that fifteen-year-old John take the entrance examination for Harvard's class of 1755.

Fear of failure pulled Adams through the exam, and now, for the first time, he took a genuine interest in his studies, at least the science taught by John Winthrop, Harvard's leading light and a colleague of Franklin's. Still, becoming a bachelor of arts did not settle the question of what Adams was to do with his life, or of how to satisfy the lust for fame that tormented him. A depressing year after graduation teaching Latin to children in Worcester convinced him that he would "die an ignorant, obscure fellow." Almost in desperation, he agreed to apprentice with one of Worcester's leading attorneys. So began the enlightenment of John Adams.

"I find my self entering an unlimited Field," he exulted to a friend in 1758. The study of law "incloses the whole Circle of Science and Literature, the History, Wisdom, and Virtue of all ages." Not to mention the opportunity its mastery gave him to "spread my Fame thro the Province." Adams's studies began with what he later recalled was "a dreary Ramble" through technical legal texts, such as Coke's *Institutes of the Common Law,* but he soon expanded his reach to include Montesquieu, Hobbes, and Rousseau, and, with them, more fundamental issues of law and civil society that would inspire him to pursue, in the spirit of Bacon, Newton, and Locke, by "Observation and Experiment," an empirical *science* of government.

The key challenge, as Adams saw it, was the protection of human liberty against the forces of oppression. He would devote his prodigious intellectual energies to comparative studies of governments historical and contemporary, where he found a wide range of conditions that influenced the condition of liberty as it emerged out of medieval oppression. He arrived at a general law that human beings in "a State of Ignorance" tended to be enslaved while those "enlightened with Knowledge" lived in freedom. Moreover, knowledge "monopolized, or in the Possession of a few, is a Curse to Mankind." It should be dispersed among all ranks, with equality preserved. Adams concluded that "whenever a general knowledge and sensibility have prevail'd among the *people,* arbitrary government, and every kind of oppression, have lessened and disappeared in proportion." To increase liberty and promote equality, he advocated universal public education as well as a free press so "easy and cheap and safe" that any person could "communicate his thoughts to the public."

It was the British imposition of a Stamp Act on the American colonies in 1765 that pushed Adams to clarify and publish his thoughts on enlightenment and liberty. He interpreted this levy of a tax on newspapers, almanacs, pamphlets, legal documents, and the like, to be a deliberate attempt by London to reduce colonists to a state of ignorance and timidity. He urged his fellow Americans to "dare to read, think, speak, and write. . . . [L]et every sluice of knowledge be open'd and set a flowing."

* * *

That Americans were increasingly willing to take up this challenge in the face of British repression was evident in the taverns and streets of the colonies, where leaders both incited grassroots activists and responded to them. Mass mobilization did not always begin with the top leadership. Local activists often took the lead in meetings where colonials had been venting concerns for years. Arguments ranged over gambling and horse racing, taxes, and even the importation of slaves. There might be no mention of Britain, save for adjournment with the customary tribute to the Crown. But as "parliamentary arrogance" mounted, people became better informed, their opinions sharper and more daring; local militants spurred strong feelings, especially over "taxation without representation." Thus the freeholders of Granville County, North Carolina, resolved that "as Free men we can be bound by no law, but such as we assent to, either by ourselves, or our Representatives." All in all, according to historian Jack N. Rakove, local resolutions created a "powerful corpus of popular opinion" behind resistance to coercion.

But the most decisive act of leadership was the forging of intercolonial cooperation against the British. This was a hard task. Even aside from their historic differences, colonial leaders were ridden with uncertainty and disagreement over the right strategy for resistance. Key to an emerging unity of purpose were the "correspondence committees" that, since the first was founded in Massachusetts in 1772, had developed as virtual shadow governments colonially and locally. They led the resistance, disseminating news and receiving grievances, organizing protests, and enforcing boycotts of British goods. They were crucial to fostering intercolonial cooperation, and, with British outrages mounting, they convened the first Continental Congress.

Conflict quickly arose in Philadelphia between leaders such as Patrick Henry of Virginia along with two tenacious Adamses, Samuel and John, who demanded a tough posture toward Britain, and moderates—most notably John Dickinson of Pennsylvania and John Jay of New York—defending a more conciliatory approach. After weeks of impassioned oratory the gathering worked out a compromise tilted toward militancy. The resolutions trumpeted the rights of the colonies—among them "life, liberty, & property"—and the claim to sole power of lawmaking "in all cases of taxation and internal polity," subject only to veto by the Crown.

That the delegates could assume collective leadership of the entire American resistance movement was extraordinary, given the multiplicity of interests and attitudes. But the leaders knew their limits. The resolutions not only recognized the ultimate authority of the Crown; a statement of grievances based on the defiant resolutions was sent soon afterward to the king in the form of a "loyal address."

All the intertwined leadership within and across the colonies could not have succeeded without grounding in popular support. That support turned initially on simple hatred of Parliament and all its works, but gradually people at all levels of society came to be animated by a belief so powerful that it was controlling day-to-day events. This was a profound faith in liberty. Before the military lines were drawn, this belief remained a rather narrow and ambiguous one. The true nature of liberty had long been debated in town meetings and country stores. It was a divisive subject because liberty might seem to be threatened on all sides, by employers, sheriffs, censors, tax collectors, landlords.

By the middle 1770s, though, the idea of liberty had become splendidly simplified and focused. It was American liberty against British imperial power.

.　.　.

The clarion call for American liberty—the Declaration of Independence approved by the second Continental Congress in Philadelphia in the summer of 1776—was the most decisive act of collective moral leadership in American history. After a series of military disasters, and with General Howe's force of 130 ships and 32,000 redcoats preparing to invade New York only 100 miles to the north, it was also the most audacious.

Collective leadership began with a most collegial act, when John Adams named a committee of five congressional delegates, including Benjamin Franklin, Thomas Jefferson, and of course, himself, to prepare a bold declaration. Adams was asked to write a draft, but he declined in favor of Jefferson, because, he said later, "1. That he was a Virginian and I a Massachusettensian. 2. that he was a southern Man and I a northern one. 3. That I had been so obnoxious for my early and constant Zeal in promoting the Measure, that any draught of mine, would undergo a more severe Scrutiny and Criticism in Congress, than one of his composition. 4thly and lastly . . . I had a great Opinion of the Elegance of his pen and none at all of my own."

This did not inhibit Adams from making his own comments on Jefferson's paper, as did Franklin and the two others on the committee, Roger Sherman and Robert Livingston. Then Congress as a whole worked it over, striking out whole sentences and tamping down a little of its heat. Jefferson—like any writer—suffered at the "mutilation" but accepted it.

Still, the collective leadership was far broader than the congressional. The city around the delegates abounded in people with strong, even radical, sentiments about the meanings and possibilities of independence. Other colonial leaders up and down the seaboard had been shaping ideas in endless writings and meetings. Adams grumbled that Jefferson had borrowed from his own thoughts and merely followed what fellow Bostonians James Otis and Samuel Adams had written and "what had been hackneyed in Congress for two years before."

"Hackneyed," yes—because the ideas of independence and liberty and equality had been intensifying among the American people for years.

SELF-EVIDENT TRUTHS

If Benjamin Franklin was the "complete philosophe"—in the American style—of the older generation of revolutionaries, then Thomas Jefferson was the same in the younger, though so far the thirty-three-year-old Virginian was best known, as Adams suggested, for a powerful way with words. His 1774 pamphlet *A Summary View of the Rights of British America* was admired for its forceful denunciation of British coercion and its reasoned, if one-sided, repudiation of parliamentary power over the colonies. He was ahead of colonial opinion in his sweeping assertion of American rights against the mother country, but not for long. "The young ascended with Mr. Jefferson to the source of those rights," remarked a fellow Virginian, Edmund Randolph; "the old required time for consideration before they could tread this lofty ground." Within a year, Jefferson was drafting a constitution for the newly independent commonwealth of Virginia whose declaration of rights and proclamation of popular sovereignty would be echoed in his draft paper for the Continental Congress.

Some years earlier, in the late summer of 1771, a Virginia gentleman named Robert Skipwith had written Jefferson asking if his fellow Virginian would create for him a catalogue of what he regarded as the best books, the total to cost not more than £50. Skipwith must have been astonished at his friend's response—scores of titles, sorted into fine arts, politics, religion, ancient and modern history, natural philosophy, and ranging from Homer and Caesar to Buffon's groundbreaking *Natural History,* "Franklin on electricity," Adam Smith's *Theory of Moral Sentiments,* and *Don Quixote.* Locke, Montesquieu, Voltaire, and Hume were well represented, as was Addison's *Spectator,* in a nine-volume edition. Jefferson included the price for every book, ranging from a couple of shillings to many pounds and totaling over £100. The Bible, classified as "History. Antient," went for 6 shillings.

Few Americans opened the sluices of knowledge as widely as Thomas Jefferson; perhaps none came nearer to achieving the Enlightenment ideal of universal knowledge. As a boy, Jefferson had roamed the fields and woodlands of Virginia with a botanist's eye, collecting plants and observing wild animals. He retained that intent curiosity, with its empirical bent, throughout his life, but the foundation of his learning—and his greatest pleasure—was in reading.

Natural aristocrats—men who earned status by merit, not, as in the Old World, those elevated by birth or wealth—should, Jefferson thought, lead society, guarding "the sacred deposit of the rights and liberties of their fellow citizens." He himself was born into Virginia's elite, son of a planter who owned thousands of acres and scores of slaves; it was from this privileged beginning that he transformed himself into a *natural* aristocrat. He accomplished it by boldness "in pursuit of knoledge, never fearing to follow truth and reason to whatever results they led, & bearding every authority which stood in their way." It also required steady application. He had what he would later describe as a "canine appetite" for knowledge. "It is wonderful," he would say, "how much may be done, if we are always doing."

Jefferson was schooled at home until age nine, then sent to a clergyman's Latin school and, at fourteen, to another small academy presided over by a minister, James Maury. Maury gave the boy a first-class education in the classics, but also, unusually, encouraged an interest in the French literature of the Enlightenment, as well as in the English language, teaching him to write with "force and elegance."

It was not yet typical for planters' sons to go on to higher education, but Jefferson, undaunted, enrolled at the College of William and Mary in Williamsburg at age seventeen and quickly came under the influence of the only non-clergyman on the school's faculty, William Small, a Scotsman who taught physics, metaphysics, and mathematics, as well as ethics, rhetoric, and belles lettres. The professor became like a father to his student, who later wrote that Small had "probably fixed the destinies" of his life, not only by setting an example of liberality and polymathy but by exposing Jefferson to the wide range of Enlightenment science and philosophy, especially its Scottish branch.

After two years at college, Jefferson apprenticed in law with George Wythe, a leading light of the Virginia bar who took delight in adorning his briefs with classical quotations. Student would outdo mentor a few years later when Jefferson, of counsel in a scandalous divorce, prepared an appeal that drew on Locke, Montesquieu, and Hume, as well as Milton and

Montaigne and, of course, the Bible. Like John Adams, Jefferson found the study of law to be a remarkably broadening, even liberating, experience. When he later advised would-be lawyers on a course of study, he went beyond philosophy, rhetoric, ethics, religion, politics, and literature to include an "extensive" dip into astronomy and anatomy, botany and chemistry—though it was not necessary, he granted, "to make yourself completely master of the whole."

"Every science is auxiliary to every other," he told an aspiring lawyer, in what could have been his enlightened creed, as well as a fair description of his mind, with its vast capacity, its thirst for order, its ability to distill the essence of his learning and to synthesize disparate topics. He was fascinated by the monumental French *Encyclopédie*, that renowned effort to gather, organize, and present to the public all of human knowledge, and he attempted a similar comprehensive survey of his native state, beginning with a bundle of loose papers on which he had jotted "any information of our country, which might be of use to me in any station public or private." Classifying this information—the land and climate, the people and their history, laws, religion, commerce, and arts—and adding pleas for liberty and education, Jefferson produced *Notes on the State of Virginia* in 1785, the only book he published.

While Jefferson's hunger for information was insatiable, it was not indiscriminate. Knowledge was tested by its usefulness. The *Notes,* for instance, was intended as an answer to Old World scientists and philosophers who contended that the New World was, in its natural features and people, inferior and blighted, doomed to decay.

But knowledge had wider, more profound uses. Jefferson subscribed to the Scottish view that human beings were naturally sociable, possessed of a moral sense, and that virtuous behavior contributed to the happiness of all. Knowledge, he believed, improved morality and hence collective happiness by leading men and women on the path of truth.

Not only did enlightenment liberate "the ideas of those who read and reflect," it was a bulwark of the liberty all people were entitled to, the basis of self-government. Like Franklin and Adams, Jefferson believed that the best way to resist the growth of tyranny was "to illuminate, as far as practicable, the minds of the people at large." He proposed an equal education—three years of free schooling—for all Virginia boys and girls. This would provide a solid base of informed citizens, capable of self-government and preserving liberty. As Jefferson wrote George Washington in 1786, "It is an axiom in my mind that our liberty can never be safe but in the hands of the people themselves, and that too of the people with a certain degree of instruction. This it is the business of the state to effect, and on a general plan."

But Jefferson was aware that, practically, laws could not be written and executed by the mass of citizens. For this, leadership was needed, that natural aristocracy of distinction based on merit. After the first three years of free schooling, therefore, inequality ruled. The more promising among the boys would continue to grammar school and, ultimately, for a select few, to college. Girls did not make this first cut. At each stage, there would be a winnowing of the survivors. "The best geniuses will be raked from the rubbish annually," Jefferson wrote. They would make up the leadership cadre of natural aristocrats, whose talents "nature has sown as liberally among the poor as the rich."

Jefferson was proposing a grand experiment. In an age when royal autocrats sat on inherited thrones in much of the Old World, propped up by priests and titled aristocrats, he called for leadership by the best minds, regardless of origins, guided by the best of knowledge and ideas. One crucial flaw in this test was its blanket exclusion of African Americans and women. Only white males, it seemed, were suitable for more than elementary enlightenment and for leadership. What Jefferson demonstrated were the limits of enlightenment as liberation. His own case showed that, however wide a man's learning and however profound his thought, he remained in crucial respects not only shaped but shackled by his environment—his time, his class, and his private interests.

* * *

In response to Adams's criticism of his "hackneyed" work on the Declaration of Independence, Jefferson said later that the object had been "not to find out new principles, or new arguments, never before thought of, not merely to say things which had never been said before; but to place before mankind the common sense of the subject, in terms so firm and plain as to command their assent." Jefferson was correct that his "common sense" was firmly grounded in the Enlightenment schools of England, Scotland, and France. But never had those ideas been employed in a public document of revolutionary import.

Jefferson was characteristically lucid and precise in setting out the "long train of abuses and usurpations" that justified rebellion against the king, whom he declared "unfit to be the ruler of a free people." But before he reached that list, he named a series of "self-evident" truths. First among them was "that all men are created equal." This was a bold statement that embraced both Locke's image of the infant mind as all "white paper" and possibility and Hutcheson's claim that all people were born with an innate moral sense. Jefferson's flat statement of equality contained unknowable potentials in a land with sharp inequalities across a host of dimensions—and with hundreds of thousands of human beings who, as slaves, could scarcely be more unequal. Next, Jefferson wrote, men were endowed with "unalienable rights" to "life, liberty, and the pursuit of happiness." These were extraordinarily rich and resonant terms, especially that enigmatic phrase at the end, but what, exactly, did they mean? Could they serve as guides to leaders? As incitement to followers?

"Life" was perhaps the most self-evident of Jefferson's truths. After all, John Locke, whose phrase "Lives, Liberties, and Estates" Jefferson adapted, defined the original purpose of government as providing security for people's lives and property. Fear of anarchy or a "State of War," Locke had written in 1689, was "one great *reason of Mens putting themselves into Society.*" Revolutionary Americans were all too aware of this peril. As Jefferson wrote his Declaration, the rebellion was already under way; battles had been lost, men and women were dying, property was being confiscated and destroyed. The leaders in Philadelphia knew that they might hang separately if they did not hang together.

"Liberty" was the "precious jewel" of the Revolution, its supreme goal and rallying cry, the object of countless paeans and tracts. Liberty's foe was easy for Americans to identify: the tyrant King George, with his parliamentary minions. But the meaning of liberty itself was less self-evident.

Inevitably, leaders of the English Enlightenment had supplied Americans with a profusion of views of liberty. Most Americans in fact were Whigs of one or another stripe, infused with the ideals of Britain's Glorious Revolution of 1689, fervent in their faith in individual liberty, liberty that protected men against oppressive rulers, liberty that could be secured only through representative government. They learned from John Locke that liberties were natural and inviolable, not granted by monarchs or legislatures, a radical idea for the time, since it meant that not they but the *people* were the ultimate sovereign power in a nation and thus had the inalienable right to resist, even rebel, in order to reclaim their liberties from tyrants.

But liberty was more than freedom from political oppression, more than the right to be left alone or to the protection of property against invasion. It was a complex combination of rights in many domains, including the intellectual, religious, social, familial. And as Locke indicated, liberty was a means, not an end. For some, it was freedom-to as well as freedom-from, expressed as a right to self-determination or self-fulfillment or, in Jefferson's term, to the pursuit of happiness. Such positive liberty could lay claim against government for the opportunity to fulfill that right, whether the opportunity be education or some minimal standard or condition of living or protection from exploitation or prejudice or, as Jefferson would later contemplate, the redistribution of property from rich to poor in each generation. Thus, positive liberty would foster the equality Jefferson held as the foremost of self-evident truths.

As America's war of liberation against the British mounted, other shackles were being loosened. Was there to be a revolution within the Revolution?

THE EGALITARIAN MOMENT

Up and down the eastern seaboard before opposition to British rule united them, people called themselves Americans, but there was not yet an American people. Rather, there were New Hampshiremen and Rhode Islanders, South Carolinians and Georgians, and more. Leaders in Boston or New York or Philadelphia or Charleston probably communicated more frequently with the British than with one another.

The economies of the colonies differed significantly. The prosperity of Virginia and the Carolinas depended largely on the toil of black slaves producing tobacco, rice, and indigo for export. To the north, cities dominated the colonial economies—Philadelphia with more than twenty-four thousand inhabitants, New York with about twenty-two thousand, Newport with eleven thousand. The port towns lived off foreign and coastal trade, finance, and some manufacturing.

Inequality was severe. The richest tenth of the colonial population owned more than half the total physical wealth, according to historian Colin Bonwick, "and within that fortunate group the richest 1 per cent owned almost 15 per cent." Meanwhile, "the bottom fifth of the population were themselves a species of property and could legally own nothing." That bottom fifth, slaves, existed in every colony—by the hundreds of thousands in the South, by the hundreds in New York City, Philadelphia, and western Long Island.

The next 30 percent of Americans just above the enslaved owned no more than 3 percent of the country's total wealth. These included landless laborers, many of them recent immigrants, in and around the northern towns. About two-thirds of all white persons were farmers, whose incomes fluctuated with the weather and local economic conditions. Native Americans, meanwhile, had been decimated by European diseases and pushed relentlessly west over the Appalachians. They had fared as poorly as any native peoples in Britain's global empire, losing perhaps half their numbers by the 1770s. Yet they remained British loyalists, earning condemnation in Jefferson's Declaration as "merciless Indian Savages"; American revolutionaries showed few signs of regarding them as equals in humanity.

As the war for independence, begun at Lexington and Concord in April 1774, quickly intensified, American leaders faced such staggering political and financial needs that discussions of equality remained little more than rhetorical bludgeons against the British with their princes, dukes, and barons. The Congress in Philadelphia had to convert itself from a protest group into a war government able to raise troops, finance an army, conduct diplomacy, and weld the new states into some kind of union. Even more daunting, those states would have to transform themselves from colonial regimes into independent republican governments. For a time Congress and the state legislatures tried to direct military operations, but, finding this wildly unworkable, they came to delegate ample discretion to General George Washington and the state militias.

But the potential for change was no less staggering. Wrote an anonymous American in March 1776: "Few opportunities have ever been offered to mankind of framing an entire Constitution of Government, upon equitable principles. Perhaps America is the only country in the world wholly free from all political impediments, at the very time they are under the necessity of framing a civil Constitution." A revolution in government was about to take effect, wrote a delegate to Congress, Oliver Wolcott of Connecticut—"a Government founded in Compact, Express and Clear Made in its Principles by the People at large."

⁃ ⁃ ⁃

Even before Congress had approved Jefferson's Declaration, reports were coming into Philadelphia about rising popular feeling for radical action. How do we know this? From the newspapers, pamphlets, correspondence, and books of the day. And from one book in particular.

Thomas Paine had arrived in Philadelphia from England late in November 1774. Born thirty-seven years before in Thetford, a small town northeast of London, Paine had worked for twelve years as a corset maker, rising from apprentice to master, before abandoning that profession for a life of

85

struggle as a teacher and tax collector. By 1774, his marriage had dissolved and his effects were auctioned off. England, he had decided, was a place of "general want" with a monarchy "too debasing to the dignity of man." Like so many others, Paine crossed the Atlantic in need of a fresh start. He found it almost immediately, quickly blossoming in bustling Philadelphia, the city with the biggest population and busiest port in British America. It was also the city of Franklin and his Junto and of a rich merchant class, but it was home, too, to a large activist movement of radical artisans, mechanics, shopkeepers, and young writers. Paine, who had left few traces of political engagement in England, soon fell in with them, and, remarkably, within a year of his arrival he published a forty-eight-page pamphlet titled *Common Sense,* intending, he said later, "to rescue man from tyranny and false systems and false principles of government, and enable him to be free." In the book, he swiftly set aside intellectual niceties. Attacking the "so much boasted Constitution of England," he especially assailed the hereditary monarchy, imagining it founded by the "principal ruffian of some restless gang," the "chief among plunderers." Paine's theme was not only independence and liberty but political egalitarianism. Radicals were rapturous in their praise, while conservatives shuddered. A colonel in Washington's army called Paine a "Crack Brain Zealot for Democracy."

Published in January 1776, *Common Sense* was an almost instant best seller, running through twenty-five editions. It reached hundreds of thousands of readers in its first year. Non-readers heard it read aloud in public places. *Common Sense* had a powerful effect on those Americans who were still uncertain about the wisdom of revolutionary war against their accustomed rulers. Paine's views were not new—they had their roots in core Enlightenment principles—but he put them forward plainly and with exceptional force. The book was more than one radical's view; it was an articulation of a wide and intense feeling that Americans, whatever their station, were as one in the fight for independence, each having an equal stake in forging what Paine called "a government of our own." Its egalitarian thrust was crucial to its appeal. As a Boston "Evangelical" radical interpreted Paine, even the laboring poor were "a vital part of God's great plan for the redemption of the world."

Paine expressed an aspiration that lay at the heart of the Enlightenment, the dream of revolutionaries everywhere, that the people "have it in our power to begin the world over again." These were the people who greeted the Declaration of Independence with pealing bells and cannon fire, the soldiers who cheered when General Washington ordered it to be read to his assembled brigades.

. . .

The Declaration's author, despite his impeccable establishment credentials, was capable of statements more radical than Paine's, including the idea that *every generation* ought to be able to begin the world over again. Years after the Revolution, writing to James Madison in 1789, Thomas Jefferson would claim as another "self-evident" truth that the earth belonged to the living and that "the dead have neither powers nor rights over it." Property occupied by any individual, he continued, "ceases to be his when himself ceases to be, and reverts to the society." Debts and even laws likewise died with the passing of individuals and generations.

Jefferson's radically egalitarian idea of property—he wrote in 1785 that to overcome the "misery to the bulk of mankind" caused by enormous inequalities, "legislators cannot invent too many devices for subdividing property"—underpinned the most enigmatic term of his trinity, *the pursuit of happiness.* Locke had included "Estates" in his own trinity and bound happiness to property, implying, as historian Jan Lewis wrote, "that human happiness proceeds from the individual's enjoyment, improvement, and use of his possessions." This was a highly individualistic conception of property at a time when most people had small plots or dwellings, if any.

Why had Jefferson substituted "happiness" for "property"? He and his fellow-rebels had read their Locke but also the men of the Scottish Enlightenment, especially Francis Hutcheson, with his vision of humans as naturally kind, faithful, virtuous, and predisposed to pursue happiness. Hutcheson regarded benevolence as collective and social. As men pursued their own happiness, as they committed and were the beneficiaries of acts of benevolence, as they were moved to further benevolence by the examples of others, the common stock of happiness increased. As with all else, the moral test of property rights was their contribution to "the *greatest happiness* for the *greatest numbers.*" They must serve the public good.

The public good! Though Jefferson himself owned extensive properties—including humans—he understood that the public good was the touchstone, the ultimate basis of personal happiness, and that, in turn, the public good rested on private happiness. For Jefferson, property ownership, as political scientist Richard K. Matthews observed, was merely an instrumental civil right, enabling men to enjoy their natural rights to life, liberty, and the pursuit of happiness and thereby contribute to the happiness of all the people. But how in reality could Locke's individual property rights be reconciled with—indeed, *serve*—Hutcheson's social happiness? Ultimately by politics and government committed to ensuring the equal rights of men and women to pursue happiness.

• • •

During the American Revolution, politics and government were not revolutionary. When state constitutions were drafted, they by no means represented the totally new political compacts that had been promised. Most crucially, virtually all of them perpetuated political inequalities by retaining property requirements for voting and officeholding. Only Pennsylvania, its constitutional convention dominated by artisans, farmers, and lesser tradesmen, abolished that requirement and opened the franchise to all taxpaying adult males. Elsewhere, most Americans were denied representation—an effective voice in government—ensuring that their interests would not be heard.

So those who had dreamed of political and social equality were to be disappointed. The changes that did occur were a consequence of the revolutionary war, not of the designs of leaders. The most direct social impact of the war was on the soldiers themselves. Suddenly men from different colonies and different backgrounds were mingling in a common effort. While many generals came, like Washington, from the social elite, others, such as Henry Knox and Horatio Gates, did not. The inexperience of much of the officer corps, and the proliferation of skirmishes along with the big battles, increasingly drew militiamen and junior officers into higher commands.

As a consequence of the Revolution, British Loyalists were driven from seats of power, offering a new class of politicians the opportunity to fill new institutions. Moreover, as many Loyalists had been members of the economic and social elite, their departure opened pathways to upward mobility for some Americans, a new elite to replace the old, with little overall effect on inequality in the new nation.

War also changed the lives of countless women, at least for the duration. Thousands of them were left in charge of fields and livestock as the men went to battle. Her husband, said Elizabeth Adkins of Culpeper County, Virginia, "was gone all summer and she had to plough, and hoe his corn to raise bread for the children." Others earned livings as soap makers, printers, tallow chandlers, tanners, net weavers, even blacksmiths. The American Manufactory in Philadelphia employed about four hundred women in spinning cloth. Still, few of the war-induced changes in women's lives carried over into peacetime. Nor were women included in the new American polity. Of the new state constitutions, only New Jersey's did not bar women from voting. Early in 1776, Abigail Adams had written her husband, John, in Philadelphia to urge Congress to "remember the Ladies." In vain she reminded him that all men would be tyrants if they could and warned that if women were ignored, "we are determined to foment a Rebelion."

Even less altered was the condition of the poor. As usual, war produced gains in jobs but also losses caused by inflation, embargoes, blockades, and the devastation of towns and whole counties. War widows and orphans joined the ranks of the impoverished. Least changed of all, of course, were the lives of the slaves. No colony or new state abolished slavery. Blacks served in state militias, some doubtless hoping to win their freedom, but in the Chesapeake region several thousand slaves fled to the British lines in pursuit of liberty—the ultimate irony.

The Revolution was a time of traumatic violence for some, small alterations in the lives of others, and of a huge potential that went unrealized. Before the Revolution, America was essentially a hierarchical society in politics and economy; despite some reshuffling in the upper reaches, it remained so. Wealth, status, and family were the great triumvirate still dominating society, even if to a lesser degree as British impositions were removed. The most common talk was of an equality of personal respect, not of money or status, or of power or condition.

Thomas Jefferson's Declaration of Independence would attain a potent universality, as freedom-seeking people cited it for more than two centuries to advance their cause. But in revolutionary America, it was less universal than it appeared and less a guide to committed leadership than a resounding statement of Enlightenment ideals that had served its purpose of uniting Americans for war. Its egalitarianism remained only a promise. Would that promise be redeemed? The outcome depended less on political reform or even military victories than on animating ideas that might propel Americans into post-Revolution revolutions.

4

France: Rule or Ruin?

The news in Paris on that day in April 1777 was mystifying at first, then shocking. The young Marquis de Lafayette had simply disappeared. How could this be? He was joyfully married to the lovely Adrienne, daughter of a duke. They were frequent guests at Marie Antoinette's salon as well as at the court of George III in London, where Adrienne's uncle served as ambassador. The couple were expecting their second child.

The mystery was solved four months later, in August, when Adrienne received a letter from America. "I am writing you from very far away, dear heart. . . . Have you forgiven me?" He had gone to America as a soldier of freedom, taking only his sincerity and goodwill. "The welfare of America is intimately connected to the happiness of all mankind; she will become the respectable and safe asylum of virtue, integrity, tolerance, equality, and a peaceful liberty."

All this was quite outrageous. The nineteen year old had left his regiment without permission. He had offended the king, who signed a *lettre de cachet* for his capture and arrest. He faced imprisonment on return. Scarcely could his friends imagine that the young marquis, who spoke little English, would boldly introduce himself to members of the Continental Congress, win his way into the heart and mind of George Washington, accompany him in major battles, and become the youngest general in the American army.

In February 1778, the French signed a treaty of "amity" with the American revolutionaries. For the royal government, it was a matter of Realpolitik, another episode in its interminable rivalry with Britain. But for much of the French public, it was an alliance of sentiments, and Lafayette returned home after Yorktown, in January 1782, to a hero's reception. Revoking the arrest warrant, the king praised him. And Lafayette was merely the most conspicuous of scores of young men, many of them aristocrats, who had sailed to revolutionary America in pursuit of both liberty and glory, and returned with admiration for the Americans they had fought beside. Lafayette's friend, the Comte de Ségur, recalled the soldiers' "personal dignity" and "noble pride" inspired by their "love of liberty" and "sentiment of equality."

How deep-seated was French enthusiasm for the revolution in America? In the country of the philosophes, paeans to Americans and their fight for liberty quickened currents of thought that had been flowing in France for decades. The mathematician and philosopher Condorcet had concluded, he wrote in 1786, that there was only one way "to ameliorate the lot of mankind" and that was to "accelerate the process of the Enlightenment." America, he believed, would become the Enlightenment's forcing-house, producing as many men as all of Europe committed to "adding to the mass of human knowledge," which would, he figured, "at least double the progress of mankind . . . and make this progress twice as rapid." But the contribution of America's rising Enlightenment was already apparent as French thinkers and opinion makers looked for intellectual ammunition not only in the Declaration of Independence but in the bills of rights in state constitutions that reflected the West's most progressive thought.

And the French had heroes of the American Enlightenment in their midst. John Adams, who was respected if unloved by the French—and the feeling was mutual—had helped to negotiate the Treaty of Amity in Paris. Later, Thomas Jefferson would serve as American ambassador, distinguished author not only of the great Declaration but also of the admired *Notes on the State of Virginia*.

But no American could compare in fame with the venerable Benjamin Franklin, who, after his contribution to the drafting of the Declaration, had been sent to Paris in October 1776 as America's envoy to the royal court and chief American negotiator of the Treaty of Amity. Franklin's baldish pate and rustic attire concealed a mind as sharp and skilled in European diplomacy as it had been in building Philadelphia into a living monument to the Enlightenment. Franklin's popularity, wrote historian Simon Schama, was virtually a mania. "Mobbed wherever he went, and especially whenever he set foot outside his house in Passy, he was probably better known by sight than the King, and his likeness could be found on engraved glass, painted porcelain, printed cottons, snuffboxes and inkwells."

In April 1778 at an open meeting of the Academy of Sciences in Paris, both Franklin and the eighty-four-year-old François Marie Arouet de

Voltaire, France's greatest expounder of Enlightenment ideas, were present. The two men, who had not met, stood apart at the gathering, each crowded by other guests. Dour John Adams also was there, observing the awkward situation. Presently, he wrote in his diary, a cry arose among the throng that the two celebrities should be introduced to each other, and so they were. But "this was no Satisfaction. There must be something more," Adams wrote. "'Il faut s'embrasser, à la francoise.' The two Aged Actors upon this great Theatre of Philosophy and frivolity then embraced each other by hugging one another in their Arms and kissing each others cheeks, and then the tumult subsided. . . ."

No incident could have better epitomized the harmonious spirit of the Enlightenment, viewed through the eyes of the acerbic man of Boston. The respect and friendship the philosophes had for one another, even continents apart, reflected Enlightenment values and reinforced them. Such a spirit bolstered philosophical optimism about liberty, progress, and happiness. Surely enlightened men and women of reason and goodwill would embrace to overcome the ills of the human race.

ROYAL PARIS

Paris, wrote the pioneering demographer Abbé Expilly in 1768, is "one of the most beautiful, the richest, the most populated, the most flourishing, and one of the biggest cities of Europe." The city had superb buildings, a wise government, and "prodigious commerce carried on within its boundaries."

Jean-Jacques Rousseau, a nineteen-year-old vagabond of Genevan origin, had imagined that Paris was such a city. But when he arrived on foot in 1731, entering "by the Faubourg St. Marceau, I saw only filthy and stinking little streets, nasty-looking black houses, the air of dirtiness, poverty, beggars, carters, cobblers, vendors of rotgut and old hats." Nothing could erase that first impression, Rousseau added. Ever after he had a secret distaste for living in Paris.

Entering the city by way of the Seine and disembarking below the Louvre, eighteenth-century travelers would have agreed with the abbé. They probably would not have tarried at the Louvre itself, a onetime royal residence now housing the royal stables, artisans at work, and the Académie Français. Rather, they would have walked on through the superb gardens of the Tuileries and then proceeded away from the river to pay homage to Louis XIV at the plaza named for him. From there they might head toward livelier parts of the city. By the 1770s, Paris was blossoming intellectually and artistically.

It was indeed a big city, with a population of probably over six hundred thousand. Its inhabitants were separated into distinct classes, according to Louis-Sébastien Mercier, the most acute urban analyst of the time: princes and great lords, professionals in the law, the church, and medicine, financiers, merchants, artists, artisans, manual laborers, servants, and—always—the abjectly poor.

. . .

But where *was* the court? Where indeed was Louis XVI? The king reigned not in Paris but a dozen miles away, in Versailles. He could be visited, although to reach Versailles was no mean feat. Wealthy personages might hire carriages, but respectable visitors with smaller purses would grab the notorious carrabas, a lumbering carriage that took over six hours. This "omnibus" did not escape Mercier's critical eye; in "its elongated cage of wicker-work twenty persons shift and struggle for an hour before they can fit themselves, and when the machine at last jerks forward all the heads go bump together, so that you fall into a Capuchin's beard or a wetnurse's bosom." Twice a day this vehicle conveyed the "lackeys of the lackeys" of the Crown.

Visitors who arrived in Versailles respectably dressed, and who were also very lucky, might be permitted to view court rituals that had changed little since the time of Louis XIV, with much of the king's daily routine conducted in public. His life was dominated by the officials of the royal household. There presided the grand master of ceremonies, who regulated his public functions; the captain of the guard, who protected his life; along with other personages who tended to his food, his clothes, his horses, his private money. Such officials almost always came from the grandest families. They dealt with the most intimate matters; thus, lighted by a huge candelabra, they escorted the king to Marie Antoinette's bedroom. The nobles presided over a retinue of "valets," most of whom had paid princely sums to gain their posts.

Louis XVI had simplified some of the proceedings endured by his predecessors, but the court in fact was larger than ever, numbering around twenty-five hundred persons in the royal household, compared to around six hundred officials in the ministries of war, foreign affairs, finance, marine, and justice. Aside from conferring with his ministers, Louis spent much of his working time receiving ambassadors and prelates and endless members of other royal households, as well as presiding over formal "presentations" at court of nobles qualified by birth. Untitled bourgeois notables, though, were not included. "No other court possessed such an extensive and exclusive caste around the throne," historian Philip Mansel wrote. Perhaps it made no difference, since the king did not use these occasions for conversation; he was not much for the small talk—often he remained completely silent.

The palace of Versailles was a place of prestige and of outrageous luxury; it was also a prison. The king was the captive of subordinates who structured his daily life but who themselves were controlled by an elaborate system of deference. The court had little regard for imagination, innovation, creativity—that is, for leadership—at a time when those qualities would be most needed in order to guide, or even understand, currents of change running faster and faster in France and outside.

* * *

If, heading back to Paris from Versailles, travelers crossed the Seine at the Pont Neuf, they might encounter the "other Paris," the narrow streets without sidewalks under protruding upper floors, the dank mazes of alleys, the dingy, windowless hovels of the "popular classes." The air was filthy with the stink of garbage, excrement, and putrefying flesh. This was a place of dark menace. The visitor would be fortunate not to come upon a public execution on the gallows or the wheel, watched avidly by gaping throngs.

No wonder Mercier called the *peuple* of Paris the saddest sight on earth. "The impoverished man in Paris, bowed by the eternal burden of his hard work, who erects, builds, and forges, who slaves in quarries or high up on roofs, who carries incredible loads, who is at the mercy of any powerful person, who is squashed like an insect the minute he opens his mouth, exerts himself by the sweat of his brow to gain his pittance—just about enough to live on but not enough to guarantee him a better lot in his old age."

Women suffered the most, along with children. Wives lost legal control of person and property on marriage. They had little protection against husbands except in cases of physical abuse—though even then redress required legal proceedings they could ill afford. Largely shut out of the guilds that dominated the crafts, women resorted to whatever work was available—at best as seamstresses or hairdressers, or as hawkers of flowers, coal, or leftovers from caterers or markets.

Some children suffered more than others. An astonishingly large fraction of the children of Paris—perhaps one-third—were foundlings, many of whom had been dispatched to institutions in the capital from the provinces. Well over half the infants abandoned before their first birthday died within a year. Those who survived would be put to work as domestics, apprentices, or farmworkers. Some got menial jobs carding or spinning wool in Paris manufactories.

Some of the more privileged dismissed the poor as a horde of ignorant, vulgar illiterates, without differentiating between vagrants and laborers. Not that the latter were much better off. The Parisian poor lived mainly on grains. White bread was preferred but expensive, so when hard-pressed the needy turned to flours of barley, rice, potatoes, or even turnips. We do not know—since the records of the poor are poor—how these Parisians supplemented their bread diet, perhaps with cheap meat, such as tongue or kidney, or else with refuse. Some shops retailed bread slices salvaged from rich households, or even crumbs to be used with soup.

We know more about the housing of the poor. Constructed from plaster over slats, the typical tenement was four or five stories, including an attic. Through subletting, huge numbers of tenants could be crowded into tiny dark rooms on each floor. Continuously rising rents created a mobile population, as some families moved every few months, leaving their meager furnishings, to foil the landlord.

Diseases promoted by such conditions of life usually could be identified, but the numbers of the afflicted remained unknown. There were the great epidemics—typhoid, malaria, smallpox—and the widespread *maladies populaires*, like the "stoppage of the bowels, dropsies, consumptions, and even a tendency to scurvy," that, according to a physician's survey, were "supported and favored among the class of indigent citizens by dearness of food, pollution of air, and filth."

We know least of all the psychology of the poor. We can judge only by their actions—or inaction. Most of the Parisian poor did not protest in the 1770s. They did not convert their deprivations into demonstrations. They were in the blind alley of the culture of poverty. Part of that poverty was ignorance amid a struggle for survival in a city that had become the European center of Enlightenment thought. Closely related to the lack of light was the absence of leadership, among themselves or from outside.

* * *

At Versailles, meanwhile, the palace theatricals and balls continued in all their old gaiety and extravagance. When a few jobless Parisians marched on the palace in 1786, the number of guards on duty was doubled, but Louis

XVI joked about it, and a marquis jotted in his diary, "This evening's ball at the palace was not at all affected by this ridiculous revolt." Nobody, Philip Mansel wrote, sensed that they were dancing on the edge of a precipice.

THE PHILOSOPHES AND THE PEOPLE

Outside the precincts of the impoverished, the development of the Enlightenment in France was driven in good part by the law of supply and demand. In his survey of Paris, Louis-Sébastian Mercier noted the host of "small bookshops, scattered here and there in little street-corner booths or sometimes right out in the open, that sell old books or some of the new brochures that are constantly appearing. You see groups of readers clustered around the counter as if held there by a magnet." Here was a sign of real change in the royal capital. A majority of Parisians now were literate, and 90 percent of men and 80 percent of women could sign their wills. This was due largely to the widening availability of elementary education. By the middle of the eighteenth century, nearly every parish in Paris had a free school for boys, though only half as many provided for girls. Most children stayed in school long enough to learn at least to read and write.

And Parisians were readers. "Gone are the days," declared the *Journal Encyclopédique* in 1758, "when journals were only for the learned.... Nowadays, everybody reads or wants to read about everything," from erotica and salacious tittle tattle to philosophy, science, and the arts. Paris dominated the nation's print trade, partly because the authorities who issued the licenses to publish and administered the censorship favored city printers. The centralized book trade made official control easier, but forbidden texts flowed into Paris from the provinces and abroad, ranging from the odd volume of Rousseau to seven crates of the pornographic *Le Libertin de qualité.* "The trade in books today," wrote Malesherbes, the government's chief censor from 1750 to 1763, "is too widespread and the public is too avid for them for it to be possible to constrain it." Malesherbes, in fact, imposed as few constraints as possible, especially of ideas. He held the Enlightenment view that ideas must keep pace with changing times and people must keep up with new ideas. Someone who read only the books favored by the king and his government, he wrote, "would be behind his contemporaries almost a century." Still, every work destined for the press passed through his department and scribblers certainly kept his censors busy: One reportedly issued *permissions de police* for as many as fifty thousand verses of pamphlet poetry each year. But the king and his officials urged on the censors to stamp out smut and subversion.

In such an atmosphere, perhaps only a noble would have dared to write *De l'esprit des lois—The Spirit of the Laws*—published in 1748 by Charles Louis de Secondat, Baron de Montesquieu. Perhaps only a noble could have penned so devastating a critique of the French monarchy, the church, and other bastions of the ancien régime and hoped to escape jail. In his thirties, like other young rebels, Montesquieu had derided the stuffy Académie Française with its membership of "Immortels" that Cardinal Richelieu had founded a century earlier to guard the purity of the French language.

In time, though, the baron's rebellion became more searching as he moved intellectually across an astonishing range of subjects, writing with assurance and authority. A consummate man of the Enlightenment who recognized no intellectual barriers, Montesquieu was an historian who analyzed the ebb and flow of events, a political scientist who evaluated the structures of governments, a moralist who explored the meaning of virtue, an anthropologist fascinated by "primitive" peoples, an economist who studied the wealth of nations and its causes well before Adam Smith, a jurisprudentialist who examined laws in their broadest contexts, a Christian who coolly evaluated religious institutions, a self-made climatologist almost obsessed by the impact of weather on history, and above all, in his broad vision and penetrating insights, a philosopher for a new age.

Montesquieu leapt into the millennia-old debate about the forms of government that had attracted the ablest minds, from Plato and Aristotle to Spinoza and Locke. He approached the subject systematically, classifying and analyzing, a method as old as the Greeks but to which he brought a new sophistication. He considered the strong and weak points of three main types of regimes: monarchical, republican, and despotic.

Montesquieu acknowledged the strengths of monarchy—it answered the twin problems of ensuring order and regularizing the succession to power. But the great risk was that monarchy could readily degenerate into the worst form of government, despotism, with the disappearance of liberty, law, and prosperity. The king's authority had to be checked and channeled by powers independent of the throne—above all, by a nobility.

Republics, too, needed balanced powers. Democracies risked popular despotism, or the rise of a dictator, while aristocratic republics became corrupt when the nobles ruled arbitrarily, detached from and unaccountable to the people.

For all the attention he devoted to the structures and operations of governments, Montesquieu's judgment of them rested on the highest standard—their underlying principle, expressed in the spirit of their laws. For lawless despotisms, the principle that united the state was *terror*. In monarchies, it was *honor* that caused men to work for the common good and defend the rule of law. Republics had *virtue* as their "soul," embracing such values as public-spiritedness, moderation, equality, and political liberty.

Montesquieu made no secret of his favorite among the many governments he studied—the "one nation in the world whose constitution has political liberty for its direct purpose." That was Britain. He admired especially its separation of powers among the executive, legislative, and judicial branches. It was this division, which he exaggerated, that protected British liberty, described as a "tranquility of spirit which comes from the opinion each one has of his security." Montesquieu's close examination of the British system—comparing it to others, relating institutions to values, ideas to legal procedures, theory to practice—was what distinguished him as a political philosopher and marked him as a leader of the Enlightenment.

* * *

Few benefited more from France's rising tide of literacy and readership than Voltaire, or contributed more to it. Born in Paris in 1694 of a prosperous notary and a mother who died when he was seven, Voltaire attended a Jesuit college in the capital where he studied literature and theater, though he claimed he had been taught nothing there but "Latin and nonsense." His early plays and verse marked him as a critic of the monarchy, which attracted audiences but also the attention of the authorities. Twice he was thrown into the Bastille, once for a satirical verse he did not write and then on a royal *lettre de cachet* an aristocratic family obtained after he dared to return an insult from one of its scions. He could have been detained indefinitely without trial, but Voltaire negotiated exile as an alternative punishment, and the three years he spent in Great Britain proved transformative. He was deeply impressed by the relative freedoms of Englishmen and the limits the English constitution put on monarchy. When he returned to Paris, he published his findings, but praise of the hated British at French expense earned him book burnings and yet another bout of exile from the city.

During his early years Voltaire had been basically a young royalist and held—as he would continue to hold—some attitudes fit for a royalist. For example, he denounced the common people of France as the canaille, an unreliable and fanatical rabble, a pack of dogs. But gradually, under British influence, Voltaire moved toward what Peter Gay called a "candid liberalism." He had—and promoted—an uncommon tolerance of diversity. He had been impressed to find the London Stock Exchange a place where "the representatives of all nations meet for the benefit of mankind. There the Jew, the Mahometan, and the Christian transact business together, as though they were all of the same religion, and give the name of Infidels to none but bankrupts; there the Presbyterian confides in the Anabaptist, and the Churchman depends upon the Quaker's word."

Like Montesquieu, Voltaire was a little starry-eyed when he looked at the British political system—no doubt because of the contrast with the French court. He celebrated the House of Commons as an Enlightenment melting pot. Centuries of struggle against tyranny, he wrote, had brought to power "the most numerous, the most useful, and even the most virtuous part of mankind, composed of those who addict themselves to the study of law and of the sciences, of merchants, mechanics, and, in a word, laborers." However fanciful that view, Voltaire made it clear that for him, liberty was the ultimate value and Britain was the model for it, despite its slave trade, which Voltaire abhorred. Against claims by defenders of slavery that an impoverished worker would sacrifice his liberty for security under a kind master, he replied that a human being would choose freedom over slavery even under the harshest conditions.

Still, Voltaire was not a philosopher of the rank of Locke or Montesquieu. In the flood of histories, plays, poems, letters, and pamphlets he produced, his joy came in pricking the pretensions of the monarchy, the clergy, and any other of the self-deluding creatures who made up the human race. At his brilliant best, he was the great publicist of the Enlightenment, sending its ideas across Europe. Another French thinker, a younger friend of Voltaire, found his own way of spreading enlightenment. Denis Diderot was born of a Champagne master cutler who was tolerant—or prescient—enough, when he caught Denis running away to Paris to avoid training for the priesthood, to take him there anyway and install him in a good college. In the heady intellectual atmosphere of the capital, Diderot developed a consuming interest in just about everything—science, nature, philosophy, politics, education, medicine, and such far-off places as Russia and Tahiti. With another young enthusiast, a mathematician and admirer of Locke, Jean le Rond d'Alembert, he conceived the idea of a grand and systematic encyclopedia that would include the latest data and thought on all these subjects and many more. The object was to put the Enlightenment in all its dimensions into print. Diderot pictured the quest for human knowledge as a great campaign to bring light where there were shadows of obscurity and error. "In the human understanding," he wrote, "everything hangs together."

His was an intellectual and publishing gambit that almost failed at the start. Prosecuted in 1749 for writings "contrary to Religion, the State, or morals," the young encyclopedist was imprisoned in solitary confinement, where he maintained his sanity by converting a toothpick into a pen, powdered roof slate into ink, and some blank pages into prison musings. Then, after he was released and the first volume of the encyclopedia appeared in 1751, Jesuit foes persuaded Louis XV to declare it an attack on royal authority, promoting "a spirit of independence and revolt." The project seemed close to suppression, only to be rescued by sympathizers at court, including Malesherbes, and by the well-connected publishers who had invested a fortune. Diderot denounced the government's censorship as a "deliberate plan" to "reduce us to beggary and stupidity." He had his revenge when the number of subscribers jumped from two to three thousand. More crises would follow, but eventually seventeen volumes were published.

"Our Encyclopedia," wrote Diderot, "will be not only the best work of its kind, but the greatest collaborative intellectual enterprise in the history of man, a synthesis of the French genius, the monument of our century." Was ever a blurb more justified?

* * *

The writings of Voltaire and Diderot electrified a widening public and spurred enlightenment and controversy in Paris, throughout Europe, and across the Atlantic. But neither had the shock value of the work of Jean-Jacques Rousseau. People were fascinated by Rousseau himself—or at least by Rousseau as he presented his mysterious, stormy, romantic past in the *Confessions,* a remarkable and novel experiment in autobiography that aimed to show "a man in all the truth of nature; and this man will be myself." The unreliability of these confessions was no deterrent to his impassioned fans, some of whom sought out the man himself in his Geneva lair, where he lived safe from the police and the censors of autocrats.

But it was his radical theories about man and society, turning conventional Enlightenment ideas upside down, that most attracted and repelled inquiring minds. In stark contrast to Hobbes and Locke, Rousseau maintained that humans had been freer and happier in their primitive state of nature, and unhappy and wicked to the degree that they had later rejected that state for the corruptions and constraints of civil society. "Man is born free," Rousseau declared, "and everywhere he is in chains." Since there could be no return to that original natural state of freedom, he proposed a new form of society, with citizenship open to all people, their freedom and equality secured by a social contract under which they could not renounce either their rights or their duties. Rousseau supposed that this good society would be governed by a "general will" that would produce purely rational policies from the unanimity of citizens.

Rousseau won wide acclaim even though his large thoughts did not always connect with—and sometimes contradicted—one another. Demanding change, he failed to make clear orderly ways of producing it. Above all, with his vision of a new society filled with good citizens, who were both rulers and ruled, working selflessly and with identical minds for the common good—no "long debates, dissensions, and tumult," he insisted—Rousseau misconceived the role of peaceful and democratic conflict as crucial to the achievement of freedom. His vision offered no protection to the rights or voices of a minority even as his own character betrayed his Utopian dream: He was a cantankerous, quarrelsome man who stood apart from the community of philosophes, scorning their faith in reason and reform and progress. Enlightenment, he would provocatively claim, was the road to slavery; true happiness and freedom came from innocence, a "sweet and precious ignorance."

Yet Rousseau himself undeniably made a dramatic and original contribution to the central project of the Enlightenment: widening the understanding of human nature, of how men and women live and how they *might* live. He was part of the change, of the transition from fatalism, passivity, and—yes—sheer ignorance to new potentials, a new optimism. It was in France itself that Enlightenment ideals met their strongest test in the crucible of revolution.

THE UNMAKING OF A KING

It is with feelings of familiarity, and yet also of hope and suspense and even dread, that an analyst of change returns to the dramatics of the French Revolution and proceeds to confront the crucial issue: In a society that the eighteenth century had only lightly altered, under a slowly evolving monarchy that had endured for hundreds of years, what caused these spasms of change in a single decade? For two centuries historians have argued about the origins of the French Revolution.

Was the collapse of the royal government caused by a failing economy? This was the simplest, most plausible explanation. One-third of the French people in the 1770s were grindingly poor—unemployed, underemployed, too old or too young or too ill to earn a living. And many who had jobs were scarcely more secure. "Day labourers, workmen, journeymen," a Norman parish priest wrote in 1774, "and all those whose occupation does not provide for much more than food and clothing are the ones who make beggars." A second or third child might mean hunger for a family. Throughout Louis XVI's reign, peasants suffered from bad harvests and price instability, culminating in a July 1788 storm that dropped hailstones big enough to kill people and wiped out crops across northern France.

If millions of the French, urban and rural, were impoverished, so was their government. By the early 1780s, France was living on borrowed money. The main reason was war. The Realpolitik of spending hundreds of millions of livres to fight the British in North America—first in the Seven Years' War and then to help Americans gain their independence—collided with the reality of a continuously unbalanced budget, which in turn accelerated the spiral of poverty. But as for the poor themselves, especially the poor in the countryside, they had neither the will nor the means, as of the 1780s, to launch a nationwide revolution. Passivity and timidity were a consequence of their poverty.

Did the Revolution, then, originate in social rather than economic conditions? Probably not, at least not directly. Whatever their living conditions, the social relationships of most of the French were deeply structured and entrenched. The system of deference at the court was reflected, albeit in less extreme form, within and between the other classes of society—the nobility, the peasantry, urban workers, the bourgeoisie, and the clergy. Deference formed the basis of hierarchies so rooted in tradition and custom as to be impervious to all but the most powerful forces of disequilibrium.

Ideas—those of the Enlightenment—played a crucial role in that disequilibrium. They sanctioned raking scrutiny of rulers who claimed to govern by divine right and judging them by human standards—their success or failure in fulfilling elemental wants and needs of their people, in guaranteeing them basic rights, in giving them opportunities for self-fulfillment, in respecting their human dignity. By these Enlightenment standards, the incompetence and repressiveness of Louis XVI's regime was glaring.

But the Enlightenment offered not only critique. It offered a justification of resistance to that regime. It offered, too, the direction for change, both end-goals and means for achieving them, as well as its characteristic optimism, its faith in the ability of men and women to transform their situations.

Above all, more than any single doctrine, it was the spirit of enlightenment that mobilized the French, opened new insights into their society, and excited them with new vistas. Talk of change, of reform and betterment, was in the air as new books poured from new presses and readers who could not afford them packed libraries and reading rooms. Newspapers also proliferated; by the 1780s, according to William Doyle, "no self-respecting provincial centre was without one." Many publications escaped the censors, who were no more efficient than most other government functionaries. Philosophes and other *hommes sérieux* communicated across informal networks of correspondence. Sometimes they traveled hundreds of miles by horse and coach to discourse with their intellectual friends and foes in their homes. As the monarchy tottered on the fiscal cliff, the conversation about its failures and the need for change was becoming general, inescapable, and urgent.

. . .

The direct, proximate causes of the monarchy's collapse were markedly political. What the French needed, as people's wants and needs deepened in the 1780s, was an effective government or social movement that could take resolute and principled action to produce needed, systematic reforms. Such a government or movement would need backing by a coalition that united elements of the different classes to generate a critical mass for reform.

And such a coalition would in turn call for another vital instrument of change—collective leadership. That was precisely what the French lacked. They had a plenitude of impressive individual leaders, such as Comptroller-General Charles Alexandre de Calonne, who boldly warned the king of the desperate financial situation and urged strong measures; the Comte de Vergennes, architect of French aid to revolutionary Americans yet a reactionary aristocrat who was effectively Louis's "first minister"; Jacques Necker, a Swiss Protestant commoner in a court of Catholic aristocrats, unorthodox and innovative in his initiatives to salvage the kingdom's finances. And—as would soon be strikingly demonstrated—France possessed a galaxy of potential leaders outside of the regime, young men in Paris or the provinces excluded from political participation by a government sealed off from society.

None of these leaders, though, active or potential, emerged to fashion a collective leadership capable of either fortifying or reforming the monarchy. The reason lay mainly in the disunity in France not only among political entities—monarchy and nobility and clergy and bourgeoisie—but within each of them. The nobility, a class of tens of thousands, ranging from the super-rich and court-connected to impoverished countrymen with only ancient titles to flaunt, was deeply divided socially and politically within itself. In the church, too, a chasm of interests and attitudes yawned between the grand prelates of the cathedrals and parish priests. And among the bourgeoisie, there was the lack of a sense of common cause between those of the professions and those in trade.

* * *

It was amid the divisions and drift of late 1786 that Comptroller-General Calonne, faced with mounting fiscal problems, came to see fundamental reform as urgently necessary. Since that would need political support he convened an Assembly of Notables—handpicked men of substance—to suggest and approve administrative and fiscal changes. The three-month gathering did nothing more than to expose the depths of France's crisis. The clergy objected to even moderate reforms—they essentially wanted just to be left alone—and nobles divided over Calonne's tax proposals. When it was clear that Calonne could not unite and lead the Notables, Louis XVI dismissed him.

Deadlock persisted. A new comptroller-general's fresh reform proposals met the same fate as Calonne's. Then the Notables, who were developing a taste for opposition, took a fateful step: a call for convening the Estates-General. The court feared the idea; if the aristocratic Notables could not be persuaded to support the king's policies, how could a gathering that included commoners? The Estates-General, an ancient institution that in theory was representative of all France, had not met since 1614, when its proceedings had been dominated by the first two estates, the nobles and the clergy, while the commoners—the third estate—had sat by powerlessly. How the Estates-General would work almost two centuries later in this environment of crisis and impasse was unpredictable.

The king and his men continued to dither until the past suddenly caught up with them. In August 1788, the government's finances collapsed. This was not simply one more deficit. The treasury was empty—the government was bankrupt. Usually dependable creditors refused to come to the rescue.

Since the levying of taxes required some kind of public approval, only one course seemed open—convening the Estates-General.

Early in May 1789 the three estates gathered at Versailles amid great expectations inside and outside the hall. They were swiftly disappointed. There was no lead from the king as the deputies tangled over the key issue: whether their voting should be by order (one estate, one vote) or in common (one delegate, one vote). Voting by order was the traditional procedure, traditionally ensuring that the Third Estate was outvoted by the two other orders. Since members of the Third Estate outnumbered nobles and clergy, conservatives saw the vote in common as dangerous. For the Third Estate, it was the only hope for reform. Agitation on the voting issue had begun months before the meeting, and now, after weeks of angry debate and quiet talks of compromise, amid fears of public disorder as bread prices continued to rise, the deadlock created a crisis.

At a critical moment the commoners took decisive action. These elected deputies saw themselves as the true representatives of the French people. With the large majority of them lawyers and public officials, they were most representative of a slowly emergent middle class or bourgeoisie, a mainly provincial elite. No artisan or peasant had a seat in the Third Estate. Even so, deputies deemed their cause patriotic and national, against the partial interests of the other estates. Under the leadership of the gifted and radical Abbé Sieyès, they voted, quite on their own and by a lopsided majority, to obliterate voting by orders. This was democratic—and would guarantee them a large and continuing majority. It was also a challenge to the other estates. Without waiting for their own order to vote, three priests came over to the commoners, then a dozen more. Emboldened, the deputies of the Third Estate on June 17 took another far-reaching step. They declared themselves and others who would follow them a "National Assembly" and claimed sovereign power in the name of the nation, which until then had rested exclusively with the king.

A few days later, when the deputies assembled for a morning meeting, they found the doors of their hall locked—by order of the king, they suspected. So they adjourned to a local indoor tennis court and vowed absolute solidarity "until the constitution of the kingdom is established and consolidated." Their oath was a declaration of independence and the assertion of a new political doctrine—constitutionalism—as well as a recognition that their unity would be tested as they and their country moved ahead into uncharted paths.

At this moment, a new and untried power center—potentially a people's power center—was born.

BECOMING REVOLUTIONARY

The Third Estate had taken over, the commoners asserting their supremacy in the king's home at Versailles. What would the deputies do with the authority they claimed? During the struggle Paris and many of the provinces had been in turmoil. Now expectations were running high. Could they be satisfied?

France was a tinderbox. Peasants still suffered from devastating weather that had killed crops the year before. Housewives were decrying the price of bread. While still loyal to the king, Parisians were increasingly hostile to the persons around him, especially the queen, Marie Antoinette, who had acquired a toxic reputation for cupidity, licentiousness, contempt for the people, and behind-the-scenes political manipulation. When Louis XVI suddenly and summarily sacked his chief minister, Necker, on July 11, 1789, for his continued efforts to conciliate the estates, a decision the queen had forcefully urged, the city erupted in outrage. Parisians struck out at a symbol of monarchical power, the Bastille.

This ancient structure, with signs of decay after three centuries of commanding an approach to Paris, was not much of a fortress. It was not even much of a jail. It had an execrable class bias: rich prisoners could command excellent meals, books—the Marquis de Sade had brought in an entire library—and walks in the garden, while commoners rotted in dark, verminous cells. So ideologically the Bastille was a fine target. And it held tons of gunpowder.

The battle of July 14 was brief but ferocious. Protesters besieged the prison; when they broke into a courtyard, terrified defenders fired at them. Over one hundred of the "citizens' army" died in this fusillade, with many more injured. But when mutinous French Guards came to their rescue armed with cannon, the governor of the Bastille had no choice but to surrender. That cost him his life as a mob dragged him away and then stabbed him to death. His head was stuck on a pole borne by surging, cheering crowds.

The fall of the Bastille electrified the National Assembly. Law and order seemed to be breaking down, and not only in Paris. Armed bands roamed the countryside, pillaging granaries and torching castles. With the king much weakened and the Assembly not yet matching actual authority to its pretensions, the country appeared on the edge of a precipice. A powerful but mysterious "Great Fear" seemed to envelop France. Hope and dread combined explosively in the National Assembly on the "mad evening" of August 4, 1789, which brought an instant revolution within the Revolution. The supports of the ancien régime were hacked away in a volatile mix of class hatred and Enlightenment idealism. The Assembly decreed that it "abolishes the feudal regime entirely"—everything from serfdom, tax exemptions, and "seigneurial courts of justice," to sinecures, pensions that were "not merited," and exclusive hunting rights. Bowing to the inevitable, eager to appease the new rulers, nobles themselves took the lead in demolishing their privileges, outbidding one another for radicalism.

In the heady atmosphere of August, deputies were eager to move on to the main business: making their laws eternal by converting them into a formal constitution. It was a bit awkward that the Assembly had not been established as a constitutional convention, but, *n'importe,* the deputies simply voted to call themselves the National *Constituent* Assembly. Naturally they looked across the Atlantic for inspiration and example. Despite America's role in the royal bankruptcy, the French had not lost their admiration for the people who had put the Enlightenment into action. The delegates intended to do the same with their own constitution. They especially admired the declarations of rights that prefaced many American state constitutions and decided their constitution must have one. Lafayette even submitted drafts to the American ambassador, Thomas Jefferson, for his blessing.

The French Declaration of the Rights of Man and the Citizen more than matched its American models. Sovereignty was held to rest essentially in the nation, not the king, and the rule of law was defined as the expression of a Rousseauist "will of the community." Privilege was abolished. Sieyès even proposed a strong draught of the positive liberty that American revolutionaries had balked at: "Citizens in common have a right to all that the state can do in their behalf." Though no such provision was approved, it reflected the radicalism that propelled some of the deputies to reimagine the state and the meanings of liberty and equality.

The constitutional structure of power the deputies fashioned was nearly as populist as the declaration. However enamored the deputies might have been with American expressions of rights, they had little regard for checks and balances. Despite pleas that France, too, should have a second legislative chamber—perhaps a senate—the Constituent Assembly voted 490 to 89 against it, some deputies deriding it as a "House of Lords."

Yet in a compromise with the king, the Assembly approved a "suspensive" veto that the legislature could override only by re-passing the law in two subsequent consecutive sessions. The concession set off a tremendous public uproar of opposition. For the first time, the Assembly was at odds with the people. But it was the court that paid the consequences. The king was being rapidly reduced from a divinely appointed absolute monarch to the creature of a constitution enacted by the people's representatives, not a few of whom lusted for a republic. Only after centuries of often bloody evolution did the British finally circumscribe their king in a constitutional role. What chance for Louis XVI amid a violent revolution that amounted to a judgment on his reign and that cut abruptly to the roots of his authority? The streets and the press had long suspected him, trafficking in rumors of a royalist counterrevolution. Was this the beginning of it?

One October morning in Paris bells rang out the tocsin that had come to serve as the people's call to arms. Hundreds of women who had been struggling with high bread prices set off for Versailles hauling cannon and brandishing anything that could serve as a weapon. More joined the procession as it went along, and by the time the women reached Versailles, they were seven thousand strong.

After intimidating the Assembly with demands for bread and for the punishment of counterrevolutionaries, the women proceeded to the palace to confront the king. The Marquis de Lafayette, commander of the National Guard since July, arrived with twenty thousand men, but even this show of force did not cow the women, now numbering tens of thousands. That night, Lafayette tried and failed to persuade Louis to surrender to the protesters' demand that he return to Paris. Next morning, a seething mob broke into the palace, killing two royal bodyguards and trapping the king and his family in a salon. Louis had no choice but to yield to what the women wanted from him—that he not hide behind the thick walls of Versailles but live like a people's king among them in Paris.

Then the most remarkable spectacle of the Revolution: sixty thousand women and men escorting the huge, swaying royal carriage to the city, some singing patriotic songs and even a ditty in praise of the king and his family. The monarch was in his people's embrace, but it was really a confinement. Inside the Tuileries palace in Paris, he and his family would live "more like prisoners than Princes," as a British observer noted. Louis would never return to Versailles.

* * *

One might expect that the National Assembly, after writing a powerful declaration of rights, fashioning a new constitution, and witnessing the king spirited away by a mob, might pause for calm and reflection. Quite the contrary. The deputies, after themselves moving to Paris, nationalized church property and, the following year, 1790, outlawed monastic vows, renounced foreign conquest, and brought the "mad evening" of August 4 to its logical conclusion by abolishing the nobility root and branch. "Incense," read the decree on the nobility, "shall be burned in churches only to honor the Divinity, and shall not be offered to any person whomsoever."

What had caused this spiraling of revolutionary ardor? The great majority of the deputies were political creatures—men who had been local officials, steeped in the problems of their constituents. Once living in Paris, they responded to people around them who were suffering from all the ills of urban existence and to radicals who claimed to be their leaders, including the sansculottes whose boast was that they were good and true patriots, as their ostentatiously plain clothes proved.

Moreover, as the Revolution deepened and deputies realized that they had the responsibility to give France a new political order, they turned to the alternatives they knew to absolute monarchy, Enlightenment ideas, which in their nature invited the deputies to ponder the relation of ends and means, the path to realization of such goals as liberty, equality, and popular sovereignty. These values were by nature radical—the abrupt change from absolute monarchy to formal constitutionalism had no precedent, even in America. Serfs in the ancien régime now had expectations of citizenship. Given such extreme circumstances, any principled change would be far-reaching. It would also be difficult to achieve except under pressured, tumultuous conditions.

Last but by no means least, the deputies were impelled to act quickly and sweepingly because they knew too well the costs of the king's inaction and were determined not to follow his example—or share his fate.

The Assembly's decisions, then, were driven by the emergence of a revolutionary psychology in a superheated political and ideological environment. This involved a crucial element of group interaction. "The assemblage of so many highly motivated and talented men, a number of whom were articulate orators," historian Timothy Tackett wrote, "generated a dynamic of mutual encouragement, emulation, and instruction," a dynamic that quickly took on a life of its own and "was amplified through the intensity and emotion of the experience" of what "all witnesses described as the most momentous period of their lives."

And the leaders? The Assembly in those historic months of 1789 and 1790 made collective leadership a key causal force. In a highly pressured atmosphere, the deputies listened to one another and actually *thought* together, improvising at one point, philosophizing at another, constantly evoking new ideas. Speeches were often intolerably long, but attended closely and rebutted vigorously. Deputies underwent a kind of conversion experience. They became revolutionary.

Conflict dominated the proceedings as a natural and rational division developed between nobles and other deputies who favored a constitutional monarchy with significant authority granted to the king, and radicals of various hues strongly opposed to any role for royalty. For a few months early in 1790, wrote Tackett, the alternation of the Assembly presidency "between candidates on the left and on the right gave political activities in the Assembly almost the character of a two-party system." But the conflict did not remain rational for long, as the Assembly grew increasingly fractionalized, with diverse forces pushing deputies into separated and often hostile blocs. That moment of two-sided equilibrium was merely a lull in an increasingly violent storm, not a harbinger of new weather.

. . .

Meanwhile, the great throngs who had brought Louis XVI back to Paris celebrated their triumph, but little change came in their lives. The challenge revolutionary leaders faced was to bring ends into alignment with means and so produce real improvements in living conditions. While the price of bread rose and fell unpredictably, unemployment soared in the cities. While patriots planted liberty trees, those symbols of revolution that had originated in Boston in 1765, and talked about equality and self-government, poor workers still barely survived in their hovels and had small hope of betterment. Revolutionary leaders proclaimed the new citizenship and the press touted various populist nostrums, arousing popular expectations that could not be met. Women, as usual, were the most rejected and dejected, their pleas for equal rights scoffed at in the Assembly.

Hosts of male peasants also failed to share fully in the new citizenship. Like domestic servants and many artisans, rural day laborers, migrants, and hired hands had the status only of *citoyens passifs* and were denied the right to vote. They responded by evading taxes, sometimes physically threatening the tax collector, or even burning chateaux—twenty-two in Brittany in one rash of protests. Peasant and worker risings often seemed so spontaneous that historians have wondered where their leaders came from. The answer: Leadership was in the *crowd*. Some of the "agitators," their names mostly lost to history, read Parisian and provincial writers, who often appealed directly to them. But the poor and the illiterate learned most from talking with activists in the street or perhaps in the National Guard, or in wine shops and market places. It was in the human relationships in their own milieux that their leadership was first generated.

In the crisis years of the Revolution, this cobblestone and grassroots leadership was sharpened, heightened, and ultimately distorted by a pandemic of panic. People feared the uncertain direction of the Revolution. It scarcely proceeded on an enlightened, rational plan, with means and ends closely bound. Instead, it jerked forward hastily in some respects and proved drastically laggard in others. Crucial and dangerous was the disconnect between what revolutionary leaders promised and what they achieved, between ideas and effective actions. Instead, to many of the French and to foreign observers, change appeared mainly as lawlessness following the collapse of authority. The poor and vulnerable variously dreaded the police, landlords, tax collectors, the hoarding miller or baker. Peasants feared vagrants and other intruders; jobholders worried for their jobs in a shattered economy; property holders dreaded the ascendancy of sansculottes. And most pervasive, the greatest fear for all except monarchists was that foreign powers might invade France to destroy the Revolution. But the Revolution's real enemy was within.

THE MADNESS OF THE FACTIONS

Around midnight on June 20, 1791, guards in the Tuileries looked on idly as a bulky man in a round hat and plain coat who appeared to be a valet, accompanied by a governess in a plain black coat, a pretty young girl, and a nurse, departed from the palace in a plain coach. In fact, the valet was Louis XVI, the governess Marie Antoinette, the girl their son, and the nurse the king's sister. The party ditched the coach after a few miles for another drawn by six fast horses. Their destination: Varennes, on the road leading to France's border with the Austrian Netherlands.

The escape had been carefully planned, but almost everything went wrong. The queen had lost her way at the Tuileries, throwing off the timing. The carriage hit a stone post while turning on a bridge, causing another delay. By the time the royal party arrived in Varennes, the astounding news had caught up with them. Excited crowds filled the streets. Soon the king was recognized. Thrust into a carriage with guards, the royal family was driven back to Paris in bitter humiliation and frustration.

The city was startled, outraged, vengeful. A radical Paris newspaper exclaimed: "He has gone, this imbecile King, this perjured King, that scoundrel Queen who combines the lustfulness of Messalina with the bloodthirstiness of the Medicis. Execrable woman, *Furie* of France, it is you who were the soul of the conspiracy!" The sansculottes felt betrayed. Louis was *their* king, to whom they had continued loyal despite their grievances. He was supposed to rule for all France, all the people. In their rage they roamed the Paris streets, smashing any sign that bore his name.

Did all this portend the final collapse of the monarchy? Tom Paine thought so. He had journeyed from the American Revolution to the French, soon making himself at home among fellow radicals. Always the stalwart republican, he decided to set up a journal to promote the abolition of the monarchy on the grounds that the king's flight to Varennes had automatically created a republic. Paine was a bit ahead of his comrades, but not for long.

France might have calmed down if the king's flight had been only an internal affair, but it was not. The sansculottes thought they knew where the royal family had been headed—to Vienna and the court of the Emperor Leopold, the queen's brother. And they knew what Austria would have done—mobilize the monarchical forces throughout Europe and the émigrés from France to restore Louis's full powers.

This perceived threat gave French public opinion an intensified fear and a fiercely chauvinistic edge that added to the rising class and factional hostility. Anyone who now expressed doubt about the Revolution was not simply a monarchist but a traitor. Tension escalated after Leopold and the Prussian king met and issued a declaration inviting other powers to restore monarchical power in France, which would become the decades-long ambition of the reactionary forces of the counter-Enlightenment. In mid-April 1792, France declared war on Austria. Two months later Prussia declared war on France. Within another few months, Britain, the Dutch Republic, and Spain joined France's enemies. By June 1792, an Austrian invasion threatened. The French Revolution—and the reaction to it—already was convulsing Europe.

*   *   *

The threat of monarchical restoration through invasion had a fatal impact on the monarch. On June 20, thousands of armed sansculottes marched on the Tuileries. Some pushed into the palace, hauling cannon up the grand staircase, to confront the king. Donning a cap of liberty and drinking to the health of the nation, Louis fended them off. But tensions rose again as two weeks later the Assembly formally declared that the *"patrie est en danger."* In the spreading anarchy, Jacobin radicals in the Paris commune consolidated their power.

Then, on August 10, the fateful tocsin sounded again. A huge crowd of soldiers and sansculottes swarmed over the king's only remaining protection, the five-hundred-man Swiss Guard. No quarter was given. The guardsmen were slaughtered, their bodies stripped and mutilated.

And now the king's fate was written. The radical Jacobin revolutionaries who dominated the new ruling Convention observed the formalities, summoning Louis before them and allowing his counsel to paint him a victim of circumstance, but they were intent on deposing and punishing him. In January 1793, the roll call on the king's guilt was almost unanimous. A narrow majority voted for his execution. On a wintry day, the former monarch was carted two hours through dark Paris streets to the Place de la Révolution and its guillotine. He was undressed, his hands tied, and his hair cut. Louis XVI was still protesting his innocence when the slanted blade fell.

* * *

A new leadership was coming to power during the months when Louis was losing the last of his. The earliest revolutionary leaders had yielded to the radicals. The moderate Comte de Mirabeau died shortly before the royal family's flight to Varennes; perhaps he was lucky. But no one fought harder for a middle way between monarchy and revolution than Lafayette. He was a moderate still idealistic enough to denounce slavery and even acquire a plantation in France's South American colony of Guiana for an experiment in emancipation. As conflict widened and his efforts at compromise failed, he faced enemies on all sides. Fearing for his life, he made a dash for the frontier only to fall into the hands of the Austrians, to whom he was a traitor to monarchy. Thrust into a dank dungeon, he was imprisoned for five years.

The radical revolutionaries now coming to the fore were not aristocrats like Mirabeau and Lafayette but, rather, middle-class professionals, factional leaders like the journalist Brissot, the editor Hébert, the two lawyers Danton and Robespierre. Most of them were widely read in current literature, urbane and cosmopolitan; they were Enlightenment men, steeped in the classics, educated in Rousseau and other philosophers. Robespierre, for instance, had early in the Revolution spoken of the general will as the source of popular sovereignty. It was, he said, following Rousseau, the legislative power: "Laws are simply acts of this general will" as exercised by elected representatives. The problem, of course, was determining what the general will was. With elections, at least honest ones, scarcely likely to yield up the unanimity that defined the general will, it must be left to the representatives to decide what it was. That in turn gave them extraordinary authority, as great perhaps and as unaccountable as those of kings who claimed to govern according to the will of God.

In the summer of 1793, the Jacobins produced a new constitution with a lengthy declaration of rights that included positive liberties—the right to public assistance when in need and to education provided by the state. But as the Jacobin Constitution of 1793 also abolished the checks and balances of its predecessor and placed all effective power in the legislature, it was a blueprint for tyranny. It created a short road to violent and fanatical Terror as the factions struggled for power among themselves and each in turn fell, each wave more radical, each washing away the last. First went Brissot and his Girondins, one-time revolutionary allies of the Jacobins who now destroyed them. They were guillotined late in October 1793, two weeks after the execution of Marie Antoinette. Next Hébert and his enragés—more extreme but less disciplined than the Jacobins—were executed in March 1794. Then Danton, who was considered a moderating influence in this brutal government—Danton, who had called for "terror to be the order of the day" and demanded "stronger sentences, more terrifying punishments"—he and his followers fell to the blade in April 1794. That left the disciple of Rousseau, Robespierre, with his Jacobins. Robespierre was chairman of the Committee of Public Safety, the dozen men who now ruled France with unlimited power and who interpreted their mandate as remorseless revolutionary justice in defense, so they claimed, of the people's liberties against counterrevolution. As Robespierre had declared at the king's trial, "A people does not judge as does a court of law. It does not hand down sentences, it hurls down thunderbolts; it does not condemn kings, it plunges them into the abyss."

With fanaticism like this gripping the leaders, could one be surprised by the Terror itself? The mobs that invaded prisons and hacked to death shackled aristocrats and other "enemies of the revolution" by the hundreds . . . guillotines so busy that gutters ran with blood . . . crowds of killers hunting down suspects . . . denunciations that packed the jails with ever more victims. . . .

This was by no means only a Paris phenomenon. In the provinces, mobs slaughtered masses of men, women, and children, and when guillotines and guns did not kill fast enough, hundreds would be chained in boats and drowned. In the end the Revolution did indeed devour its children. And the devourers, from the Jacobins at the center of power to countless bloody-handed cadres in the provinces, were themselves in turn devoured.

So breathtaking was the pace, so terrible the events that it seemed as though Robespierre must have ruled for an age. In fact, he survived Danton by only three months, taken down by colleagues fearful that he was aiming the people's thunderbolt at *them*.

. . .

How could France have become a slaughterhouse? What had happened to the original, splendid vision of a peaceful and just, libertarian and egalitarian nation? How could men espousing the highest ideals send thousands of innocents to their deaths?

One answer must be the utter failure of leadership among the radical revolutionaries, their failure to channel the outrage of the people into effective, enduring reform that would satisfy their wants and needs. They abandoned the moderate legacy of the Enlightenment expressed in the 1791 constitution, which gave a principled basis to a government pursuing liberty and equality for its people. The declaration of rights in the new Jacobin constitution was twice as long as its predecessor, with sweeping guarantees of a panoply of rights, even as revolutionary tribunals were condemning dozens of French people to death each day, destroying the first and most basic right of all, to life, with minimal due process or regard for evidence. Lofty Enlightenment ideals became a cover for organized and disorganized slaughter, for power struggles among a rapidly shrinking elite. For all their philosophical pretensions, for "all their talk of virtue and energy, the legacy left by Jacobin leaders was a barren one," historian Susan Dunn wrote. With their "illogical maxims, ferocious calls to love the people, paranoid denunciations, and delirious odes to suicide," the Jacobins "bequeathed to France no exemplary models of courageous political leadership or creative, visionary intellectual leadership."

Why, then, this failure of the leaders? It was due in part to their absolute conviction that they were right. This is a habit of political animals around the world, but the Jacobins believed that only *they* understood the "general will" of the French people, hence they were *morally* right. Opposition was considered not merely mistaken but evil and traitorous and hence punishable, even lethally. The Jacobins asserted a monopoly of virtue which meant to them a license to kill those who held up other values.

Differences over moral values contributed to the factionalization of the revolutionary movement, in turn eroding collective leadership and responsibility. As revolutionary activism quickened and flowed into separate channels, factions not only multiplied but split internally, with every side denouncing others for betraying the cause. Instead of uniting into some kind of collective effort with coalition leadership facing a coherent opposition, the Jacobin factions of the Terror disintegrated into spokesmen truckling to the crowds, then becoming their victims.

Still, the sheer ferocity at every level must have originated more in psychological forces than political. This was the psychosis of fear, which can arouse savage hatreds. If a Great Fear gripped people in the early years of the Revolution, a Greater Fear rose later. To a degree it was a rational fear in response to the foreign powers threatening France from all directions, land and sea. It was also a fear based in severe economic insecurity. But above all it was a fear of the radical instability—even chaos—that was overtaking the Revolution, the lethal game politics had become, the knowledge that victors in factional struggles could propel losers to the guillotine. Distrust blanketed the land. French civil society had collapsed into a nearly Hobbesian state of nature. It was all against all; no one was safe.

· · ·

In 1790, after Benjamin Franklin's death, the French Assembly asked the Marquis de Condorcet to eulogize the American philosophe. The marquis was the perfect choice for the task—a philosophe himself, a mathematician who wrote major works on the progress of the human mind, an internationalist who knew the American literati well, a moralist who took advanced positions on the rights of women and the abolition of slavery. In soaring oratory, Condorcet praised Franklin for his faith that enlightenment would lead to "a slow but lasting perfection" and "contribute to the happiness of all."

Four years later the marquis ran afoul of the violent fanaticism of the French Revolution. In hiding from the Jacobins, writing his masterwork, the *Sketch for a Historical Picture of the Progress of the Human Mind,* Condorcet imagined a future when men would "appreciate their true title to glory and take full pleasure in the progress of their reason." He added that this vision of human perfectibility consoled the philosopher "for the errors, crimes, and injustices that still defile the earth, of which he is often the victim!" A superb tribute to reason—by a thinker who would soon be captured and die in prison, a victim of the Terror.

5

Transforming American Politics

Early in 1794 American supporters of the French Revolution were shocked to hear that Tom Paine had been thrown into a Paris jail. Paine, friend to revolutions on both sides of the Atlantic and a representative in the national Convention from Calais: How could this have happened to *him*? More news followed from across the ocean.

Despite Paine's support for the monarchy's abolition, he had passionately opposed the execution of the king, suggesting he be banished to America—perhaps for rehabilitation. Furious Jacobins took their revenge as for almost a year Paine languished in Luxembourg prison, watching with sorrow as day after day the Terror devoured the Revolution.

From their distance, American friends of France had also watched that Revolution with rising anxiety and dismay. They had been enthralled by their ally's abolition of the monarchy a decade and a half after they had rejected their own king. But as the French descended further into the maelstrom, as they repudiated leaders admired in both countries, such as Lafayette, many Americans turned away in revulsion.

Mixed in with this dismay in America was a degree of complacency—it couldn't happen here. American activists clearly were more tolerant, rational, conciliatory. This self-satisfaction would prove exaggerated, but, despite unrest and partisan turmoil in the postrevolutionary years, America had no Terror. Why not?

The answer lay in the capacity of the American revolutionary leadership to both manage and exploit conflict, to respond to people's fears and hopes, to mediate among contending leaders, to tolerate faction and "interest" but to rechannel it, to forge new political institutions grounded in Enlightenment principles during and after the Revolution, while keeping broader goals and visions in mind. In short, they were able to conduct transactional leadership even as they pursued transformational goals reflecting the Enlightenment values they held dear.

For over two centuries, Americans have celebrated a holy trinity of transforming leadership—George Washington, a model as both Father of his people and Founder of the new nation; John Adams, as militant and steadfast in his principles as he was proud and prickly; and Thomas Jefferson, the visionary of Monticello, who could descend from his hilltop of books and speculative thought to play backroom politics with the best of them. The Founders, it was said, while well bred, fed, read, and wed, were above all well led, not by this trio alone but by an unprecedented depth of diverse leadership. There was an extraordinary array of "secondary" leaders typified by Alexander Hamilton and two fellow New Yorkers, John Jay, jurist and diplomat, and Robert Livingston, who helped draft both the Declaration of Independence and the New York state constitution. Beyond Washington and Jefferson, Virginia's contribution to America's founding leadership included George Mason, a delegate to the Constitutional Convention in 1787 who refused to sign the new charter because it lacked a Bill of Rights; Patrick Henry, fiery orator and fierce opponent of the Constitution; and James Monroe, who also opposed the new Constitution because he feared a too strong presidency. A Philadelphian, Robert Morris, raised millions to finance the Revolution but ended up in debtors' jail. Many others were almost equally influential; leadership in this era was remarkably deeply layered.

Often viewed as a lesser figure next to the three giants, James Madison probably had as much impact on American history as any one of them. No other American brought such incisive critical and constructive powers to the complex dilemmas of human government. No one so brilliantly linked means and ends, broad goals to institutions that would promote them. Madison's quiet, undramatic, but momentous participation in great events reads like a short chronicle of his time. As a Virginia delegate to the Continental Congress he saw the deficiencies in the revolutionary government and the need for a stronger system. He played a central part in framing the Constitution and served as the Philadelphia Convention's best chronicler. He, along with Hamilton and Jay, wrote the *Federalist* papers, which were seductive appeals for the proposed Constitution as well as brilliant contributions to the theory of government. In a splendid oratorical contest with Patrick Henry, he played a critical role in Virginia's ratification of the Constitution. As a member of the House of Representatives in the new government, he helped establish the Treasury department that Hamilton would build into a powerhouse. In his most notable feat Madison drafted and pushed through Congress the Bill of Rights amendments to the Constitution. He authored some of President Washington's notable statements. Working closely with his lifelong comrade Jefferson, he led in the building of America's first opposition party, the Republican, and helped manage its defeat of the Federalists in 1800. He went on to become Jefferson's secretary of state. His two-term presidency as Jefferson's successor was almost an anticlimax.

Madison was far from a philosophe on the model of Franklin or Jefferson, and indeed much of his greatest work was done in the shadow of more celebrated figures. But no one had a greater role in fashioning the American experiment, basing the government on Enlightenment principles and then testing them in action.

THE LIFE OF THE NATION

War poses the harshest test of leadership. The ultimate measure of its success is to win not only victory in the field but the ends fought for. The revolutionary leaders met this test. They won the war *and* their supreme goals— independence and liberty.

Yet American leadership went into decline after the Revolution. The leaders were generally the same men, many far-famed and even venerated, but they were projected now into a different situation. They had been united behind transcending goals. Now they divided over mundane policies. They had offered a striking example of bold, collective—even transforming— leadership. Now they were expected to practice piecemeal, transactional leadership.

The weaknesses of the Articles of Confederation, enacted during the war to create and control America's first national government, now in peacetime doomed that government. The Confederation had been established by the states rather than by the people and hence was not bottomed on popular sovereignty. Members of Congress were elected annually and faced term limits. The approval of nine of the thirteen states was required to ratify treaties or pass laws on war, peace, and spending. In a government that needed reform from the start, amendments could be adopted only with the unanimous approval of the states. Strong executive leadership was almost impossible.

Power and leadership were left to the "sovereign states." Yet state governments suffered from the same executive weaknesses as the national confederation. In most states, governors had one-year terms. Executives were chosen by legislatures in eight of the states, and most had limited appointive powers.

Legislative majorities—sometimes fleeting or unstable, elsewhere overbearing and rampant—led these hobbled governments. On the key issues facing the Confederation—trade, revenue, expansion—the states pursued their own interests, quarreling and competing with one another and leaving Congress all but irrelevant.

Many Americans liked it this way. They scorned strong government and the taxes and curbs that came with it. They were republicans of the Whig variety whose principal aim had been to limit the power of kings. But as the top leadership in a state or the nation was denied the authority to act, more power fell into the hands of factional and local leaders, most of them grounded in narrow and self-seeking interests. If, as New York artisans had proclaimed back in the 1760s, "*Self-Interest*" was "the grand Principle of all Human Actions," the Confederation had no powers to transcend it.

How, then, could leaders act at all? How could anything get done, even from day to day? To the degree that the Confederation acted on practical matters, it was because national and local leaders became adept at negotiating, bargaining, exchanging—at transactional leadership. But while somewhat effective in placating contending interests and maintaining political consensus, this kind of leadership often produced halting, ineffectual, and unprincipled responses to the accelerating velocity of technological and social and economic change.

Unrest, too, was accelerating in the postrevolutionary years. America's farmers were to be the enlightened and virtuous yeomen who, as Jefferson and others imagined it, would provide the backbone of the new republic. But in a depressed economy, they were overwhelmed by taxes and debt, with demands that payment be made in hard money—gold or silver. They faced the loss not only of their property but of their liberty if they were convicted and sentenced to jail in debtors' courts. From desperation, they became rebels instead. In the fall of 1786, Vermont farmers tried to close courts in two counties to block judgments for debt. The governor of New Hampshire called out two thousand militiamen to disperse several hundred farmers demanding the issuance of paper money. Tenants threatened an uprising in New York. Virginia farmers burned down a county courthouse.

The climax came in western Massachusetts, in Shays's Rebellion. Hundreds of poor farmers, many of them war veterans, organized into squads and companies to stop courts from functioning. Early in 1787, over fifteen hundred rebels marched under Daniel Shays to the Springfield arsenal to seize military stores. Massachusetts militiamen gunned down a score of them and sent the rest fleeing. The militia caught up with them again, captured most of Shays's men, and finally hunted down and killed the remnant in a southern Berkshire woods. Shays escaped with a price on his head.

At least one national leader seemed unperturbed. Turbulence in protest prevented the degeneracy of government, Jefferson wrote James Madison. In a characteristically radical effusion, he added, "I hold it that a little rebellion now and then is a good thing, and as necessary in the political world as storms in the physical."

But many other Americans feared that the upheaval and violence would doom the republican experiment. Something must be done about the impotent Confederation and the state governments that seemed active only in calling out militias. But what? And how? Leadership was pulverized and hence government was near paralysis.

. . .

It was James Madison who diagnosed the direst and toughest dilemma facing the new nation—the tendencies toward disunity inevitable in a diverse society, a fault the Confederation had made all too vivid. Madison's Tenth *Federalist* paper is an example of Enlightenment thought at its finest, combining the philosophical and the empirical to reach a profound insight into human nature and its implications for society. The Tenth's most penetrating, famous paragraph should be memorized along with Lincoln's Gettysburg address:

> *The latent causes of faction are thus sown in the nature of man; and we see them every where brought into different degrees of activity, according to the different circumstances of civil society. A zeal for different opinions concerning religion, concerning Government and many other points, as well of speculation as of practice; an attachment to different leaders ambitiously contending for pre-eminence and power; or to persons of other descriptions whose fortunes have been interesting to the human passions, have in turn divided mankind into parties, inflamed them with mutual animosity, and rendered them much more disposed to vex and oppress each other, than to cooperate for their common good. So strong is this propensity of mankind to fall into mutual animosities, that where no substantial occasion presents itself, the most frivolous and fanciful distinctions have been sufficient to kindle their unfriendly passions, and excite their most violent conflicts. But the most common and durable source of factions, has been the various and unequal distribution of property.*

Madison has been portrayed writing the Tenth with David Hume's *Essays* lying at hand. He had studied Hume at Princeton, whose president was also his mentor, John Witherspoon, a Scot who had himself been a student of Francis Hutcheson and became a leading advocate for the ideas of the philosopher of happiness. Both Hutcheson and Hume taught that the sociability of men was crucial to understanding how they might best govern themselves. Hume's influence on Madison was of a solidly realistic bent, especially with Madison's adoption of the idea that faction's perils were overcome more effectively in a large republic than a small one. If the power of faction were dissolved in a wider polity, Madison reasoned, "factious leaders" might kindle a flame, but they could not start a "general conflagration." No single faction would be "able to outnumber and oppress the rest."

As they gathered in Philadelphia in the early summer of 1787, the delegates to the Constitutional Convention wanted not only a more broadly based politics but also a more stable one—and most of them believed that the one strengthened the other. The new Constitution they framed granted extensive powers to the new presidency and to Congress. Yet, like Madison and Hume, they were realists about human nature, trusting neither in the natural benevolence nor the disinterested reason of leaders. Guided by Madison, they provided that would-be tyrants or rampant legislatures would be curbed by a system of checks and balances contrived as carefully as the balances in an old grandfather clock. The new Senate and House would have an absolute veto over each other, while the new presidency would hold a partial veto over both. And the judiciary would serve as yet another dampening layer against the feared autocratic or democratic excesses.

What the Framers—and probably the American people—wanted first and foremost, after the chaos of the Revolution and the unrest following it, was *order*. Order promised personal as well as national security—and a durable government. Jefferson had put "life" first in his trinity of values, and if life meant order, he was right to do so. Without it, liberty would constantly be imperiled and the pursuit of happiness a chimera.

But order by itself was dangerous, even tyrannous, unless curbed by the other values—above all, liberty.

* * *

Who could resist this glorious new Constitution that embodied Enlightenment qualities of both idealism and caution, the work of a glittering array of leaders, both old revolutionaries and new thinkers? Many Americans did. They protested the dwarfing of state and local power by a national government, the establishment of a Senate so removed from the people as almost to constitute an American House of Lords, the erection of an independent federal judiciary with untold authority, above all the absence of a bill of rights that would protect people's liberties from invasion by this powerful and centralized regime, especially those of minorities.

Against the relatively unified ranks of the Federalists in support of the Constitution and its proposed government, opponents to the new order were drawn from diverse sections of American society. Each believed that the Constitution threatened their own ideals and interests. A small elite of republicans warned that the new government must become either an aristocratic cabal or a mobocracy. Populist "plebeians," farmers and artisans, also republicans and often egalitarians, were devoted to democracy and local control. The "middling sort" of merchants and other middle-class people looked to their state governments to protect liberty and promote their own interests, as well as the common good.

For all their differences, these Anti-Federalists were united enough in their fears of centralized power to threaten to stop the Constitution short of ratification by the states. Through lively county meetings and their own newspapers, local Anti-Federalist leaders mobilized people especially in the "back country" of New England, the middle states, and the South. Lacking national heroes, they appealed to the "common man."

But the Federalists won ratification of the Constitution in state conventions during late 1787 and 1788, though in several states—Massachusetts, New York, and Virginia among them—it was a close-run thing. Rhode Island was the last to ratify, in May 1790. A number of states followed the example of Massachusetts in coupling ratification with "recommendations" of amendments—especially relating to a bill of rights—on Federalist promises that the new Congress would consider them.

In the end, the crucial political act of the Anti-Federalists was what they did *not* do—they did not resort to violence. There were local incidents as feelings rose. In Carlisle, Pennsylvania, a crowd of "plebeians" took their fury out on James Wilson, a leading Federalist, who was denounced for "despising what he calls the inferior order of people." They made an effigy of Wilson, held a ritual trial, paraded the effigy through the streets, whipped it, hanged it, and burned it on a funeral pyre. Still, it was just an *effigy*—how the French terrorists would have laughed.

Anti-Federalist leaders saw that their best—indeed, their only—recourse lay not in rebellion, but in taking leadership of the rising public opposition to the Constitution. They did so in part by attempting to enlighten people by the written word. While far outshone by the *Federalist* authors, Anti-Federalist thinkers produced tracts of lasting value, powerful minority reports on the Constitution that would shape later interpretations of it and fuel many a partisan battle. Indeed, the war over the Constitution exposed the lineaments of a party system that would emerge in the next decade. If Federalists like Hamilton were moving toward a "court" party, the Anti-Federalists would help shape an emerging "country" party that eventually, under the leadership of Jefferson and Madison, would become the Republican party. The Anti-Federalists would operate within the new republic, not outside or against it. Ultimately they acted for order, protecting the stability of the nation.

By rejecting violence and helping to form the emerging party opposition to the Federalists, by using the new national institutions such as Congress to press for their specific aims and policies, above all a bill of rights, the oppositionist Anti-Federalists took on a vital and indeed indispensable role in the Founding era. They helped build a future democracy that would tame and channel conflict. Hence, in this respect, their leaders became co-Founders.

THE LIBERTY OF A PERSON

The critical Anti-Federalist objection to the Constitution was the absence of a bill of rights. Since their emergence in the early Enlightenment, rights had become the most powerful claims citizens could raise against government, the most powerful limitations on its reach. By 1787, most state constitutions featured guarantees of fundamental rights. Why did the proposed federal charter fail to secure the specific liberties the revolutionaries had fought for? Thomas Jefferson, watching developments closely from his post in Paris, asked this question, too. After waiting impatiently to hear from Madison about the new Constitution, finally, late in 1787, he received a transatlantic letter of many pages, which he read through with mounting anxiety.

Jefferson politely praised his fellow Virginian for what he liked in the new charter: A federal government that could stand on its own feet.

"I will now add what I do not like." What Jefferson liked least was the "omission of a bill of rights providing clearly and without the aid of sophisms for freedom of religion, freedom of the press," and other securities. When Madison wrote back with a defense of the Constitution, Jefferson responded to his points with sledgehammer certainties. A declaration of rights might not be broad enough? "Answer. Half a loaf is better than no bread. If we cannot secure all our rights, let us secure what we can."

Limited federal power and opposition from jealous states would combine to protect liberty? Answer. A declaration of rights would set a standard for both levels of government. Experience had proved that a bill of rights was not always an effective protection? "True. But tho it is not absolutely effica-cious under all circumstances, it is of great potency always." Madison still was not sure—a bill of rights, he had said, might offer no more than "parch-ment barriers" when "its controul is most needed." Yet he had acknowledged that, should danger of "subversion of liberty . . . exist at all, it is prudent to guard against it, especially when the precaution can do no injury."

◦ ◦ ◦

James Madison desperately wished to serve in the first Congress. Persuaded in part by Jefferson and by the national strength of Anti-Federalist senti-ment, as well as by contacts with prospective constituents in his Orange County district of Virginia, he came to think that "the Constitution ought to be revised" by promptly adding "the most satisfactory provisions for all essential rights, particularly the rights of Conscience in fullest latitude, the freedom of the press, trials by jury, security against general warrants &c." In the 1788 election, Madison was opposed for a seat in the new House of Representatives by another rising Virginia politico, the Anti-Federalist candidate James Monroe, whom Madison beat mainly by cultivating Bap-tists and other sects who sought the guarantee of full religious liberty. Soon he was making the long trek to New York, temporary site of the new capital.

Seated in the House of Representatives in May 1789, Congressman Madi-son tried to gain the floor to offer his carefully prepared package of consti-tutional amendments. Again and again he was put off for more urgent business—taxes, tariffs, and, of course, members' salaries. Finally, after a month, he seized his chance. Slight in build, moderate of voice, Madison was not a captivating speaker, but his presentation of the case for expressly declaring "the great rights of mankind secured under this constitution" ranks as one of the most consequential congressional speeches. His defense of a bill of rights ranged from the philosophical to the political, but he ar-gued most passionately that passage of the amendments would "extinguish from the bosom of every member of the community any apprehensions, that there are those among his countrymen who wish to deprive them of the liberty for which they valiantly fought and honorably bled."

There followed a brilliant legislative achievement—and an act of trans-forming leadership too little celebrated in history. In the debate over his proposed amendments, Madison and his allies stayed in control of the floor most of the time, proposing, demanding, yielding, placating. The Constitution's authors, as agents of change themselves, realized that the United States might in future need to improve the charter, but since they did not share Jefferson's calm faith in continuous change and periodic revolution, they had made passage of constitutional amendments difficult. Madison won the required two-thirds majority of the House by late August. Next he succeeded in mobilizing a two-thirds Senate majority as well, again working closely with Anti-Federalists, though they vociferously indicated that they would have preferred a wider range of proposals. After differences between the House and Senate bills were adjusted, the amendments could finally be submitted to the states. The approval of three-quarters of states was required, and a groundswell of popular support pushed them through, though Virginia politicians embarrassed Madison and Jefferson by claiming to find the amendments inadequate and being the last to ratify.

Finally ratified on December 15, 1791—a date that should live in fame— the ten amendments of the Bill of Rights contained those liberties and protections that, happily, echo through most of the days of our lives: rights of speech and religion and press and assembly; to bear arms; for security against intrusion in our homes; for open trials with proper procedures and protections against excessive bail or fines and "cruel and unusual punishments."

And the man who came down in history as the Father of the Constitution, when there were many fathers, earned the title that truly honored him: Father of the Bill of Rights.

THE HAPPINESS OF THE PEOPLE

For all their majesty and power, their epochal significance, the lustrous Bill of Rights were of limited value to the poor of America. First Amendment freedoms of speech and press and religion? These they did treasure. Even if illiterate, they relished argument and debate, and most were churchgoers. But the right to bear arms? Many of the poor lacked the means even to buy a gun. The right to be secure in their homes? What soldiers would want to be quartered in their hovels, and what papers could the poor be hiding? The right to counsel? They couldn't afford it. Excessive bail? They couldn't even put up fair bail.

For some classes of Americans, the Constitution itself, even with its new bill of rights, was almost irrelevant. Slaves were nowhere explicitly mentioned in the charter, but Madison in 1787 had assured the Virginia ratifying convention that the Constitution gave no powers to the federal government to interfere with "property" held in the states. That meant slaves, who were endowed not with unalienable rights but with the status of a possession, like a rocking chair. Women went unmentioned in the Constitution, and since suffrage qualifications were not made the business of the federal government, the voting rights of American women were left to the callous mercies of the states. And that meant states also were free to maintain their property requirements for suffrage. In some, more than a quarter of adult white men were ineligible to vote.

These inequalities persisted from the revolutionary era. They stood as violations of basic Enlightenment principles as embodied in Jefferson's flat declaration that "all men are created equal." That they were not remedied in the new charter demonstrated the extent and limits of the Constitution and its new Bill of Rights.

*   *   *

Even so, with a new central government in operation and with President George Washington, hero of the Revolution, reassuringly at its head, the 1790s bade well to mark a sharp and welcome break from the turbulence of recent decades. Later our school texts would treat it as a time of easy transition and consolidation. They were wrong. The 1790s proved a tough, sweaty, violent decade, scarred by deep anxieties and even hysteria over what was seen as the highest possible stake—the fate of the American experiment in bringing the Enlightenment to life on a national scale.

The decade indeed seemed to mock the hope of life, liberty, and happiness. Life as unity, harmony, and security? As the war triggered by France's revolution convulsed Europe, its echo across the Atlantic fueled a bitter hostility between Republicans and Federalists. Republicans called Federalists "Tories" and "monarchists," while Federalists denounced Republicans as "Jacobins" and "impious traitors." Class conflict sharpened. Early in the decade a few dozen Democratic-Republican societies sprang up around the country. Exercising their First Amendment rights, the grassroots leaders launched militant though nonviolent attacks on "High Federalists." Federalist gentlemen, including President Washington, denounced the societies, as did a "Virginia lady" who termed the Kentucky branch a "hellish school of rebellion and opposition to all regular and well-balanced authority."

Liberty? In 1798 Congress passed and President John Adams signed the Alien and Sedition Acts. The measures aptly reflected Federalists' fears of dangerous immigrants and wartime conspiracies, as well as their raw partisanship. The Sedition Act had teeth; critics of Adams and the Federalists were jailed, including one Luther Baldwin who sat by in a tavern as the president and Mrs. Adams paraded down Newark's Broad Street to chants of "Behold the Chief who now commands!" and an accompanying roar of cannons. Old Luther merrily remarked, "I do not care if they fire thro' his arse!"

Happiness? In the general prosperity of the nineties most property holders did well. Washington extolled the *"aggregate happiness of society"* as "the end of all Government," but the kind of public, social happiness Francis Hutcheson had so evocatively celebrated was lacking. Enormous inequalities still existed between men and women, between men of property and farmers and artisans, between white men and black slaves—between opportunities for the pursuit of happiness.

There was little outright violence. When Pennsylvania farmers rose in wrath over a federal excise tax on the jugs of whiskey they often used as currency, two persons were killed and some offices destroyed—a minor disturbance that provoked a massive overreaction. Washington mobilized thirteen thousand militiamen to quell these "rioters and delinquent distillers." But the potential for violence was rising, especially after the magisterial Washington left office in 1797 and John Adams took over. As the Sedition Act and its prosecutions illustrated, the always combative and insecure Adams tended to regard his political foes as enemies, including his old comrade-in-arms Thomas Jefferson and, increasingly, his fellow Federalists, like Alexander Hamilton. The question now was whether conflict inevitable in a free republic could be led into constructive channels. The Democratic-Republican societies had faded away, leaving a dangerous void in the balance of conservative-radical politics.

What could fill this void? Ideas as varied as ways that Americans were pursuing their happiness. For some in the 1790s, this meant above all personal security and public order. Others cherished most their liberties under the Bill of Rights. Still others saw happiness as a fair share of material well-being; they took seriously the equality promised by the Enlightenment and in America's great documents. The Revolution, historian J. R. Pole wrote, had put a weapon, the stirring ideal of egalitarianism, into the hands of the oppressed. But how pursue equality in America? With revolts à la Daniel Shays or the Whiskey Rebellion? Attacks on Federalist nabobs that could land a man in jail? Or some far more comprehensive strategy that might convert people's wants and needs into Hutcheson's public happiness?

It was clear to James Madison that people were becoming disenchanted with Federalist rule. But what could they do about it? In 1792, Madison had written an odd article on "Parties" for the *National Gazette*—odd because political parties did not yet exist as such and because Madison did not yet see them as more than a potential evil to be combated. But he knew the goals—to find a common ground in society not only by "establishing a political equality among all" but by denying the wealthy *"unnecessary* opportunities" to increase the inequality of property, while raising, through "the silent operation of laws," the extremely indigent "towards a state of comfort." Madison understood the ends but was groping for the means.

He was nothing if not a "contemplative statesman," though, and within a year the train of his thought and the surge of popular feeling and ideological combat led Madison to perform an intellectual somersault. In the Tenth *Federalist* he had warned against popular majorities prone to threatening people's liberties and minority rights. To curb the majority he had advocated federal checks and balances that would splinter the power of leadership. But now he was coming to see that wealthy men could exploit those checks and balances to override popular majorities seeking equality and happiness. Such men made up, in effect, a party of the "opulent" class of society, with the aim that government "by degrees be narrowed into fewer hands." These were the Federalists. To check them—to save republican government— the "mass of people in every part of the union," united around "common sentiment and common interest," must form a party of their own and use their superior numbers to re-take power. Strangely, Madison still thought parties an evil, even though as a realist—and as a partisan—he recognized that organized opposition was both inevitable and indispensable.

It was not Madison or Jefferson who first fashioned the means to oppose Federalist control of the national government but grassroots and street Republicans under their own leadership. Conflict in the national, state, and local contests of the mid-1790s increasingly swirled around Federalist and Republican ideas and interests, especially where Republican insurgents challenged Federalist incumbents. Adams, with his Federalist policies and High Federalist hauteur, hardened the rivalries.

The tightening of party lines as the climactic election of 1800 approached produced a new ferocity of partisan language, but amid the rhetoric the parties offered a fairly clear choice. The Republicans promised to restore the "Principles of the Revolution" and bring "unity, peace, and concord" to the country, as well as to reduce the debt and taxes, eliminate corruption, and avoid foreign entanglements. Their appeal rested heavily on Jefferson himself, portraying the presidential candidate as "a sincere and enlightened republican"; though Jefferson gave no speeches, he made his views clear through pamphlets and letters. The Adams Federalists, always evoking the patriot Washington, presented themselves as the party of order and safety, with the ablest, most experienced leadership. And they raised the cautionary cry of all incumbents: in such "critical and turbulent" times, it was unwise to be "making experiments on the administration of our government." But while the Republicans were fairly unified, Adams had to deal with dissension among Federalists, culminating with an open attack by Alexander Hamilton on his own party's candidate, the president. As a whole, though, the ranks of each party stood firm.

No long evening of breathless election reports brought the campaign to an end. The Electoral College count trickled in slowly by horseback and riverboat. By late December 1800, the total vote put Jefferson over Adams, 73 to 65. But Aaron Burr, Jefferson's running mate, also had 73 votes, and the slippery New Yorker, while protesting loyalty to Jefferson, made it known that he would be happy to serve as president. It was a reassuring test of the infant parties that the Republicans faced Burr down and leading Federalists did not try to exploit the situation as a means of subverting Jefferson's election.

So the Republicans had their victory over the Federalists. But both parties also shared a triumph. During the months of counting ballots amid paranoid threats and rumors of armed violence out in the country, party leaders remained steadfast in promoting stability. In the end the election might have been most dramatic for what did *not* happen—a coup of the sort that had become all too common in France through the 1790s. And Adams and his Federalists scored another moral victory. They established the principle that the losing party must yield power to the winners and surrender control of the government. That principle would serve as a bellwether—not always heard—for elections around the globe during the next two centuries.

THE FIRST TRANSFORMATION?

In the last quarter of the 1700s American society changed steadily, though not dramatically. Only three new states, Kentucky, Tennessee, and Vermont, joined the original thirteen. Total population had grown to above five million in 1800, an increase of about 35 percent in a decade. Counting slaves, about a third of its population, the South remained the most populous region, with almost as many inhabitants as the middle states and New England combined. The Industrial Revolution had yet to come to America, but industry and commerce were expanding, and more and more farmers rotated their crops and used experimental methods.

The most significant change over that quarter century was in ideas, and they in turn changed Americans' attitudes and behavior. The stupendous idea of the 1770s was the right to rebel against illegal or oppressive authority. But rebellion for what *positive* goals? Morally the revolutionaries' beliefs centered on their concept of virtue—the readiness of Americans to place the common welfare above their personal needs, reflecting the Enlightenment assumption that human beings had it in their power to shape their world with shared values at the basis of the social order. "For Americans," historian Robert Shalhope wrote, "the moral character of their society formed the prime measure of the success or failure of their revolution: republicanism blended indistinguishably with political revolution and moral regeneration." Though American savants liked to look to the Greek and Romans of antiquity for such republican ideals, they were in fact modern concepts with Enlightenment origins.

American republicans stressed this need to subordinate individual wants to the collective needs of the community or country. Self had to yield to the bonds of unity forged in families, churches, and schools. Communal harmony and order were crucial. Personal virtues such as frugality and temperance were emphasized, too. Since the productive person was thrifty but sharing, this benefited the community as well.

Republicanism of this kind had significant political implications. In general, republicans imagined polities incorporating a small, homogeneous area such as a county or state where the best government might be the least government, curbed through an independent judiciary, popular assemblies, rotation in office, a small military. American republicans pointed scornfully at the inflated British monarchy and empire, full of corruption, selfishness, ambition, and pomposity.

Would Americans ape the British? Slowly, incrementally, almost invisibly, the expanding markets of the enlightened economy rewarded individual initiative rather than collective virtue. Mobility from town to city weakened village homogeneity. People became more materialistic and competitive as economic opportunity expanded. "The people grow less steady, spirited and virtuous," John Adams had already warned in 1775, decrying greed for money and power, "the seekers more numerous and more corrupt, and every day increases the circles of their dependents and expectants, untill virtue, integrity, public spirit, simplicity, frugality, become the objects of ridicule and scorn, and vanity, luxury, foppery, selfishness, meanness, and downright venality, swallow up the whole society." Leaders like Alexander Hamilton, Washington's treasury secretary, were now more intent on building a national government capable of guiding the growth of industry and trade in competition with Europe than with guarding the republican ideals.

Thus the concept of virtue at the heart of republicanism lost force as the revolutionary impulse faded and private interests reasserted themselves. Virtue came to be linked to personal ambition and interest. The old values of frugality and industry were translated to the new Protestant work ethic of competition and productivity. And as Americans became more entangled with Great Power rivalries, they had to come to terms with uses of power that republicans had shunned as manipulative and Machiavellian.

Republicanism, in short, was yielding to a competitive individualism that came to be called liberalism, emerging as the dominant ideology of the Enlightenment, with the industrialization of the West leading to the creation of an assertive middle class. Republicanism and liberalism did not wholly differ from each other, unsurprisingly given their common roots in the Enlightenment. Liberal qualities of individualism were evident early on in republicanism, which in turn was a potent element in liberalism for decades. Indeed, the era abounded in multiple "discourses," according to historian Isaac Kramnick: republicanism, Lockean liberalism, work-ethic Protestantism, state-centered theories of power. Historians, he noted, are uneasy with this clatter of ideas. The Framers, all men of the Enlightenment, were not.

Certainly James Madison was not. He seemed to have the broadest vision, recognizing the complexity of ideas and politics and arriving at practical truths. In the *Federalist,* he defended the Constitution but without Hamilton's extreme nationalism. He not only authored the Bill of Rights but guided it through Congress. He saw the emerging liberal democratic tide and responded to it without sacrificing republican principles. He had the intellectual honesty to shift from a concern over factions to a recognition that conflict could be best channeled through a two-party system, and he had the political skill to build the Republican party and help guide it to victory in a brilliant collaboration with Jefferson. Again and again, it was Madison to the rescue—a problem solver of the highest quality, both intellectually and practically.

A man of realism and hope, rational and impassioned, activist and philosopher—among all his brilliant colleagues in the collective leadership that transformed America, Madison most thoroughly embodied both the spirit and the practical achievement of the Enlightenment in the New World. While other Founders may have brought more fire in forging the American experiment, surely Madison brought the most light.

6

Britain: The Rules of Rulership

Nothing succeeds like success, we are told, so presumably nothing fails like failure. But sometimes nothing succeeds, or endures, like failure. In the aftermath of Britain's humiliating surrender at Yorktown, a few English radicals castigated their political and governmental system. They demanded at least a reexamination of the polity responsible for such bungling government.

Britain had had its Vietnam, Americans could recognize two centuries later. The proud empire—the victor over France and other powers, possessed of the strongest navy in the world—had succumbed to ill-equipped, ill-trained colonials fired up by their dream of personal liberty and national independence. And just as Vietnam led to years of bitter recrimination in America in the 1970s, so did Yorktown precipitate sulphurous conflict in Britain in the 1780s.

But Britain's failure did not empower the radicals. As in the United States, there was no major reevaluation of a governing system that excluded the poor and guaranteed the domination of cliques of aristocrats, magnates, and their hangers-on. Why not? For all its disarray, British politics remained closed tightly against outsiders and therefore against new ideas. The rules of admission were jealously guarded. Parliamentary constituencies continued to be bought and sold like property. Sons and dependents of aristocrats sat on Commons benches, reliably supporting the factional interests of their patrons.

British political power still was overwhelmingly in the hands of a single class, and, in the absence of meaningful conflict over ideas and issues, lackluster rule was the outcome. The British had not forged the foundations of strong leadership: unified cabinets headed by effective and accountable first ministers; intensely competitive parties seeking wide popular support for their ideas and issues; militantly united oppositions; a Crown that knew its authority and its limitations—all grounded in an informed and active electorate. Instead, Britain still had a heavily personalistic system, monopolized by factions that combined in fleeting coalitions. Could the British find or forge a new leadership to meet the challenges and opportunities of a time of crisis and ferment?

THE INSIDE GAME

One benefit of handing parliamentary seats to young aristocrats was that it brought fresh blood to the Commons—the youthful beneficiaries bypassed the boring process of winning competitive elections and gaining experience. Born in 1749, Charles James Fox was descended from Charles II and connected with a half dozen of England's greatest families. Delicate in infancy, he grew up enjoying "one of the most indulged childhoods in English history," his biographer L. G. Mitchell wrote. From his early years he was adored by his family, while seen by others as a conceited bumpkin.

Though he had the obligatory stints at Eton and Oxford, "France was Fox's university," Mitchell observed, where he had the standing to attend the most sophisticated salons and meet with the likes of the visiting David Hume. Early in life he displayed his dualisms—a lover of the classics and of Paris brothels, a notorious rake who paraded the mistress he seduced away from the Prince of Wales, an earnest interlocutor of Dr. Johnson and Edmund Burke, a habitual gambler who assured his father that he had "a most fixed Resolution never again to play," which always became unfixed.

Oddest of all, this scion of royalty and aristocracy turned into a political romantic who devoted much of his long career to tilting against kings and knights. Elected to Parliament as a Whig at the age of nineteen from a borough given him by his father, he first won attention for his garrulity and excesses in debate. Because of the noises he made, Fox, as historian John Derry noted, "appeared more radical than he was." He was, in fact, a moderate Whig who encouraged very cautious reform of parliamentary representation, among other issues. But even these positions he would sacrifice in political maneuver and sometimes, it seemed, for the sheer pleasure of embarrassing a foe. His opportunism and waywardness, together with his undeniable charisma, made him less the leader of his faction of Whigs than the object of a personality cult.

Fox's relationship with Lord North, first minister to the Crown during the American war, tells much about the young MP—and also about British politics. Fox's parliamentary skills, passionate commitments, and talent for invective—described by Derry as a "seemingly tireless capacity to heap insult, contempt and ridicule upon his opponents"—made him a keen and unrelenting thorn in the side of a floundering administration, a role he would relish throughout his political career.

The more the young political freelancer attacked North, the more he antagonized George III, who saw this whippersnapper as an unscrupulous opportunist. In the whirligig of British politics, however, the king dropped North in March 1782 and turned to a new line-up. Fox was briefly foreign minister before resigning in a storm. A few months later he was back with a new partner: the man he had harassed from every direction for years, Lord North. They formed a coalition, putting the Duke of Portland up front as chief minister, while they themselves held the real power. Moreover, they presented the king with a fait accompli—not only was he denied his prerogative of choosing the first minister, the new coalition nominated men for even petty offices, reducing the king's patronage to nothing.

Immediately denounced as infamous, the new government was not built to last. After eight months in office, "King Fox" introduced a controversial bill to rein in the corrupt East India Company. This needed measure sailed through the Commons, but George bullied the Lords into rejecting it. Scarcely had the votes been counted before the king demanded the coalition's resignation. But with Fox and North still holding a majority in the Commons, George was hard-pressed to find a replacement. Finally, in December 1783, he asked young William Pitt to form a new government. Outraged by the king's reassertion of his prerogative and confident of his own majority, Fox bet Pitt would last a week.

* * *

Few indeed would have seen strong leadership potential in William Pitt early in 1781 when he first took his place in the Commons. Of course, he was the son of William Pitt the Elder, but eminent men did not often spawn great leaders—more often they produced the opposite. The young man had shown no great distinction at Cambridge, yet a year after taking his parliamentary seat, Pitt the Younger became Chancellor of the Exchequer. And the year after that, he accepted George III's summons to head his government. Pitt was not yet twenty-five years old.

Worries about Pitt's age soon evaporated. He took office with the self-assurance and astuteness of an old cabinet hand. He mastered Parliament with eloquent and powerful addresses that strengthened him in dealing with backbench and frontbench alike. Long concerned about the government's loose financial arrangements, he took on administrative reforms and is even credited with sponsoring the first income tax, though things got a bit out of hand when he proposed levies on hats, perfumes, hair powder, maidservants, and bachelors, leading to hilarious caricatures.

Pitt even proposed parliamentary reform: shorter sessions, curbs on bribery, additional representation for London and the larger counties, and more. He came up with a scheme that would pay a million pounds in compensation to thirty-six of the most "rotten" and unrepresentative boroughs for their loss of seats. Pitt was no radical: He believed that the British constitution was essentially sound. Its institutions needed not revolution but a vigorous cleansing to rid them of corruption and make them truly representative and effective. But Pitt's appeal to both tradition and reform could not persuade members to tamper with the basic electoral system that had put them into office.

Still, Pitt's toughest problem was not Parliament but the king. George III was a formidable ally—and opponent. Defeat in America had not diminished the Crown's constitutional authority. The king selected and dismissed cabinet ministers, and during his reign, general elections were typically seen as appeals by the monarch and his ministers for votes of confidence rather than as chances for parties to set the future course of the nation. The king also claimed a broad but undefined executive veto. After some early stumbles Pitt grasped the fact that in his balancing act as a leader among Parliament, his cabinet colleagues, the nobility, and court and country interests, King George represented a powerful, volatile, even destabilizing threat.

Learning from the experience of his father, whose poor relations with the young George III had hastened his departure from office, Pitt soon fashioned a working partnership with the king. As for George, whatever his misgivings about this tyro, he hated Pitt's foes far more. In 1784, he dissolved Parliament at a time of maximum disadvantage to the disorganized opposition, leading to major losses for Fox and North. The next four years saw a continuing association between the king and his first minister, while the opposition opposed—furiously but impotently.

Then a thunderbolt: George had gone mad. At least he exhibited symptoms of madness—delirium, foaming at the mouth. He had to be straitjacketed. In all likelihood, it was porphyria, a metabolic disorder. This blow touched off a political as well as a personal crisis. The Foxites had long looked forward to the king's death and the enthronement of their friend and ally George, Prince of Wales, the king's eldest son and heir. Now that King George was ill, a regency was called for, with Prince George as its natural leader. Their big chance seemed at hand. But the king annoyingly declined to die, and Pitt, asserting that a regency could be set up only by an act of Parliament, played for time. The monarch, so physically robust that he could survive the emetics and blisterings the doctors forced on him, resumed the throne in a few months.

In these years as the king's first minister, Pitt played his weak hand so smoothly that he remained secure in office, despite grumblings on all sides, including the king's. A masterful political negotiator, parliamentary broker, and cabinet head, Pitt continued as the consummate transactional leader of the time.

And transactional leadership was perhaps the best that could be expected in a system where most politicians were Whigs of indifferently distinct colorations. Whigs were less a political party than a disarray of factions. They had no coherent set of beliefs. To be a Whig was to continue to take credit for the Glorious Revolution, now a century past, while declaiming vaguely forward-looking, reformist sentiments. To call oneself a Tory, by contrast, was to appear backward and even somehow unpatriotic. Yet the Whig advantage in numbers brought no unified majority capable of the collective leadership that produces principled, transformational change.

Politics abhors a vacuum. If politicians could not fight each other as soldiers in two political armies, they competed for control of the one dominant party. It was an inside game. Most members of Parliament were mute followers, with little influence on Whig policies and only passive involvement in the rise and fall of factions. Amid vast economic change in the country outside, Parliament seemed stagnant at best, attuned to no principle but self-perpetuation. The same old political merry-go-round blared out its patriotic ditties while the country gentlemen rose and fell on their rocking horses and the powerless crowds looked on, bemused by the flamboyant horsemen until the music ended, the lights dimmed, and the spectators returned to their dark streets and hovels.

What could shake Britain out of its stalemate?

THE REVOLUTION THAT WASN'T

The tempests of British politics appeared petty beside the great storm slowly gathering across the Channel. It was with fascination and hope that British radicals, most liberal Whigs, and a few politicians followed the breathtaking events in Paris. Charles James Fox, the romantic who had fallen in love with France and its highlife and lowlife, greeted the French Revolution with rapture. A month after the fall of the Bastille he told a friend, "I say nothing of french News but if I were to begin I should never finish. It is I think by much the greatest Event that has ever happened in the world, and will in all human probability have the most extensive good consequences."

Seventeen eighty-nine! The British could relish this year—it was the centennial of their own Bill of Rights, climax of the Glorious Revolution. But there was a real revolution exploding *now* in Paris. Richard Price, the noted Dissenter, seized the coincidence to demand of Britain's rulers that they quickly restore and enlarge the rights of Englishmen and "consent to the correction of abuses before they and you are destroyed together." The light of liberty, he sermonized, "after setting America free, reflected to France, and there kindled into a blaze that lays despotism in ashes, and warms and illuminates Europe!"

The revolutionary frenzy across the Channel sent shivers of excitement even through Whigs of Fox's bent as well as more radical Whigs, and of dread into Whig conservatives. When those Parisians talked reform they really seemed to mean it! As though awaking from a decades-long slumber, radical Whigs turned back to the old Wilkesite cause of parliamentary reform. Leaders founded the Society of the Friends of the People to build grassroots support. Some believed that reforms within Parliament might lead to a transformation of the whole political system, though not too fundamental a one, of course.

But it was the hope of fundamental change at home that more and more transfixed British working people as they followed the drastic actions in Paris. Most artisans and laborers had little interest in the intricacies and compromises of "Whiggish" reform, and even less faith that the men of Parliament would transform the system that empowered them. By the mid-1790s a groundswell of radical feeling was rumbling through the ranks of urban workers and some country people. Amid scattered strikes and food riots, protest was turning to constructive action. Together with middle-class radicals, workers founded the London Corresponding Society and blasted out their ideas, less in books than in a storm of pamphlets.

What were those ideas? That the Glorious Revolution was still unfinished, that the Rights of Man must be vigorously pursued, that the government itself was guilty of suppressing liberties, that the crucial need was real reform acknowledging the unmet wants and needs of human beings, and, finally, given the unlikelihood of such change coming out of Parliament as it was, that an extra-parliamentary National Convention must be convened, just as in France.

Few Englishmen sounded forth such radical ideas more eloquently and extensively than a leader of the time, later almost forgotten, John Thelwall. Son of a London silk mercer who died when John was nine, he became entranced by literature he read by the light of a candle he held as he walked the streets of London. Soon he was drawn into the heady world of urban reformism. At first he leaned toward Whiggish criticism of oligarchical rule and factional politics. But soon, as a leader in the London Corresponding Society, he moved toward a radical emphasis on social and economic problems of poverty, labor, and the rights of workers.

A devotee of Adam Smith, Thelwall was not hostile to enterprise—he wanted working men and women to enjoy its ample fruits. Those were, he argued, their fruits, too; they had a natural right to their share. Echoing Locke, Thelwall insisted that property was "nothing but human labour. Most estimable of all property is the sweat of the poor man's brow—the property from which all other is derived." As he emphasized, "*the property of the country is* NOT THE COUNTRY." Rather, "*The population of the nation is the nation!*" Yet, in England, inequality was growing more profound. At its heart, Thelwall thought, was the inequality of power between employer and worker, even as the "arts and inventions" of modern industry were accelerating "the progress of accumulation." That left the worker isolated, with urgent needs, in "absolute subjection," helpless to earn a living wage. It was, Thelwall thundered, "robbery committed by the rich and powerful upon the defenceless poor."

He drew on Adam Smith for his portrait of working men and women degraded by industry. For Smith, as it would be for many socialists later, this was an inevitability of capitalism. But Thelwall thought differently. The key to preserving enterprise, while taking the first step to a just society, was to overcome the owning class's "monopoly of knowledge." Because "*Knowledge is Power,*" he said, it was the policy of the rulers "to keep the mass of mankind as ignorant as possible"—ignorant of their rights, incapable of understanding their oppression or any means of redress. But the swelling forces of industry provided their own remedy. Man, Thelwall said, was naturally social and communicative, "proud to display the little knowledge he possesses, and eager, as opportunity presents, to encrease his store." By pressing men together—literally and figuratively—the factory system was creating conditions "favourable to the diffusion of knowledge." So "every large workshop and manufactory is a sort of political society, which no act of parliament can silence, and no magistrate can disperse."

Thelwall practiced what he preached—by preaching. His medium in the early 1790s was his voice, despite a stammer from childhood. To masses that grew ever larger, Thelwall eloquently explained the crisis, the challenges they faced, the opportunities they had. Thus, he was enlightening all those within reach of his voice, and in so doing smashing the rulers' monopoly of knowledge. How long before they struck back?

◆ ◆ ◆

As horrific reports began to flow in of the Terror—the executions, mass drownings, lethal conflict among the Jacobin leaders themselves—many English lost sympathy for the French Revolution. Some reasserted their own patriotism as "loyalists" and inflicted their fear and insecurity on allegedly disloyal fellow citizens through private threats or local harassments: a tenant farmer faced with loss of his livelihood; a brilliant chemist denied a prestigious Oxford chair; a parish constable in Norfolk dismissed for showing disrespect to the government. A Halifax staymaker sacked her "Jacobin" assistant to placate a customer. A "vile democrat" was accused of wearing his hair powder without a license!

Dedicated above all to the maintenance of order and stability, Pitt could not countenance free-ranging patriotic assaults on "Jacobins." But he shared loyalist suspicions that there was subversion and sedition among his people. In May 1792, the government issued a royal proclamation targeting "wicked and seditious writings," aimed in fact mainly at one book—Thomas Paine's explosive new *Rights of Man*, which drew fire even from Whig liberals like Fox for its powerful assaults on the British constitution and its institutions.

As Britain joined Austria and Russia in war against revolutionary France in 1793, Pitt's line hardened. The next year, he took his most drastic step—suspension of habeas corpus, the writ that had guaranteed English liberty for centuries. That move was as much a psychological punch as legal. "The suspension, together with a series of arrests," historian Clive Emsley wrote, "terrified some into quitting the popular societies; and some small provincial clubs closed as a direct result of the suspension." Like most "suspensions" of rights in Western experience, this bill had been rushed through the legislature before many in the populace could realize what was happening.

Tension rose in 1795 in the streets and at open-air political meetings attended by large crowds. One day in October, as the king rode in state to the House of Lords, angry mobs appeared, throwing stones at his carriage and shouting, "Peace and Bread! No War! No King! Down with George!" On his return from Parliament to St. James's Palace the crowd pursued him again. The door to his carriage opened, probably by accident, but word spread of an attempt on his life. The incident created a storm in the country and in Parliament, especially against the London Corresponding Society, which the government blamed for inciting the mob. Pitt took the opportunity to push through, over the vigorous opposition of Foxite Whigs, two "Gagging Acts"—a bill making it treason to incite hatred of king, government, or constitution, and another that restricted public meetings to fifty persons.

Repression neared its peak in the late 1790s as fears of French invasion stoked hatred of English radicals. Scores were arrested for "Treasonable Practices." Many of them were jailed indefinitely; one was hanged. Protest meetings were banned, while "Jacobin" newspapers and bookstores became favorite targets of the authorities.

The hardest blows to workingmen's efforts to forge a role in Britain's political and economic order came in 1799. First Parliament outlawed such political organizations as the London Corresponding Society. Then trade unions were declared illegal under the Combination Act, which, as Emsley noted, was for the first time "directed against working men as a whole, indeed as a class." Before this, combination laws had banned organizing within individual trades like hatters, paper makers, or tailors.

Did the government not realize that its class approach might have ominous implications for future political struggles?

For the time being, though, repression worked. Radical action dwindled late in the decade. Even before it was banned, the London Corresponding Society had faded in numbers and influence. The press turned more cautious and "patriotic."

Thelwall's fate epitomized the decline. Police harassed his meetings. His handbills were torn down; some of his relatives were thrown off their farms. Detained and denied habeas corpus in 1794 together with a number of other leading radicals, Thelwall was charged with treason, interrogated by the Privy Council including Pitt himself, put into solitary confinement for five months, shunted off to a Newgate cell with little light or air, arraigned for "conspiracy to overthrow the Government and perpetrate the King's death," subjected to a three-day trial—and acquitted. He returned to a hero's welcome and published his most significant book, *Rights of Nature*. But then he entered a long twilight. His audiences shrank as mobs and police harassed his talks. Booksellers feared to peddle his work. Ultimately, he was silenced, prevented from increasing his followers' store of knowledge. He scored one final victory: He lived long enough to see passage of the Reform Act of 1832.

Repression in Britain in the era of the French Revolution succeeded because it was rarely too nakedly repressive. The enforcement bite appeared fainter than the statutory bark. Prosecutors seemed not always that enthusiastic, jurors not all that militant. In this respect the British could enjoy the defects of their repressive system. For those with no means of redress, that was perhaps the one chink of light on the horizon.

THE FRACTURED DEBATE

The scene appeared set in the 1790s for a grand intellectual confrontation that would transcend the day-to-day debates in Parliament and the tumult in the streets. The French Revolution was testing radical and reformist ideas as never before. Some British radicals gamely defended the Revolution's excesses on the grounds that vast change had never taken place without a lot of broken crockery, while conservatives used every outrage to say, "We told you so."

No man both polarized and elevated the confrontation more grandly than Edmund Burke, the old advocate for America. A leading figure in Fox's parliamentary faction, he was shocked by the starry-eyed tributes to the French Revolution by his longtime friend and ally and others inside Parliament and out. Repelled by doctrinaire enthusiasm, Burke in early 1790 asked how they could wish to emulate "an irrational, unprincipled, proscribing, confiscating, plundering, ferocious, bloody, and tyrannical democracy"? How could they abandon good, stout English principles for the wild ideas imbibed from Enlightenment savants like Voltaire and Rousseau? Burke himself did not exclude the possibility for change—"a principle of improvement"—"but even when I changed, it should be to preserve."

For Burke, the revolution across the Channel was as much an ideological challenge as it was a political and military threat. He felt a fierce urgency to meet that challenge with force, to annihilate the subversive doctrines of the French before they would overturn "the true principles of our own domestic laws." Speeches were not enough now. He mobilized his most potent weapon—the pen. *Reflections on the Revolution in France* became an immediate sensation, selling seven thousand copies within six days in London, going through eleven editions in one year, finding ten thousand buyers in Paris and thousands more in Germany. Only Spain's Inquisition, fearful of any discussion of new ideas even in a vehement condemnation of them, saw fit to ban the book, placing it on its *Index Liborum Prohibitorum*—a boost to Burke like the "Banned in Boston" label that American booksellers later prized.

Though Burke set himself up as the Enlightenment's most destructive critic, his concepts—his very language—were based in that despised movement. The state of nature, the social contract, the original rights of man, the power of reason, the perfectibility of man, the necessity for change— these ideas comprised Burke's thought. The difference came in the vociferous insistence that, in his usage, they were not mere "abstract ideas" with no reality except in the minds of dishonest philosophers and lunatic revolutionaries. *His* usage was grounded in the authority of tradition and of religion. In other words, Burke neutralized the liberationist potential of Enlightenment ideas and harnessed them to the service of conservatism.

For instance, his first priority was social and political order, without which no community could survive intact, as the "fresh ruins of France" sadly proved. Order, in his view, was rooted in tradition and custom. In society, that meant a stable, hierarchical class structure, which might allow for limited social mobility. In politics, it meant that a small number of men would govern in the interests of all. It also meant an established religion— the Anglican for England—as the foundation for civic harmony and moral and political consensus.

For Burke, though, order was necessary but not enough on its own. What would order uphold and perpetuate? Here again his answer was clear and emphatic—*liberty*. But, unlike the liberty peddled by philosophes, Burke's liberty was not license; it was defined not by what men could do but by what they *ought* to do. Liberty without wisdom or virtue was, Burke declared, "the greatest of all possible evils; for it is folly, vice, and madness." A man's freedom was measured not by his distance from other men or from social obligations but by his willingness to control his passions and recognize the reciprocal claims of others. Far from the inborn, individualistic liberty celebrated by most Enlightenment philosophers, Burke's liberty was communal, formed and hedged by social, political, and legal institutions.

Those institutions guaranteed respect and protection not for the novel "pretended rights" of "theorists" but for the *real* rights" of man, ancient, according to Burke, and therefore genuine—rights to the fruits of his industry, to his property, to do what he could for himself without trespassing on others, "to instruction in life, and to consolation in death." He had a right "to a fair portion of all which society, with all its combinations of skill and force, can do in his favour." Men had equal rights in these respects "but not to equal things."

Burke's *Reflections* challenged Whig grandees, Britain's greatest beneficiaries of the inequality of "things," to choose between his cause of tradition, loyalty, and safety, and the Foxite fling with anarchy. But although many of his warnings about the course of revolution in France were prescient, Burke's vehemence as the prophet of counterrevolution lost more followers than it won. He became more and more impassioned about—even obsessed with—his dire vision of an apocalyptic conflagration that would leap the Channel and consume England. Increasingly he turned into the kind of ideologue he had deplored—so dogmatic that he gravely warned his party colleagues that he could not allow personal friendship to interfere with saving Western civilization from the contagion of France.

He and Fox made an effort to reconcile; they even walked to the House of Commons arm in arm. But the gulf was too deep. Burke was left frustrated, isolated, powerless, a "politician without a party."

. . .

Thomas Paine, who appeared equally at home among American revolutionaries, French republicans, and British radicals, seemed an unlikely friend to Edmund Burke. In *Common Sense* and other writings, Paine had long waged war on some of Burke's most heartfelt beliefs. But the two had found common cause in support of American independence and, given Burke's cooptation of Enlightenment concepts, they shared a common language. In the late 1780s they met several times, dining together in the country, Burke introducing Paine to Whig grandees. They corresponded even as the French Revolution raged, and in January 1790, Paine sent Burke an account of events based on the eyewitness of the American minister in Paris, Thomas Jefferson. While Paine found reason for optimism in Jefferson's news—indeed, he saw the French Revolution as the happy forerunner of others to come—the letter only confirmed Burke's fear and loathing of the upheaval across the Channel.

The Revolution made an irreparable breach between the two men. The intensity of Paine's attack on the *Reflections* may in part have been due to feelings of betrayal. In *Rights of Man,* published just four months after Burke's book, in March 1791, Paine championed the Revolution for carrying out the principles of those natural rights Burke so scorned. For Paine, rights were not abstractions; they were as real as human life and essential to it. They could be "neither deviseable, nor transferable, nor annihilable." Indeed, they spanned all that involved "man in right of his existence," including intellectual rights, "or rights of the mind," and civil rights, which were natural rights that needed society for their fulfillment. Above all, and crucial to the rest, was the right to participation and representation in government. People also had an "inherent indefeasible right" to abolish any government that did not accord with their "interest, disposition, and happiness." Scorning Burke's vain labors "to stop the progress of knowledge," Paine celebrated the revolutions in America and France for having "thrown a beam of light over the world, which reaches into man." And Paine confidently asserted that there could be no counterrevolution: Once ignorance was dispelled, it would be impossible to reenthrone it.

Rights of Man was an even greater publishing phenomenon than Burke's tract, quickly selling some fifty thousand copies. Not even Pitt's bill against it could stop its circulation. The force of Paine's riposte sent radicals into raptures and ensured that his core principles of equal natural rights and of popular sovereignty would, as historian Mark Philp wrote, "be firmly lodged at the centre of radical politics throughout the decade." But if together Paine and Burke set the parameters for the ideological confrontation between loyalists and radicals, many others took up the battle. The 1790s detonated a burst of creative polemics. As usual in the course of the Enlightenment, those challenging the status quo were more heterogeneous than its defense, ranging from extremes of radicalism to radical Whigs, from neo-Lockeans to Rousseauists, feminists and republicans to millenarians, unitarians, egalitarians, and fledgling utilitarians. Many radicals believed that it was in their power, as Paine had written, really to begin the world anew.

· · ·

It was a paradox—a profusion of fresh, creative ideas about human nature, rights, government, yet the reality in Britain as the eighteenth century neared its end was political stagnation, disarray, and repression. The cause of parliamentary reform had been tainted with Jacobinism, while reform's great hope, Fox, with his dwindling group of followers, was absorbed in parliamentary maneuvers. The popular radical societies that had flowered in the early, hopeful days of the French Revolution disappeared under government pressure, though a "revolutionary underground" of activists persisted.

Pitt continued to lead that government and Fox continued to harry him on the parliamentary flanks, charging him and the king with stoking fears of French invasion to carry out their "invasion of the constitution." But his condemnations of the war brought accusations of disloyalty and defections. Unable to offer effective opposition, Fox in 1794 led his remnant band out of Parliament.

With the support of the king, Pitt kept his office. But that support came at a price—the threat of monarchical veto. As long as Pitt and George III could agree on the prosecution of the war and of radicals, Pitt was secure. But then intruded another issue to rouse atavistic hatreds and fears—Catholic emancipation. The monarch was adamantly opposed, Pitt conciliatory. The issue marked a reversion to the ancient battle over the powers of the Crown. With Catholic relief unpopular in Commons and country, Pitt lost. His resignation in 1801 left a leadership gap in British politics his successors could not fill.

Were more proof needed, the disarray that followed Pitt's fall exposed the bankruptcy of the political system. The king could still intervene at will. Factions and personal followings still dominated political action, as the departure and return of Fox with his followers showed. The essentials of a modern democracy—disciplined party leadership and followership confronting a united party opposition—had not yet been achieved at the start of the nineteenth century. Whig optimism, with its Enlightenment faith in progress and in beneficial change, seemed a mockery as the status quo ruled and reigned without foreseeable end.

Nothing better reflected the inability and unwillingness of British rule to adapt to emerging challenges than the old and new social and economic problems that plagued the underclass. The poor could not vote, they could gain no representation in Parliament. Their organizations were outlawed, their speech proscribed, their leaders jailed and harried. As industrialization began to gather pace, they were helpless to improve their work and living conditions. When food riots—that most primitive and elemental protest—broke out in 1800, the nation that Montesquieu and Voltaire had glorified as the model of political modernity seemingly reverted to a land that the Enlightenment had passed over.

7

Napoleonic Rulership

It seemed a bit odd, on the face of it. After decades of wars, revolutions, and migrations, the map of Europe appeared hardly altered by 1800. Almost ceaseless war between Britain and France had left the two countries essentially intact. Despite incursions, the loose German array of states still sprawled across central Europe, bordering on the Austrian Empire, which embraced Hungary and Galicia and ended on the frontier of the Ottoman Empire. Iberia remained split between Spain and Portugal. In contrast, the political geography of North America *had* changed, with the rise of an independent United States flanking Canada, which after the Seven Years' War had shifted from French to British control, as had the Louisiana territory, from France to the Spanish.

Still, much had happened within some European borders. During the 1780s and 1790s the smaller nations of Europe had fought for their independence. Threatened by the French, the Dutch had to call in Prussian troops in 1787 to restore the authority of their king. The Swiss Confederation, forsaking for a time its traditional bent for neutrality, allied itself with France in the 1770s; it then flirted with Prussia and Austria, and, later, reverted to isolation until a rebellion in Geneva brought a renewed friendship with France. In Sweden Gustav III established a dictatorial government to fend off Russia and Prussia—then he came out as an "enlightened despot," sponsoring reforms to end torture, strengthen the poor laws, proclaim liberty of religion and the press, and promote trade. His commitment to the Enlightenment was exposed when dread of France's revolution swung him back to autocratic conservatism, only to be murdered by a conspiracy of nobles infuriated by his reforms.

Common to many of the countries in the last quarter of the eighteenth century was the seesaw between enlightened, reformist leadership and authoritarianism that safeguarded the regime's power. In Austria, Joseph II, son of Maria Theresa, epitomized this dichotomy. He methodically pursued reforms even as he tightened his hold on every corner of the empire. The result was resistance and rebellion, concessions and brutal repression, ending in the loss of many of the reforms.

Reform came even more haltingly in the lands of Goethe and Schiller. In 1793, with the German city of Mainz under French occupation, local Jacobins led by a group of Enlightenment intellectuals set out to "revolutionize" the southern Rhineland countryside, enthusiastically planting liberty trees. Prussian and Austrian troops soon seized Mainz, jailed the Jacobins, and put the city under Prussian occupation. In the mid-1790s, Dutch republicans drafted a constitution, elected a national assembly, and established the Batavian Republic, not only modeled after the French but dependent on France to keep counterrevolution at bay. Native Jacobins emerged in Italy and Switzerland and other countries and bravely raised tricolor flags, but with enthusiasm dampened by repugnance toward the French Terror and its military aggressiveness.

Foes of the French Revolution had feared that the fires of the Jacobins would start conflagrations all across Europe. This did not happen. Could the fires of revolution be stoked from below in indigenous risings? They flared up sporadically, only to die or be put down.

LA GRANDE FARCE

If the French Revolution failed to produce sweeping changes in the rest of Europe, how much did it transform France itself? Politically it gave citizens legal equality and men a qualified right to vote. Socially most aristocratic privileges had been abolished and landownership broadened to some degree. But real social reform was limited. When the Terror finally waned, millions of peasants and urban laborers remained in poverty and misery.

It was a paradox of the French Revolution that its transforming impact was more thoroughgoing in the military than in the civilian sector. In February 1793, a month after the king's execution, facing nations bent on revenge, the national Convention turned desperately to a winter draft of three hundred thousand men and then a *levée en masse* in August, mobilizing another half-million recruits. Amid patriotic excitement, the government created not only a new army but a new *kind* of army, an "enlightened" army that cast out old props for authority and embraced fresh approaches to organization, training, and battle itself. The grip of class on the officer corps was broken. Promotions were given for merit. Political reliability counted for more than social background. Soldiers could now elect their junior officers, in effect creating their own leadership. Equally transformational was the new army's rejection of the traditional tactic of advancing in serried ranks. Commanders now called for daring and speed, replacing, for instance, frontal attacks with flanking maneuvers.

Some of these changes were improvised necessities since the Revolution had driven out much of the ancien régime's officer corps. The army, like everything in France, had become a political battlefield. The Jacobins in the Convention explicitly politicized it. As citizens, soldiers were now allowed to vote, join demonstrations, form political clubs of their own, or join clubs outside their garrisons. They were encouraged to read revolutionary newspapers. Bulk orders—"some seven and a half million copies in all—were bought for the armies," according to historian Alan Forrest, "and every effort was made to ensure that the men were made aware of the major political issues of the day." The new liberty brought license as well—indiscipline, desertions, pillage. But punishment, too, was levied with a sense of equity; some commanding officers were guillotined for incompetence.

The new-fashioned French army emerged from revolutionary disorder and survived the Revolution's collapse. History would record that Napoleon created powerful armies. But it was the revolutionary army that created Napoleon.

♦ ♦ ♦

It was an early indication of Napoleon Bonaparte's relentless self-discipline that he could rise in the French army even before the revolutionary democratization of the mid-1790s. With his Corsican name and dialect, he had to overcome the gibes of fellow students at Brienne, an austere military academy for the sons of poor nobles in the northern province of Champagne that he entered in 1779. For over five years he was virtually incarcerated there, unable even to visit home, but he had all the more time to read deeply in stories of the valiant heroes of classical history. He excelled in mathematics. Winning a scholarship to the elite Royal Military School in Paris in 1784, he found his reception there somewhat warmer, and whatever snobbishness and prejudice he still suffered and resented seemed only to steel him and sharpen his ambition. Graduating at sixteen, he was posted to a regiment and then to an artillery school that trained a picked section within the regular army.

Huge opportunities were opening up for young officers in the chaos of

French politics of the mid-1790s. With veteran officers in exile or opposition, men in their thirties or even twenties were made generals. The government that took power in late 1795, after the Terror was extinguished and under a conservative constitution written in reaction to it, was desperately fending off a royalist resurgence on the right and Jacobin threats from the left and finally turned to the army for support. The five-man executive, the Directory, used troops to purge the government of rightists, at a time of ever mounting pressure on France's borders by the armies of Europe's monarchs. Napoleon, who had shown his mettle in several engagements, was given command of fifty thousand soldiers and sent to invade Italy.

Now the twenty-six-year-old general demonstrated his lifelong knack at creating order out of apparent chaos. Taking charge of the campaign from older officers who disdained the Corsican upstart, he systematically smashed through Piedmont and Lombardy. Leading troops hungry for glory and booty, he moved so swiftly that he outran orders from Paris and thus could operate with the latitude he wanted. But it was in the settlements he exacted from his vanquished foes that he demonstrated his budding political skills. While demanding heavy indemnities, including a "tribute" from the pope of 21 million lira and one hundred works of art, Napoleon was determined not to leave chaos in his wake. He created a "Cisalpine Republic" with a constitution modeled after the French Republic that united over three million Italians under a single French-monitored government.

Enthusiastically hailed as a hero by the people of Paris, Bonaparte looked around—literally—for new fields to conquer. That he chose Egypt revealed another dimension of the revolutionary wars. Militarily it was risky, since the British fleet patrolled the Mediterranean, but the hope of cutting Britain's lifeline to India seemed to outweigh the danger. Even more audacious was Napoleon's plan to export the Enlightenment to the Near East and to import knowledge obtained there back to Paris. In the wake of his invading army he sent a battalion of 167 intellectuals—geologists, historians, and scientists, including noted chemists and mathematicians. And to his troops, he declared:

"Soldiers! The peoples with whom we are going to live are Mahometans; the first article of their faith is this: 'There is no other God but God, and Mahomet is his prophet.'

"Do not contradict them. Behave towards them as we dealt with the Jews, or with the Italians. Respect their *muftis* and their *imams,* as you have respected rabbis and bishops."

To some, such a show of tolerance seemed to be the Enlightenment in action, but the experiment proved short-lived. Napoleon could control the land but not the sea. In the summer of 1798, he seized Alexandria and crushed the Mameluke army; soon, however, Nelson's warships found the French fleet at anchor in Aboukir Bay and destroyed it. Cut off from home, Napoleon spent time discussing the Koran in Cairo with Islamic dignitaries, introducing windmills to grind flour, and improving the drainage system. After a failed French assault on the Turkish fortress of Acre in Syria in spring 1799—only half of his plague-ridden army returned alive—Napoleon abruptly abandoned the war, his comrades, and his Enlightenment mission. Slipping through the British blockade, he returned to Paris.

He received another hero's welcome since it was not yet clear that the Egyptian campaign would end in disaster. He returned also to a government in extreme crisis. Once again France's enemies were threatening its borders. Again the Directory resorted to repression, now against the left, which aroused the Jacobins, while also raising taxes, which infuriated property holders. Peasants, meanwhile, were rebelling in the southwest. Napoleon's ambitions soared with every crisis. Would a coup be very difficult? he asked a moderate royalist. No, came the reply; it was already three-quarters complete.

Napoleon had allied himself with some old revolutionaries: Abbé Sieyès, the veteran constitution maker and now a Director; Charles Maurice de Talleyrand-Périgord, Bishop of Autun, who had served the Revolution as a diplomat; and Joseph Fouché, a onetime Jacobin who had played a bloody role in the Terror and now was minister of police. As he triggered the coup of 18 Brumaire, Napoleon had two key cards: support by the military and popularity with the masses who feared a return to chaos. Appointed commander of all troops in the region of Paris, Bonaparte secured the resignation of the five Directors and then invaded the legislature, whereupon the lawmakers surrendered. On November 10, 1799, the Directory died with hardly a whimper. What had begun a decade earlier with the highest hopes for human betterment through principled self-government, with liberty, equality, and fraternity as guideposts, ended in a squalid military coup by the era's most brilliant opportunist and his henchmen.

• • •

At the turning of the new century the French leadership staged a pseudo-transformation that made a mockery of old revolutionary ideals and postrevolutionary hopes. On the one hand, leaders solemnly but quickly went about the business of writing a new constitution with a carefully wrought division of powers. On the other, the actual ruler was methodically accumulating personal power that would make the new constitution a sham. It was hypocrisy on a massive scale—*une grande farce.*

The drafters seemed determined to fashion a structure that would avoid the excesses and chaos of the past decade. They feared both a runaway legislature, like the Convention, and an overbearing executive. They delegated lawmaking to a *tri*-cameral legislature—an upper and lower house, plus a new senate to serve as a "constitutional jury" and rule on the legality of the government's actions. The executive was likewise divided among three consuls, of whom the First Consul—Napoleon—was much the most equal. On paper, the new constitution seemed a blueprint for deadlock and inaction.

The drafters were as cautious when it came to voting. The franchise was grandly set out in the new charter as open to all male adults, but an elaborate multitiered system of indirect elections would thwart popular democratic forces and demands, leading to conservative outcomes. The alternative was more to be feared: The direct democracy that had driven the Revolution down such violent courses.

In the end, all these careful plans took place in a never-never land. To validate the new constitution a plebiscite was held, its results announced almost two months after the constitution took effect: three million *oui* and fifteen hundred *non*. The new regime won a landslide, but in an excess of caution by Napoleon's men, almost half the votes were manufactured out of thin air. With this mandate for dictatorship, the Revolution, as the constitution's authors said, indeed was over, though hardly because, as they claimed, it had now finally been "established on the principles with which it began."

The new order was in fact established on the principles of its First Consul—and his first principle was the consolidation of his power. Napoleon showed no hesitation in bypassing or overriding the legislative chambers or for that matter interfering in the elections of legislators. He exploited an assassination attempt against him to compel the senate to grant him emergency powers. He controlled the ministry of police through Fouché, who employed a small army of informants.

Why would the French people, after centuries of monarchical rule and a decade of furious struggle, let Napoleon steal their Revolution and betray it? Despite the electoral fraud, the First Consul had overwhelming popular support. It was partly because he still preached and personified change. But mainly he vowed to end a decade of chaos, misrule, and corruption, and to protect the people's primary need and value, *order*. He suppressed violent Catholic and royalist uprisings in the Vendée. And he won wars. Early in 1800 he ordered his army to cross the Great St. Bernard Pass in the Alps—a feat compared to Hannibal's—and then crushed the Austrians at Marengo, north of Genoa. To be sure, the general rode the pass on a mule rather than on the great white steed portrayed in Jacques-Louis David's famous painting, *Napoleon Crossing the Alps*, and the decisive battle against the Austrians was won six months later at Hohenlinden near Munich by another general—but Napoleon reaped the glory back in Paris.

POWER: THE SUPREME VALUE

What did Napoleon believe in, apart from himself? He was enough a child of the Revolution to have absorbed its faith. But as he amassed power, little of that remained.

Liberté? "Political liberty, which is so necessary to the State," he lectured the newly created Italian legislature in 1805, consisted of "a visibly stable and secure system of good administration." Liberty as necessary to the *state*? Napoleon had it upside down. He did not see liberty as necessary to the people. Consequently, "it can be repressed with impunity." And repress it he did—speech, the press, even religion.

Égalité? Napoleon voiced the usual catchwords, but he was far more careful of the property rights of the rich than of the equal rights of the poor. No egalitarian, he believed in a sharply stratified and hierarchical society. Jefferson had put happiness in place of property in the Declaration of Independence; Napoleon substituted property for equality.

Fraternité? This was the most compelling but most ambiguous term in the holy trinity of the Revolution. Napoleon had little use for it, either, except for fraternizing in the army. The Convention had in 1792 declared its will to accord "fraternity and assistance to all peoples who wish to recover their liberty," but neither the French nor any other peoples under Napoleon would be inundated with liberty or fraternity.

Revolutionary ideals decayed under Napoleon because he prided himself on being neither a theorist nor an ideologue but an administrator, an organizer, a *doer*. His key value—perhaps his only one—was security and survival. He saw himself as a pragmatic, opportunistic leader bent on creating an efficient, technocratic state. Politics was administration, leadership the top of a pyramidal command structure. Napoleon could not accept or even really understand the idea of an opposition, loyal or disloyal—organizations don't need oppositions. Hence he was more dictator than leader.

Still, Napoleon persisted in considering himself a man of the Enlightenment. He held long discussions with Goethe, a great admirer of his, and other intellectuals and artists, and he could talk the Enlightenment talk. He has been called an "enlightened absolutist" along with other European rulers, but the term was a self-contradiction. Enlightenment values such as liberty and democracy could not be legitimated or achieved by absolutist means without perversion or corruption. Indeed, if Napoleon had ever pretended to believe in democratic means to lofty ends, he showed his true colors on December 2, 1804, in his most dramatic and revealing act— crowning himself emperor of the French and converting French citizens into his subjects.

How did a commoner become the emperor of a nation that had violently abolished royalty little more than a decade before? For Napoleon it was simplicity itself, a matter of timing. He had already won executive and legislative power adequate for an absolute monarch. In 1802, at age thirty-three, he made himself consul for life. The next year's renewed warfare with Britain made many of the French anxious for even stronger rule. A royalist plot with English backing to murder Napoleon had been easily foiled, but it gave him an opportunity. Though the First Consul would not say so himself, his lieutenants pointed out that the incident proved the pressing need for an hereditary monarch with clear successors—Napoleon with his three eligible brothers, whom he would soon make kings of nations within his domain. So prodded, the legislature voted for Napoleon's elevation and a plebiscite duly ratified it, by the now usual almost-unanimous vote. Despite the corruption, the ballot revealed that a large majority of the French welcomed a return to royal government. Pius VII was summoned from Rome to officiate.

. . .

A general who becomes an emperor mainly through his military prowess must prove his continuing mastery of war, and Napoleon's enemies promptly gave him the opportunity. By 1805, all of Europe's powers—Austria, Prussia, and Russia—were combined against France, together with the nation that had become Napoleon's most detested enemy, Britain. For the emperor, this meant it was time to go on the offensive. He had the finest fighting force in Europe, historian George Rudé wrote, even though it was ill-paid and even ill-shod. Fervor distinguished these troops. Moving quickly without a baggage train, Napoleon led 190,000 soldiers across the Rhine within a month and three weeks later encircled 50,000 Austrians. Six weeks later, on December 2, 1805, the emperor cornered a huge Russian force in Auster-litz and cut it in two. Peace negotiations brought France much-expanded power in central Europe. In July 1807, Napoleon met Russia's Tsar Alexan-der in Tilsit, and the two emperors in a secret alliance in effect divided Europe into two spheres of influence, east and west.

Napoleon's "half" of the continent opened a glittering landscape of people and polities. In some, his brothers ruled—King Louis in Holland, King Joseph in Naples, King Jérôme in Westphalia. Eventually the empire would stretch across Europe, from Madrid to Warsaw. How govern such a diversity of peoples? How make, as Napoleon told his police chief Fouché he would, "all the peoples of Europe one people"? As a sometime revolu-tionary, the emperor might have practiced creative leadership to unite them behind Enlightenment ideals. But he did not want revolutionary change—he wanted order and control. Emperor Napoleon's most modern trait was his organizational skill, which, for a time at least, made him a far more effec-tive autocrat than his predecessor on the throne. Indeed, the emperor ap-peared less interested in ruling his subjects than in reorganizing them. His effort to impose a bureaucratic ethic and technique on the unmodernized countries he had captured inevitably encountered ancient systems of privi-lege, with entrenched classes and tribal networks of loyalty, as well as guilds impeding free trade, archaic legal procedures, and ecclesiastical resistance.

Napoleon wielded a potent weapon of legal and administrative change— the Civil Code he had engineered in France. Designed to create a unified legal system out of the variegated ancient and revolutionary laws of France's provinces, the Code gave "permanence to the essential accomplishments of the French Revolution: national unity and civic equality," in historian J. Christopher Herold's view. But that equality was only for some; the Code effectively erased women from civil society. "They should stick to knitting," Napoleon had once said. Husbands were granted extensive control over wives and children. For the emperor, the Code became a tool for his own control over France. A French legal historian saw it as a measure of social pacification and wrote that it was "as if the citizens had exchanged their po-litical rights for the guarantee of a fixed and egalitarian civil statute."

Napoleon even tried to impose uniformity on that most sensitive yet tough intersection of ideas and power—the Catholic Church. After humili-ating the papacy in his Italian campaigns, he found it expedient to make peace. To do so, he dismissed the longstanding campaign by Enlightenment leaders, rooted in the terrible wars of the Reformation, to disentangle the state from religion. This was essential, they believed, to enlightened and effective government. For the emperor, conciliation was simply opportunistic. By restoring Catholicism, Napoleon bound the church to his own rule, which undermined the monarchist counterrevolutionary cause. As he candidly told a meeting of ultra-Catholic leaders, "I intend to reestablish religion, not for your sake but for mine." The Concordat he signed with the Vatican in 1801 confirmed Catholicism as the faith of most of the French, permitted public worship, and allowed normal parish life. But church property confiscated during the Revolution was not restored, and the church had to accept subordination to the state, with the clergy on the public payroll and bishops nominated by Napoleon himself. Meantime, in the expanding empire, French administrators sought to carry out secular reforms, which in some satellite countries broke on the rocks of Catholic resistance.

It was taxation and conscription, though, that most pervaded and unified Napoleon's Europe. Resistance to both was strong both inside and outside France, but the imperial bureaucracy was stronger. A dizzying array of taxes—on land and movable property, industry and consumption—was devoured by Napoleon's perpetual warfare machine. Conscription, adopted by the revolutionary government at a time of peril, was enthusiastically augmented by Napoleon and extended to the satellite lands. The old revolutionary fervor no longer stirred many young Frenchmen, especially those in rural areas, and they dodged military service by fleeing or hiding or mutilating themselves or paying off officials. Still, conscription worked—between 1800 and 1814, some two million Frenchmen and hundreds of thousands of other Europeans served in the Grand Army.

As Napoleon strengthened his grip on most of Europe, one lustrous prize lay beyond his reach—Britain. Any thought of invading the island nation—and the emperor thought about it obsessively—was checked by the Royal Navy's complete command of the Channel. Could he, then, defeat Britain economically if not militarily? From the beginning of their wars in the 1790s, the two countries had been blockading each other, though with limited effect. In 1806, Napoleon tightened the screws, and the British replied in kind. The mutual blockade had its own momentum—the longer it lasted, the wider the impact, as new ports and shipping routes and neutral ships were drawn in.

But economic warfare was all too slow for Napoleon, compared to the lightning victories of his armies. He had the burden of regulating shipping through the numberless ports of his empire, which entangled him all the more with the complex economics and petty politics of allies and satellites. Few of them, of course, were *voluntary* participants in the grand design, which depended on his continued military control of the continent.

For all his sweeping continental schemes, Napoleon was, as in France, far more occupier than liberator, in some places restorer and in others modernizer, but nowhere a transforming leader. Many Europeans inspired by Enlightenment ideals had sought to lead their people as indigenous reformers or revolutionaries and had failed. Now they hoped that the emperor would be a benign transformer of their backward states into enlightened democracies. But they found Napoleon a fanatic apostle of order and, above all, a compulsive warrior.

"Kings, and Persons of Soveraigne authority," wrote Hobbes, "because of their Independency, are in continuall jealousies, and in the state and posture of Gladiators; having their weapons pointing, and their eyes fixed on one another; that is, their Forts, Garrisons, and Guns upon the Frontiers of their Kingdomes; and continuall Spyes upon their neighbours; which is a posture of War."

THE ABDICATION OF THE PEOPLE

Where did Napoleon's fall begin? Was it on the battlefield, with his defeat at Leipzig, or at Moscow, or in Spain? Was it on the seas, with his naval disasters at the hands of the British? Or was it in the character of a man who became so heady with victories that he could not imagine defeat until the mounting successes became unmanageable? Or was it in the leadership of an emperor whose appeal to the people rested on the power and glory of his arms, not a grasp of their real wants and needs?

It was the people of Europe in the end—their abdication from his imperial vision—that brought him down: the peasants and the landowners, the artisans and the laborers, the merchants and the lawyers, the priests and the nonbelievers, the patricians and the servants, the villagers and the urbanites, the royalists and the Jacobins, the soldiers and the sailors. They, in the end, collectively determined the emperor's fate. Napoleon is so vivid historically, so sharply illuminated, that we lose sight of the people in the shadows, in the city streets and the distant countryside. It is impossible to capture them in their endless complexities, economic and social, political and religious, but we do know what Europeans were *not*—they were not profoundly revolutionary. But neither was Napoleon bringing liberation; he imposed subjection to a new authority, an occupier. He brought not Enlightenment but the sword.

On the periphery of his empire, Spain provided a sample of the maze of conflict that would destroy him. French hegemony in Spain was vulnerable to British domination of Portuguese ports. The rural population was profoundly Catholic and hostile to Enlightenment ideas that wafted over from France. Despite the emperor's promise to deliver "the benefits of reform without annoyances, disorders or convulsions," the Napoleonic regime in Spain gave them little reason to change their minds. The small party of liberal intellectuals and politicians who fought Catholic domination in the name of liberty and tolerance could gain little traction as patriotic feeling was aroused by the invaders. Compounding all was a throne brutally contested by King Charles and his usurper son Ferdinand, a conflict in which all rival forces took sides.

So intense was that struggle that Napoleon abruptly plucked his brother Joseph from his Neapolitan kingdom and made him king of Spain. But before Joseph could reach his new capital, Madrid was rocked by popular rebellions that swiftly spread to Seville in the south and the Asturias in the north and then across the country. Opposition became organized when peasant guerrillas and regulars, with backing from the Catholic Church, began to attack French convoys and Spanish collaborators. In July 1808, a Spanish force of thirty thousand, aided by guerrillas, overwhelmed two French divisions. The emperor dispatched more troops from the Grand Army and came himself to assume command. But now the British saw their chance. Landing thirteen thousand men in Portugal under the command of the Duke of Wellington, they began to supply the Spanish insurgents. The British avoided pitched battles, but the ensuing stalemate served them: Spain became a running sore for Napoleon, a bloody drain of men and materièl.

Liberalism in Spain, fragile at best, caught between French imperialism and Spanish patriotism, was crushed in the war. Hundreds of miles to the east, the situation was quite different. Their catastrophic defeat at Jena, the university city in central Germany, in 1806, drove home to Prussian officers the superiority of the dynamic French fighting style over their traditional rigid formations. Now they pushed tactics of skirmishing and advancing in columns rather than fronts. But the defeat spurred broader reforms in Prussia. Liberals took a radical step in abolishing serfdom. They attacked the power of the guilds, strengthened secondary education, and ended discrimination against Jews, who now would be legally free to work where they wished and serve in the military. While the changes were mixed in impact, often short-lived, and destined to be swallowed up in wars to come, an advanced guard of enlightened liberals demonstrated what could be done even amid the devastation of Napoleon's wars.

. . .

Napoleon's assault on Russia has long served as a classic example of a military campaign gone disastrously wrong. It was a disaster of leadership, too, as the emperor threw away an opportunity that might in the long run have helped produce a transformation in Russian life and liberty. It might also have altered his own fate. When Napoleon invaded Russia, Herold wrote, he did not anticipate "that in addition to the Russian army, of whose command he had a low opinion, he would have to fight the Russian people— that 'blind and apathetic mass' of superstitious barbarians." Russia's oppressed and impoverished serfs might have been aroused by a leadership that offered hope. Perhaps Napoleon could have also mobilized another element indispensable to a revolutionary effort in Russia—that part of the nobility and intelligentsia that had been exposed to Enlightenment values. But as elsewhere he came as a conqueror, not a reformer.

It had been Tsar Alexander's grandmother, Catherine the Great, reigning from 1762 to 1796, who brought the Enlightenment to Russia—or at least some measure of it to a small circle of Russians. Like a good student she schooled herself in advanced ideas, including her "prayer-book" lessons from Montesquieu's *Spirit of the Laws,* which, along with Tacitus, "produced a revolution in my thinking." Her keen mind was stimulated by a long and spirited exchange of letters with Voltaire and a visit from Diderot. Still, in her time, the ideas of the philosophes hardly penetrated Russia beyond a few nobles, functionaries, and educated bourgeois. Even Catherine's close advisors fought off reform. She complained they had "erased more than half" of her "Instructions" to a committee she had created to codify Russia's laws in the spirit of Montesquieu, including her reformist remarks on serfdom. But though she had once proclaimed liberty "the soul of everything," Catherine herself never dreamed of yielding her autocratic powers or of freeing the serfs, whose oppression in fact deepened during her reign.

Her grandson Alexander, who as a youth had been tutored in the most modern ideas by a Swiss republican, had been known to talk even about leading a Russian revolution—the "best sort of revolution," he said, creating a constitutional monarchy supported by an enlightened people. His first years after he became tsar in 1801 also seemed promising, though his reforms made little progress. He sought to carry out the codification of Russia's laws, with the eventual goal of bestowing civil rights on his people. A new Ministry of Public Enlightenment began planning for a general, classless school system. And Alexander promised to improve the lot of peasants. He claimed he would risk his life to emancipate the serfs—when the time was right.

But Alexander's ambitions turned increasingly to the world stage, and the right time, much to the frustration of the growing number of enlightened Russians whose expectations he had sent sky-high, receded into the future. He was enthralled by his confrontation with the great French conqueror, and what Herold said of Napoleon—that he regarded "war as a personal contest for power among sovereigns," a concept that was a relic of feudal times—could also have been said of the tsar.

· · ·

Alexander's prestige in Europe swelled as his relationship with Napoleon deteriorated. Emperor and tsar, so flirtatious at Tilsit in 1807, now, three years later, viewed one another with disdain and suspicion, sharpening mutual grievances. Napoleon, for instance, had earlier carved a "Grand Duchy of Warsaw" out of Prussian Poland. On Alexander's doorstep, the Duchy challenged his domination of the turbulent Poles, while also serving as a ready base for a potential attack against Russia. Most unacceptable to Napoleon was the tsar's breach of the Continental System. He decided on war when, late in December 1810, Alexander opened Russian ports to neutral ships and hence to English trade. After massive preparations, the emperor led his army across the Niemen in June 1812.

Napoleon's Russian campaign was an epic, catastrophic instance of one man's hubris and folly: French and allied troops pushing into Russia on a broad front seeking to encircle and destroy the tsar's army in one climactic battle, with Napoleon so sure of a quick victory that he issued his troops a four-day bread ration with a three-day backup of flour; the Russians retreating, retreating, leaving empty villages and plowed-up fields until their commander, Kutuzov, finally turned on his pursuers at Borodino, inflicting—and suffering—heavy casualties before retreating behind Moscow; the emperor vainly waiting for Alexander's surrender rather than doing "the one thing," according to George Rudé, "that might have turned the scales against his opponents by liberating the Russian peasants from serfdom." Napoleon waited too long, to the onset of an arctic winter.

Only a Tolstoy could do justice to the nightmarish retreat: the miles-long train of soldiers loaded down with loot; women, refugees, children, prostitutes, and other camp followers choking roads that passed through battlefields full of skeletons and rotting corpses; mounting deaths and desertions from cold and hunger; the remnants of the Grand Army staggering back across the Niemen, reversing the triumphal march of six months earlier. Since then, 370,000 French soldiers had died, and 200,000 more were in Russian captivity.

Amazingly, back in Paris, Napoleon was able to muster tens of thousands more recruits and field a new army. But his prestige and his luck were now up for question, and he appeared to have lost his old steadfastness and skill. He faced a vast array of enemies, not only Russians but Prussians and Austrians and Swedes, all of whom united to defeat him decisively at Leipzig in October 1813. With much of his empire forfeit and the allies ready to march into France itself, Napoleon raised the old revolutionary cry of *la patrie est en danger,* but, as Rudé asked, how *could* he?—after parading for years "his contempt for '*la vile populace,*'" governing by decree, and discouraging popular initiatives? After almost a million war deaths and all glory faded, the weary French would not respond. Soon his foes closed in on Paris and, rather magnanimously, offered him a haven on the Mediterranean island of Elba.

* * *

During his ten months of exile on the tiny isle, Napoleon—ever the organization man—busied himself with tidying up its budget and administration. But mainly he waited for news from Paris, which proved encouraging. The allies were already bickering with one another. Louis XVIII, brother of the late king, installed by the coalition in the Tuileries, was rapidly losing popularity. Hosts of Frenchmen, Napoleon was told, already wanted him back. In February 1815 he embarked with a thousand men and two cannon, miraculously eluded patrolling British cruisers, and landed on French soil. Then began the storied Hundred Days.

Earlier, en route to exile, Napoleon had encountered hostile mobs in southern France and heard screams that he was a butcher who had lost them their husbands, fathers, sons. He had finished his flight in disguise. Now, on his way north, his trip became a triumphal procession, with old soldiers rallying to his summons: "Come and range yourselves under the flags of your leader! He has no existence except in your existence; he has no rights except your rights and those of the people." Louis XVIII fled from

Paris with his ministers and courtiers. Reinstated in the Tuileries, Napoleon drafted a new constitution and had it ratified by a plebiscite that attracted far fewer voters than the plebescites of his glory years. This apathy suggested the people's abdication, so he pumped up his appeals to them. It was the "men born in the upper classes of society who have dishonored the name of France," he told a delegation of workers.

Once again he turned to the art in which he excelled—raising an army. Starting with only fifty thousand battle-ready troops, he called up veterans, the National Guard, naval units, part of the constabulary, and ordinary workingmen. Meanwhile, his enemies were scarcely idle. His nemesis, the Duke of Wellington, was forming an Anglo-Dutch army in Belgium, and the Austrians and Prussians prepared to take the field against their old foe. With some of his former aggressiveness, Napoleon fell upon the allied forces and tried to separate them; after some initial successes he concentrated on Wellington's defenses near the village of Waterloo in Belgium. In a six-hour battle on June 18, 1815, Dutch and Belgian forces fell back, but not Wellington's infantry. Desperately Napoleon threw his prized Old Guard reserves into the fray, but to no avail; the allied infantry, reinforced by late-arriving German troops, held their ground under intense fire. Napoleon suddenly quit the field and, with the Prussians in hot pursuit, fled to Paris.

There, extraordinarily, people were still with him. He was urged to dismiss the Chamber of Deputies, which was demanding his abdication, and to rule as a populist dictator. But Napoleon refused to become "Emperor of the rabble," final proof of his contempt for those who had backed him for so long and from whom he had demanded so much. Probably, even this scorned title was not an option—the allies, Louis XVIII in tow, were approaching the gates of Paris. He had little real alternative to abdication—and flight.

What haven now could the fallen emperor find? America beckoned. A frigate was available at Rochefort, but that port was under British blockade. For four agonizing days he awaited favorable winds. But, alerted by the turncoat Fouché, the British closed in. Soon Napoleon was their guest on a ten-week voyage not to America but to St. Helena, a speck of land in the south Atlantic. The emperor was even denied a conspicuous exit.

And what might he have dreamed about as he looked to exile in America? Simply to retire and write his memoirs? Possibly. Stage yet another return to France, as he had done from Elba? Or plot some kind of backwoods adventure? He would confide to his captive audience at St. Helena plans for creating his own state somewhere near the Canadian border. There, he vowed, he would reignite the Revolution, first with French Canadians unhappy with British rule and then the tens of millions of enlightened Europeans disgruntled with the restoration—yes, restoration—of the prerevolutionary order.

RESTORATION?

What had begun as an ideologically charged war between the forces of revolution and the armies of reaction nearly a quarter century earlier was finally over, after millions of deaths and turmoil that touched every continent on earth. Meeting in congress at Vienna after Napoleon's first abdication and again in Paris after Waterloo, the victorious monarchs and ministers swiftly rearranged territories and distributed prizes. Each of the major allies—Russia, Austria, Germany, and England—made gains that improved their security while swearing solemn pacts to act in concert to restore order in Europe and preserve it far into the future.

Order—that was their common purpose, their obsession. Order was the negative, the negation of a revolution whose last embers they were determined to stamp out, along with the spirit—the enlightened ideals—that had lit the fire. This was the dream of transforming leaders, but transformation in reverse, the restoration of a former regime.

The years after Napoleon's collapse indeed came to be known as the age of Restoration, with kings regaining their authority and liberal ideas suppressed. To reactionaries, the French Revolution had been a monstrous aberration imposed by unscrupulous fanatics on an unwilling or deluded people. They denied that it was inevitable or the fault of the ancien régime. They denied that it had popular support or that conditions had been all that bad back in 1789. The bloody Revolution in fact confirmed their faith that order and security were the only foundations of government and policy.

Against Enlightenment ideas of reason and democracy, of liberty, equality, fraternity, the men who vanquished Napoleon countered with a renewed and robust conservatism. The anarchy of popular rule would yield to monarchies hedged about by submissive but strong aristocracies and even stronger and larger corps of police. Instead of the "leveling" of Enlightenment egalitarianism, strict, even severe, class differences would be undergirded by reverence for private property. Rather than possessing rights, people owed their rulers obedience. The counter-Enlightenment claimed the sanction of "tradition," rooted in medieval times and brandished against any threat of progress.

Tradition's bastion was Restoration Christianity. The Catholic Church, recovering after its Napoleonic humiliations, regained confiscated lands and control of education. Following ancient fashion, it blessed kings as God's earthly agents. In Protestant countries, too, churches often served reaction. Prussia forced the union of Lutheran and Calvinist churches to strengthen religious resistance to liberalism. England's Anglican Church, with its monopoly of power, its wealth and aristocratic leadership, formed a natural alliance with the enemies of reform.

Among the royals gathered at Vienna, strangest yet most telling and tragic was the turn taken by Tsar Alexander. Hope of Russia's small but growing cadre of liberals, Alexander had become a fervent reader of scripture, gradually surrendering to mysticism under the influence of a Latvian baroness who doubled as a prophet. He left Vienna dissatisfied with the Realpolitik practiced at the conference. The agreements there did not promise moral or intellectual regeneration but rather a perpetuation of the corruption responsible for the catastrophes of the past quarter century. The tsar grew determined to set the future course of Europe on a virtuous Christian plane.

So, when allied leaders met again in Paris in the fall of 1815, after Napoleon's second abdication, the tsar suddenly presented his fellow sovereigns, the Austrian emperor Francis and Prussia's King Frederick William, with the draft of a "Holy Alliance." This manifesto opened with a statement of repentance and reform: The monarchs agreed, it said, that "the course, formerly adopted by the powers in their mutual relations had to be fundamentally changed," urgently replaced "with an order of things based on the exalted truths of the eternal religion of our Saviour." As his biographer Alan Palmer wrote, Frederick William, "whose dreams at times soared similarly to the sublime, welcomed the project, though he barely disguised the fact he did not understand it." But Francis concluded that the tsar was mad, and his foreign minister Metternich muttered that the proclamation was a "loud sounding nothing." The Duke of Wellington, listening to Alexander's presentation, could hardly keep a straight face.

Yet Metternich saw how he might turn the tsar's idealistic draft to his own purposes, tainting Alexander's high-minded Christian principles with a dose of cold policy. The tsar graciously agreed to changes of wording suggested by the Austrian foreign minister that, though he failed to see it, transformed the character of his manifesto. Under Metternich's hand, the finished "Act of September 26, 1815" was less a repudiation of Realpolitik, less the call for "urgent" and "fundamental" reforms, for Christian statesmanship—less, in short, the "proclamation of a new era," in Henry Kissinger's words, than "an attack on the transformations wrought by the Revolution, as a promise to return to order." Subscribed to by all the monarchs of Europe except the British regent, the Ottoman sultan, and the pope, the Holy Alliance boldly put reaction under the cover of religion, with Metternich himself as chief priest and policeman.

* * *

Millions across Europe who had been born into a world that differed little, politically, economically, intellectually, from their ancestors' in the Middle Ages, regarded Napoleon Bonaparte as an embodiment of modernity and progress in the age of Enlightenment. In his aftermath, that grand movement of ideas and action appeared to be on the defensive, almost as beaten as the man himself. As counter-Enlightenments flourished, tradition seemed to be in the saddle. Yet even as ideas of progress were under heavy assault by ruling elites and their apologists, the force of progress was bursting through old restraints.

The monarchs who had gathered in Vienna and Paris with their retinues would soon discover that boundaries could be reset, government reestablished, order imposed, but that another revolution—with no headquarters, no central direction, proceeding by unknown laws to create a new world—was beyond their power to contain.

As it slowly radiated outward from its British core, the Industrial Revolution was a transforming, ultimately irresistible force, breaking and remaking economic and social structures and revolutionizing politics. While it originated in Enlightenment ideas of science and technology, of human striving and self-fulfillment, the Industrial Revolution would transform the Enlightenment itself as its diverse impacts on individuals and societies made themselves felt. New ideas—among them a rich, complex liberalism of the emerging middle class and a panoply of socialisms rising from the plight of the new urban working poor—would inspire new leaders to seek change in a renewal of the spirit of Enlightenment.

8

Britain: Industrializing Enlightenment

The origins of the Industrial Revolution lay in the scientific speculations and day-to-day innovations of thousands of Western European thinkers and tinkerers, in a remarkable display of mutuality between theory and practice. The "natural philosophy" of Isaac Newton, with its revolutionary physical laws of gravity, mechanics, optics, and the like, as well as the example of Newton's painstaking methods, helped make the British the leaders in economic transformation, far outdistancing their continental rivals.

A House of Lords Committee questions Richard Roc, a surveyor, over the diversion of water power by a proposed canal:

> *Suppose two shutters of a Mill of 4 feet are elevated 17 [inches] with 4 feet over them. What quantity of water flows in a minute?*
> *287 Tons per minute.*
> *That is when the water is 4 feet high from the bed of the river?*
> *Yes.*
> *Do you speak from observation or calculation?*
> *I calculated it from the Dimensions given by Mr. Snape.*
> *How do you ascertain it?*
> *By known Hydrostatick Principles . . .*

The "Principles" that men like Roc followed were typically drawn from Newtonian science. Mechanics, pneumatics, hydrostatics, hydrodynamics were useful to practical men who had to calculate how to move huge objects across hills and valleys or design waterwheels or harness steam to engines.

Often the practical men were dismissed as mere tinkerers, operating at a level far below the lofty scientists. Mostly they were self-described engineers or mechanics who found that science did not offer blueprints applicable to any and all needs. Perhaps following folk theories or a hunch, proceeding "by guess and by God," they would fashion their own working principles as they ran into endless problems of mining coal or channeling water. So they were forced to become innovators, and their successes—and mistakes—might in turn inform scientists.

This kind of linkage between high and low had been praised earlier by Francis Bacon, the seventeenth-century pioneer of empiricism, who observed that it was deemed a kind of "dishonour unto learning" to descend to practical matters, but in fact the "history of nature wrought or mechanical" was "the most radical and fundamental" natural philosophy, "operative to the endowment and benefit of man's life." Theorists and craftsmen could learn from one another, offering a classic example of a leader-follower interaction that converted followers into leaders of the original initiators.

Britain's extraordinary industrial leadership did not grow in a vacuum. Technological progress occurred in an environment where experimentation and innovation were becoming a way of life, embracing a wide diversity of skills. There was excellent schooling in both principles and practice, and a culture of enlightenment peopled by itinerant lecturers, booksellers, printers, librarians, and members of scientific, philosophical, and literary societies.

John Watt was a barely literate artisan who filled notebooks with an astonishing range of learning and speculation, from the theories of Copernicus to explorations in Newtonian mechanics, experiments to determine the weight of smoke, detailed sketches of an invention to measure the distance traveled by a ship at sea. Watt also offered himself as a teacher with a formidable curriculum: "square and cube roots, trigonometry, navigation, sailing by the arch of a great circle, doctrine of spherical triangles with the use of both globes, astronomy, dyaling, gauging of beer and wine, making of globes," all of which, he added, he could teach "either arithmetrically, geometrially or instrumentally."

It was a scrappy life and John Watt died poor. None of his inventions succeeded, and if not for a nephew who carefully preserved the notebooks, Watt would be entirely forgotten. But he represented the powerful drive for knowledge and the search for new ways to apply it that made eighteenth-century Britain a vast mutual education society that propelled economic development.

IDEAS AS CAPITAL

The rising demand for motive power spurred innovations that quickened eighteenth-century economies, overwhelming the feeble energies of man and animal. Water was a force of extraordinary potential but so far it had been harnessed only crudely. For centuries the waterwheel had powered flour mills and fulling operations and the bellows and hammers of iron-masters. The first steam engines, developed in the late seventeenth century, were essentially water pumps, ungainly contraptions modernized as min-ers dug deeper and needed more power to expel the water that flooded into the pits. Very inefficiently, the pumps also turned the grindstones of mill-ers. In 1711, a Devonshire blacksmith produced the Newcomen steam en-gine, which had a larger capacity and simpler mechanics than the pumps. By the 1770s, Newcastle alone could boast of almost seventy Newcomen engines. But these were still inefficient; the world was waiting not for incre-mental changes but a transformation.

Born in Scotland in 1736, grandson of a mathematics teacher, son of an architect and shipbuilder, and nephew of John Watt, James Watt even in his twenties was a model Enlightenment man. Settling in Glasgow, he first be-came a maker of scientific instruments, meanwhile mastering French, Ital-ian, and German. As his interests broadened he undertook investigations of such disparate phenomena as salt, water, and weather. Somehow during his busy middle years he became versed in ancient history and the fine arts, with a particular enthusiasm for poetry and music.

But James Watt was above all a practical, determined innovator when it came to steam engines. Much was later made of the story that he gained inspiration from watching a kettle boil, but in fact he learned most from continuing experiments in steam pressure and from studying the deficien-cies of existing technology. Eighty percent of the steam heat of a Newcomen engine, he found, was wasted. Watt's solution—his revolution—was to de-sign an engine that harnessed the steam power so that, with its property of expansion, it would drive the pistons, acting as a direct motive force in it-self.

His complex design was not easy to produce, requiring parts that were carefully measured, machined, and assembled. The practical Watt saw he needed workers of new skills to replace the tinsmiths and millwrights of old. The human task was tougher than the mechanical. He also needed financial backing. His initial partner, John Roebuck, provided capital for the first steam engine, set up near Edinburgh—a defective machine appropriately called Beelzebub. The venture failed when Roebuck became insolvent. The second investor had deeper pockets: Matthew Boulton, a manufacturer who owned a huge factory in Birmingham employing six hundred workers. Boulton's close involvement with Watt began in 1773 when he cancelled a debt Roebuck owed him in exchange for Roebuck's share in Watt's patent. The new partnership thrived quickly and was soon grinding out perfected "fire engines."

They gained a host of new partners as demand for the engines soared—not only other investors but the talented foremen and machinists, engineers and suppliers, who helped make Birmingham for a time the center of the Industrial Revolution. And at a critical juncture Watt won unusual allies—members of the House of Commons. Threatened by competition, he had appealed to Parliament in 1775 for an extension of his patent rights. Just before the vote Edmund Burke rose to attack Watt's "monopoly" as a threat to liberty, but the inventor won a patent extension of twenty-five years, which ensured that his steam engine design would supersede hydraulic power.

* * *

James Watt was first an inventor, but he became a supremely successful example of a new breed of men who were at the cutting edge of change in the Industrial Revolution: the entrepreneurs who saw the economic potential in new ideas and then went about raising capital, selecting managers, recruiting labor, securing supplies—all with an eye on the markets. Few if any were themselves as creative as Watt, but entrepreneurs were at the juncture of all the creative forces, putting them to work in tandem.

Where did such leadership come from? A century before Horatio Alger Jr., successful entrepreneurs boasted that they were "self-made men," rising from humble circumstances. Yet fewer than 10 percent of factory owners could claim fathers who had been factory hands. Most came from middle- or upper-class backgrounds, although there were striking exceptions. Textile baron Richard Arkwright was the thirteenth child of a poor barber, and William Hirst, born of impoverished parents, went to work at seven years of age, advanced to journeyman cropper, and finally built his own large mill. But the myth of rags to riches made the success of the entrepreneurs more than a story of opportunities seized and chances taken. It became a moral tale, of good character, hard work, and just reward. It was a story of heroism, not luck—or access to capital and credit. "It was among the fictions of Coketown," Charles Dickens would write in his novel *Hard Times*. "Any capitalist there, who had made sixty thousand pounds out of sixpence, always professed to wonder why the sixty thousand nearest Hands didn't each make sixty thousand pounds out of sixpence."

Few inhabited the role of entrepreneur more successfully than Matthew Boulton, Watt's business partner. His was no rags-to-riches story. The son of a manufacturer, he married an heiress. He had attended a religious academy in Birmingham and acquired a rudimentary knowledge of science and languages. On his father's death in 1759, he inherited a buckle business that he quickly expanded into the manufacture of buttons, silverware, steel jewelry, shoe ornaments, and a host of other such items. To power his factory, Boulton experimented with steam and even sent an engine model to an American acquaintance, Benjamin Franklin, appealing to his "fertile genius" to "preserve me from error." Still, Boulton's own genius was entrepreneurial. Even before he and Watt established Boulton & Watt in 1775, he demonstrated his creative business judgment and drive in securing funds, grasping the needs of the market, competing furiously with rivals in Britain and outside. He had no compunction about conducting patent battles, enticing skilled workers from home and abroad, exchanging trade secrets, or spying on competitors, who had their own tricks. But Boulton won friends as well as enemies—enough so as to be received more than once at the court of George III.

Josiah Wedgwood, "vase-maker general to the universe," rivaled Watt and Boulton in entrepreneurship and outdid them as a self-made man. Son of a potter, Wedgwood left school to join the family business at age nine when his father died, and a few years later he became an apprentice potter under an older brother. The apprenticeship was derailed when Wedgwood contracted smallpox, which gave him time to read voraciously, ranging from the arts of Greece and Rome to Rousseau. Smallpox left his right leg enfeebled; no longer able to work the foot pedal of a potter's wheel, he turned to the design of pottery. He was still in his thirties when he built a new factory that employed hundreds of artists and craftsmen. His experiments in the measurement of high temperatures helped win him membership in the Royal Society. He made the "Wedgwood" stamp famous, providing table china to inns and mansions across Europe. Insisting on the highest quality, Wedgwood, it was said, would roam the factory floors and smash any piece that was not perfect.

Yet he was more than a rugged capitalist. As an Enlightenment man, he held liberal views, opposing slavery, supporting free trade, sympathizing with the American Revolution and, for a time at least, with the French. He should rejoice, he said, "to see English liberty and security spread over the face of the earth, without being over-anxious about the effects they might have upon our manufactures or commerce, for I should be very loth to believe that an event so happy for mankind in general could be so injurious to us in particular." His most direct impact was on his own Staffordshire community, transforming scattered, impoverished villages into a land of prosperous potters.

* * *

A striking force that propelled the Industrial Revolution in the late 1700s was its collectivity—its philosophical internationalism, its community of intellectual leaders who crossed national borders, the interplay of scientific disciplines, the constant and close interaction of scientists, innovators, and entrepreneurs. To an extraordinary degree, considering travel conditions, leaders in these fields visited one another, despite fears of stolen ideas and pirated technologies. Much of the cross-fertilization took place in new scientific institutes, learned academies, and discussion groups. In Britain, these intellectual enterprises were by no means monopolized by London. Societies variously titled "literary" or "scientific" sprang up in smaller towns across the country. In the manufacturing centers of Manchester, Liverpool, Bristol, among others, inventors and entrepreneurs joined scientists and literary men for discussions both civil and contentious.

The most notable of these was the Lunar Society of Birmingham, so named because the members met during a full moon to ensure lighted journeys home. The dozen or so active participants included not only the luminaries Boulton, Watt, and Wedgwood but Erasmus Darwin, a poet, physician, and natural philosopher (and grandfather of the evolutionist); Joseph Priestley, the radical Unitarian clergyman who experimented in electricity and chemistry and was a discoverer of oxygen; and William Small, scientist, metallurgist, onetime teacher of Thomas Jefferson at the College of William and Mary. The group originated in shared admiration for that other famous American, Benjamin Franklin.

The Lunar Society has been called a forerunner of the modern science/technology research institute. Its members embraced an awe-inspiring array of scientific fields: metallurgy, chemistry, steam, optics, ornithology, geology, electricity, as well as their practical applications. They were creatively helpful to one another. "Wedgwood supplied chemical utensils for Priestley's experiments," historians A. E. Musson and Eric Robinson wrote, "while Priestley analysed minerals of possible utility in pottery." Patents and the tools of the clockmaking trade were topics of common interest, and the society naturally investigated improved designs of the steam engine. Boulton consulted with Darwin as well as with Franklin on a new engine he had developed.

The "Lunatics," as they referred to themselves, did their main collaboration through intensive correspondence; the meetings were reserved for general conversation that often ranged deeply into the moral issues of the time. Reform-minded, most members welcomed the American and French revolutions. Incensed by Priestley's support of the Jacobins, a Birmingham mob sacked his house, destroying his library and laboratory. The Lunatics strongly opposed slavery, with Wedgwood making hundreds of cameos of a kneeling slave in manacles crying out, "Am I not a man and a brother?"

THE TYRANNY OF THE MACHINE

The men of the Lunar Society, glittering successes in the economic revolution of the late eighteenth and early nineteenth centuries, were liberal, compassionate, and benevolent, yet the new enlightened economy of Britain that enriched them had a devastating impact on vast numbers of their fellow human beings. Too often the lives of the new English working class were indeed solitary, poor, nasty, brutish, and short. Working days in Manchester factories ran from twelve to fourteen hours, even for children thrown into mills at the tenderest age. "The nervous strain," wrote J. L. and Barbara Hammond, two British scholars who almost a century ago made an exhaustive study of the early Industrial Revolution, "of watching machinery and working with machinery aged men and women faster than the heaviest physical exertions." But the machines never tired.

Work in the mines was especially ghastly. Men, women, and boys labored hundreds of feet underground in foul air and constant danger from explosions or floods. At the Clan Down colliery, a Somerset magistrate wrote to the Home Office in 1817, where scores of laborers worked at depths of twelve hundred feet, "it is in the power of an idle or mischievous Engine Boy to drown the whole of them without destroying or injuring the Fire Engine." Machines of course could be salvaged.

A Tyldesley textile mill imposed fines of a shilling or more on any spinner who was found with his or her window open or who was heard whistling or arrived five minutes late or failed to find a substitute in case of illness. The latter reflected the new labor discipline: The time clock ruled. Factory women in Lancashire hardly had the opportunity to learn the basic tasks expected of them in domestic life. Existence in the ugly factory cities and mining towns was mean and squalid. The filthy, slapped-up housing and monotonous diets, together with the grueling labor, brought markedly higher mortality rates in "unhealthy districts," more than double among children, whose long working hours led to what one report described as "permanent deterioration of the physical constitution" and "the production of disease often wholly irremediable."

＊　＊　＊

The Industrial Revolution, the Hammonds memorably concluded, separated England from its past as completely as the French Revolution had severed France from its past. The pulverizing impact of this new world on work, community, and family, indeed on thought itself, intensified the chronic struggles of the poor as they attempted to improve their lives—above all, the challenges of fashioning an ideology that offered hope and direction for change and of developing their own leadership and mobilizing collective action. Social disorganization, stress, exhaustion, illness, illiteracy, inarticulateness, lack of self-confidence—these were hardly conditions for empowerment. The laboring poor were desperately dependent on others. In the Enlightenment world of the late 1700s, they found very few friends of high standing, for England was in the hands of men who, the Hammonds charged, "deliberately sought to make the inequalities of life the basis of the state, and to emphasise and perpetuate the position of the workpeople as a subject class." Far from offering leadership to the poor, the British ruling classes were intent—with their measures outlawing unions, political societies, public meetings—on denying those in need the means to take action together.

One result was an outburst of machine-breaking, a protest against the mechanization of traditional crafts that displaced skilled workers and pushed them into the maw of the mammoth new factories. Resisters took their name from a boy named Ludlam who "when ordered by his father, a frame-work knitter, to square his needles, took a hammer and beat them into a heap." Luddite outbreaks in Britain were far more extensive, varied, and dangerous than elsewhere. They also had a longer history. When entrepreneurs in the seventeenth century had imported Dutch engine looms, Londoners complained about the use of machines "for workinge of tape, lace, ribbon, and such, wherein one man doth more amongst them than seven English men can doe." In 1675, Spitalfield weavers had rioted against devices feared capable of doing the work of twenty men. But it was not until a century and a half later that Luddism erupted across England and, to a lesser extent, Scotland.

For the most part the Luddite outbursts of the early nineteenth century were local and short-lived, reflecting intense grievances, and were so varied by place and type of machine as to defy generalization. Croppers and stockingers appealed vainly to constitutional rights and Christian principles. Beset by spies and agents provocateurs, petitioners for redress were answered by a bill that made frame-breaking a capital offense. Frustrated workers became more and more violent. Luddism's climax came in attacks by crowds of hundreds in the industrial north. Food riots that broke out in Leeds, Sheffield, Nottingham, and elsewhere sometimes turned to machine-breaking. When a Yorkshire mill owner and notorious enemy of the Luddites was assassinated, the authorities responded with alacrity, sentencing a large number of workers to transportation to Australia for life and over a dozen to the noose.

In the end, the main significance of Luddism was its insignificance as a causal force. The violent response to mechanization was understandable yet self-defeating. Protesters struck out impulsively at immediate targets of their wrath, diverting them from political strategies of reform that might address the roots of their impoverishment and disempowerment. Local, uncoordinated, and spontaneous, machine-breaking reaped a few temporary victories but no fundamental change. While violent outbreaks probably sharpened class feeling, outrage was not channeled into a strategy of class struggle. In the early 1800s, reform required new strategies based on new political ideas.

PROPERTY AND POVERTY

Rarely have such large numbers of people confronted such harsh dilemmas of strategy and ideas as faced the workers of Britain in the early 1800s. The repression of the 1790s still worked for the rulers. Politicians with reform sympathies could gain no traction in the factionalized Parliament. Luddism was ultimately self-defeating. Alternatives still seemed limited.

Should reformers appeal as Englishmen to moral principle? Workers still were quoting Tom Paine and other radical thinkers, especially the idea that power that did not originate with the people inevitably violated the rights of man. But in the long wake of the French Revolution the noble concepts of popular sovereignty and natural rights still smacked too much of the Jacobins and their guillotines to be useful in public campaigns. And radical economists were only beginning to formulate theories along lines that John Locke and John Thelwall had advanced, that a man or woman's labor was the basic source of wealth, even the sole source of rights in property.

So, should activists focus on day-to-day trade union pressure and negotiation? Despite the Combination Acts, workers had formed unions, often labeled "friendly societies," and, despite frequent prosecutions, some survived. There were occasional strikes—Glasgow and Lancashire weavers, London shipwrights, Durham miners, Sheffield cutlers, and others walked out. Still, these were widely separated acts, often conducted by exclusive crafts and lacking national unity and impact. The Combination Acts were at last repealed in 1824, but the next year an Amending Act tightened restrictions on the newly legalized unions.

Should they concentrate on specific problems and policies? Like all good Englishmen, workers hated taxes. Most levies unfairly burdened them, especially on day-to-day articles of consumption, the necessities of life. Pervasive government corruption made that burden seem even heavier. But grumbling about taxes did little good when you couldn't vote.

What about revolution? Most impractical in the average worker's mind— but had not the Americans freed themselves of a king and the French beheaded theirs? Revolution was indeed considered seriously by a few leaders. As it stood, the odds clearly were daunting, given the power of the army against scattered revolutionary groups lacking any organized mass base. How could that mass base take form? Could even the bleakest misery of hundreds of thousands of workers support an uprising? Suffering was not automatically converted into militancy. Above all, revolution demanded brilliant and imaginative leadership and fresh, forceful ideas to kindle spirits of would-be revolutionaries.

But such ideas were as rare as transforming leaders. Britain's intellectual leadership of the time offered a formidable obstacle to any worker-based challenge to the status quo.

· · ·

Adam Smith's intellectual stock was rising in these years, at least in government and commercial circles. There was no greater apologist for capitalism at a time when the wealth of most industrializing nations was increasing sharply. Production expanded, foreign trade resumed after the wars, while workers' pay remained fairly static. Smith's classic findings on the virtues of "free enterprise" reverberated in people's minds and were trotted out by his disciples in debates over economic policy. His ideas were crucial to the growth of liberalism as the ideology of the Industrial Revolution's rising classes.

Less remembered were Smith's concerns about the potential failures of the system—his blunt statement in the *Wealth of Nations* that "no society can surely be flourishing and happy, of which the far greater part of the members are poor and miserable." Smith, like his philosophical Scottish brethren, had called for the happiness of all the people. But many disciples, though aware of the brutal effects of industrialization, shrugged them off as growing pains. In general, the Scottish economist J. R. McCulloch wrote complacently, "factory work-people, including non-adults, are as healthy and contented as any class of the community obliged to earn their bread by the sweat of their brow."

Another heir to Smith, David Ricardo, would grow more pessimistic about capitalism's benefits to working people. His Wage Fund theory held that wages should be limited for fear of damaging future production; hence the solution to poverty was not higher pay but harder work and greater productivity. Twelve hours a day evidently was not enough. But even the famous Ricardo could change his mind. In the first two editions of his *Principles of Political Economy and Taxation,* he contended that mechanization of production benefited all members of the community; a few years later, in his third edition, he conceded that machines could cause not only temporary hardships to workers who lost jobs but permanent displacement and migration of labor. If this concession disappointed his more conservative colleagues, he would receive a tribute years later from another economist. It showed, said Karl Marx, Ricardo's characteristic "scientific impartiality and love of truth."

The most formidable conservative thinker in the early decades of the Industrial Revolution, Jeremy Bentham, was all the more formidable because he did not loom as a conservative. Bentham liked to tell of stopping in as a young man at a coffeehouse in Oxford, his alma mater, where he had run across a pamphlet by Joseph Priestley that blazoned the words "the greatest happiness of the greatest number." Never mind that Priestley had probably never used the phrase, or that Bentham probably took it from an Italian philosopher who had borrowed it from Francis Hutcheson. Seized by the words, Bentham made them his own, even as he gave their meaning a hard twist.

For Hutcheson, happiness was grounded in sociability, empathy, and benevolence. For Bentham, it was an intensely individualistic quality, though scarcely recognizable as a feature of enlightened liberalism. He placed human beings under "two sovereign masters, *pain* and *pleasure*," that "govern us in all we do." Happiness was the maximization of pleasure, the avoidance of pain—the "only right and proper and universally desirable, end of human action." For Bentham, happiness was grounded in security, abundance, and equality, values that were not delivered from heaven or derived by reason but emanated from the practical arrangements—especially the laws—of a society. Bentham listed security in the first place, as essential to the others. And security was based on the stabilizing social effects and individual liberties derived from private property.

But unlike Locke and most of the political thinkers who followed in his wake, Bentham did not call private property a natural right. He disdained the very idea of the natural rights preached by American and French revolutionaries. Of the articles of the French Declaration of the Rights of Man and the Citizen, with their assertion that the purpose of all political associations was to protect people's natural rights, Bentham wrote scornfully in 1789 that they "must come under three heads—1. Unintelligible; 2. False; 3. A mixture of both."

Bentham's crucial objection to natural rights rested in the awesome power he vested in legislatures. They should not, he insisted, be restrained in any way from making such laws as they thought necessary to the greatest happiness of the greatest number. The doctrine of natural rights, however, held that such rights were superior to law, a check and limit to legislation, a standard to which men might appeal against unjust or oppressive government. To Bentham this was absurd nonsense: "to talk of what the law—the supreme legislature of the country, acknowledged as such—*can* not do!—to talk of a *void* law, as you would of a void order or judgment!—the very act of bringing such words into conjunction is either the vilest of nonsense, or the worst of treasons:—treason—not against one branch of the sovereignty, but against the whole:—treason not against this or that government, but against all governments."

Bentham described Englishmen as "lords of their own property," subject "only to the regulations of the legislature." But Parliament could "dispose of any part or all of it" without consent, if needed for "the public good." Despite this qualification, Bentham believed that property was more secure when protected by positive law than by the "nonsense upon stilts" of natural rights. What "his utilitarianism took away in theory," political scientist Thomas Horne wrote, "it gave back in practice, providing an extraordinarily strong defense of private property combined with a defense of a legal right to aid" to the poor. Bentham based the latter in the utilitarian principle of relieving suffering, though his plan for "pauper management improvement" was characteristically severe and unbending. The poor were to be incarcerated and kept at work under a cunningly—even cruelly—devised system of constant supervision. All this left Bentham looking like a hard-edged philosophical Tory, appropriate for a young Londoner living on a comfortable income. But the new century would see the emergence of a new Bentham with new ideas as he confronted the practical problems rising from the Industrial Revolution.

The challenge for Bentham as for other reformers was to convert his many plans into action. If Parliament was to be fit to make wise and just laws, its members must be men of sound principles, which in turn meant that they must be selected not by aristocrats or—increasingly—capitalists, but by the people. And if the voice of the people was to be controlling, they must have wide suffrage, annual elections, equal electoral districts, the secret ballot. Such concerns inevitably enmeshed Bentham in the growing agitation for parliamentary reform. He had long believed in voting reform, but with crippling restrictions. Then in 1817 he produced a *Plan for Parliamentary Reform* that came out for suffrage leading to the representative democracy he believed would provide the strongest security for property, suffrage that was virtually universal, practically equal, free, and secret—except for the exclusion of women. Women's suffrage, he argued, was perfectly just and inevitable, but "altogether premature."

Bentham was at pains to make clear that his plan was no radical innovation. Quite the contrary: The restoration of rule by "freely chosen deputies of the body of the people" that had disappeared in the War of the Roses would bring "political salvation." That, he insisted as he surveyed the centuries-old corruption and misrule of British government, must be the "ultimate end."

THE NEW RADICALS

Jeremy Bentham offered intellectual firepower to the cause of parliamentary reform, but who would inspire activist leadership to improve the lives of working people? Few could surpass Robert Owen in diverse, even antithetical talents and principles—a self-made employer of thousands who sought to be just to his factory workers, a capitalist who took leadership of the trade union movement, a rugged individualist and free enterpriser in practice yet a prophet of "Co-operative Socialism," a foe of the Christian churches who bored listeners with his own nonstop moralizing. Born in central Wales in 1771, the son of a saddler and ironmonger, he became such a successful manufacturer in Manchester that he was able to purchase the huge New Lanark cotton mills and turn them into enormously profitable enterprises.

Though he epitomized entrepreneurial achievement in the early Industrial Revolution, Owen was appalled by the devastation the new economy brought to working men, women, and children, and by the indifference, at best, of his own new class of entrepreneurs—factory owners, financiers, mining magnates—and of most politicians in Parliament. Owen was an instinctual reformer, a native problem solver, with a deep faith in the malleability of men—that they could be changed and improved by transforming their environment.

So Owen became an activist in industry and politics. He first tried to set an example at New Lanark by maintaining good working conditions and paying proper wages, even though his partners disagreed with him and almost managed to freeze him out. With his view of human educability, he preached the need for better popular schools. And he worked with Sir Robert Peel and political reformers for passage of the Factory Act in 1819. The first law to regulate factory conditions, it made nine the minimum age for employment in the textile mills and twelve hours the maximum working day for children under sixteen!

The Act did little to temper the inhumanity of factory work and Owen was dissatisfied. Prospects for further reform were dim, the conservative bastion appeared virtually impregnable. Was there a better reform strategy? To help the jobless, Owen had proposed "Villages of Co-operation" that would enable the indigent to earn their own keep through collective farming. But this was not enough, either—world regeneration was needed to overcome cruelties of the profit system. His new solution was to extend the cooperative village idea to the whole globe and to include industrial settlements, along with agricultural.

He would begin in America, leaving the "Old, Immoral World" behind him as he experimented in the "comparatively uncorrupted atmosphere of the United States." Journeying to Indiana in 1824 he visited a community called New Harmony, which so met his ideals that he bought it lock, stock, and barrel from the Rappites, a religious group that had arrived from Germany twenty years earlier. Here Owen would establish a truly communal form of living that would elevate village harmony even over conventional marriage and family life.

The discipline Owen would impose on his villagers was severe, total, and heavily moralized. They would have no choice but to live communally, in closely planned settlements, under complex self-regulations. Moral improvement was the goal, with labor and education as exercises in character building. Owen's ultimate aim was to replace "the habits of the individual system" with those of the "Social System."

According to Josiah Warren, a pioneering American anarchist and member of the colony, it was this discipline that doomed New Harmony to failure after only four years. So rigid were the colony's rules of cooperation that they prevented the "compromises and concessions" necessary for true cooperation. Instead, Warren concluded, "the difference of opinion, tasks and purposes *increased* just in proportion to the demand for conformity," and thus common interest was put "directly at war with the individualities of persons and circumstances," leaving the experimenters "in despair of all reforms."

. . .

For all the stringencies of Owenism, it quickly attracted working-class disciples in England. Societies, newspapers, and discussion groups devoted to Owen's ideas appeared in the early 1820s. His vision of an orderly community working cooperatively for the common good appealed to many people as a new religion. But the response also reflected the persistent lack of alternatives. Nothing better epitomized Parliament's idea of the place of workers in the British political economy than its response in 1808 to a petition from Lancashire cotton weavers for a minimum wage. A "select committee" sternly lectured the weavers on their "perfect Liberty" to earn what their employers chose to pay them under conditions employers imposed. Interference with that "Freedom" would threaten the "prosperity and happiness of the community."

Blocked at every turn, increasing numbers of workers were joining hands with the middle-class radicals who for years had been agitating for the reform of Parliament—expansion of suffrage, elimination of rotten boroughs, curtailment of patronage and corruption. The reform campaign had suffered defeat after defeat in Parliament. Efforts to create a unified party committed to reform collapsed. After a particularly bitter defeat in 1812, one radical leader decided to take reform to the people, on a platform of universal manhood suffrage.

John Cartwright was a prime example of the versatility of Enlightenment leaders—naval officer, militia major, experimental farmer, liberal-minded mill owner, and indefatigable reformer. His first pamphlet on reform had been published in 1776, envisioning a national movement that embraced all classes. Nearly four decades later, in the 1810s, Cartwright set out on a series of "missionary tours" to the provinces, to build the broadest popular base for reform. For a petition campaign, he collected a million and a half signatures through a new network of reform societies. Their members, according to historian Naomi Churgin Miller, included "small manufacturers and artisans: cobblers, weavers, framesmiths, mechanics, cutlers, printers, hatters, drapers." Still, it was not enough. Parliament turned away the petitions with disdain and Cartwright was threatened with prosecution for conspiracy.

In late 1816, another leading radical, Henry Hunt, accepted an invitation from a group of working-class radicals to address a demonstration at London's Spa Fields. From a prosperous country family, Hunt had arrived at radicalism from Whiggery through disillusion. A powerful speaker, he was viewed by many more moderate radicals as a demagogue too eager for the applause of the "dangerous classes." But workers adored him. At Spa Fields, the crowd was so great that Hunt had to speak from a window overlooking the fields. That meeting gave new urgency to the radical campaign for universal manhood suffrage.

Hunt's strategy was to serve Parliament not with petitions—humble prayers—but with remonstrances. As one working-class leader said, "Why not go forth as the Barons of old with a Sword in one hand and the Bill of Rights in the other and demand your Birthrights." A series of outdoor meetings climaxed in August 1819 when a huge crowd of protesting millworkers and handloom weavers gathered in St. Peter's Field, near the center of Manchester, to hear Henry Hunt's call for parliamentary reform. It was a largely peaceful, disciplined affair until the local authorities tried to arrest Hunt. Hussars rode into the packed crowd with swinging sabers, "cutting most indiscriminately to the right and to the left," wrote one witness. As people fled in "utter rout and confusion," hundreds were trampled. Eleven persons were killed and 160 were reported to have suffered saber wounds.

To a shocked British public, St. Peter's Field came quickly to be known as the "Peterloo massacre." It was also class war, provoked by Manchester capitalists and the intransigence of Britain's political elites. Above all, E. P. Thompson, historian of the English working class, concluded, it was a defining event, "a formative experience in British political and social history." It raised fundamental questions about what remained of the liberties of "free-born Englishmen." "No one," Thompson wrote, "could remain neutral."

At least protesters and reformers could retaliate in the press. The satirist William Hone parodied a "speech from the throne" at the opening of Parliament.

> *Reform, Reform, the swinish rabble cry—*
> *Meaning, of course, rebellion, blood, and riot—*
> *Audacious rascals! you, my Lords, and I,*
> *Know 'tis their duty to be starved in quiet.*

An awakening class of workers saw their real duty as demanding their rights as Englishmen and women. They sought political equality and working conditions that reflected and respected their central place in the new economy. For leading them—for, that is, inciting the king's subjects "to contempt and hatred for the government and constitution"—the hero of Peterloo, Henry Hunt, was sentenced to thirty months' imprisonment.

9

France: The Crowds of July

On a February day in 1819, not far from Lyon, police were spotted escorting a wagon carrying a huge, ungainly contraption to a Vienne factory. As it crossed a riverlet the wheels stuck in a mudbank. From their houses along the stream, village locals showered the police with rocks. Soon some attackers plunged into the cold water, clambered up on the wagon, and struck heavy blows on the contraption with their big shearing scissors. The object of their wrath, the Grande Tondeuse, was a new machine for shearing, glossing, and brushing large measures of cloth far more quickly than human hands could—and it needed only three operators.

Mounted dragoons stormed in. When fainthearts in the mob dithered, women urged them on. "The men are cowards," cried out wool workers Marie and Marianne Mange. "Ah, if we were only men!" Charging with drawn sabers, cavalrymen wounded several rioters and drove others away. Soon the Grande Tondeuse was pulled out of the water and repaired. It began operating a few days later, while shearers long known for their craft skills looked on in fury.

* * *

France seemed poised to challenge British scientific and technological leadership in the Industrial Revolution. Both nations were large and populous, with extensive resources at home and abroad, huge domestic markets, great cities and trading ports, and a capable and intelligent working class. Each was a home to the Enlightenment. Yet the British were at least a generation ahead of the French in industrial innovation and development.

Why the difference? A crucial reason was the top-down leadership of the French compared with bottom-up British innovation. The French state, whether monarchical, revolutionary, or Napoleonic, played a more central role in the economy than did the British government. Yet the focus of the ancien régime had been on defense-related enterprises such as military engineering; aside from "scientific farming," royal Paris did not actively promote key economic sectors or encourage what historian Margaret Jacob called the "gentlemanly zeal for practical science" so widespread in England. Nor did it make haste to clear away obstacles, especially those put up by the church; the Jesuits resisted Newtonianism until the order was expelled from France in the early 1760s.

French revolutionary leaders proposed to set up a "Factory for Improvement" open to all for mechanical training and to learn the "rapport" between theory and practice, but as the Revolution sank into chaos, little came of such initiatives. It was not until the Napoleonic era, amid much talk of "enlightenment in the principles of the arts," when young, thrusting men under imperial leadership shook up entrenched methods and hierarchies, that the French began to catch up with their British competitors in key fields.

Yet the chasm in economic leadership between the two nations remained profound. Their differences were fundamentally intellectual and cultural, reflecting the contrasting forms Enlightenment took in the two countries. French science education tended to be abstract, showing its Cartesian roots; British engineers innovated water power development, while mathematicians led the French effort. Moreover, French academicians lacked the freedom of inquiry enjoyed by British universities, including Oxbridge. On balance Britain was a looser, more individualistic society, open to experiment and change, more willing to reward its innovators like Watt.

The response of workers to industrialization also reflected cultural differences. In a less individualistic society, with labor controlled for centuries by powerful guilds, French workers were readier to band together in militant action to defend their collective interests. For instance, while worker combinations were banned during the Revolution, informal associations played a significant role, including the sansculottes with their populist demands to take the Revolution in ever more radical directions. As in Britain, most of these informal associations were transient, but the deep French instinct for collective action prepared workers for interventions in politics in the decades after the Revolution and inspired intellectual leaders as they shaped their responses to industrialization.

Authority's answer to worker unrest, however, was no less brutal than in Britain, even as old habits of thought and deference remained. In 1819, some desperate shearers appealed to the Vienne police for protection against the

Grande Tondeuse. One spoke of Louis XVIII as "a good king, a paternal king who loves his subjects," and said that if the king understood "that this machine would reduce many of us to beggary, he would not let it be introduced." It was Paris, of course, that had sent the cavalry to protect the machine against the people.

THE LIBERAL REVOLT

Louis XVIII, unlike his brother, the deposed and decapitated Louis XVI, did not seek to govern France like the kings of old. He was painfully aware that the Bourbon "restoration" had been imposed on a defeated nation by the bayonets of the allies. Immediately the new king confronted political polarization between Ultra-Royalists agitating for a return to the ancien régime in full and those who still looked for inspiration to the Revolution in one or another of its many faces. Louis's policy was conciliation, a role to which this king, an old man described by historian D. W. Brogan as "fat, lame, gouty, impotent," and also lazy, selfish, intelligent, even Voltairean, was especially well suited. He refused, he declared, to be "the king of two peoples"—the reactionaries and liberals—so "to the ultimate fusion of these all the efforts of my government are directed." He would rule constitutionally, issuing a Charter that he proclaimed was his gift to France. While avoiding the revolutionary language of rights, the Charter flaunted its enlightened character, recognizing principles of liberty, equality, and property, as well as freedoms of religion and, to a limited degree, of the press. On the other hand, it reestablished Catholicism as the state religion.

Among royal compromises was the creation of a bicameral legislature that guaranteed public representation in permanent institutions. But the king retained the authority to initiate and promulgate laws and the suffrage was so narrow—limited to men over age thirty who paid at least 300 francs in taxes—that only one hundred thousand of thirty million citizens were eligible to vote.

In its moderate, mixed principles, Louis's Charter bore a resemblance to the first Constitution of 1791. This infuriated the Ultra-Royalists, whose aim was to erase any trace of enlightened government in France. Though the Charter did not satisfy liberals, either—their aim was to extend and deepen its liberties—they defended their generous interpretation of it against the assaults of reactionaries. In the first years of his reign, Louis was able to check and balance these opponents, but by 1820, as he succumbed to the charms of a certain Madame du Cayla, an Ultra plant in the royal household, the reactionaries were in the ascendant, their repressive policies driving liberals to conspiracy in the secretive Carbonari movement. Composed of republicans and Bonapartists, soldiers and civilians, young politicians and old revolutionaries like the Marquis de Lafayette, the Carbonari tried to organize uprisings against the Ultra-dominated administration. But their campaign was short-lived, destroyed by the government's violent response and their own divisions.

Quickly though the movement collapsed, it proved a training ground for liberals who would act when the crisis of the regime approached. The death of Louis XVIII in 1824 brought his brother to the throne, the Comte d'Artois, who had been the leader of the Ultras since the Restoration. He made his intentions clear with a traditional coronation in the Cathedral of Reims, complete with the new king's prostration before the archbishop. A monsignor gave a sermon denouncing his predecessor's Charter.

But the determination of Charles X to rule as kings had in bygone days faced two perils from the start. One came from monarchist circles, where moderates opposed the king's attempt to centralize power in the throne. A more serious threat came from France's rapidly growing middle class—the bourgeoisie—and its liberal beliefs.

As industrialization gathered pace in France, it brought prosperity to ever larger numbers of merchants and shopkeepers, entrepreneurs and professionals. Class structures, at least beneath the titled elite, grew more fluid, and much as in Britain and the United States, a doctrine of individualistic striving took hold. This "demand for self-determination," as R. R. Palmer called it, was the essence of liberalism. It embraced the freedoms of thought, speech, religion, and press, the Enlightenment's panoply of "negative liberties"—freedom from governmental or other institutional restrictions—expressed in the Declaration of the Rights of Man. Economically, it was expressed as laissez faire in the vein of the physiocrats and Adam Smith.

French liberalism's most formidable theoretician was Benjamin Constant, who contended that the abandonment of feudal privileges and economic regulations had liberated France's entrepreneurial energies and opened pathways of opportunity to men of ambition. Crucial to that opportunity, indeed to the political and economic life of advanced society, was the safeguarding of individual rights. Constant was no radical; he epitomized the liberal's propensity for tolerance, compromise, and moderation. Thus he believed in the idea of popular sovereignty and the people's rights but also in restricting suffrage to property owners. He supported a constitutional monarchy based on the principles of 1789 but stood opposed to the Ultra crusade for a resurrection of the ancien régime.

In their struggle against an overweening king with claims to absolute power, Charles's adversaries had a ready weapon—the Chamber of Deputies established in the Restoration. The right to vote, severely restricted in the Charter, grew still rarer as reactionaries used fraud and deception to shrink voting lists. Even so, liberals pulled off a striking swing to the left in the fall election of 1827, in turn setting off street riots in Paris. When the new Chamber loosened restrictions on the press, Charles, acting like a proper Bourbon, began to plan for a ministry that would take a tougher line toward what he saw as insurrectionary plots. When the Chamber refused to yield, he abruptly suspended it, providing his opponents with fresh ammunition. The next election, in late June and early July 1830, further drained the king's backing in the legislature.

Conciliatory ministers urged compromise, but Charles would have none of it. All the Bourbon memories of miscalculation and tragedy surfaced in his response. His enemies, he said, were trying to overthrow the monarchy. He admonished his ministers: "Unfortunately I have more experience on this point than you, gentlemen, who are too young to have seen the Revolution; I recall what happened then; the first retreat that my unfortunate brother made was the signal for his downfall. . . . [T]hey asked of him only the dismissal of his ministers, he gave in and all was lost."

So the king and his ministers resorted to drastic actions, the July Ordinances that suspended press freedoms, dissolved the newly elected Chamber of Deputies, and ordered yet another election under a rigged system that effectively disenfranchised the middle class.

How would France respond to these dictatorial decrees? How would *Paris* respond? When the edicts were announced on July 26, opposition journalists declared at once that they would defy the new press restrictions. There was a lull as word of the Ordinances radiated out to cafés and shops, reading rooms and households. The next day, the city seemed to explode. Crowds of ordinary Parisians—mainly artisans and other workers—spilled out of homes and factories, crowded into the streets, shouted out their anger.

The government seemed paralyzed; deputies and other liberals met and deliberated; cobblestone leaders took over the streets. At the invitation of liberals, the National Guard was revived, under the command—as in 1789—of Lafayette, a heroic figure to liberals, who now as then attempted to negotiate between a king and his people. Too late—a revolution was under way. As royal troops sought to march across Paris, people found the ideal weapon—barricades in street after street. They piled up furniture, ancient carriages, tree stumps. Struggling to get through, soldiers were pelted by debris raining down from upper floors and rooftops. Paris fell into chaos. No army could be mobilized in the face of such resistance.

Following these events with mixed eagerness and apprehension was another royal, Louis-Philippe, duc d'Orléans, who had read in the newspaper of Charles's decrees. The duke, a cousin of the king, had long been considered a rival to the throne. But though he had courted liberals, playing the good bourgeois and contributing to their campaigns, he had never conspired against Charles. Also riding the whirlwind of events was Lafayette, whose National Guard was charged with maintaining some order in the city. It was increasingly clear to him and other leading liberals that Charles must go.

At the climax of the "three glorious days," on July 31, Louis-Philippe coolly rode through often angry crowds of republicans crying down all royals and dismounted in front of the Hôtel de Ville, where Lafayette and other officials received him. Then the duke and the general mounted the steps to the great hall above, where their embrace brought shouts of "Vive Lafayette!" and "Vive le Duc!" Two days later, Charles X abdicated, and on August 9, the Chamber of Deputies proclaimed Louis-Philippe king of France.

The revolution in France outside Paris was less fratricidal than in the capital and more formless, partly because the news came in bits and pieces. People clustered at the coach stops to grab newspapers and eagerly question travelers. Wild rumors of bloodshed swept some towns. Prefects, normally controlled by the national government, had tried to enforce Charles's decrees but with mixed success. Now they tried to maintain order, often with even less success. Riots, mutinies, attacks on property erupted. Priests suspected of royalist loyalties were threatened, their churches attacked. Still, there was no nationwide rebellion against Charles's rule.

Limoges would become known as the "red city" later in the century, but it typified France's stability before the July Revolution. With its chamber of commerce protecting business interests and its municipal council composed of the city's noble and bourgeois elite, the city had little to fear from its mild religious dissenters or poor but resigned citizens. Despite some liberal activity and the founding of a newspaper that challenged conservative rantings against "misled children of the century of light," the city pursued a steady course. While liberals made some gains, "official" candidates trounced them in the 1827 election, due in part to a restricted suffrage.

Even so, in the 1830 elections liberals won a stunning victory—a premonition of the crisis ahead. When a month later news arrived of the Paris revolt, some three thousand workers gathered in the city to cry, "Long Live Liberty." And when word came of Charles's abdication the local National Guard triumphantly lofted the revolutionary tricolor.

TRIBUNES OF THE PEOPLE

During the July days, liberals and workers had separate but mutually supporting roles—liberal deputies negotiated in the halls of power while the "common people" fought in the streets. The sacrifices of the workers were reflected in the grim accounts of casualties—the *Constitutionnel* listed a total of 2,860 killed or wounded, including 185 locksmiths, 158 cobblers, 108 joiners and masons, 70 coachmen, 50 tailors, 35 domestic servants, 34 cabinetmakers, and 31 clerks, among many others. Workers by no means fought alone—medical and law students, artists, and *jeune gens de commerce* shed blood in the barricaded streets, in contrast to liberal politicians who issued pronunciamentos from safe havens.

Many workers, lacking leadership and a strong arsenal of ideas, as well as any access to power, had looked to these liberal deputies and intellectuals in the Restoration's last decade to lead the fight against the common enemies—the king, the church, the aristocracy. Liberals, though, with their campaign for restricted government and entrepreneurial liberty, preached what historian Edgar Leon Newman described as "a doctrine of individual self-help which offered no hope to the poorly educated and penniless masses. Liberal politicians and journalists, who defended property rights with one hand while attacking the nobility and clergy with the other, represented the narrow interests of the propertied middle class." Nevertheless, workers believed their economic aspirations might be fulfilled through the liberals' constitutional ones.

And the street fighters could only admire—sometimes to the point of hero worship—the liberal soldier who shared their hopes and dangers, General Lafayette. So it was with mingled confusion and concern that they had witnessed this staunch republican embrace the duc d'Orléans. Were they to have another king? Sure, Louis-Philippe had a reputation as something of a liberal, but that was before he wore a crown. The stage was set for another struggle after the July Revolution, as the new regime gradually became more repressive. Younger and more radical workers and liberals began to see how little they had gained, as older, conservative liberals, businessmen, upper bourgeois, and the like—the "men of order"—took power and made the most of it.

This denouement spurred radicals into opposition, sharpening their often inchoate ideas. Their activism took varied forms. Luddism reemerged, as female shawl-workers and tobacco workers attacked the machinery they said was putting them out of work. Print-workers broke machines at the Royal Print Workshops, urging the government to buy and destroy presses that, they cried, "serve only the interests of a few." Between 1830 and 1833, in Paris alone there were eighty-nine strikes.

Gradually a new labor consciousness was emerging, propelled by an ever-rising opposition to increasingly remote monarchical rule, by workers' pride in themselves as the truly productive element in society, and—still faintly—by a sense that they were a separate, but not yet proletarian, class. Two months after the July days, three newspapers were founded in Paris written and edited by workers, some in prison. "Without a tribune," *L'Artisan* proclaimed, "where they can expose their grievances and their complaints, how can workers make themselves understood by the government?"

*   *   *

For those workers who might have sought a tribune of their own, for fresher ideas and newer strategies than machine-breaking or alliances with middle-class liberals, what could they have found in the torrent of books and newspapers, lectures, and discussion groups addressed to them?

Among the earliest thinkers to confront the pulverizing, demoralizing impact of the new industrial order on human beings and society and who offered up solutions of breathtaking audacity were the Comte de Saint-Simon and François Marie Charles Fourier, who had developed their strange and radical systems amid the regimentation of Napoleonic France.

The most grandiose visionary was Saint-Simon. Crank or genius? Nothing about the man smacked of self-doubt. Born in 1760 into an old aristocratic family, Saint-Simon enlisted in the American Revolution and returned to France as a colonel. During the French Revolution he styled himself Citizen Bonhomme while barely escaping the deadly attentions of Robespierre, suffering arrest but not execution during the Terror. He was certain of his destiny as among the world's greatest leaders. He believed he could integrate all the sciences and discover a Universal Law that would safeguard world peace. He glorified two earlier eras—Greco-Roman antiquity and the medieval Europe of Christian unity—even while he represented a superheated strain of the modern Enlightenment. Now, after revolutions, after Napoleon and world war, the West was poised for the most glorious epoch of all.

What would it bring? Above all, comprehensive enlightenment and the death of superstition, the supremacy of science, an orderly and rational world. Scientists of morality would invent common values to replace archaic Christian doctrine. Cooperation among all producers—employers and workers alike—would replace class war. Rational leaders would plan the economy and integrate intellectual work with the help of a "New Encyclopedia," promote and exploit scientific discovery, relegate unproductive people to minor status, and, not least, avoid politics. Saint-Simon even urged Louis XVIII to grant finance powers to a council of ten top industrialists who would plan colossal public enterprises. But his ambitions soared above France—he called for global unity through federation.

To a remarkable degree he was preaching leadership—bold, comprehensive, and committed leadership—without using the word or knowing the concept. But leadership is impossible without followership. Saint-Simon inspired prominent producers and engineers, as well as middle-class readers seeking some new kind of universalism transcending the messy disputes and divisions of everyday life. But few workers were persuaded—and it was the working class that he most hoped to enlist in his quest for cooperation and harmony.

Fourier was Saint-Simon's near opposite. Born in 1772 of a middle-class family that had lost most of its possessions in the Revolution, he put his faith not in grandiose institutions but in small communities, not in large-scale planning but in decentralization, not in technology but in human initiative. Fourier's reformist faith began in a sustained critique of the ravages capitalism inflicted on people and the environment. He would win Friedrich Engels's praise for pitting the material and moral miseries of the modern world against "the earlier philosophers' dazzling promises of a society in which reason alone should reign," for pointing out "how everywhere the most pitiful reality corresponds with the most high-sounding phrases."

Never mind that few Enlightenment philosophers could have outpaced Fourier in "dazzling promises." He himself was an Enlightenment thinker, albeit one on its outer reaches. In historian Nicholas Riasanovsky's summary, Fourier's Enlightenment included his claims to have discovered universal laws and a faith that society could be transformed by the use of reason, which would yield a "scientifically correct theoretical model" that if realized would result in an ecstatic peak of human happiness. Like his Enlightenment predecessors, Fourier grounded his reform views in a theory of human nature. He saw all people as having passions—psychological needs—in common. In his systematic way, he enumerated twelve basic or "radical" passions, ranging from the five sensual appetites to the four "appetites of the soul," including love and ambition, and finally the three "compound appetites," including the "most romantic" longing for a happiness that blended spiritual and physical pleasures. The harmonization of all the passions Fourier called "Unityism," a "boundless philanthropy" that was something like Francis Hutcheson's benevolence. Fourier thought all passions were in themselves good and their satisfaction pleasurable to men; it was their repression or perversion that caused misery in the world. The object, then, was to create an environment that allowed the passions their fullest play. Labor, education, leisure—all of life was to be organized rationally to meet people's natural inclinations, enabling them to pursue happiness, which for Fourier was the highest value, "the full development of Unityism." Like Saint-Simon, he was no student of leadership as such, but his view of the motivating force of human wants and needs was akin to later concepts of the foundations of leadership.

To achieve his ends, Fourier offered tantalizingly Utopian means—communities that he called *phalanstères*. These would typically consist of perhaps sixteen hundred persons farming five thousand acres of land, a large enough establishment to offer members a variety of occupations. People would be housed in communal buildings with common services. But Fourier was no absolutist. He did not bar private property, insisting only that it be put to communal use. Nor was he for any kind of state socialism—the *phalanstères* would be financed by voluntary contributions.

The ever-optimistic Fourier devoted much of his life to the promotion of his ideas, above all through followers whose enthusiasm matched his own. Eventually, he became notorious for some of his wilder visions—imagining that the planets shared the joys of copulation and that salty seas would turn to lemonade—and Parisians nodded knowingly when he became insane in the years before his death in 1837. Still, his visionary hopes attracted supporters not only in France but in Germany, Britain, and, especially, America, where over a dozen short-lived Fourierist colonies were founded.

The dream worlds, as historian Pamela Pilbeam called them, of the early Utopians, including the cooperative vision of Robert Owen, were strikingly similar—all promoted solidarity, mutual aid, sharing, community, and, ultimately, happiness. And their dreams all were a recoil from what they agreed were the costs of the emerging liberal order: the competitiveness and greed of unbridled selfishness that trampled the mass of people unable to keep pace in the chaos and conflict of the market economy.

* * *

Most workers shared little of the Utopian dreams. They knew firsthand the costs of capitalism and wanted higher wages, shorter hours, better working conditions. They, too, wanted brotherhood and companionship, but mainly at the workplace. In France as in Britain, the United States, and elsewhere, workers were barred early in the century from forming associations. Later they won more freedom to band together, but the time had yet to come for militant nationwide trade unionism.

It was between glorious but impractical Utopias and practical but mundane trade associations that socialism emerged. Its origins were in the Enlightenment, but it exposed the movement's differing strains, while giving it a fresh turn as the new circumstances of the industrializing economy demanded. At first the idea, centered in France, was as hazy as other beliefs floating across the continent. For some socialists, it meant taking over the state, for others abolishing it. To some, liberty was the overarching idea, for others equality, while still others—indeed most socialists—insisted the two were inseparable. At the heart of socialism lay radical programs for redistributing economic and political power, democratizing the industrial order, overcoming poverty and unemployment, all under collective leadership that would emerge from the working class. But socialist aspirations went far beyond the satisfaction of material needs. Whether they meant to reform or to destroy existing society, socialists insisted that the change would not only redress inequalities but also undo the damage done by capitalism to the minds and spirits of human beings, redeeming their moral natures.

Indeed, socialism had its moral foundations in the concern for the poor in Christian doctrine. For centuries, while the hierarchy paid little more than lip service, many of the working clergy had ministered to the poor. And now, in the early 1800s, as the ravages of industrialization left multitudes jobless and destitute, there were ample poor to minister to. Most lived in hovels: In Paris, wrote Fourierist leader Victor Considérant, "one bedroom for all, bereft of window or floor, also served as kitchen, dining room, cellar, grain store, stable and farmyard." Not only were the dreadful conditions visible to those who cared to look, but they were translated into statistical terms in investigations organized in the early 1830s by the French Ministry of the Interior—the age of the social science survey had begun, thanks in part to Saint-Simon's influence. Works such as Victor Hugo's 1831 *Notre-Dame de Paris* dramatized these dark enclaves.

* * *

Until he died in 1825 Saint-Simon persevered in his effort to create a science of man, but he was making his own turn to Christianity, whose regeneration was needed to provide the moral underpinnings of a society devoted to fulfilling every human need. Not surprisingly, perhaps, he imagined himself the new messiah. But Saint-Simon's true legacy was to socialism. His identification of inequality and class conflict as the central features of modern industrial society became gospel to the socialists now finding their own voices.

Among the first was Étienne Cabet, who combined an acute critique of industrialization and a practical program of reforms with a vision of the Utopia toward which gradual enlightenment would lead. Cabet boldly labeled himself a communist as well as a socialist even as he sought to distinguish himself from a notorious communist precursor, François-Noël Babeuf, who had emerged from the rubble of the Terror to become the leader of a "Conspiracy of the Equals." Babeuf demanded violent class struggle and the redistribution of wealth to achieve the fullest social and economic equality in what historian G. D. H. Cole described as "an almost fully fledged scheme of proletarian Communism." But in the 1790s, with industrialization in only a rudimentary stage, there had been little in Paris to resemble a proletariat—the militancy of the sansculottes, who were mostly independent artisans, was aimed at improving their chances of economic security, not a thorough redistribution of wealth. Babeuf's attempt to lead workers into violent rebellion against the state was doomed; he was guillotined by the Directory in 1797.

Cabet would agree with Babeuf's assertion that "private property is the source of all the calamities upon this earth," but he recoiled from revolution as the answer to inequality. He favored instead a democratic transition to an ideal, happy communist state in which capitalism's vices—greed, envy, poverty, crime—would be extinguished by equality in all things. But Cabet was more activist than dreamer. After July, he was elected to parliament and started *Populaire,* a newspaper for workers that was produced by workers and aggressively defended labor associations even as the government was repressing them. In 1834, Cabet was charged with lèse-majesté for writing that Louis-Philippe would do anything to keep power, including ordering "French men shot, gunned down in the streets." For this "affront to the king," Cabet faced a prison sentence of two years. Instead, he chose a term of exile in England.

Far closer to Babauvism in spirit and methods was Louis Auguste Blanqui. He was of middle-class origin and high-level education. While his older brother Louis Adolphe became a loyal civil servant and antisocialist, Louis Auguste flaunted his zeal for revolution and appetite for violence. He participated in the July revolt and then in every rising against the July regime, almost pulling off an armed coup in 1839. Impatient with theory, Blanqui was no more restrained in his ideas and rhetoric. He derided the "scarecrow spectre" of the Jacobin constitution: In his rage against capitalism and the market economy, he himself would go much further. Charged in court with inciting the poor to rebel, he proudly admitted that his profession was "proletaire," claiming identity with thirty million French people. Violent of speech, contemptuous of authority, this "most Jacobin of the Jacobins" would spend many years of his life in prison.

Louis Blanc, too, grew up in a bourgeois family—his grandfather had been guillotined by the Jacobins and his father earned a pension from the Bourbons—but his rebellion took the form of a faith not in revolution but in democratic reformism. For his moderation, he was condemned as a bourgeois socialist. Turning early to left-wing journalism, Blanc was appalled by the poverty he witnessed, especially by the plight of women workers. He came to see the capitalism of his merchant forefathers as the root of all evil. In search of an alternative, Blanc wrote a study of the "organization of labor," an early attempt to work out the practical economics of socialism. It led him to his own answer to inequality and poverty—a vast program of "social workshops" in the form of self-governing producer cooperatives, ateliers that had Fourierist undertones. Unlike Fourier with his dread of government, though, Blanc insisted that it was necessary to use the "whole power of the state" to provide the proletariat with what they "lack to free themselves"—the means of production. But then government was to step back and allow workers to lead themselves.

Pierre-Joseph Proudhon cut a different figure from socialists of noble or middle-class origin, coming from a family of peasants on his mother's side and artisans on his father's. He became a printer, even setting the type for Fourier's 1829 treatise *Le Nouveau Monde Industriel et Sociétaire,* which fortified his radical ideas. Proudhon was opposed not to the private use of property but to the unlimited acquisitiveness secured by laws that bred gross inequalities of economic power and exploitation. His ideal was almost Jeffersonian, a republic of small landholders living simply and cooperatively on terms of independence and equality. This gentle anarchism was the work of an exceptionally combative man, an adept at verbal extremism, whether his targets were "proprietors," fellow socialists, or feminists who thought women might have a place in public life.

The attacks on property, inequality, and oppression spearheaded by early socialists helped dramatize the failings of industrial society and framed the needs of the dispossessed in terms of the noblest values of the Enlightenment—liberty, equality, justice. Yet as these men recognized, the economic plight of the French working class was inseparable from their political powerlessness. After the July Revolution, socialists and others renewed the issue that had been a source of conflict since 1789: How was France to be governed?

REPUBLICAN REVIVALS

Republicanism as an antimonarchical creed had fallen into low repute during the reigns of Napoleon and the restored Bourbons, monarchs whose propaganda relentlessly linked the idea to the Jacobins and revolutionary terror. Charles X's Ministry of Justice kept republicans under surveillance as seditious, but after the Carbonari were repressed, there were few culprits to be found. Far more feared by authorities was a revival of Bonapartism, for the Napoleonic legend remained potent, especially in the military. It was supremely ironic that a dictator who had failed so catastrophically should continue to resonate so strongly and even sentimentally in the French heart, to be glamorized in songs, plays, medals, bric-a-brac, even hats and neckties, while a genuinely populist revolutionary movement should be remembered only for its extremists and excesses.

The July Revolution had not begun as a republican effort, even though republicans like Lafayette were among its leaders, but after July, as the regime of the "Citizen King" took root in conservative ground, a more coherent, ideological, radical republicanism soon emerged. In the four years after July, Pamela Pilbeam wrote, "networks of opposition societies, of an increasingly republican nature, sprang up in France, challenged by Orleanist persecution." Decisive in the emergence of this opposition was the impact of radical ideas that went far beyond the abolition of monarchical rule and beyond French liberalism.

They were Enlightenment ideas, brimming with fresh philosophical and political implications proclaimed by new thinkers living in a time of deep-running social and economic change. They included durable liberal values such as free speech and press, but economic and political causes were joined with a new egalitarianism to construct a platform of parliamentary reform and broadened suffrage, a more equal division of property, aid to the poor, and even more radical programs for economic and social justice.

Workers did not have to look far for such transforming ideas. Cheap editions of the works of Rousseau and Voltaire, produced by the tens of thousands, could be bought for 10 sous when a four-pound loaf of bread cost about 13 sous. If Enlightenment philosophes widened minds to the broadest intellectual ranges, there were plenty of republican papers and pamphlets that addressed immediate, day-to-day needs, while also appealing to workers to take back *their* revolution from those who had betrayed it. At a time of widespread unemployment, the republican message resonated. The well-organized Société des Droits de l'Homme enlisted thousands of committed members in working-class Paris and enrolled thousands more in its free schools for working people.

Many Utopians and socialists were activists, taking part in the republican revival of the early 1830s. Saint-Simonians founded republican clubs in the provinces and organized evening classes. Cabet's *Populaire* promoted the free schools of the Droits de l'Homme and he himself served as their secretary. Blanqui was a leader in the Amis du Peuple, agitating for a constituent assembly. Blanc shunned the radical societies but promoted worker education in his democratic weekly *Bon Sens*.

Most radical republicans made little secret of their Jacobin sympathies and allegiance to the republican Jacobin constitution of 1793 with its long declaration of rights, including both negative and positive liberties, that the Terror effectively negated. The Société des Droits de l'Homme echoed the most salient assertion in its own defiant declaration: "When a government violates the rights of the people, the people have a sacred right and indispensable duty to rebel." Filippo Buonarroti had survived participation in the "Conspiracy of the Equals" to become, nearly four decades later, a revered sage to young republicans, a living link to the heroic age of revolutionary radicalism. Buonarroti defended the Constitution of 1793 as a democratic and egalitarian manifesto, the blueprint for a new republic. This, he argued, was the heart of Jacobinism, not the Terror, which he—vaguely—regretted.

Yet it was this close tie with Jacobinism that made the prospect of a republic frightening to many of the French, including the laboring poor, whose goals were far more modest and practical than total revolution. Moderate republicans, bourgeois liberals, were tarred with the same Jacobin brush, and it was the failure of the republican movement to overcome popular suspicion of its means and ends that made it all the simpler for the government to allege that a scattering of riots in 1835 represented a massive conspiracy to dethrone Louis-Philippe and declare a republic. Police arrested two thousand alleged leaders. In September 1835, the Chamber of Deputies passed a draconian press law that banned the word "republic" from newspapers and made an insult to the king's dignity punishable by a year in jail. Together with a measure passed the year before requiring political and labor societies to register with the government, these laws destroyed the republican movement, forcing its remnants under ground.

The promise—and betrayal—of French republicanism had been captured in a conversation between Louis-Philippe and Lafayette on August 1, 1830, the day after their famous embrace at the Hôtel de Ville. "You know," Lafayette had declared, "that I am a republican and that I regard the constitution of the United States as the most perfect that ever existed."

"I think as you do," the duke replied; "it is impossible to have spent two years in America and not to be of that opinion; but do you believe that in France's situation, in the present state of opinion, it would be proper for us to adopt that constitution?"

"No, what the French people must have today is a popular throne surrounded by republican institutions, completely republican."

"That is precisely what I think," was the reply.

Perhaps Lafayette believed Louis-Philippe, but four years after the July days the old revolutionary was dead and republicanism was giving way to reaction, leaving the "bourgeois king" secure on his throne, for the time being. But now there would be no question of a "restoration." In their different ways, liberals and radicals would see to that.

In the almost half-century since France's original, earthshattering revolution, the nation had swung from enlightened constitutionalism to terror to dictatorship to restoration and reaction. Now, with liberals securely within the circle of power, if not fully in charge, and radicals mobilizing on the outside, France faced a new contestation, which produced different visions and expectations of change, different conceptions of the ultimate goal of human happiness. The Enlightenment provided a framework for the pursuit of happiness. Leaders and followers—citizens—were left to fight over the meanings of happiness and the path for pursuing it.

10

The American Experiment

A small crowd had gathered in front of Conrad & McMunn's boarding-house in Washington. It was March 4, 1801, Inauguration Day. Soon Thomas Jefferson quietly emerged from the front door. A tall, lean, loosely framed man, he hardly cut a heroic figure. He felt ill at ease in a crowd, even though people were attracted to his open countenance and pleasing manner. No coach-and-eight waited to carry him to the Capitol. He would walk. Shortly before nine, followed by a motley throng of officials and politicos, he set out for the north wing of the as yet unfinished building.

Several hundred persons had crowded into the Senate chamber to witness Jefferson's inauguration. His old Virginia adversary, Chief Justice John Marshall, administered the oath. Conspicuously absent was the man Jefferson was succeeding. John Adams had slipped out of Washington before dawn.

The new president turned to the audience.

"Friends and Fellow-Citizens." At this some good Federalists in the crowd must have stirred. "Citizens"! This was the language of Paris Jacobins!

Jefferson spoke in such low tones that many in the audience could not make him out. In any case much of the speech was familiar from the campaign. After lauding a "rising nation, spread over a wide and fruitful land," he laid out Republican positions: "Equal and exact justice to all men" . . . support for state governments as bulwarks of republicanism . . . economy in public expense . . . help to agriculture and commerce. These principles would guide him and the country through an age of "revolution and reformation."

But Jefferson also offered an earnest plea for conciliation. Every difference of opinion was not a difference of principle. "We are all Republicans, we are all Federalists," he said. "If there be any among us who would wish to dissolve this Union or to change its republican form, let them stand undisturbed as monuments of the safety with which error of opinion may be tolerated where reason is left free to combat it."

Addressing Federalist concerns, he went on, "I know, indeed, that some honest men fear that a republican government cannot be strong, that this Government is not strong enough; but would the honest patriot, in the full tide of successful experiment, abandon a government which has so far kept us free and firm on the theoretic and visionary fear that this Government, the world's best hope, may by possibility want energy to preserve itself?"

The ceremony over, President Jefferson walked back to his lodgings at Conrad's, where friends, political colleagues, foreign diplomats, and others greeted him. There he would stay for two weeks, until he moved to the President's House, eating at table—and sometimes at the foot of it—with thirty or so friends and officials. He was not one for a big public celebration, so ardent Jeffersonians celebrated on their own. In Virginia an inaugural pageant depicted Liberty as a beautiful virgin, threatened by a king and a bishop and other assailants, until a trumpet sounded proclaiming Jefferson as president, whereupon the evil men took flight and sixteen comely women, one for each state, protected Liberty. In Philadelphia sixteen horses, driven by a youth dressed in white, pulled a carriage bearing the resplendent schooner *Thomas Jefferson*. A "Patriotic Song" rang out:

> *Rejoice! Columbia's sons, rejoice!*
> *To tyrants never bend the knee,*
> *But join with heart, and soul, and voice,*
> *For* JEFFERSON *and* LIBERTY.

WE ARE ALL REPUBLICANS

Jefferson's presidency is often seen as inaugurating a new epoch. It was also a continuation of the longest-running dynasty in American history—one that began with the influence of the Virginia notables in winning the Revolution and shaping the Constitution. Then followed the fashioning of the presidency by its first occupant, and after the single term of a non-Virginian and Federalist, John Adams—Washington's approved successor—came a *quarter century* of presidential rule by Virginia Republicans. These leaders hardly held on to power by their teeth. Washington had been elected and reelected unanimously; his Virginian successors did almost as well. After narrowly besting Adams in 1800, Jefferson went on to reelection in 1804 by taking 162 of 176 electoral votes. Madison won by comfortable margins in his two presidential elections, while James Monroe had a landslide victory in 1816 and then went on to run unopposed for reelection four years later—a deplorable spectacle in a democracy.

Great election winners, but how strong was the rule of the Virginians? Washington has come down through the ages as a stiff and formal executive standing above politics, cautious in policymaking, remote from the people. More recent scholarship has revealed a highly political president who read both the Constitution and the *Federalist* papers as granting considerable authority to the chief executive. Washington built a strong presidential structure where the Constitution had left gaps, while also leading an aggressive Federalist faction even as he condemned partisan excess. He not only occupied the office, some said, but conquered it.

Did Jefferson, then, restore the presidency to the weaker office suggested by the Madisonian checks and balances of the Constitution and by his own doctrine of limited government? Only to a small degree. Jefferson was quite serious when he told the inaugural crowd that he proposed to be a "strong" chief executive. But he would not "swell" the presidential office. He had a different plan, a political strategy: He would govern not outside and around Congress but through the Republican majorities in each chamber, involving himself centrally in the Republican leadership of the two houses.

Still, how could the new president unify a group of legislators who, both by constitutional design and the realities of electoral politicking, were so sovereign in outlook, so dependent on their state and local constituencies, so independent politically of *him*? Jefferson had carefully worked out his tactics: to gratify the self-esteem of lawmakers by deferring to the doctrine of congressional supremacy, while asserting himself in the crucial phases of lawmaking and thus to become chief legislator. And all this he meant to do quietly and adroitly so that the Federalists would not be aroused nor his fellow Republicans feel overpowered. George Washington had provided collective leadership through close collaboration with his cabinet; Jefferson would do so through close interaction with his partisan Republicans.

Jefferson proved to be a transforming leader in drawing Republican followers behind the transcending Enlightenment principles he had long preached. He was also a transactional leader in his dealings with both friendly and rival politicians. His initial leadership was made easier because his first acts followed directly from his campaign stands, repealing Federalist measures, cutting federal spending and the national debt, breaking away from actions that might unduly "entangle" himself and the nation in foreign affairs.

It was supremely ironic that Jefferson and his presidential successors faced "entanglement" almost from the start—indeed, that foreign relations would dominate their agendas year after year. They were entangled willy-nilly, by events beyond their control, above all by the Napoleonic wars that convulsed Europe and the world.

But happily for Jefferson his first entanglement with the Old World would offer an opportunity of vast proportions in the New. This was Louisiana, an immense territory of eighty hundred thousand square miles that ranged north from the Gulf of Mexico to the border of Canada, west from the Mississippi River to the Oregon country. To Americans, Louisiana was their western borderland, nearby but mysterious, peopled by roving Indian tribes but rich in fertile land for settlers headed west. Fronting this area was the mighty Mississippi, rising somewhere in the far north, swelling miles wide as it approached the Gulf of Mexico and providing a boulevard to the world for husbandmen and flatboatmen. To westerners, Secretary of State Madison said, the Mississippi was everything—"the Hudson, the Delaware, the Potomac and all the navigable rivers of the atlantic States, formed into one stream." And at the foot of the river lay New Orleans, a place of exotic peoples and erotic temptations, a commercial center vitally necessary to American traders for shipping their goods abroad.

The problem was that America did not control Louisiana—France did, or soon would when the secret agreement Spain signed in 1800 to surrender the territory it had acquired from France after the Seven Years' War took effect. When rumors of the deal reached him, Jefferson wrote that this was "very ominous to us." French control of Louisiana would place Napoleon's armies athwart America's western frontier, under the control of a man Jefferson detested as a "moral monster" and whose dictatorship had delivered the final blow to Jefferson's hopes for France as an Old World counterpart to republican America. The president already had reason to fear Bonaparte's imperial ambitions. The dictator was organizing an expedition to Haiti in order to overthrow the regime of General Toussaint L'Ouverture, the black leader who had seized power after a bloody slave rebellion. Jefferson did not object to the attempt to suppress Toussaint—he feared the impact of a successful slave revolt on America's slaveholding states—but would Bonaparte stop there? If the French ruler could send twenty thousand soldiers to the West Indies, could he not dispatch even larger armies to Louisiana, a far greater temptation?

When Spain in autumn 1802 abruptly suspended the treaty rights of Americans to deposit their goods in New Orleans before shipment to Europe, the outrage of westerners and Federalist clamors for war led Jefferson to send James Monroe, who was just ending a term as Virginia governor, to negotiate with France and Spain. To some, Monroe's mission seemed impossible: Haiti and Toussaint were in French hands, and Napoleon was mobilizing a huge fleet to pursue his ambitions in the Caribbean and perhaps Louisiana. On reaching Paris, however, the envoy found the situation remarkably altered. Napoleon had received two pieces of staggering news: His army in Haiti had been almost annihilated by yellow fever, while the fleet carrying reinforcements had become ice-bound in Holland. With his hopes for a western empire dimming, Napoleon now was ready to deal. The United States gained all of Louisiana for $15 million plus some minor concessions. It was perhaps the most momentous real estate deal in history.

Jefferson had pursued it with both determination and flexibility. Since the Constitution contained no grant of authority to acquire territory, he faced the question of whether he should seek a constitutional amendment. He knew that the amendment process would be slow and risky—and might give Napoleon time to change his mind—but he headed the party of strict and narrow construction of the charter. After extensive consultations, he yielded to what he later called "the laws of necessity, of self-preservation." In a statement that would be echoed later by Abraham Lincoln, he wrote: "To lose our country by a scrupulous adherence to written law, would be to lose the law itself, with life, liberty, property and all those who are enjoying them with us; thus absurdly sacrificing the end to the means." His close collaboration with his cabinet, his envoys, and the Senate, which voted the treaty through by a handsome majority, made the Louisiana purchase a memorable achievement of collective leadership.

*   *   *

Louisiana was but one instance of America's entanglement with European powers in the age of Napoleonic wars. The ever-intensifying Franco-British rivalry remorselessly sucked Americans into its vortex. Jefferson and Madison patiently sought a posture of neutrality on the high seas but success was elusive as long as American merchants pursued profitable trade and expected the small U. S. Navy to back them up. Clashes with Britain's aggressive navy and other "incidents" were inevitable. In desperation the Virginians turned to the weapon of economic coercion. The 1807–1809 Embargo first banned the departure of American vessels from U. S. ports, and then was expanded to include all trade across American land frontiers. The idea was that British merchants, denied their best customer, would pressure Parliament to respect American neutrality.

The embargo brought dire economic distress to Americans, especially New Englanders. Its main result was to alienate the British even further and help precipitate the War of 1812. That conflict was fought over vast distances by incompetent American generals and ill-trained troops, which led to the humiliating sack of Washington by British invaders and a peace that restored the status quo antebellum—no gains or concessions on either side. Given the course of the war, that was perhaps reason enough for Americans to celebrate. They had fought the "conqueror of Europe" to a bloody standstill and had earned, as a French observer noted, "what they so essentially lacked, a national character."

In domestic policy Jefferson led the Virginians in a display of resolute and enlightened leadership. Those who feared—or hoped—that the relaxed, casual Virginia patrician would let others run his administration could hardly recognize the decisive figure in the President's House. Jefferson did not need to bestride a white charger or bark out orders. As chief executive, he had a quiet air of authority, a steadfastness of purpose, and the capacity to look ahead.

Buttressed by Republican support in Congress, he was a strong legislative leader as well. Even more, as head of an organized majority, he also led a wide party of Republican followers throughout the nation. He was a firm believer in majority rule as the proper expression of "government by the people," but he also recognized, as he said at his inaugural, that "though the will of the majority is in all cases to prevail, that will to be rightful must be reasonable; that the minority possess their equal rights." Implicit, too, in the idea of majority rule was the Madisonian understanding, contrary to the assumptions of other Enlightenment thinkers, that, in a large and pluralistic country, the majority would embrace so many diverse interests, sections, and attitudes that it would pursue a moderate and balanced program. That is what Jefferson did.

Madison and Monroe inherited Jefferson's philosophy, most of his popular backing, and some of his leadership skills. What they lacked was a potent opposition to generate political conflict that would clarify ideas and empower leaders and followers to pursue transformational change. After Adams, the Federalist party never again won the presidency or lasting majorities in Congress. The main reason for this decline was found in the ideas that underlay and defined their leadership—in hallowed but increasingly anachronistic beliefs in the stewardship of gentlemen of learning and virtue, in a natural hierarchical order among citizens, in the need for balance and harmony among classes and interests. Such ideas appeared elitist and outdated at a time of rising democratic sentiment. Moreover, Federalist opposition to the War of 1812 gave them the cast of, in historian Sean Wilentz's words, "a pro-British American Tory party."

At least they went out with a small bang. In December 1815, a number of genteel, prosperous-looking men strode into the council chamber of the Connecticut State House in Hartford. This was a group of antiwar New England Federalists gathered to consider "a radical reform in the national compact." Rumors spread that the convention was plotting secession. But these were cautious men, merchants and lawyers, whose motivating concern was the war's impact on the New England economy. They ended up merely recommending a handful of constitutional amendments to address longstanding Federalist grievances, including one that would bar successive presidents coming from the same state, a swipe at the Virginia dynasty. It was said that when President Madison read the recommendations, he roared with laughter. But to many Americans, the Hartford meeting smacked of treason in wartime. Soon the Federalist party began its quiet death watch.

THE DEMOCRATIC MAJORITY

The Virginia dynasty came to an end in 1824 in one of the wildest presidential elections in American history, an election that signaled and helped trigger a transformation in national politics. The leading Republican aspirant was no Virginian but rather John Quincy Adams of Massachusetts. What was an Adams—son of *the* Adams—doing in the Jeffersonian camp? For one thing, with the fading of the Federalists, almost everyone—at least, everyone with ambition—was a Republican now. And Adams had ambition. He had served brilliantly as Monroe's secretary of state, a position from which Jefferson, Madison, and Monroe had moved to the presidency. Why shouldn't he?

Adams's competitors for the job were all avowed Republicans. Henry Clay of Kentucky was as hearty and disarming as Adams was forbidding. At forty-seven, Clay had served for years in both houses of Congress and had made a name for himself as an ardent nationalist, calling for the federal government to sponsor "internal improvements"—roads, bridges, canals that would knit the union together. John C. Calhoun of South Carolina,

Monroe's secretary of war, was another committed nationalist. This was the same Calhoun who only a few years later metamorphosed into a fiery defender of states' rights and even secession. Calhoun would soon withdraw from the presidential contest and win election to the vice presidency.

Most formidable of the candidates was Andrew Jackson. American presidential politics had not seen the like of him. All five presidents to that time had been raised in genteel homes ranging from the comfortable to the affluent. Jackson was born in 1767 in the Carolina backcountry. His father died days before his birth while clearing land for a farm, and his mother perished of cholera in 1781 while nursing nephews incarcerated in British prison ships in Charleston. Orphaned at fourteen, Jackson became an angry, dueling frontiersman given to gambling and drink and violent defenses of his masculine honor. Brief stints in the House and Senate in the 1790s did not tame him. He oversaw shocking massacres of Indians as commander of the Tennessee militia. Then came the Battle of New Orleans in 1815 and fame for saving the city from British invasion. He won more notoriety when he conquered Florida three years later without direct authorization from Washington, slaughtering Indians, humiliating the defeated Spanish, and executing two British subjects he accused of inciting the Creeks against his new rule.

Having organized a new government in Florida, boasting that he had granted the right to vote to every white male in the territory, Jackson returned to Tennessee in 1821 resolved to mobilize the poor and the needy. At the same time he enlisted the less needy—southern and western planters, traders, speculators, lawyers, slave owners like himself. Jackson had long championed what he termed "good old Jeffersonian Democratic principles," which attracted those who opposed the Bank of the United States and the Eastern elites as well as the nationalism of Adams and Clay that drained power from the states.

Jackson also aroused the less affluent with his vociferous majoritarianism. "The people are the government," he would say, "administering it by their agents." They were the "sovereign power" whose will must be obeyed. In state after state, Jacksonians proclaimed that their cause was the people's cause—to recover a government that had grown corrupt and distant from the people. They mounted mass rallies that portrayed Jackson, flamboyant war hero and Indian killer, as the people's candidate. The contrast with his main opponent in the campaign, the aloof and "aristocratic" Adams, could not have been greater, and the verdict was unmistakable. Jackson won almost as many votes as Adams and Clay combined, showing strength in every region save New England, where Adams dominated. While class lines were not yet clearly formed, it was evident that the Tennessean had mobilized a national constituency of low-income farmers and workers.

Because Electoral College votes had been split among four candidates, though, Jackson did not have an outright majority. Under the Constitution this threw the election into the House of Representatives, where Clay, who had finished a distant third in the popular vote, yielded his electoral votes to Adams, enough to give him a solid majority—and next became new President Adams's secretary of state, that stepping-stone to the presidency. A roar of indignation swept the country over the presumed bargain. "The *Judas* of the West," Jackson called Clay.

Now the sharpshooters of the west and south had a clear target—the Adams-Clay administration—and a fine moral issue. Jackson's people, including an easterner, Martin Van Buren, who had demonstrated masterful skills in building a coalition in New York state, worked out a strategy of consolidating the general's personal support and embedding it in the agrarian ranks of the Republican party, Jefferson's old base. Jackson would exploit the extension of the suffrage that widened that base, as states eliminated property-holding qualifications for white men. Thus was precipitated a rupture in the Republican party between Jackson's Democratic Republicans, or simply Democrats, and the National Republicans of Adams and Clay.

The Democrats' strategy won out. Jackson's rout of Adams in 1828, sweeping both the popular and Electoral College vote, was sweet as a victory of the vengeful, but it was above all a seismic shift in national politics as a new party—dramatically different in composition and character—charged to power. The magnitude of the 1828 election as a democratic watershed could be measured in the over one million white men who cast their ballots, three times as many as had voted in 1824.

* * *

An image has come down through history of a hard-riding Jackson sweeping into the White House and boldly seizing the reins of leadership. It did not seem so at the time. The only immediate change after the March 4, 1829, inauguration was in some of the White House crockery and furnishings broken and torn as thousands pressed into the public rooms to celebrate the first "people's inaugural." Jackson's address that day had been by contrast almost sedate. Evidently distrustful of the government he was taking over, he promised to respect states' rights and limits on executive power. Vowing to remove all those "appointed against the will of the people," the new president soon indulged in what the opposition called a "Reign of Terror," stuffing the executive branch with his own partisans, which created a new normal in American government. The stability in the country's small civil service had been the result of decades-long one-party rule. In the only previous transition between parties, John Adams, after his loss to Jefferson, tried to cram the executive and judiciary with Federalists before he left office. Jefferson himself made the executive an arm of the Republican party.

President Jackson presided over a capital filled with noisy clashes often signifying little. The main issue was an old one, the Bank of the United States, headed by an ex-Federalist patrician, Nicholas Biddle of Philadelphia. Ever since Alexander Hamilton first conceived a national bank, it had provoked bitter political wars, pitting, in popular terms, democratic republicanism against aristocracy, the poor against the rich, agrarians versus capitalists, liberty versus tyranny. To its defenders, the Bank of the United States represented the stability needed to encourage investment and expansion. To its enemies, the bank represented a dangerous concentration of economic power in the hands of eastern financiers of Biddle's stripe, giving them, in Jackson's words, "power to control the Government and change its character." With his hardscrabble western roots, populist following, and ferocious temper, Jackson was the bank's perfect enemy, and his furious effort to kill it helped propel year after year of intense, often hysterical debate, not only about the bank but about the course of the country's political and economic development. And the nonstop bank fight precipitated a vigorous and organized opposition to Jacksonian leadership.

That Whig opposition reflected the continuing diversity and tentativeness of American political life. The birth of the Whig party, mainly out of Adams's short-lived National Republicans, was so obscure that historians have placed it at some time in 1832 or 1833 or 1834. But there was nothing obscure about the early opposition leaders who were coming to call themselves Whigs.

Henry Clay was the most conspicuous oppositionist. Celebrated for his sharp intelligence, compelling congressional leadership, and unpredictable combination of political daring and compromise, he planned to challenge Jackson's reelection bid in 1832. His platform would center on what he called the "American System," based on an active federal role in shaping national economic development, the road, he promised, "to riches, to greatness, to glory." The jewel in the Whig diadem was Daniel Webster of Massachusetts, incomparable Senate orator, champion of New England commerce—but a failure in converting his celebrity and ambition into national political support.

South Carolina's John Calhoun was becoming the most anomalous member of the opposition. He had managed to serve as vice president both to Adams and to Jackson—a remarkable feat. With equal adroitness, he abandoned nationalism to stand as champion of states' rights extremists, coming into bitter conflict with Jackson when the president stunned his Southern backers by furiously denouncing South Carolina's assumed authority to "nullify" federal tariffs. Jackson threatened that "if one drop of blood be shed there in defiance of the laws of the United States, I will hang the first man of them I can get my hands on to the first tree I can find." In Jackson's view, nullification was the destructive extreme of the states' rights the Constitution had properly guaranteed. Nullification equaled secession and the dissolution of the United States. The president vowed to use force to crush it.

After his foes bombarded Jackson from all directions, it was Clay who won the privilege, as the Whig presidential nominee, of running into the juggernaut of the president's reelection campaign of 1832. Undaunted, the Whigs barreled back into the fray—actually three frays, as Webster and his backers stumped for the bank, business groups rallied behind Clay and his American System, and states' rights advocates lined up behind Calhoun, who, characteristically, began to edge toward the Democrats. Jackson's party maintained its unity when the president chose Van Buren as his Democratic successor in the White House.

The anti-Jackson coalition adopted a daring strategy for 1836: not to unite behind a single nominee but to choose three candidates with strong regional followings in hopes of throwing the election into the House of Representatives, where Whigs had more strength. It seemed a realistic move that recognized fundamental political divisions in the country. But politics has its own realities. The Democratic majority held while the Whig coalition imploded. The three regional candidates—William Henry Harrison of Ohio, New England's Webster, and an anti-Jackson Tennessean, Hugh L. White—won a total of 113 electoral votes; Van Buren carried fifteen of the twenty-six states to gain victory with 170 electors.

The chastened Whigs had learned a vital lesson—a coalition is not a party. They resolved to unify their ranks and "win next time."

LIBERTY AND EQUALITY

In the restless young American nation change seemed always to be in the air, palpable and irresistible—change that was personal, economic, social, political, attitudinal. Most indelible was the image of a people constantly on the move, rapidly increasing in number. The population leaped from 5.3 million in 1800 to some 13 million in 1830 to 17 million a decade later, rising especially rapidly on the western frontier. The floodgates of immigration opened, numbers swelling from 5,400 newcomers in 1820 to 23,000 in 1830 to 84,000 in 1840. Lured by tales of abundant jobs and opportunity as well as expectations of political freedom, more than half a million British, Irish, and Germans debarked in New York City alone in the 1830s.

Those immigrants most often became fuel for an American Industrial Revolution. The nation's progress in science and technology was in the Enlightenment's empirical mode best exemplified by Benjamin Franklin and Thomas Jefferson. Francis Bacon, along with Newton and Locke, was enshrined in Jefferson's pantheon; he carried Bacon's picture with him wherever he went. The aim of American empiricism was, in inventor Nathaniel Ames's words, to develop an "Infinity of Utensils, improved in the exercise of art." Americans took inspiration and method from Britain, as well as its technological breakthroughs, sometimes by outright theft. Still, they typically used imported technologies as the starting point for further advances. Native invention drew on what historian Brooke Hindle described as a spirit of competition and emulation, infused with a general enthusiasm for mechanization and a "folk understanding of the ways of technology."

While still trailing the British, Americans had already produced a remarkable number of technological breakthroughs, which were followed by a large crop of entrepreneurs who exploited them. The nation was developing an infrastructure that began to connect distant points on the vast continent, binding them together in the new market economy. Eli Whitney had brought about a transformation in cotton processing with his invention of a machine that used rotating wires in a cylinder to push lint through holes too small to pass the seed. Patented in 1794, the cotton gin enabled one worker using a hand crank to produce fifty pounds of cleaned cotton in a day. Expanding sixtyfold from the 1790s to 1815 largely in order to feed the voracious mills of England, the cotton trade gave a huge economic boost to the rural, slave-powered South while northern textile factories, perched over rushing streams, competed strenuously with established British counterparts.

Indeed, the first modern factory in America was a cotton mill established in 1815 by Francis C. Lowell, who had gone to Britain to gather its industrial secrets and returned to America with plans for large-scale production. With other Boston capitalists, he built a textile mill in nearby Waltham that integrated all the cotton cloth manufacturing processes under one roof. Then, during the 1820s, woolen factories began to replace the hand-loom weaver. Another vital new industry took root with Pittsburgh's establishment of rolling mills that produced iron goods and industrial machinery.

Even more than Britain or France, the United States with its vast area, profusion of rivers, and abundant mountain ranges offered both rich possibilities and daunting obstacles to heavy transport. While American leaders were meeting in Philadelphia to unify the country politically in 1787, John Fitch was experimenting on the Delaware River with a rudimentary type of steamboat that later would help unify the country economically. Within a quarter century ships able to churn upstream on the Ohio and Mississippi rivers began to open up the fertile lands of the Northwest Territory stretching from the Appalachians to the Mississippi.

That was where Robert Fulton, who had experimented with steamboats on the Seine in France and the Hudson in New York State, saw his chance. As migrants poured westward over the Appalachians after the War of 1812 he glimpsed the enormous potential of trade up and down the lengthy Mississippi. He noted that western farmers floated their products downstream to New Orleans on flatboats, sold off the boats for a pittance, and usually hiked back home. Why not steam back with paid passengers and cargo? Fulton and other inventors tested new types of vessels. To navigate through the low water, falls, and floods of western waterways, they had to be lighter than steamboats that navigated more protected rivers of the northeast. Obstacles overcome, 69 steamboats, averaging about 190 tons each, were operating on western rivers by 1820.

Where there were no rivers, Americans dug canals—the greatest connecting Lake Erie with Albany and then with New York City via the Hudson. Since Americans not only lacked the experience of the great canal builders of France and Britain but the excavating machinery used abroad, the Erie Canal was dug by men with shovels and crude derricks. Beginning in 1817, hundreds of Irish "bogtrotters" and other laborers struggled for endless hours amid the muck, building scores of locks with big broad gates where water was plentiful enough to fill and empty basins several times a day. By 1825 the job was done—a canal 363 miles long, 4 feet deep, 28 feet wide at the bottom, with 83 locks lifting boats to heights of up to 600 feet, and costing over $7 million, paid for by the state of New York. The canal was one of the most impressive and consequential public works in American history, opening a pathway to the American Middle West for people and commerce. Its inauguration inspired celebrations all along the line.

By the time of Andrew Jackson's election to the presidency, America's enlightened economy appeared poised for explosive growth. The output of pig iron—a good gauge of the overall economy—was rising from 55,000 tons in 1810 to more than triple that two decades later. Other industries were rapidly expanding: papermaking, printing, glassmaking, shipbuilding, and of course textile manufacturing. Much of the expansion was due to technological innovation, along with increased demand, but the private enterprise was not always entirely private. While the federal government encouraged domestic manufacture through tariff policy, the states could provide direct support to industry by buying stock in favored enterprises, limiting the liability of investors, and giving premiums to "home" industries. Just as New York subsidized the Erie Canal, so Pennsylvania invested heavily in the multilock Main Line that connected Philadelphia to Pittsburgh.

As the economy grew, so did inequalities. Class lines were forming, though the lines of cleavage were not yet sharp. The upper classes in some cities were newly minted with industrial money. In Boston, old Brahmin families like the Lowells and Cabots refreshed their status with the proceeds of industry and, Philip S. Foner wrote, "controlled the Bay State, its press, pulpit, schools, factories, legislature—in short, its economic, political, and cultural life." While this was an exaggeration, the "Lords of the Loom" did wield power to a degree far beyond their numbers.

These modern Medici were found wherever the Industrial Revolution erupted, as were the new classes of exploited and downtrodden workers who endured hours often as long as seventy a week, low pay, and wretched working and living conditions. But, in America as elsewhere, situations might differ widely. Skilled craftsmen—cabinetmakers, glaziers, pewterers, shipwrights, caulkers, sailmakers, riggers—usually had the leverage to command higher pay and a measure of economic security. Unskilled laborers, especially immigrants, worked in the most miserable jobs for the lowest pay as they competed with thousands of others. Women and young children, as usual, made out most poorly. The paternalistic mills of Lowell, which recruited New England farm girls, were praised by some observers, including European visitors, but more common elsewhere were harsh penalties for lateness or absenteeism or for any indication of union sympathies.

Unions remained only a potential challenge to employers in America, despite precursors. During the Revolution, journeymen printers in New York had united to demand a wage increase, which they received—and at once disbanded. During the 1790s, carpenters, hatters, bricklayers, and other craftsmen combined with their employers in mutual aid societies. Later, when bosses and workers disagreed over pay and hours, craftsmen created their own associations with such graphic names as the Journeymen Cabinet and Chair Makers and the Society of Journeymen Shipwrights.

Early on, these associations had also used the strike weapon. Philadelphia house carpenters and cordwainers as well as sailors in New York and Baltimore staged walkouts. The press stoked fears of worker solidarity. The *New York Daily Advertiser* was appalled that a 1795 strike by carpenters and masons might "not only excite similar attempts among all other descriptions of persons who live by manual labor but induce reiterated efforts to increase their wages at seasons when they find their services most wanted." The most striking aspect of these early union efforts was their brevity. Few outlived the grievances that had sparked them into being. Most that did had disappeared by the 1820s.

By the 1830s, workers in the Northeast were developing a leadership idealistic about such social reforms as education while trying to be practical in the quest for better conditions. Still, while desperate and often bitter walkouts brought some gains, strikes probably hurt union workers more than their employers. With the law against them and employers able to fire at will, they had little leverage. Politicians showed scant sympathy for organized labor. The parties were dominated by "overwhelming monied influence," said labor radical Theophilus Fisk, and made laws "in favour of wealth, instead of honest industry." Some leaders experimented with embryonic labor parties and issued fiery manifestos, but, historian Daniel Feller noted, "even the trade societies reflected their members' individualized aspirations and their reticence to accept a separation of classes." They simply wanted their share of their country's new wealth.

. . .

Individualism, indeed, was far more typical of the times than collective action by low-paid laborers. "Every man for himself" was the guiding ideology of Americans in the age of Jackson. Workers were strikingly heterogeneous, competitive, enterprising, pragmatic, and self-promoting, with little time for ideas or even reflection. Such attitudes hardly formed a foundation for strong, collective leadership. Yet some historians have called the era a time of revolution, with the potential of a mighty transformation.

The overriding issue, the one with the most radical potential, was the meaning of the first value mentioned in the Declaration of Independence: equality. One approach would focus on equality as a matter of equal

rights—civil, legal, political, or simply personal. It was this equality, bound
so closely to the idea of liberty, that was least controversial. Far tougher
and deeper were arguments about equality in its economic and social
dimensions—equality of *opportunity* and equality of *condition*.

Almost all Americans backed the principle of equal opportunity. It was a
crucial part not only of the liberal creed but of the United States as the land
of the fresh start, where people were given the opportunity to get ahead using their own brains and brawn and will. Many Americans believed that
equal opportunity was a reality for all, and for most Americans, including
most Jacksonians, that was equality enough. "Distinctions in society will
always exist under every just government," Jackson had said. "Equality of
talents, of education, or of wealth cannot be produced by human institutions."

Whatever the reality, equality of opportunity was hardly a radical idea.
Far more radical—so radical that few except radicals took it seriously—was
the idea of equality of condition, of how people actually lived. And the most
radical of such proposals came from a self-educated political theorist in
New York, Thomas Skidmore, whose readings of Locke and Rousseau, Jefferson and Paine, convinced him that the unequal distribution of property
was at the core of all social evils. Like Jefferson, he proposed to ban the inheritance of property, but Skidmore went further—to "a full and General
Division" of all existing property, its expropriation and redistribution in
equal shares to all, continuing until "there shall be no lenders, no borrow-
ers; no landlords, no tenants; no masters, no journeymen; no Wealth, no
Want."

Skidmore's shocking plan inspired the founding of the New York Workingmen's movement, an independent political party that ran candidates for
state and city offices in 1829. With a platform that watered down Skidmore
but was still radically egalitarian, the party won more votes than the National Republicans and elected two of its members to the state legislature.
Skidmore himself fell just 23 votes short of election. But the party's very
success made it a target for a pro-Clay faction that seized control of it and
expelled Skidmore and his most daring ideas. Stripped of its distinctive appeal to workers, the party was dead a year after its triumph at the polls.

For most workers, "leveling," despite its powerful appeal to those whose
labor was producing wealth for a few while they themselves were impoverished, remained a chimera. The equality they sought was more modest,
though no less compelling. Before the gaping, grinding maw of industriali-

zation, workers faced a different sort of leveling; their fight was to preserve their independence, to have their labor respected and fairly rewarded. The National Trades' Union Convention, meeting in New York in 1836, proclaimed that its aim was to secure for the mechanic "sole and absolute control over the disposal of his labor."

. . .

That hope was hardly inconsistent with the vaunted liberal principle of individualism, including the right to express and pursue one's interests freely. Self-determination was one of the Enlightenment's most powerful principles. But how could such individualism be protected and enhanced in an age when industrialists with their appetite for the cheapest possible labor reigned? What role did government have? Both Whigs and Jacksonian Democrats would invoke Bill of Rights protections against arbitrary government, but beyond that the parties differed. With their emphasis on national development and the expansion of opportunity, the Whigs favored a stronger role for government—especially the federal government—in broadening the field for individual choice and action. This position would gain its classic expression years later in the statement of an old Whig, Abraham Lincoln, that the "legitimate object of government, is to do for a community of people, whatever they need to have done, but can not do, *at all,* or can not, *so well do,* for themselves—in their separate, and individual capacities."

Jacksonians could hardly disagree more. To them government—especially the federal government—could do little to promote, and much to harm, individualism. Rather, people should be set free of government so far as possible, free of impersonal and artificial bonds and duties, free of private as well as public authority, free from that upper-class privilege and domination that in Jacksonian eyes characterized government. People were to be left free to live their own lives, to create their own opportunities and to fashion their own social relationships, to work and play—and vote—as they wished.

And equality? Conflict over the role of government impacted heavily, in ways that Jacksonians did not fully understand, on this transcending issue. Whigs saw equality of opportunity emerging from a free and fair play of economic forces and institutions, such as private property, with government in the crucial and ostensibly neutral role of promoting initiative and enforcing the rules. But what did this mean in practice? The optimistic Whig faith in laissez faire, qualified though it was, and in the capitalists who most benefited from it, effectively limited the party's commitment to keep open the pathways of opportunity to the hard-pressed working poor. Whig blindness to their needs was reflected by its leading economist, Henry Carey, son of a prosperous publisher. He promoted economic diversification and interesting work as the remedy for the ills of industrialization, as the path to human enlightenment and fulfillment. "The more perfect" a person's development, "the greater is his desire for knowledge, the greater his love for literature and art, the greater his desire to see for himself the movements of the world. . . ." A noble sentiment, an Enlightenment-worthy goal, but for whom was Carey writing? Factory labor was stifling indeed, but the urgent problem for workers was that their "whole physical and mental powers" were sacrificed to industry as they eked out an existence by the penny. "Diversity of employment"—yes, but only the middle classes, the Whig base, could even dream of this opportunity, of stretching through interesting jobs to "the higher enjoyments of life."

What, then, of the "people's" party that claimed to speak for dignity and interests of the downtrodden? One labor leader would say he found no fault with Whig politicians. "[T]hey were sent to make the rich richer and the poor poorer, and they obeyed the will of their constituents. But the Democrats, what shall we say of them?" They were even more obtuse than the Whigs and more self-defeating. With their dogmatic assumption that government, even, it appeared, governments they controlled, naturally served the interests of "aristocrats," Jacksonians rejected the huge federal potential to serve the interests of the poor and forgotten and thus shunned the real political struggle. For it was in the field of politics, with its vast potential of men who could use their voting power, that the Jacksonians had their only opportunity to bring about transforming social reform.

If the Jacksonian leadership was so self-defeating, if it continued to enjoy mass support yet had no strategy of active government, what could ordinary people do? Their only practical alternative was to turn to the vehicle they potentially could control, the Democratic party. This was a time, after long dormancy, of party renewal. Partisan combat was already sharpening at the state and local levels. Party activists were reaching out to voters, building alliances with regional interests, establishing infrastructures of local committees and state conventions. Political invective both reflected and shaped party mobilization.

Yet as parties mounted in significance, it was the elite, not the ordinary people, who controlled their direction. Professional party managers were taking over at the national level. The most notable of these was Van Buren himself. A proud party man since the age of seventeen, educated in the lusty politics of the Empire State, he reinforced his leadership of the national Democratic party when he succeeded Jackson in the White House. But he was more effective in strengthening the machinery of his party than in reorienting its antigovernment philosophy. Slow to respond to the Panic of 1837, the nation's worst depression yet, and unwilling to allow direct government intervention in the economy, the president came to be called Martin Van Ruin.

His failure gave the Whigs their chance at last to win the top office. Rejecting Clay and other divisive leaders, they united behind William Henry Harrison, one of the party's 1836 candidates and a national hero since 1811 when he won a famous battle along the Tippecanoe River in Indiana against Shawnees who had ambushed his army. Though he was the son of a wealthy Virginia slave owner and had served in many high public offices since he was first elected to Congress in 1799, Harrison ran in the Jackson mold as the homespun hero, adopting the log cabin and hard cider as his campaign's symbols. It was a reversal of expectations, a Whig pitch for the Democratic vote. Van Buren, meanwhile, was tagged as an exquisite who sipped *soupe à la Reine* with a gold spoon. Behind the hijinks of the 1840 campaign, the Whigs were deadly serious and targeted. Harrison was intent on undoing Jackson's legacy. He won, but sometimes nothing fails like success. When Harrison died within a few weeks of taking office—from a malady caused by a frigid inaugural day, it was said—the Whigs were left with John Tyler, who in the White House turned out to be as much a Democrat as a Whig. Indeed his own party tried to impeach him for vetoing national bank legislation and other heresies.

Nevertheless, the Whig victory of 1840 marked far more than a typical party shift. It signaled the rise of a vigorously competitive two-party system that would regularly offer the "outs" a good shot at ousting the "ins." That election demonstrated that fiery party competition could bring out the voters—an unprecedented 80 percent of eligible white males flooded the polling stations. But would future hot and tight races with highly mobilized partisan followers really force party leaders to respond to their wants and needs with steady economic and social reforms?

Had Americans in fact forged a "Second Constitution" by the end of the 1830s—a people's charter that embraced the political parties the Founders had shunned? If the 1787 constitution was in part a charter for inaction with its checks and balances, the people's constitution could energize government, connecting the separated circuits by uniting Senate, House, and presidency, sharpening party competition, and taking credit or blame at the next election. What James Madison and the others had put asunder in the 1780s, less known party men sought to put together fifty years later. But would this Second Constitution in fact prove more responsive to American realities, to the needs and interests of *all* the people? Would it empower action—or would fire be needed to bring light?

THE NEW WORLD

The age of Enlightenment, historian Gita May noted, "was also the age of travel." Montesquieu, Voltaire, Johnson, and many others had explored lands foreign to them in the 1700s and written of their observations and conclusions in voluminous letters and journals. Travel intensified in the next century, and the new world of the United States was a popular destination for those curious about the American experiment, eager to check its realities against lofty Enlightenment values. Among them was the Scots-born social reformer Fanny Wright, whose outrage over slavery inspired her in 1825 to found a socialist colony of free blacks, the Nashoba Commune, near Memphis. Frances Trollope's 1832 *Domestic Manners of the Americans* was based on acidulous observations in Cincinnati and became a sensation in London. Still more acute were the reflections of Harriet Martineau, an abolitionist and feminist and pioneer of sociology, whose groundbreaking *Society in America,* published in 1837, was the result of two years' travel around the United States. Martineau was especially appalled by the poor state of women's education, which reflected the nearly complete exclusion of American women from civil life. To men, women's intellectual activity was "dangerous: or, as the phrase is, unfit." American women and slaves had in common, she concluded, that "justice is denied on no better plea than the right of the stronger."

Large numbers of Englishmen and Frenchmen visited America, too, but without leaving observations as vibrant and incisive as those of the famous trio of British women. The exception was Alexis de Tocqueville. This French aristocrat arrived in America in May 1831, less than a year after he had watched Charles X in his carriage being driven into exile from Versailles. The July Revolution prompted the bitter observation that "[a]s for the Bourbons, they have behaved like cowards and do not deserve a thousandth part of the blood that has been spilled over their cause." Tocqueville became the most celebrated of all foreign observers, largely because his enlightened ideas caused him to probe deeply into the most fundamental questions about what he saw as the historic experiment in the New World—questions of life, culture, religion, government, political parties, and above all of liberty and equality—and even to question those ideals themselves.

His observations of America gathered in less than a year of travel and published in two volumes were endlessly fascinating to readers of the time, and to us today. Central to his study was majority rule, which he called the "unlimited power" of the majority, its "irresistibility," even its "tyranny." His concern seemed to reflect an aristocrat's fear of mass rule, a fear engendered by the cruelty and irrationality of the Jacobins who had arrested his parents and killed many of his relatives. Tocqueville recognized the remarkable efforts the Framers—and state constitution makers—had made to tame naked majority rule through the establishment of checks and balances in the new governments. But these, he thought, were inadequate to the ultimate danger of majority power—the tyranny of opinion, the silence observed by a minority when the majority had made its decision. In such cases, when the dissenter was to be shunned "like an impure being," no checks or balances could bridle a majority, especially if, as Tocqueville feared, authority tended to become centralized in the federal government rather than dispersed among the states, and in towns and villages. The powers of enlightenment, of liberty of mind and speech, would be of no avail. Freedom of opinion—that value so indispensable to the Enlightenment project, so hard-won and as yet so precarious in Europe—would disappear.

But how could proud, self-reliant American individualists fall into a submissive silence when confronted by the voice of a majority? How could American democracy become mob rule? Tocqueville acknowledged that the dynamism of American democracy contrasted with the stasis and inertia of aristocratic societies like France. The "equal liberty" of Americans underpinned individualism—men were equal in their freedom to pursue their own forms of happiness and, in a commercial society, that meant the pursuit of wealth. The fluidity of American class structures meant that any man might hold the highest aspirations—and with pluck and perhaps some luck achieve them. That, after all, was the founding legend of the New World, a place of apparently limitless vistas of opportunity.

Yet this individualism exacted a heavy price from both individuals and society. Its defining feature, Tocqueville wrote, was that it "disposes each member of the community to cut himself off from the mass of his fellows." Indeed, others were regarded as competitors. Pursuing private interests, untethered to the thick social structures of old aristocracies, lacking deep familial roots, free of tradition and inherited beliefs, constantly on the move, democratic man, in Tocqueville's portrait, was profoundly *alone*. "Absorbed in downright selfishness" and egotism, he endured ever-multiplying wants, as well as frustrations and resentments over unfulfilled aspirations. His vaunted self-reliance was more a burden than a liberty, and his freedom of opinion extended no further than his own reason as the "most obvious and proximate source of truth." As Tocqueville put it, "Everyone shuts himself up tightly within himself and insists upon judging the world from there." Cut off from those nearest him in matters of judgment, where was democratic man to turn? To the mass, the public—to a conformity with the multitude, with "the enormous pressure of the mind of all upon the intelligence of each."

That, he indicated, was how a society of individualists could paradoxically become a herd, a tyrannous majority, a democratic despotism, if there was no middle passage between the isolated self and the multitude, such as the vast array of associations—political, commercial, religious, and many others—that Tocqueville found in the United States. Lacking them, people would be crushed under the hypertrophy of selfhood; they would suffer the full consequences of the liberal society that made the isolated *self* the measure of all things personal and political and of the market economy that made *money* the measure of all things economic and social.

Tocqueville was writing from the perspective of a disillusioned aristocrat, convinced that his class was doomed, studying the New World in troubled anticipation of transformations of the Old. Europe's early socialists, the agitators and would-be revolutionaries, though, were looking at the old world around them, with its factories and slums, and dreamt of a new world built on justice and virtue. Yet the critiques by agitator and aristocrat of the effects of industrialization and liberalism were remarkably similar in crucial respects. Both deplored their atomizing, isolating impact on human beings and the greed and envy the market nurtured. Rooted as they were in Enlightenment thought and methods, both believed that individualistic values had dangerously overbalanced collective ones, tearing at the fabric of civil society, privileging the distinctions that kept people apart rather than the commonalities that brought them together in mutual need, especially the human happiness that Francis Hutcheson had located in sociability. That posed a question both to thinkers and to practitioners: How might the Enlightenment itself be transformed to confront the Industrial Revolution and the transformations it wrought?

11

Britain: The Fire for Reform

By the 1830s, Tories had ruled Britain almost continuously for four decades, during which time the country experienced massive change, economic and social and attitudinal. Though the rulers had to cope with revolutions abroad and riotous outbreaks at home, they governed with apparent serenity through good times and bad. All this pointed up a paradox. How could a conservative government sit securely on a little island of stability while the currents of change around it were so fast-flowing?

Not least because its leaders were supremely self-confident men, accustomed to governing, resourceful in manipulating power, experienced in employing little expediencies to overcome obstacles. They had, after all, survived not only revolutions in America and France but the direst military threat in centuries, Napoleonic aggression. For them, to rule was an instinct. It was not only a duty but a profession. Hence they achieved a unity and collegiality remarkable in a society riven by ideological, religious, and sectional hatreds, and in the process strengthened cabinet government as a tool of collective leadership.

Still, a key reason for their long rule was that they were Tories who did not always behave like Tories. Historian Christopher Harvie well placed them as sitting "edgily on the right center." They believed in laissez-faire economics but passed regulatory laws when practicality demanded it. They bargained and coalesced with their Whig adversaries on lesser matters when need be. But on the transcending issues—above all, electoral reforms that might open Parliament to outsiders and break their own grip on power—they vowed never to budge.

No one personified this Tory rule more steadfastly, or exercised it more strategically, than Lord Liverpool, prime minister from 1812 to 1827. Unlike prime ministers exposed to the turbulence of the House of Commons,

Liverpool ruled from the backstage of the Lords. Long viewed as a medio-cre reactionary, he later came to be respected as a politician's politician, a team captain who managed to harness more celebrated men. He and his cabinet had their luck, too, enjoying weak opposition in the divided Whig ranks. And, as many a government before and since failed to do, they learned from their successful war leadership and applied its lessons to their domes-tic battles.

The Tories presided over startling growth in people and selective pros-perity. The United Kingdom's population, almost sixteen million in 1800, rose by more than eight million during the next three decades. The brilliant industrial inventions of previous years—the water-powered spinning frame, steam engines, locomotives, machine tools—were now paying off, creating a new middle class that would fuel political reform. Factory own-ers, of course, fared best. The calico printer Robert Peel, reformer and sire to a future Tory prime minister, had fifteen thousand hands on his payroll. Robert Owen boasted that over the first three decades of the nineteenth century, his New Lanark mills brought him and his partners a £300,000 profit. The partners complained that that figure would have been much higher had not the firm been burdened by Owen's determination to im-prove the material and moral conditions of his workers. Cloaked by such titanic profits was immense poverty and wretchedness. That offered a po-litical challenge to any who would take on the men in power. But what kind of leadership would accept this opportunity?

STRATEGIES OF REFORM

Whigs after Waterloo were still living off memories of yesteryear—of their hero, Charles Fox, dead since 1806, of gallant struggles against Pittite re-pression and Crown excesses, of continuing fights to protect the constitu-tional legacy of 1689, of appeals to Enlightenment ideas and values in ringing parliamentary speeches. In the political landscape of the 1820s two things remained constant—Tory supremacy and the dilemma of overcom-ing it. Everywhere Whigs turned, the implacable figure of Liverpool loomed, bolstered by his solid cabinet team and his loyal supporters in Par-liament.

Whigs tenaciously stuck to their own political keystone of liberty, their belief in individual liberty against government, a conviction harking back to Magna Carta and ancient struggles against the Crown. Whigs celebrated religious liberty for Catholics and Dissenters. They supported independence movements in Europe and Latin America. The liberty they believed in, though, was negative liberty, and their great fear was of government's arbitrary power, along with mob rule. That liberty might be enlarged and enriched through the *exercise* of power was rank heresy. Whig liberty was a "rational liberty" regulated by laws, infused by a certain liberal temper, grounded in social hierarchy, well hedged against anarchy. It reflected aristocratic values, best protected by aristocrats. The Whig conception of liberty was not wholly unlike that of the Tories but was grounded in Enlightenment ideas of individual rights and of civil society. This liberty was a natural right that stood under the protection of law, where the settlement of 1689 had lodged it.

The political problem was that this noble vision of liberty from the seventeenth and eighteenth centuries had little hold on hosts of nineteenth-century workers and farmers, entrepreneurs and tradesmen. Popular wants and needs had changed over decades of urban growth, industrial expansion, and radical protest. Negative liberties offered small hope for machine tenders paid starvation wages, factory children standing at their looms twelve hours a day, farm laborers at the mercy of owners and overseers, all denied a share of English liberty—as were women, everywhere excluded even by radicals in their bugle calls for "universal" suffrage.

The philosophical limitations of Whigs raised crucial practical—that is, political—questions. Where were their constituencies? How could they be mobilized? And if Whig leadership could not attract support, would rivals— reformers and radicals and even moderate Tories—steal followers away?

*   *   *

"The feeling in favour of Reform is no meteor flash," a Birmingham newspaper observed in 1831, "no transient burst of passion—but a deep seated, fervent unquenchable fire—a fire that has long been smothered but never extinguished." The reform impetus in Britain went back at least to the 1760s and 1770s, when John Wilkes began to mobilize impoverished Londoners against their exclusion from their government and Christopher Wyvill led a call for more equal representation and broader male suffrage, while "Rockingham Whigs" tried to limit Crown patronage. In 1785, even Pitt had called for the redistricting of seats but, unremarkably, had failed. With the radical Corresponding Societies of the 1790s and emerging working-class consciousness came the belief that economic and social reforms could be achieved only if workers had their own representatives in Parliament. Such a change in turn needed electoral reforms, and in that respect the radical program resembled that of the more advanced Whigs. But the prospect of an independent labor strategy for reform threatened to widen the breach between working people and the Whig party, with its aristocratic and middle-class base of support.

The cleavage turned on what backers hoped to gain from reform. Rising industrial interests were of course more concerned with bolstering their own influence in Parliament than extending political rights to their working-class employees. They demanded that booming business centers like Birmingham receive representation in the House of Commons proportionate to population, as compared with the overrepresentation of declining counties. As late as the 1820s, Leeds, Manchester, Sheffield, and Birmingham had *no* seats in Parliament of their own.

The "unquenchable fire" for reform had ignited bursts of outrage over Britain's most horrific problem—child labor—but no real betterment, even as more and more children were crowded into the "Satanic mills." Parents could be of little help; impoverished themselves, they were expected to train their young for a childhood of factory work. Would Parliament then intervene? Robert Peel's Health and Morals of Apprentices Act of 1802, restricting pauper apprentices in the cotton industry to twelve hours of daily labor, appeared a breakthrough, except that Parliament failed to insist on its enforcement, as it also failed to do in the case of Peel's 1819 Act to limit all child labor in cotton mills to twelve hours.

Who might then rescue countless thousands of children—and women and men—from barbarous conditions of labor? Only radically minded workers and their leaders. It was they who finally stoked the fire of reform that forced regulation.

They were a feisty lot, these radicals, and courageous, too, willing to risk jail or exile or even death in their determination to produce serious reform. Joseph Swann, a hatter condemned in 1819 to several years in gaol for selling seditious pamphlets, spoke up to the sentencing magistrate, "Han ye done? Is that all? Why I thowt ye'd got a bit of hemp for me, and hung me." His wife was arrested when she continued to sell the pamphlets, and after release she had to survive on a parish allowance of 9 shillings a week, with some help from radicals still at liberty.

Communication was crucial for workers needing solidarity, but how could poorly educated or illiterate protesters keep in touch? Largely by reading the radical press or having it read to them. Workers also connected with one another through church groups, countless reading societies, and even ballad singers performing in coffeehouses or on the street.

Publishers, editors, and booksellers often ran the highest risks. Before a 4-penny stamp duty on newspapers was imposed in 1819, the radical press sold in remarkable numbers—Cobbett's *2d. Register* above twenty thousand each week, the *Black Dwarf* around twelve thousand. The duty had the specific aim of putting such periodicals beyond the means of most of the working class. Circulation of stamped papers dropped sharply, but in response a new "unstamped"—illegal—press flourished. The gravest threat to the radical press was direct repression. In one year alone, 1817, twenty-six prosecutions were conducted for seditious and blasphemous libel. One editor languished in jail for months because he could not raise the £1,000 bail. But nothing could stop people *reading*.

＊　＊　＊

The most direct link between reformers and masses of workers were the great demonstrations, featuring celebrities of the stump like Henry Hunt. How could even this orator reach tens of thousands stretched over many acres, gabbling among themselves, joking and flirting, buying or peddling wares? His eyes seemed to distend and protrude and as "he worked himself furious," a colleague wrote of Hunt on the platform, they "almost started from their sockets.... His voice was bellowing; his face swollen and flushed; his griped hand beat as if it were to pulverize; and his whole manner gave token of a painful energy, struggling for utterance." Others, though, felt that Hunt was a mere platform radical, a showman who overly personalized issues. And his issues, some said, were too often popular and simplistic, neglecting the fundamental causes of major social problems.

No doubt Hunt's popularity owed much to the clarity of his message. He minced no words. What was the cause of unemployment? Hunt had demanded at the great demonstration in Spa Fields in late 1816. "Taxation," he replied. "What was the cause of taxation? Corruption." Everything that concerned the people's subsistence or comfort was taxed—bread, beer, "everything they ate, drank, wore and even said." Taxes "were imposed by the authority of a boroughmongering faction who thought of nothing but oppressing the people, and subsisting on the plunder wrung from their miseries."

William Cobbett could not rival Hunt as a platform force, but he had a bluntness and common sense that attracted working-class audiences without putting off more educated listeners. Cobbett liked to talk shillings and pence. He would tell workers how much of their wages they paid in taxes on the necessities of life—about half—and how much of the money "placemen" holding sinecures would put in their pockets—enough to "maintain *a thousand families.*" Then he would thunder, "And yet the insolent hirelings call you the *mob,* the *rabble,* the *scum,* the *swinish multitude,*" and say "that *you* are, and ought to be, considered as nothing in the body politic!"

But as the 1820s wore on, Cobbett appeared to lose some of his popular appeal. He seemed to lack a principled set of ideas, rather firing off in all directions. The writer William Hazlitt contrasted him with Tom Paine, who reduced issues to first principles and self-evident truths, while Cobbett occupied himself with details. Still, he had an enduring base, workers and farmers, who liked him because he had been a farmer and a soldier, because he dressed not like a snobby journalist but like an old-fashioned gentleman, because of his obvious compassion for the poor. Cobbett's main disadvantage was that, large as it might have been, his following was not solid or organized but dispersed, even isolated. It seemed unlikely that Cobbett could mobilize workers in the event of a political crisis requiring firm and yet compassionate leadership.

Could anyone? Robert Owen, back from America in 1828, rejoined militant ranks. His strategy of change and reform stayed fundamentally the same—all, employers and employees, landlords and farmers, should unite to help the poor and oppressed. He still put community over competition, collective order over individualism, socialism over capitalism. Other radicals could hardly disagree more. Cobbett called Owen's Village of Co-operation a "parallelogram of paupers." Some charged him with proposing a "community of slaves." The differences among reform leaders were deep and portentous. The radicals saw open political war between workers' movements and a formidable coalition of Tories, industrialists, and landowners as the only feasible strategy. By bringing conflict to a crisis, workers would gain at least a hearing for their ideas and perhaps win over Britons who had been taught to regard unfettered capitalism as part of the natural order and shake the government into meaningful concessions. Owen and others rejected "class war" in favor of national unity, the cooptation of all good men behind good causes, relying on both rational persuasion and innate human sympathies. This conflict over reform strategy would stimulate and complicate reform efforts for years to come.

IDEAS AS WEAPONS

"There is an important distinction between thoughts and ideas," the German legal philosopher Hermann Kantorowicz wrote. "Men possess thoughts but ideas possess men." In the early nineteenth century, Western thinkers were still resonating to the ideas of Hobbes and Montesquieu, Locke and Rousseau, and a host of other grand theorists. But possessed as they were by ideas, they were also arming ideas as weapons, few more aggressively than the remarkable father/son team of James Mill and John Stuart Mill.

Among eminent Enlightenment intellectuals, James Mill had strikingly low class origins—born in 1773 of a Scottish shoemaker and a servant girl. This humble start in life and the exertions required for Mill to escape it doubtless fueled his passionate hatred for the aristocracy, which he would describe as both filled with mental defectives and exercising almost dictatorial power in Britain. A precocious child, James got a push by his mother over her other children, and then by his parish minister and a local aristocratic couple who sponsored him at the University of Edinburgh. There he flowered intellectually, drinking in Enlightenment ideas during the 1790s as the Revolution in France escalated. Disappointing his mother's hopes that he would join the ministry, James set out for London to make his name and living as an intellectual. He first worked as a journalist, writing on a wide range of topics. Needing to support a wife and growing family, he plunged into writing a history of British India. This work helped him win a well-paid post at the East India Company, which in turn gave him a secure standing both as a civil servant and among the London intelligentsia. And it was in London that he came under the influence of Jeremy Bentham, who would dominate young James Mill's intellectual development for years.

Mill and Bentham first met in 1808. Their disparate ages—Bentham's sixty years to Mill's thirty-five—seemed only to cement their relationship. "Bentham needed an intelligent disciple and a forceful man to make a political philosophy and party out of his Utilitarian doctrines," Mill's biographer Bruce Mazlish wrote; "Mill needed—psychologically and economically—a patron and a philosophical mentor under whom he could serve with security." Their intense relationship was to last almost twenty years. Bentham was by now renowned for his utilitarianism, yet the political impact of his central precept and ultimate goal—the greatest happiness of the greatest numbers—was yet to be tried. In Mill, Bentham found an ambitious and relentless political agent for his ideas.

◦ ◦ ◦

Gathering around him a small band of followers, James Mill aimed at nothing less than a revolution in British government, the transformation of a political system controlled by a self-serving aristocracy into a government by and for "the people." But Mill was no populist. Just as he refused to distinguish between Whigs and Tories—they were one aristocratic party—so he denied that there was any meaningful class conflict, or clash of interests, except that between the rulers and the ruled. "The people" were simply all those who were not of the aristocracy—what his disciple Francis Place called "the masses and millions." As intellectual historian Joseph Hamburger noted, Mill's political doctrine was "impersonal," not grounded in the needs, fears, or aspirations of any particular class in society. Though he shared the radicals' agenda for democratization—universal suffrage, the secret ballot, shorter parliaments—Mill shunned their economic and social goals. He stood apart from radical leaders, the Hunts and Cobbetts and Owens, whose advocacy for the working classes blurred that war-to-the-death against aristocracy.

Mill's chosen weapon was a campaign in the press, to rouse "the people" against their rulers. "Nothing is more important," he wrote, "than the frequent recounting of those evils, which they who suffer them always know, but of which they lose the accurate and pungent sense, if the thought of them is not frequently and vividly renewed." Because Britain's rulers had in the past successfully deflected—or repressed—discontent, protest must be raised to an intensity "the rulers do not think it prudent to disregard."

When Mill's band of "Philosophical Radicals" went to war in the 1820s, their pressure campaign—articles in newspapers, books, pamphlets, and journals, as well as public debates—inevitably merged with the efforts of other radicals. They were not the only ones warning of dire consequences if reform was denied. But James Mill pioneered the menace of revolution as a deliberate *tactic* in the fight for reform, to steel the nerve of parliamentary supporters and to intimidate opponents. Mill never promoted violence but rather, as one of his followers, Charles Buller, said, "such a fear of it as to render its use unnecessary." Rational self-interest would bring the aristocrats to heel; at the brink of destruction, they would see, Buller went on, "that property and life are worth preserving, even by the sacrifice of their political power."

. . .

During these years James Mill was undertaking a venture almost as extraordinary as overthrowing the aristocracy—he was educating his first child, John, born in 1806. He had begun when the boy was two years old. For three or four hours a day the father drilled him not only in languages and literature but in philosophical doctrine. In his *Autobiography*, John

Stuart Mill claimed that he had learned to read Greek at the age of three and by eight had studied "a number of Greek prose authors, among whom I remember the whole of Herodotus, and of Xenophon's Cyropædia and Memorials of Socrates. . . ." Not to mention "the first six dialogues" of Plato. Was this mere boasting? Probably not. A preserved letter John wrote to Bentham at the age of six has been described by a scholar as "unsettlingly mature." As a teacher, though, James Mill was demanding and didactic and joyless. A friend and admirer said later that John was a boy who "never was a boy."

Today all this would seem a recipe for disaster, but it was not, at least for a time. "There is abundant evidence," Mazlish wrote, that young Mill "thought his father the most wonderful and intelligent, the strongest and wisest, person in the world, and that he continued in this belief beyond the age of most adoring children." This father-son closeness persisted into John's teenage years, and the father procured his seventeen year old a clerkship at the East India Company. The son's duties were so routine that he could dispose of them in a few hours, leaving the rest of the day for his reading and writing—no doubt to the satisfaction of his father.

For some years John kept up his roles of good son and faithful Benthamite. From his early teens, indeed, he spent happy summers at Bentham's vast house in Somerset. By sixteen he was moving into a broader orbit, first by organizing peer groups of young Utilitarians who would discuss diverse thinkers such as Ricardo on economics, Hobbes on logic, and a range of other works, including James Mill's *Analysis of the Phenomena of the Human Mind*. By the mid-1820s, John was a principal recruiter for his father, bringing in the core of a younger generation of Philosophical Radicals.

To some, the younger Mill appeared headed toward a prominent political career, but his main interests lay in ideas rather than activism. Then, in 1829, the critic and preeminent Whig Thomas Babington Macaulay brutally attacked Utilitarian pretensions. Macaulay mocked claims that such concepts as the "felicific calculus," a computation Bentham developed to measure precisely the pleasure or pain derived from any action, rested on a science of human nature. Reviewing James Mill's *Essay on Government,* he castigated "that slovenliness of thinking which is often concealed beneath a peculiar ostentation of logical neatness." Once people "begin to talk of power, happiness, misery, pain, pleasure, motives, objects of desire, as they talk of lines and numbers," Macaulay wrote, "there is no end to the contradictions and absurdities into which they fall."

Macaulay's attack on Utilitarianism—and on his father—gave John Stuart Mill "much to think about." He was already in the midst of what he later called "a crisis in my mental history," a deep depression that was causing him to lose faith not only in his father and in the ideas he had been born to but in himself. To a degree, and under Macaulay's goad, the twenty-three year old rejected his father's philosophy as narrow and coldly abstract. "The true system" of philosophy, he now believed, "was something much more complex and many-sided than I had previously had any idea of." Aspiring to "Goethe's device" of "many-sidedness," he turned to the world of feeling, poetry, beauty, love, and joy. These were the real conditions and substance of happiness!

John Stuart Mill's new world did not shut him off from events around him; rather, his political interests seemed to intensify and broaden. On hearing of the collapse of Charles X's monarchy in July 1830, Mill and two friends sailed for France. His later account of the trip in his *Autobiography* was, alas, highly abbreviated: "I went at once to Paris, was introduced to Lafayette, and laid the groundwork of the intercourse I afterwards kept up with several of the active chiefs of the extreme popular party." One of his companions, though, reported an incident that reflected Mill's new joie de vivre. When Louis-Philippe visited the opera, the English threesome incited the audience to demand the playing of "La Marseillaise" and shouted, "Debout! debout!" until the whole throng, including the new king himself, rose to its feet for that revolutionary call to arms.

In Paris, Mill met also with some disciples of Saint-Simon who impressed him with their principled leadership of the working class in the July Revolution and their belief in the "perfect equality of men and women." He was even more inspired by workers who, even though starving, had committed no excesses during the July days. The question remained whether, back in Britain, a rapport between intellectuals and workers could produce equally telling results.

STUMBLING TOWARD REFORM

Would the Tories rule forever? Liverpool died in 1827, but conservatives could fall back on a phalanx of experienced leaders. Not least of these was Wellington, hero of Waterloo, who took over as prime minister the following year. The Iron Duke inherited a relatively unified party but also the burning issue that had unhorsed Pitt almost three decades before, Catholic emancipation. Wellington faced a formidable foe in Daniel O'Connell as the champion of Irish resistance and the founder of the powerful Catholic Association, a reform movement that had taken on the character of an alternative Irish government. In a supreme effort to forestall O'Connell's intransigence and even revolution in Ireland, Wellington won Tory support for an emancipation act admitting Catholics to Parliament and to virtually all offices—while also banning the Catholic Association. The king, George IV, reluctantly went along.

Catholic emancipation was a direct affront to a large band of Tory Ultras, 173 of whom voted against it. Tension was high; Wellington fought a duel with a peer who charged him with deceit, and Oxford took out its anger against the duke by ejecting his lieutenant, the younger Robert Peel, from the university's parliamentary seat.

The deep rift among Tories was a fine opening for the Whigs, if only they would exploit it. But the Whig party remained in a parlous state. Trapped for so long between Tory parliamentary domination and assaults from radicals, the party was badly fragmented, especially over parliamentary reform, to which Whigs had, at least in principle, been committed for generations. With reform agitation rising in the country, Whigs could not agree on what to do. Some thought reform an opportunity, others a dangerous gamble. Some feared going too far, others not going far enough.

Whig leadership could hardly have been weaker. The chief, Lord Grey, a handsome and wealthy patrician of the kind that inhabits novels, himself embodied the long Whig vacillations over reform. As a young man in the 1790s, he had collaborated closely with radicals to present a sweeping reform plan to the Commons. By 1810, though, he was warning that "the examples of the other nations of Europe should deter us from any precipitate attempt to hurry on to premature or violent operation a measure on which the best interests of the nation so essentially depend." Seven years later he remained haunted by the threat of radical change; his embrace of even gradual and moderate reform was at best half-hearted. In any case, he noted, among Whigs "agreement upon that question is hopeless." At about the same time, his colleague William Lamb said that he would support reform *if* "the people should ever become seriously and perseveringly desirous of it." But, he concluded, "the people did not wish it."

Lamb (later Viscount Melbourne) was voicing Whig cant about deference to the popular spirit. At the heart of their dilemma was precisely their mistrust of the people, their anxiety about mob rule. Most Whigs stood away from the radical claims to popular sovereignty voiced by Paine and echoed by agitators of the 1810s and 1820s. Yet they also worried they would find themselves, as Charles Fox had once warned, isolated between "the Court and the Democrats."

For long, the result was irresolution, inaction, with sound and occasionally fury that signified nothing. By the late 1820s, though, Whigs realized that action was necessary. Macaulay noted that economic and social changes had created a "pressure almost to bursting" between "the young energy of one class and the ancient privileges of another," with "the new society under the old institutions." But how yield to the people without yielding control? Lord Holland, Fox's son, set the objectives: Reform must extend "a real and positive and not a mere nominal representation" to the broad public, while also securing "the tranquility and subordination of the people."

Could Whig leaders find that narrow path to safety before events, or the people, took over?

. . .

It is a dream of democrats that in the face of massive injustice a united people under enlightened leadership will rise in indignation, overcome the opposition, and sweep on to total victory in the form of fundamental change. This was not the happy lot of British reformers, at least during most of their struggles. People were passive and divided, leaders uncertain and indecisive, the ultimate change partial and fragile. Still, that change marked the start of crucial alterations in British government and politics.

From the start reformers lacked a simple, dominating goal such as toppling a tyrant. Instead they confronted a *system* deeply entrenched in British history and culture. Consider the notorious "rotten boroughs," with only a few inhabitants eligible to vote. Or the "pocket boroughs," where a rich patron could control the nomination process through his family and dependents and a discreet use of funds. Or seats that were simply purchased. Long embedded in local political cultures and ferociously protected by their beneficiaries in Parliament, these little power systems could not easily be uprooted. Directly fortifying them was extreme malrepresentation, allowing tiny counties to have more votes in the Commons than booming population centers.

Reform hopes had risen and fallen during the 1820s as Whigs and radicals confronted a Tory leadership as intractable as the system it ruled. Toward the end of the decade Grey had even considered joining Wellington's government rather than replacing it. Then, in June 1830, King George IV died, precipitating a general election. With Wellington standing against reform, the stage seemed set for a showdown. It was not to be. With both Tories and Whigs internally divided, the election results were mixed, but his party carried enough seats for Wellington to cling to office. Then, after winning some support from moderates, he unaccountably made an utterly polarizing speech that repudiated reform in categorical terms. Soon after, in November 1830, the old general lost a parliamentary vote on a lesser issue and resigned office.

At last Grey and his fellow Whigs had gained the government bench, but without a clear mandate. The new prime minister selected a committee to draft reform proposals, insisting that the package must be broad enough to satisfy the public but also must "afford sure ground of resistance to further innovation." This was the new Whig dogma; it ruled out universal manhood suffrage and other radical proposals. After Lord John Russell proudly offered the modest product to the House of Commons, it passed its second reading by a single vote. Even this limited measure was bound to be so cut up in its further progress through Parliament that Grey insisted on a dissolution and new election. He was rewarded for his firmness when Whigs won a sweeping victory in the Commons in 1831.

Now Grey had the majority he needed—but not in the House of Lords. Despite warnings that a stubborn English aristocracy might meet the same fate as the French nobility forty years earlier, the peers voted the reform bill down. Grey's only recourse was to seek the assent of King William IV to create enough peers to carry a majority in the Lords. The new king, despite earlier professions of support for reform, refused and invited Wellington to form a new government. But even many Tories were unwilling to oppose the overwhelming wishes of the people for reform. William had no choice but to turn back to Grey and consent to his scheme to pack the Lords. Grey, a peer himself who once had said that in a crisis he would "stand by his order," hesitated to use the ultimate constitutional weapon. He decided it was best deployed as a threat, as a show of both power and patience, because then appreciative peers would support reform. Grey was right. His clear message that he would advise creation of peers *if necessary* brought a close victory in the Lords, 184 to 175. Reform was law.

* * *

The Great Reform Act of 1832, as it came to be called, was both great and not so great. Fifty-six pocket or rotten boroughs lost their parliamentary representation altogether, and thirty more were reduced from two seats to one. Twenty-two new boroughs, mostly in the north and in the Midlands, were awarded two seats each and twenty others one. Cities gained better representation, but inequalities remained: While some London constituencies had 7,000 voters, nationwide 115 boroughs had fewer than 500. A uniform voting right was established, enfranchising all males who owned or rented property worth at least £10, thus extending the vote to hosts of middle-class townspeople and at once enlarging the electorate by 50 percent. As in France, it was the new middle class that benefited most from workers' exertions and sacrifices. Millions of those who had the direst need of government attention to their interests, the working and unemployed poor, were left with no vote and no representation. Women not only remained barred from the polls, the act put into law the existing practice of denying them suffrage. And the secret ballot was not won because Grey and his cabinet opposed it.

The obstacles to reform of Parliament within Parliament itself had been so forbidding as to raise the question of why even the half-measures were passed. The answer lay not in the turmoil in Parliament but turbulence in the country. On the eve of the parliamentary struggle, Cobbett and Hunt had issued a joint manifesto to workers urging them to reject compromise. Never mind the adage that "*half a loaf is better than no bread*; in this case half a loaf *is no bread*."

Workers in London who established the "National Union of the Working Classes and Others" accepted the Whig proposals, but only as a first step toward universal suffrage and broader goals. The NUWC and other groups had effectively pressured Parliament with threats of upheaval and even revolution if reform failed. When the bill was languishing in the Lords, NUWC leaders called on "all the working classes to immediately arm themselves" and the *Poor Man's Guardian* urged workingmen to "form your millions" into a "Popular Guard."

James Mill's followers used their connections to leading Whigs to convey alarming estimates of popular feeling, including "apprehensions" of "a violent revolution." Francis Place organized the London-based National Political Union and played a key role in uniting middle and working classes behind the bill. If the Tories prevailed, Place had warned a Whig MP, "we shall have a commotion in the nature of a civil war"—"towns will be barricaded, new municipal arrangements will be made by the inhabitants." Most ominously, Place added that "in less than five days we shall have the soldiers with us." While the threats of violent revolution were more a brilliant exercise in fearmongering than anything real, historian Michael Brock noted that the intensity of the militants "staggered the politicians on both sides."

Country people had awaited the daily reports of the bill's progress from London with excited interest. "Artisans in country places tramped miles after work to hear the news," Brock wrote. "Six or seven farm hands or miners clubbed together to buy a paper at half price when it was a day or two old; and one of them would read it aloud to the group." Sitting in the village ale-house or around a single candle in a shed, they learned about the historic events in London. While great festivals celebrated passage of the Reform Act, Cobbett chose to mark the day with a group of activist farm laborers who earlier had remonstrated "with the farmers, the parsons, and landowners" over wages "that had reduced them to a state of half-starvation."

The big surprise of the reform bill agitation was the eruption of middle- and working-class people in "Political Unions." Beginning in Birmingham in January 1830, at least one hundred of these organizations mushroomed across England. They spread to London and Liverpool and Manchester and Leeds, creating a truly national campaign for the radical reform agenda. The Political Unions prided themselves on offering a model of democratic processes, with the open election of leaders, free debate, and grassroots organization. Pointedly inclusive, they reached out to farmers and workers, professionals and merchants, local officials and soldiers, radical Whigs and moderate Tories. They perfected the art of the mass action, organizing "monster" rallies and marches of tens of thousands.

The Political Unions were controversial from the start—more in the fighting among themselves than in the eyes of Wellington's administration, which ignored them until an informant warned that they were likely to become "a most dangerous body." Within and between the widespread unions, conflicts blazed over strategic questions—how closely to work with the Whigs, whether to press for economic as well as political reforms, whether to require members to possess "good moral character," and, above all, whether to support Grey when the Whigs compromised on reform. When the struggle was at its peak, with riots in Derby, Bristol, and elsewhere, some unions discussed organizing themselves along military lines, but they made a point of decrying violence—their aim was self-defense and "the preservation of tranquillity"—and of repeatedly affirming their loyalty to "His Gracious Majesty." Still, the unions thrived on conflict and controversy, turning every setback in Parliament into a renewed recruiting drive.

Naturally the Political Unions with their mass mobilization took the credit for passage of the Reform Act, while Cobbett boasted that it was pressure from the "Country Labourers" that achieved the breakthrough. James Mill and his allies claimed that without their use of the press to raise, at key moments, the specter of revolution, reformers "might have talked and petitioned for an age to come." The press itself, able now to turn out thousands of cheap copies of newspapers in a few hours, had shown new powers to agitate and to soothe, to act as a vital channel between the public and political leaders. Inside Parliament, moderate Tories not only supplied crucial votes for reform but undermined Tory Ultra warnings of its dangers, while advanced Whigs applied steady pressure on their leaders. And that Whig leadership, weak and fumbling for so long, culminated in Grey's patient and even imaginative transactional leadership at the crucial junctures that produced a transforming outcome.

Victory had many fathers. Who was responsible for reform? The easy—and probably correct—answer is all of them, fortifying one another. But in broadest perspective, it was the *idea* of reform, in the air for generations, that at times dimmed but never died and finally gathered an irresistible force to win through in 1832.

It is relatively easy to quantify election returns, parliamentary votes, poverty rates, strikes, while the impact of ideas or ideologies is more speculation than science. Still, we learn enough from an era's books, newspapers, sermons, speeches, demonstrations, and even more fugitive data to have a fairly good understanding of what may have been on the minds of a people. And in Britain in the 1820s and 1830s, that was an array of ideas about political rights and political power, about liberty and self-government, about equality and representation, the claims of human dignity, of social order, and of happiness. And we gain some hints of the linkage between these ideas and the politics of reform when we know that the principles propelling the Political Unions were drawn from Tom Paine and the Corresponding Societies of the 1790s and still farther back, from John Wilkes and the American Revolution, whose own intellectual roots reached to the transforming ideas of the seventeenth and early eighteenth centuries. As elsewhere, the Enlightenment offered both ends and means for transforming leadership. The Reform Act of 1832 was the work of generations of principle and conflict and compromise, of leaders and followers thinking and acting like children of the Enlightenment.

THE DAWNING OF A LIBERAL PARTY

It was a band of battle-hardened Whig leaders that celebrated the passage of the Reform Act. But the celebration was short-lived. After the first general election to the reformed Commons a few months later returned a huge Whig majority, the gritty realities of governing brought the leaders back to earth. Their mandate was for more reform and the agenda was long and formidable—slavery, child labor, poverty, education, the church, local government, the secret ballot.

Were the Whigs capable of mastering such wide reform tides? The answer soon became clear. After leading Parliament to refashion itself, Lord Grey returned to form. His stately phrase-making, delivered in the Lords "with a manly bearing and with the Blue Ribbon and Garter prominently displayed," in historian Jonathan Parry's words, belied his real traits: "fastidious, timid, fatalistic, gloomy and strikingly indecisive." Lacking in resolution and energy, overly conciliatory and philosophically divided, Grey remained a reluctant reformer.

Putting together a new cabinet tested his mettle—whether to choose a small, unified, efficient leadership or a broader array of politicians that reflected the diversity of the Whig cause. He chose the latter. His cabinet included a tough but down-to-earth workhorse in Viscount Althorp, a smooth political operator like Viscount Melbourne, a young and dedicated reformer such as Lord John Russell, and the ever self-promoting populist Henry Brougham, created baron in 1830. All told, the cabinet ranged from radical Benthamites to conservative Whigs who hardly differed from moderate Tories. Not only were many of these men members of the peerage, but they had extensive family connections. Grey, in particular, had two sons in government office, a son-in-law in the cabinet, and two in-laws serving in turn as parliamentary whips, as well as a brother who was a bishop.

The Whig leaders might have stood together if they had merely to carry out the familiar policies they had struggled for over the years. But looming over them was a phantom that would plague British governments for another century and more: Ireland. Centuries of British rule had brought little but endemic poverty, ignorance, and religious strife to the eight million Irish. According to contemporary estimates, over a quarter of Ireland's people lived below a "rock-bottom" poverty line. Little more than a third of its men and less than a fifth of its women were literate. Sometimes the state of affairs was grotesque. Doon, in Limerick, had but one Protestant inhabitant, the clergyman, who nonetheless claimed, as the law entitled him to, tithe from the five thousand Catholics in his parish. To get some of the money, the authorities seized the Catholic priest's cow for auction under government supervision, protected by hundreds of troops from the 12th Lancers and 92nd Highlanders. But no parishioner would bid for it. Little could better symbolize the obtuse, futile meanness of British rule. The government kept the cow.

The man who led the Irish people and who for years had bedeviled both Tory and Whig leaders was Daniel O'Connell, the fiery barrister who had been the effective author of Catholic emancipation. O'Connell was, according to historian Oliver MacDonagh, "in the mainstream of the historic liberal tradition of the enlightenment and the *philosophes*—and he transmitted many of its values and assumptions to his awakening countrymen." Elected to Parliament but unable to take his seat until emancipation, O'Connell launched a campaign for repeal of the 1800 Act of Union that bound Ireland into the United Kingdom, a union with the character of an occupation. As the Grey government struggled for parliamentary votes, O'Connell was feared not only for his control of thirty or forty Irish followers in the Commons but because he had shrewdly formed alliances with the middle-class English radicals that the Whigs had counted on for support.

To deflect Irish resistance, the Whigs passed a bill in 1833 to allow the "appropriation" of surplus Irish Protestant church revenues to meet such broader needs as education. Four of Grey's ministers resigned over this concession, revealing the folly of the prime minister's all-in cabinet-making. Then Grey tacked the other direction, deciding to renew the notorious Coercion Act, authorizing the lord lieutenant to ban public meetings, in the face of O'Connell's blustering and bullying opposition. Again the cabinet split, and in 1834 Grey resigned, to be succeeded briefly by Melbourne.

The Irish failure of the Grey regime was all the more depressing in the light of a historic legislative victory the Whigs had won—the abolition of slavery in 1833; a year later, eight hundred thousand slaves throughout the British empire became free. Another, far more mixed, achievement of Whig government after the Reform Act was an extensive revision and modernization, on Benthamite principles, of the Poor Law. It was a daring measure to replace patchwork local relief with a uniform national system, but the new workhouses were designed to be, an official said, "as like prisons as possible," with "severe and repulsive" discipline. The reformers assumed that poverty was caused by "work-shyness" and other character defects, so they intended that no able-bodied person would willingly seek incarceration in the workhouses, while those driven there by utter desperation would be shocked and humiliated into moral improvement. Here was Bentham's utilitarianism institutionalized as "pauper management," on the premise that the human brute was motivated by little other than the allure of pleasures and, in workhouses, the disagreeableness of pain.

These "new Bastilles" spreading across the country stirred powerful resentment among working people. To some, they represented class war at its most naked; to others, the dissolution of old community bonds, of responsibility and caring for unfortunate neighbors, or, as one opponent put it, of "the legal and ancient title of the poor to existence."

*   *   *

A short Tory interregnum followed the collapse of the Whig government, until one more switch of the pendulum brought Melbourne in again as prime minister in April 1835 to establish a new reform government with another opportunity for transforming leadership. If there was an identifiable moment when a new and coherent Liberal party emerged from the factionalized Whigs and their reformist allies, it came in 1835. Whig leaders had an illustrious history of fighting overbearing monarchs and domineering Tories but a less illustrious history, too, of fighting as brutally among themselves, and Melbourne now needed and insisted on a more solid base to support a firm and lasting government. After all, Robert Peel was, at the same time, forging a counterpart—a new Conservative party—from the divided and disorganized Tories. Melbourne's partnership with the more liberal Lord John Russell, who took over the vital post of leader of the Commons, brought together two no-nonsense professionals. Prima donnas like Brougham had no place in their cabinet.

The new party leadership could be strong because of the depth of its support in both Parliament and country. The big reform majority in the Commons wanted clear direction after the chaos of the Grey ministry. New whips enforced discipline among the rank and file. Stronger party unity and direction invoked a sharpening of party spirit at the grass roots, encouraged and coordinated by a new reform association, which in turn empowered the leadership.

Russell soon emerged as the outstanding leader. Firm in his liberal convictions, clear and convincing in his oratory, flexible in tactics, he united elements that had divided and immobilized Whigs in the past—old guard Whigs, committed reformers, outspoken radicals, Catholics, Dissenters—together with the new liberal middle class emerging from the Industrial Revolution. His principled leadership had its source in practical experience but even more, perhaps, in his intellectual background. He had written a Whiggish history of the British constitution and a biography of Charles James Fox, as well as a survey of Europe's history since 1713, and he had both a secure sense of the relation of ideas to events and an optimism that liberty would steadily expand in its reach and dimensions through gradual reform. He had his shortcomings, too, such as a certain haughtiness and petulance, but the "ultimate fact about Russell," Parry wrote, "is that a combination of name, achievement, talent, fearlessness and principle left him without serious rivals as the greatest Liberal statesman of his age."

Such leadership was needed as the reformers tackled the acute needs of the 1830s. After the Grey ministry had confronted problems dammed up for decades by the Tories, such as slavery and the Poor Law, the Melbourne government proceeded more cautiously to deal with less dramatic and clear-cut issues. Still, Russell and his Liberal colleagues had an abiding faith in the capacity of government and law to improve human behavior through the reform of institutions. Children (or grandchildren) of the Enlightenment, they were members of such bodies as the Society for the Diffusion of Useful Knowledge and the British Association for the Advancement of Science. They even hoped that reforms like more scientific prison management and the extension of public education—improving the moral characters of criminals and children—would help revolutionize the condition of humankind. They believed in *systemic* change as well as specific reforms—in transforming the structure of government as well as its powers. They tackled the chaotic and archaic array of local governments through such legislation as the 1835 Municipal Corporations Act. It was the capacity of these reformers to link governmental means to human ends that would typify the transformations that lay ahead.

The tenacity of embedded institutions, though, is such that reform movements seem destined to limited terms of office. Liberal party support dwindled in successive elections, and in 1840 Peel and the Conservatives won a parliamentary majority. Much of the reform agenda remained uncompleted. But, after decades of deadened aristocratic rule, a grand political structure had slowly been shaped since the Napoleonic wars—a vigorous, competitive system of two political parties that over two centuries would offer real choices to an expanding electorate, broaden representative institutions, and provide the Western world a model of democratic leadership that, with all its perfections and imperfections, glories and failures, would endure.

12

The Negative of Liberty

If the reach and richness of the Enlightenment could be captured in a word, it would be *freedom*—the revolutionary assumption that human beings had a natural right to personal liberty, which went hand in hand with Enlightenment thinking about human nature, human autonomy and educability, self-determination, equality. Though, in Lockean principle, all human beings should have the potential to enjoy freedom in its fullness, in practice there were strong, even gross limitations that affected large numbers of people in Europe and the United States. The debate in Britain over the Reform Act, for instance, had exposed the disdain for and fear of the uneducated, impoverished masses who were, in most countries for much of the era, the overwhelming majority of the population.

Of the "populace which has only its hands to live by," Voltaire had written sourly, "I doubt that this order of citizens will ever have the time or capacity to educate itself; they would die of hunger before becoming philosophers." It was, in any case, "essential that there be ignorant wretches" to labor on the estates of enlightened *honnêtes gens* like—well, like Voltaire himself—without becoming dissatisfied with their humble, exploited station.

In the new United States, the fate of the republic was thought to rest with an enlightened citizenry capable of rational debate and principled decision. Thomas Jefferson and other reformers promoted universal education in state-supported schools, to give, as Noah Webster put it, "every citizen an opportunity of acquiring knowledge and fitting himself for places of trust." Yet education remained exclusive. Virginia repeatedly rebuffed Jefferson's proposals "to illuminate, as far as practicable, the minds of the people at large" by state subsidies for elementary and higher education. And as the republican ideal of an ordered and virtuous citizenry faded beneath the rush and clamor of an industrializing and commercial nation, men like Webster turned against universal education. In his *American Dictionary,* published in 1828, Webster defined "people" as "the vulgar; the mass of illiterate persons" and "the commonalty, as distinct from men of rank."

Suspicions of "the people" were etched into the constitutions of the age of Enlightenment, with provisions that blocked and diffused majority power. Everywhere, suffrage was linked to property or to taxes paid or, in some cases, to a virtuous character. Even as democratization slowly spread, the argument over the capacities of "the people" for real majority rule was vigorously debated.

So much for white men—at least they were in the conversation. It was they whom Enlightenment thinkers typically meant when they talked about the people. There were millions of others in the West or in its control who were not included, whose full humanity and capacity for freedom were ignored, marginalized, or denied in the Enlightenment, and who faced a long, daunting battle to be regarded and treated as *people.*

PEOPLE AS PROPERTY

By the late eighteenth century, British investors and shipowners had long been managing one of the largest forced migrations in history, profiting enormously from their global traffic in bodies. They believed they thoroughly earned their wealth. Organizing slave-collecting expeditions on a continent far to the south, recruiting captains and seamen for the monstrous task of delivering bound captives into slavery, dealing with shifting slave markets in the Americas—all this took ingenuity and hard work.

The British did not simply manage slavery from afar. King Charles II had bought a personal servant for £50. In 1765 a Liverpool newspaper advertised: "To be sold at George's Coffee-house, betwixt the hours of six and eight o'clock, a very fine negro girl about eight years of age, very healthy, and hath been some time from the coast." Yet within a few decades the British would not only revolt against the well-entrenched and hugely profitable slave trade—they would ban it. How could such a drastic reversal come about?

Partly because of the sheer horror of the trade itself. By the late eighteenth century, expeditions were reaching deep into the African interior to buy men and women—who often had been kidnapped or captured in war—from tribal chieftains or at markets. Then the captives would be forced on long marches from "catchment areas" to the African coast, where they would be imprisoned in "slave castles" until they were sold again. The fate of human cargo on the high seas was well known: shackled together, often left naked to the elements, flogged for "misbehavior," sometimes dumped overboard when dying.

The British people stood for this infamy for much of the eighteenth century because they had few contrary guidelines from their political leadership, for whom slaving was excellent commerce. And much literature confirmed stereotypes. A *Universal History* published in midcentury showed Africans as "proud, lazy, treacherous, thievish, hot, and addicted to all kinds of lusts." Not to mention that they were "quaffers of human blood."

Yet it was finally the "common people" of Britain who took leadership in the counterattack against the slave trade. Shaking off their own prejudices, they could not ignore the increasingly graphic accounts in the press of the inhuman treatment of black people. Nor could they close their ears to the entreaties of grassroots religious leaders. Dissenting churches abandoned long-held Christian rationalizations that slavery was part of God's plan or fitting punishment for the descendants of Cain or missionary opportunity. The great Methodist John Wesley had lived in Georgia and knew slavery firsthand. He condemned the trade in slaves as "a scandal of religion, of England, and of human nature" and led his growing flock firmly into the abolitionist cause. Even more committed were the Quakers. For them, slavery was at the root of all human sin, the negation of the Quaker values of love and brotherhood. As a leading Quaker abolitionist put it, "If this is not an Evil there is no Evil in the World." Quakers took to the streets to denounce the iniquitous institution and soon allied with other activists, while the Cambridge-educated Evangelical and MP William Wilberforce took the lead of what quickly became a mass campaign.

From another kind of holy writ, though, that of Enlightenment philosophers, the guidance was far from infallible or, often, enlightened. John Locke expounded the natural and inalienable rights of men, among them the right of a man to his own person and labor. Yet while he called human bondage "vile and miserable," he used a philosophical sleight of hand to justify slavery by placing it outside the social compact, as "*the State of War continued, between a lawful Conquerour, and a Captive.*" In the real world, though, slavery was very much a creature of society—with the slave as legal property, as a source of profit for those who traded and owned her—as Locke, with his stockholdings in the Royal African Company, the powerful slaving firm, surely knew.

David Hume considered slavery a losing economic proposition, a brake on progress, but he was not inclined to struggle for the liberation of those his study of "National Character" had revealed "to be naturally inferior to the whites." Hume put the power of Enlightenment empiricism in the "proof" of dehumanizing prejudices. Adam Smith, like Hume, attacked slavery as economically inefficient, as an artificial restraint on free enterprise. Slaves had little incentive to work: "A person who can acquire no property, can have no other interest but to eat as much, and to labour as little as possible." Owners would generally be better off employing free labor because, as Smith concluded, "the work done by slaves, though it appears to cost only their maintenance, is in the end the dearest of any." That was why slavery had disappeared from western Europe. Why, Smith asked, did it persist in the Americas? Mainly because the economics of sugar, tobacco, or cotton cultivation made slave labor marginally less inefficient than did the cultivation of other crops, and "wherever the law allows it, and the nature of the work can afford it," men's pride and their love of domination would generally cause them to "prefer the service of slaves to that of freemen." Emancipation would come, he was convinced, only when the economic disadvantages of slave labor clearly outweighed the psychological benefits of mastery.

Francis Hutcheson also pointed out the economic irrationality of slavery, but for him it was preeminently a moral question whose answer rested in his conviction that *all* human beings possessed a moral sense and natural rights to life, liberty, and the pursuit of happiness. Slavery perverted the fundamental principle of utility by producing the greatest *un*happiness for the greatest number: "Permanent power assumed by force over the fortunes of others," he concluded, "must generally tend to the misery of the whole."

As the global slave trade came to a peak in the late 1700s, as slavery outrages aroused the people, a huge movement coalesced in Britain. Year after year, protesters sent pamphlets, letters, and poems through the mails or handed them out at street corners. They showered petitions on Parliament. Defenders of the trade, especially West Indian planters, were no less vocal, justifying it as in the national interest, as ordained by Providence—and, anyway, did not the poor of Britain live as badly as slaves?

The primary argument was, of course, economic. Slavery had enriched many Britons, not least the planters. Abolition, they said, would devastate West Indian agriculture and trade. For years, as planters objected even to a moderate, gradual approach to abolition, they were able to block parliamentary action. But the reformers had two great strengths: commitment and persistence. Moreover, they had the moral argument, which, even if slow to gain traction against the money argument, reached tremendous force through the relentless propaganda of the reformers. Gradually the votes against the trade mounted in Parliament, approaching a majority, then slipping back, then surging again. It was in 1807 that Parliament finally outlawed the trade in slaves.

A glorious victory. But Parliament had abolished only the slave *trade*—it would be another quarter century before slavery was banned from all British colonies. Elections after the Reform Act, conducted amid what the diarist Charles Greville called a "rage for emancipation," strengthened the abolitionist bloc in the Commons and overwhelmed the ambivalence of Whig leaders who had among them slaveholders and investors in slaving companies. The man who had led the crusade for so many decades, William Wilberforce, lay dying as abolition was at last approved in 1833; a year later all slaves throughout the British empire became free.

◆ ◆ ◆

In the age of Enlightenment, powerful denunciations of slavery were met with excruciatingly slow progress toward outlawing it. In no country was that gap so egregious as in France. Its philosophes struck at the heart of the problem. "Everything concurs to let man enjoy dignity, which is natural to him," wrote the Chevalier de Jaucort in Diderot's *Encyclopédie*. "Everything tells us that we cannot take away from him that natural dignity which is liberty." Rousseau was even blunter, declaring that slavery was "incompatible with human nature." "To renounce liberty," he wrote, "is to renounce one's essence as a man, the rights and also the duties of humanity." And in *Candide*, Voltaire wrote a moving description of a slave in Surinam maimed by his master. "This is the price for which you eat sugar in Europe," the slave told Candide.

Montesquieu's was among the most influential voices against slavery, in part because he was the first among philosophes to apply Enlightenment methods of inquiry to the institution, considering it in the round, from the impact of climate and geography to sociology and psychology to politics, arguing up from facts to principles.

Montesquieu denied that any human being could be a "natural slave," recognizing that the enslavement of Africans was rationalized on racist grounds that denied their humanity, which in turned created an especially vicious relationship between master and slave, harmful to the character and morals of each, as well as to the public good. It was this *marginalization* of slaves, as both human and social beings—their treatment as property, to be owned and traded—that was so radically contrary to Enlightenment ideas and assumptions.

Even before the Revolution a number of enlightened French leaders, including Condorcet, Mirabeau, and Lafayette, had founded the Société des Amis des Noirs. In the National Assembly in early 1790, the society pressed for reform, to little avail. Later the Convention decreed the emancipation of slaves, though without outlawing the trade. Soon the cause was lost in the chaos of the Terror, its leaders dead or scattered.

Since Napoleon while seizing power represented himself as the enlightened heir to the Revolution, abolitionists might have hoped for his sympathy. Instead, the dictator not only proceeded to revive the French slave trade, he restored slavery itself in his empire. In 1799, the Société des Amis was suppressed; not until the 1820s would an equivalent to it appear. After Napoleon's final downfall, the British persuaded the Restoration's "Concert of Europe" to agree that the trade was "repugnant to the principles of humanity and universal morality." Louis XVIII actually approved a ban in 1815, but France's enforcement was lax. Nantes continued to send out its expeditions, more than three hundred in the next decade. The slave trade remained immensely profitable.

But the main reason that France, the vaunted seat of the Enlightenment, dragged its heels in suppressing its slave trade was the failure of antislavery leaders to mobilize popular backing for their cause. The Société des Amis was an elite group and, as historian Lawrence C. Jennings wrote, its leaders "had much difficulty bringing themselves to resort to the tactics of popular appeal, mass mobilization, and large-scale petitioning" of the kind that ultimately succeeded in Britain. Then, too, both patricians and proletarians feared that antislavery militancy might carry the Jacobin taint. In the end, ironically, the French Revolution did not advance—perhaps even damaged—the abolitionist cause.

. . .

American exceptionalism extended, at tremendous human and social cost, to slavery. Unlike Britain or France, the United States had huge numbers of slaves on its own soil, and the economy of the South, especially after the introduction of the cotton gin, was deeply dependent on enslaved cotton pickers. In a great evasion, the Constitution did not address slavery directly, but as part of the compromises that made union possible, Congress was given the choice of banning the trade in slaves after twenty years, in 1807.

That Congress would choose the ban seemed unlikely. The South held close to a majority of seats in the House of Representatives and substantial representation in the Senate. But many slave owners, including Thomas Jefferson, opposed the trade, some on moral grounds—to own human beings who were born into slavery was justifiable, if not natural and good, but to enslave Africans born free was to commit what Jefferson called "violations of human rights" against the "unoffending inhabitants of Africa." Others favored a ban for economic reasons since curtailing the importation of Africans would preserve the market value of their own slaves. So President Jefferson in December 1806 called for the trade's abolition, and both houses of Congress with remarkable expedition approved the ban, effective in 1808. But this was the beginning, not the end, of a turgid era of American politics.

The situation was full of ironies. The internal commerce in slaves was not banned, only the international traffic; this was in part why the act was approved. Of course, resourceful ship owners found ways to smuggle slaves. But planters typically possessed so many that they were not heavily dependent on imports. To increase their "stock," they could exploit "breeding women"—female slaves producing slave infants. In fact, the slave population of the United States rose by a third in the decade after the trade was banned. By 1825 the United States possessed over one-third of all slaves in the Americas. How long could this anomaly continue in a nation that claimed to be founded on—and still proclaimed—the liberating values of the Enlightenment?

THE CANKER OF BONDAGE

Many philosophes realized that "females" were oppressed and powerless but did not know quite where to go from there. Some felt women were so deficient in the basic Enlightenment trait, *reason,* that they could contribute little to the public worlds of ideas and politics, even as they granted that women might be superior to men morally, and at the very least absolute mistresses of their household domains. During the French Revolution, women were powerful collective actors—in 1789, they invaded the National Assembly to demand that deputies address food shortages, and they led the famous march to Versailles that captured the king. But when it came to a formal political role, sexism prevailed. Not only was there no serious discussion of women's suffrage in the National Assembly's debates over the 1791 constitution, but that charter denied women citizenship, grouping them with such others of the excluded as children and convicted felons.

"True patriotism," the Jacobin journalist Louis-Marie Prudhomme lectured in 1793, consisted not of wearing a liberty cap and pantaloons or carrying pike and pistol but of "fulfilling one's duties, and only wanting those rights allotted to each according to his sex." Leave the patriotic regalia to the men, who were "born to protect you and to make you happy."

Still, the Revolution inspired British philosopher Mary Wollstonecraft to produce *A Vindication of the Rights of Woman,* which inveighed against "the weakness of mind and body" in women "which men have endeavoured, impelled by various motives, to perpetuate." She insisted on treating women as "rational creatures, rather than flattering their *fascinating* graces," and demanded a "REVOLUTION in female manners" promoted by equal liberty. "Let woman share the rights and she will emulate the virtues of man." A work both profound and impassioned, the *Vindication* was a sensation on publication in 1792, caught in the swift currents of radicalism the French Revolution had unleashed in Britain. But as the reform impulse ebbed under government repression, so did the cause of women.

The struggle over parliamentary reform inspired new women's groups like the Female Radical Reform Society of Manchester, as well as participation in marches and mass rallies. Disappointed by the Reform Act's failure to legislate women's suffrage, activists were spurred to take prominent roles in the campaigns against the New Poor Law and slavery. Still, suffrage was the acid test; it would give women a real weapon in political combat. Progress was glacially slow. R. J. Richardson, a master joiner who authored *The Rights of Women* in 1840 while in prison for riot, demanded civil and political rights for women but resorted to cheery stereotypes in hoping for "good laws, happy homes, cheerful hearths, loving husbands and prattling children."

Britain at least had a woman ruler after 1837, though hardly an elected one. Americans had an all-male presidency and Congress year after year. Even as male suffrage broadened, American women had no vote or promise of it. In 1790, seizing on the absence in the New Jersey constitution of a provision barring female suffrage, women had successfully urged passage of a state election law that referred to voters as "he or she." This anomaly inspired a male counterattack, including charges that ignorant women were being herded to the polls by partisans. In 1807, the New Jersey legislature limited the ballot to adult white males. Three decades later, Harriet Martineau noted on her travels that American women remained firmly under male domination: "woman's intellect is confined, her morals crushed . . . her weaknesses encouraged, and her strength punished."

Some courageous women, led by Elizabeth Cady Stanton, carried on the struggle. Her "Declaration of Sentiments" approved at the 1848 Woman's Rights Convention in Seneca Falls was modeled on Jefferson's Declaration, proclaiming "that all men and women are created equal." The "Declaration of Sentiments" listed the denial of women's "inalienable right to the elective franchise" among the "injuries and usurpations" men had inflicted. Stanton, along with Frederick Douglass, urged women to emphasize the "sacred right" of voting. But the convention's voting rights plank was controversial because to many women it seemed a radical step that would invite public ridicule. It was the only proposal not to pass unanimously; indeed, it barely won a majority.

The outcome dramatized a bitter dispute among the delegates about the strategy of reform. Should they focus on a host of specific social and civil problems such as the oppression of women in marriage and unfair divorce laws, or should they venture into the forbidden realm of politics and wage a single, concentrated campaign for the suffrage that if successful would make all their other goals more attainable? This dilemma not only bedeviled and split the women's movement before the Civil War but would continue to do so for many decades after it.

*   *   *

Most leaders of the early women's rights movement in America had served an apprenticeship in another great crusade for liberty and equality: abolition. It was not only that women saw, in the denial of their natural rights, an analogy to black slavery. In that respect, Frederick Douglass would later remark, the women's suffrage movement was continuous with the fight against slavery. "We have the same sources of opposition to contend with, we must meet them with the same spirit and determination, and with much the same arguments." Denied a place in public life, women were turning to the "moral crusades" deemed more appropriate to them—on behalf of the poor, prostitutes, prisoners, and above all enslaved African Americans—where they learned the arts of activism and the confidence in their political capacities that they would turn to the cause of their own liberation. Douglass witnessed the effect on women of involvement in the battle: "there is more intellectual life and vigour" among abolition activists, "and much more happiness."

He also recognized that women's "heart and conscience have supplied in large degree" abolition's "motive and mainspring." Led by black women in Salem, thousands of northerners formed female antislavery societies in the

1830s, collecting tens of thousands of signatures on petitions to Congress. They faced down resistance, too: mobs in Philadelphia and Boston, disapproving clergymen and editors, an indignant southern congressman who demanded to know how women had dared assume the "imperious duty" of asserting "the great right of petition."

As both female and male abolitionists confronted their foes, they had to be struck by the fire of the counterattack by slavery's defenders—and the perversity of their doctrines. One of the most forceful of the apologists was English-born Thomas Cooper. A radical at Oxford who authored a pamphlet against the slave trade, an avid supporter of the French Revolution, rejected for a post at the University of Virginia because of his contempt for the clergy, a veteran utilitarian, Cooper was in his sixties when he took up the "sacred duty" of defending slavery. Bentham himself had denied that slavery could promote the general happiness, pointing out that "[no] one who is free wishes to become a slave, and there is no slave who does not wish to be free." In a mockery of Enlightenment science, Cooper conducted his own "careful analysis and comparison" using such techniques as phrenology and "organology" to demonstrate the natural inferiority of blacks. His premise seemingly was that a "population of free blacks is the most idle, debauched, thievish and insolent that we have ever witnessed in the United States." Therefore, by restraining their barbarism and improving their morals as far as was possible, slavery was beneficial to slaves. Since it also best served the economic interests of slave owners and the South, Cooper concluded that slavery was "on the whole" consistent with the happiness principle, producing "a balance of good."

It was certainly good for James H. Hammond, who married into ownership of 148 slaves. Hammond also served South Carolina as its governor and senator and imagined himself something of a philosophe. In his judgment, every society needed its class of menials to support the master class that stands "in the broadest light of the knowledge, civilization and improvement of the age." The South's "patriarchal scheme" of slavery was itself "well calculated to awaken the higher and finer feelings of our nature. It is not wanting in its enthusiasm and its poetry." As for the slaves, they "are the happiest three millions of human beings on whom the sun shines." Yet into this Eden was coming "Satan in the guise of an Abolitionist." And what was this threat? That the mutual bonds between master and slave (few ties could be "more heartfelt, or of more benignant influence") would be destroyed by arguments against slavery, that the minds of slaves would be liberated by the "all-devouring flame" of enlightenment. He demanded of abolitionists, "Allow our slaves to read your writings, stimulating them to cut our throats! Can you believe us to be such unspeakable fools?" Indeed, as the testimony of Frederick Douglass movingly demonstrated, for a slave to seek enlightenment was a subversive and heroic endeavor.

Abolitionists could fire back with a squad of impassioned intellectual and moral leaders. Of these, William Lloyd Garrison appeared the most formidable. Editor of a Vermont newspaper that backed John Quincy Adams in 1828, Garrison had shown limited interest in the cause of abolition, but Andrew Jackson's election seemed to confirm fears that the slave states would perpetually monopolize the national government. He won fame when, on July 4, 1829, he spoke to a Boston audience with such moral fervor and blunt candor, declaring that "our politics are rotten to the core" with "hypocritical cant about the unalienable rights of man" and "unmeaning declamation in praise of liberty and equality," that the address became a springboard to his leadership of the abolitionist cause. Other intellectuals and orators—Wendell Phillips, Theodore Dwight Weld, the sisters Sarah and Angelina Grimké, along with Whig politicians—joined the movement and broadened its impact.

A divisive issue had long complicated the struggle against slavery: colonization. Gradual emancipation followed by a "return" to Africa had been offered as a benign compromise, a solution, moreover, that had been favored by some of the Founders. Free or freed blacks, some said, could never feel at home in white America, while Africa was their natural living place. Abolitionists, though, saw no solution in dumping ex-slaves across the Atlantic. Indeed, blacks themselves were divided. Some were sorely tempted by the prospect of instant relief from oppression via exile. Garrison, who earlier had been attracted to the idea, dropped it after staying for a time in the large and vibrant community of free blacks in Baltimore, people living lives as rich, settled, and committed as was possible in a racist society—and passionately opposed to expulsion from their own country.

. . .

To many white Americans, the prospect of colonization was too good to be true. The canker would not be so easily expelled, the negation of Enlightenment principles caused by the enslavement of millions not so easily overcome. In half the nation, slavery supported an economy that was nearly feudal. Masters were a law unto themselves. "On our estates," declared Governor Hammond, "we dispense with the whole machinery of public police and public Courts of Justice. Thus we try, decide and execute the sentences, in thousands of cases, which in other countries would go into the Courts." And the slave could have no recourse, as a North Carolina judge pointed out in 1829: "The power of the master must be absolute to render the submission of the slave perfect. . . . The slave, to remain a slave, must be made sensible that there is no appeal from his master."

As abolitionism mounted in the North, the South only retreated further into perversions of Enlightenment principles or their rejection altogether. John Calhoun, South Carolinian defender of states' rights, insisted that liberty and equality meant the preservation of slave owners' rights. George Fitzhugh, in his 1854 *Sociology for the South,* dismissed his fellow Virginian Thomas Jefferson's declaration of equal rights. Where Jefferson had said that men were not born to be ridden like horses by other men, Fitzhugh retorted that "it would be far nearer the truth to say, 'that some were born with saddles on their backs, and others booted and spurred to ride them. . . .' They need the reins, the bit and the spur," not only blacks but the mass of whites as well who, unable to complete with slave labor, were impoverished. Still, southerners liked to boast, as Senator Albert Brown from Mississippi proclaimed that same year, that "nowhere in this broad Union but in the slaveholding States is there a living, breathing exemplification of the beautiful sentiment, that all men are equal. . . . I mean, of course," he hastily added, "white men" since "negroes are not men, within the meaning of the Declaration."

Congress was paralyzed. To most senators and representatives, as it had been for the Founders, slavery was the price of union. The two institutions were fatefully intertwined. Terrified that the union would explode, Congress fashioned one compromise after another in an attempt to bridge the divide between freedom and slavery. Except for John Adams and his son, every American president up to and including Andrew Jackson was a slave owner. Among them, George Washington was regarded as a paragon of political leadership, while Thomas Jefferson and James Madison were leading figures in the American Enlightenment. Nearly all claimed to detest slavery; some provided for the emancipation of their slaves after their deaths. But none held a lamp to guide the United States out of its moral darkness.

Andrew Jackson thought he could lead on slavery. On the one hand, the self-made southern planter had a special scorn for northern abolitionists. Convinced that they were attempting "to stir up amongst the South the horrors of a servile war," he attempted to censor abolitionist materials sent through the U.S. mail. At the same time, though, he fiercely challenged the southern nullifiers and secessionists who would destroy the Union in order to protect their peculiar institution. So the old frontiersman remained hopeful about the future of the American democracy. "All is safe," he said just before he died in 1845. There would be enough patriots in the land "to maintain sacredly our just rights and to perpetuate our glorious constitution and liberty, and to preserve our happy Union."

But the institution that divided the United States against itself, that gave the lie to Jackson's noble sentiments and to those of the founding documents—that negation of the Enlightenment, betrayal of its most fundamental principles—that deep canker could not easily be cut out from the body politic.

It would take only fifteen years to prove Jackson wrong.

13

The Transformation

One fair day in September 1830, happy, excited crowds in Liverpool Station were celebrating the inauguration of Britain's most important railroad to date, the Liverpool and Manchester. A glittering party headed by the prime minister, the Duke of Wellington, and adorned by such celebrities as Fanny Kemble, mounted the train for the gala trip to Manchester. The Iron Duke, though, was not in a wholly celebratory mood. He disliked these newfangled railroads, the noise and smoke that polluted the countryside. But his spirits appeared to lift as the iron horse whizzed along at the astonishing speed of thirty miles an hour to the cheers of thousands of commoners who lined the tracks.

Awkwardly for the duke, a member of the party was his former colonial secretary, William Huskisson, whose resignation he had welcomed two years earlier when Huskisson had shown undue sympathy for reform. Huskisson was an enlightened Tory, virtually Whiggish in his enthusiasm for capitalism. As a student in Paris in the 1780s he had known Franklin and Jefferson and had closely observed the fall of the French king, pondering the lessons of both reactionary and revolutionary governments. Unlike Wellington, Huskisson believed that "[t]he government and legislature must keep pace with the spirit of the age. They should neither be behind it, nor before it."

Still, it was a day for celebration, not confrontation, and Huskisson joined the dignitaries who crowded around Wellington when the train stopped for watering. Huskisson had just grasped the duke's hand, eyewitnesses remembered later, when a shout rang out: "Clear the tracks!" The locomotive *Rocket* came roaring in on a parallel track. The celebrities scattered to their carriages but Huskisson stumbled, uncertain whether to turn to Wellington's carriage or his own. The *Rocket* smashed him down, crushing his leg "to a jelly." He died in agony a few hours later.

After the grieving, people moralized. Huskisson's last-minute vacillations, someone cruelly said, were typical of his political career. Others saw a broader message—the crushing of the individual under an increasingly impersonal industrial society. Collisions, derailments, explosions—the iron horse dealt a new kind of death by technology. Moreover, entire communities could fall. Villages or towns bypassed by rail lines withered, while those that were wound into the network flourished. Soon, authors like Dickens and Ruskin would protest and mourn the ravaging of the countryside by the iron monster. Wordsworth asked plaintively, "Is then no nook of English ground secure / From rash assault?"

There was, in truth, ground secure. It belonged to grandees whose wealth and power shielded them from these changes. Publicly Wellington favored cheap trains for the masses. Privately he would travel in his own railcar, isolated from those masses. When a railroad was planned that would run near his Hampshire County mansion, he demanded that no station be located within five miles of his home.

Yet nothing could hold up the ramifying railroads. They were too important to the surging British economy, there was too much money to be made by their spread. Britain had built its first steam railroad, 27 kilometers long, in 1825. By the end of the 1830s the United Kingdom had 1,454 miles of functioning rail lines, compared to Germany's 291 and France's 255. Russia, meanwhile, had a single line that ran 17 miles from St. Petersburg to the tsar's summer palace.

As for the United States, it was far advanced in steamshipping, with an immense network of canals, huge lakes, and navigable rivers. But railroads soon followed, as entrepreneurs competed furiously for investors and government support while engineers wrestled with the infinite challenges of the American terrain. By the mid-1840s, the United States had nearly 3,000 miles of track. The Western Railroad, a 150-mile line from Worcester, was pushed through to Albany by 1841, overcoming the mountainous Berkshires.

The railroad transformed economies, and as everything in the Industrial Revolution, the changes brought, unevenly distributed, both immense benefits and severe hardships. The trains revolutionized transport not only of commodities but of people. Before the iron horse, travel was a slow and dirty, dangerous, costly proposition. As rail networks expanded, trains permitted comfortable and swift passage to more and more remote places, opening new horizons for settlement and exploitation—and for tourism, widening people's experience and knowledge. The rails brought people together by spreading their spidery webs far and wide or by pumping masses into and through vast urban aggregations. At the same time, though, they tore men and women from ancestral farms and villages, casting them loose and alone on the great tides of humanity to sink or to swim. In its capacity to change utterly people's lives and prospects, their hopes and needs, the railroad represented industrialization's challenge to thinkers and statesmen. How ensure that these changes benefited all human beings?

THE LIBERAL TRIUMPH

People cut loose from their homes, their customs, their past—it depended on your vantage whether this was a terrifying or an empowering image. For Enlightenment pioneers, it meant a rejection of centuries of repression, when church and state combined to impose obedience and conformity. It meant also embracing mankind as the measure of all things—not authority, not custom, not faith, but *individual* perception and reason were the foundation of truth. I think, therefore I am—"Nothing can be more evident to us, than our own Existence," Locke wrote, nothing more beyond doubt, no foundation firmer for knowledge and action.

The implication of this for politics was staggering—it tore up deeply rooted assumptions. Now the *individual* was, as historian Anthony Arblaster wrote, more "'real' or fundamental than human society," with "a higher moral value." Society existed to serve men, not men society. The individual, not king or prelate, was the central factor—the cause of society's existence. To explain this, thinkers as diverse and even opposed as Hobbes and Rousseau deployed the social contract, a fiction that pictured society as an amalgam of individuals, created wholly by their mutual consent.

But Hobbes and others had written that men were not by nature social creatures, not like bees and ants, and they entered into the social contract only reluctantly, to protect their supreme value—their lives—by escaping nature's anarchy, the Hobbesian war "of every man against every man." In doing so, though, they agreed to sacrifice only a portion of their autonomy, as much as was necessary to secure their lives.

What that meant—what liberties the individual would surrender and what retain, what society would do to protect individual liberty and what not do to limit it—became the object of enduring dispute, both when liberal individualism existed only in the dreams of philosophers and later when it became the dominant political idea of the West.

Though liberalism had roots in the seventeenth century and had been at the center of the three great revolutions of the West—British, American, French—it faced competing strains of Enlightenment, notably those of Hutcheson and the Scots, who built their philosophy on the premise that people were indeed sociable by nature, a twist with implications for the Enlightenment's political, economic, and social ideas. But as industrialization gathered pace, liberalism rose in tandem with laissez faire to become the dominant ideology of the age of the enlightened economy. In liberal doctrine, property was the third great value of the trinity, with life and liberty; it became identified with the pursuit of happiness. Political economists of the day justified a nearly absolute right of property—that it could be employed as its owner saw fit, without limitation by society. They insisted not only that prosperity depended on it, but that the right of property was, as the Scot J. R. McCulloch wrote in 1824, "a rampart raised by society against its common enemies—against rapine and violence, plunder and oppression." Though McCulloch argued otherwise—"the institution of the right of property gives no advantage to any man over any other man"—it was hardly a revelation that property rights empowered the propertied.

But liberalism was the doctrine not only of the great property holders—McCulloch's "few favorites of fortune." The chief beneficiary of the major changes of the first third of the nineteenth century—the Great Reform Act, France's July Revolution, the passing of the old Founding elite in the United States, and above all the acceleration of the Industrial Revolution—was the burgeoning middle class, which James Mill asserted was "universally described as both the most wise and the most virtuous part of the community." As it began to displace Mill's despised aristocracy in political, economic, and social power, it also inherited the nobility's ancient fear of the mob. As its wealth grew, so did middle-class fears of losing it. "The necessary aim of those without property," warned France's liberal apologist Benjamin Constant, "is to obtain some," so political rights, "in the hands of the greatest number, will inevitably serve to encroach" upon it. When reform in Britain and revolution in France opened government to the middle class in the 1830s, the newly empowered closed the gates to those who had been their allies in the struggle, workers and the poor. Enlightenment and political power were placed beyond their reach. "It is not by mere numbers," argued Britain's liberal apologist Thomas Babington Macaulay, "but by property and intelligence, that the nation ought to be governed." As it had been in the age of aristocratic rule, property remained the test of worthy citizenship; only the propertied were deemed to have a sufficient stake in the social order to be trusted with the suffrage, and thus with actual political power; only they enjoyed in full rights to life and liberty.

Liberalism was, above all, an ideological defense of the power, wealth, and status of this newly authoritative middle class. The British had their Liberal party, while American liberals dominated the Whig party. And the French—doing as usual nothing by half—overthrew one king, Charles X, and installed their own, Louis-Philippe. French liberals became the king's party.

* * *

Liberal individualism had long been the target of intellectual counterrevolutionaries, from the defenders of James II and monarchical rule to Burkean traditionalists who drew a straight line from liberals to the Terror. So heated was the postrevolutionary reaction against liberalism that a leading French Ultra-Royalist called it "a fight between life and death." Attacks from the right could devastate when backed by state power, as they were in France and elsewhere in the Restoration. Liberals were confident, though, that their reactionary foes were a wasting force, on the wrong side of history.

But even as they won their greatest victories yet in the 1830s, liberals came under heavier fire from the opposing flank. Radicals denounced their erstwhile partners as the reactionaries of a new order founded on the exploitation of the mass of workers for the enrichment of a minority. The exaltation of property ensured that the unpropertied would remain second-class citizens—as surely subjects of liberal government as they had been of kings. Liberalism was, in short, a self-serving middle-class fraud. What could prattle about self-determination, about glorying in one's individuality mean to people unsure of their next meal or how to keep a roof over their heads? Radicals liked to tell the story of the French premier who, when complained to about the high property requirement for voting, replied, "*Enrichissez-vous*"—Get rich!

The grievances of the working poor were becoming more audible and focused in the 1830s and 1840s. But despite the powerful voices of Saint-Simon, Robert Owen, Louis Blanc, and others, there was as yet no analysis of capitalism and its impact on the lives and minds of workers that could rouse passion among partisans while provoking respect and fear in opposition ranks. There was no body of ideas to fuel radical leadership and empower militant followers. Who would be the left's Locke? Who the Adam Smith of the working class?

THE CLASH OF IDEAS

During the 1830s, Karl Marx was attending high school in Trier, in the Rhineland, and then the universities of Bonn and Berlin. Born in 1818, he grew into a darkly handsome youth doted on by his parents and siblings, in a middle-class family of Jewish origin now converted to Protestantism so that the children might attend Christian schools. Karl, alas, was only a fair student, partly because he was pursuing the lovely Jenny, daughter of the Baron Ludwig von Westphalen, who headed the area's police and internal security. Aside from Jenny, young Karl's passion was poetry, which he end-lessly discussed with schoolmates at a restaurant-bar near Trier's cattle market. Gradually his interests turned to history and philosophy. In Berlin, Marx began to gulp down Hegel and other philosophers of law and history, while taking courses in inheritance and criminal law and other practical subjects. And it was in Berlin that he came into close contact with radicals, Utopians, and revolutionaries challenging authority.

Even then, though, there was little foretaste of the future Marx. If he could be labeled in those years, it was as an Enlightenment man in familiar mode, enlightened in his home by two cultured parents, in his high school by exceptional teachers, in Bonn and Berlin by the range and depth of his voracious reading and by heady ideas out of France and Britain blazing through the Rhineland. He was not yet an original thinker. Early in the next decade he and Jenny married and moved to Paris.

In Marx's nightlong wrangles with fellow students, no philosopher had so dominated the proceedings as did Georg W. F. Hegel. The German sa-vant's provocative ideas touched with creative ambiguity kept credulous and hair-splitting youths in happy argumentation long after Hegel's death in 1831. Embedded in his heavy prose was an idea crucial, in a revolution-ary time, to explaining the role of inevitable and unstoppable conflict as an agent for progress in history. This was Hegel's concept of the dialectic. An idea, he argued, inevitably gave rise to its opposite, or antithesis, and the conflict between them was resolved by a synthesis of the two, whereupon the process started again, ever moving forward. Hegel's followers, as if to prove their master correct, split between right and left, between conserva-tive believers in statism and Christianity and radical "young Hegelians" on the left. But in Paris, Marx took another course, striking at the essence of

Hegel's philosophy by substituting the conflict between ideas as the dynamic force in history with the brute conflict of *classes*. "Oppressor and oppressed," he would write in the 1848 *Communist Manifesto,* had through successive epochs "stood in constant opposition to one another," in a fight "that each time ended, either in a revolutionary reconstitution of society at large, or in the common ruin of the contending classes."

This recognition of historical materialism proved the key to Marx's vision of social transformation, of capitalism as, merely, another epoch in history, the outcome of the triumph of the bourgeoisie over feudal lords temporal and spiritual that would, in its turn, be swept away. Marx's economic focus was relentless—the "modes of production" dominated men's lives and determined their political and social structures. "The handmill gives you society with the feudal lord; the steam-mill, society with the industrial capitalist." But the harshness of capitalist labor conditions, the impoverishment of workers even as their masters fattened on profits wrung from the sweat of their brows, would, Marx forecasted, give birth to a new burst of enlightenment, of "ideas that revolutionize society," transforming the class consciousness of proletarians. The revolution would overthrow the capitalist order and usher in a next new society—communism. But in Marx's reckoning, that would be the final new society, the end of history—a society of equals who owned the means of production in common and gave to each according to her needs, would be classless. There would be no more of history's engine, conflict.

Did Marx, then, repudiate the Enlightenment? Did he dismiss its ideas as products of—and a defense of—the economic forces of capitalism? His innovative, radical take on the modern economy owed much to Enlightenment forebears. In the first place, he embraced the Enlightenment's insistence on the linkage of thought and action, writing that "the philosophers have only *interpreted* the world, in various ways; the point, however, is to *change* it." Moreover, his belief that change in history was not only possible but inevitable was derived from early Enlightenment optimism about social progress. And the ideas of the human mind as conditioned by education and experience and of the mind's malleability also had roots in the early Enlightenment, with Locke in particular; looking around him at capitalism's pervasive force, Marx concluded that human minds were determined by economic conditions—but he also believed that they could be liberated by revolution. Finally, and most characteristic of the Enlightenment, was Marx's faith that the study of economic history could be a science, with grand theory built on scrupulously marshaled evidence. Marx gathered facts and figures with a tirelessness that Francis Bacon would have admired, making close observations of industry and working conditions, especially in London, where he lived for thirty years. He virtually inhabited the British Museum, inhaling dry economic statistics along with the ideas of lofty Enlightenment thinkers like Locke, Hume, and Adam Smith. All of this research Marx poured into his writings, most notably in his massive study of capitalist production and the exploitation of labor, *Das Kapital,* whose first volume would finally be published in 1867. It was an epic, excursive, exhaustive work, encyclopedic in the Enlightenment sense of the term.

Yet despite this clear line of descent, Marx's writings were a rebuttal to the Enlightenment's original contribution to politics and economics—liberalism. One by one he dismissed liberal values as meaningless to workers in capitalist society. Individual liberty, self-determination, and democracy were, he insisted, delusions and frauds under capitalism, belying the absolute economic power of the capitalist class, even as industrial production methods "mutilate the laborer into a fragment of a man, degrade him to the level of an appendage of a machine . . . estrange him from the intellectual potentialities of the labour-process." In contrast to the relative independence of the old class of artisans—skilled tradesmen such as masons, shoemakers, chandlers, and printers—the lives of factory workers "have become something extraneous, something over which they, as separate individuals, have no control, and over which no *social* organization can give them control." But, despite their power and freedom from brute labor, the bourgeoisie of the master class were no more fulfilled—enslaved by money, driven to maximize wealth, in a fierce struggle for economic survival.

Marx's vision could hardly have been more bleak or more contrary to Enlightenment hopes and expectations. He wrote of people trapped in their circumstances, dissociated, blank figures in the great drama of history, their existences defined by membership in a class in conflict with another class. But, when the last act of his drama was played, Marx's ultimate faith in Enlightenment principles was stunningly displayed. With the triumph of communism, a man or woman, nestled in and nourished by a community of equals, would burst forth in rich, full, autonomous, and *individual* humanity. *Then* would the Enlightenment reign.

* * *

It is an irony that the greatest spokesman for liberal individualism—and Karl Marx's most powerful intellectual adversary—should have considered himself a socialist. For John Stuart Mill, capitalism's enormous class differences had little to do with "merit and demerit, or even with exertion"; they were "obviously unjust." He was repelled by the materialism of the new industrial order, by the "trampling, crushing, elbowing" of laissez-faire competition. Marx himself allowed that Mill was not one of "the herd of vulgar economic apologists."

That was apt, since the hero of Mill's philosophy was not the herd or an economic class but the autonomous *individual,* whose very distinctiveness and creativity were progressive: "The unlikeness of one man to another is not only a principle of improvement, but would seem to be almost the only principle." Individualism was, in fact, at the heart of Mill's socialism. His aim was not to make the distribution of property a matter for government, dominated as he feared not by workers but by "a combination of rich men, armed with coercive power." Rather, by fostering worker cooperatives, he would enable all working men and women to become entrepreneurs, competing in the marketplace on the basis of each "individual's own energies and exertions." Mill agreed that laissez faire should be the "general practice" and that the burden of making the case for "government interference" should be "on those who recommend it," yet he argued that the "exclusive & engrossing selfishness" accompanying the pursuit of wealth produced "moral insensibility."

That insensibility spurred Mill to seek an alternative, a philosophy that viewed the complexities of the new industrial age through the moral lens of individual freedom, which Mill equated with autonomy and self-development. Rejecting Marx's economic determinism, Mill maintained that *ideas* were history's driving force, not on Hegel's equally deterministic model but with the gradual revelation of truths, as contending opinions were subjected to rational scrutiny and debate. Enlightenment was the backbone of individual freedom as well as of social leadership by creative individuals—exceptional individuals.

Mill understood that he was suggesting a new class division based not on economics but on education, opposing an intellectual elite to what he called the "mass of brutish ignorance." More dangerous in his eyes, though, was the empowerment of that ignorance. Like Tocqueville, whose study of America he read closely, he feared the unchecked rise of a "tyranny of the prevailing opinion," a "social tyranny more formidable than many kinds of political oppression" because it would "penetrate much more deeply into the details of life" and enslave "the soul itself." The risk was that a tyranny of a majority over a minority might effectively wipe out the autonomy of all.

"What is right in politics," he insisted, "is not the *will* of the people, but the *good* of the people," and what was needed were "some restraints on the immediate and unlimited exercise of their own will." He proposed a democracy narrowed by a weighted voting system that would give some persons more than one vote, according to their education, not their property. "The people ought to be the masters," he wrote, "but they are masters who must employ servants more skilful than themselves."

Mill and Tocqueville were both writing in a time of gradual democratization across the West, the expansion of suffrage to those who had previously not been regarded as stakeholders in civil society because they owned little or no property. Their political impact was feared both because of their numbers and because of their interests, their claim to equal participation and equal dignity as human beings.

Mill shared—indeed, exemplified—the Enlightenment faith in the transforming power of ideas and education, as well as in individual liberty, and he was attempting to adjust the means and ends of the liberal Enlightenment to meet the intellectual challenges of a new, industrial age. He sought to navigate between the greed and cruelties of laissez faire and the threat to liberal values posed by a growing, impoverished working class with its radicalized leadership. His middle way led in nearly Hegelian fashion to a synthesis that was not entirely clear-cut. He seemed, in certain ways, Marx's mirror opposite. While Marx pushed workers forward as the heart of radical change, Mill would sideline them in order to safeguard the middle classes.

As a spokesman for middle-class liberalism, Mill was sometimes groping, often tentative—much as that class itself remained uncertain about its role and status, set as it was between the great industrial magnates with their interests and the working class, with *its* distinct wants and needs. For both Marx and Mill, the lodestar of the Enlightenment guided them only so far before they set off in radically different directions—Mill the intellectually generous philosopher and activist, both utilitarian rationalist and Romantic, and Marx, tirelessly combative, more and more the ideological bully and sectarian, estranging friend and foe with his hammering disputation. Even greater, of course, grew the abyss between them in their philosophical ideas, Mill with his liberalism, the focus on individuals, education, liberty, reform, against Marx's communism, the focus on classes, economics, equality, revolution. The two set up an intellectual dialectic that came to dominate the thought and politics of the West, and eventually the world, for at least a century and a half. Neither man alone had the key to an Enlightenment project that would give definite conceptual and practical direction in the face of modern complexities.

A NEW AMERICAN ENLIGHTENMENT?

For the young republic across the seas, that dialectic appeared as the tension between two values Americans loudly professed, liberty and equality. As in Europe, conflict over these values pitted a rising middle class against industrialization's rapidly burgeoning working class. But, in the bondage of millions of human beings that scarred its society, Americans faced a far harsher and more divisive case of the complex interplay between the ideals of liberty and equality. And few leaders were so nakedly at odds with themselves as Thomas Jefferson, slave owner and author of the Declaration of Independence's claim that all men were created equal. Writing before the depths of industrialization had been sounded, Jefferson saw a distinctly different route to the future than Mill or Marx. Like Marx, he thought gross disparities in wealth injurious to people and societies. Like Mill, he believed in enlightened leadership. But to Jefferson, the people were neither helpless victims of economic forces nor an unruly, potentially threatening mob to be marginalized or repressed. Instead, he spoke of common people who, with education and experience, would act as responsible citizens fully capable of self-rule. Among the aims of primary education, he wrote, was for every citizen "[t]o understand his duties to his neighbors and country, and to discharge with competence the functions confided to him by either; [t]o know his rights; to exercise with order and justice those he retains; to choose with discretion the fiduciary of those he delegates; and to notice their conduct with diligence, with candor, and judgment." A government closely accountable to the people, attuned to their wants and needs, would be, he thought, naturally dedicated to enlightenment for all and thus to maximizing equality and liberty and happiness for all. Entangled in his clashing roles of democrat and master of slaves, Jefferson abandoned the problem of abolition to the future, "to the rising generation, and not to the one now in power."

How can we, generations far into Jefferson's future, long after slavery's end, assess progress in achieving life, liberty, and the pursuit of happiness? Defining life most literally, we in the United States can celebrate the enormous medical and social and agricultural advances that nurture, protect, and prolong the lives of those to whom they are available. Defining liberty most simply, and despite many shortcomings and complexities, we can applaud the protection of civil liberties in most dimensions of the personal and public lives of most Americans. This has truly been the work of centuries of evolution and struggle. But the pursuit of happiness? Happiness would, of course, be defined by different people in countless ways, including those unable to obtain adequate medical care or whose liberties are not respected. How, then, think about its pursuit?

The answer is to borrow from the most vibrant idea in the French revolutionary call for action—*égalité*. As we have seen, no European nation—certainly not France—could boast a meaningful commitment to egalitarianism. Nor were Americans better, despite their veneration of Jefferson's Declaration and his assumption of natural human equality. Even apart from slaves, gross differences among men abounded in income, property, education, speech, social status, and political power. To Jefferson, this represented a threat to the republic: the rich—men of landed wealth, bankers, capitalists—would overpower common farmers and workingmen, stamp out democracy, and rule in their own interests. Most Americans embraced with increasing fervor the idea that theirs was the land of opportunity, where, with luck and pluck, any man could pursue happiness in his own way; he could become rich and powerful by his own merit. Inequality, though, was the normal order, widening and deepening as industrialization displaced the old economy. The change was marked in John Adams's thought as he abandoned his own revolutionary egalitarianism; by the early nineteenth century he was dismissing the efforts of philosophes to show "the natural Equality of Mankind" in every respect, snorting that he had never heard "Reasoning more absurd."

It was Adams, too, though his wife, Abigail, insisted that she could never consent "to have our sex considered in an inferior point of light," who described the empowerment of women as a Pandora's box in a kidding-on-the-square letter to his son Thomas. Adams wrote that the "source of revolution, democracy, Jacobinism . . . has been a systematical dissolution of the true family authority. There can never be any regular government of a nation without a marked subordination of mothers and children to the father." He asked Thomas to keep this argument for female inequality from his mother, who would "infallibly raise a rebellion."

* * *

The American Enlightenment, at least, was a demonstration by those who made it of opportunities seized, of inequalities overcome. For every planter-philosopher like Jefferson or Madison, there was an Adams, whose father made shoes to add to his small living as a farmer, or a Franklin, who had begun as a printer's apprentice, or a Paine, whose first career was as a maker of corsets, or an Alexander Hamilton, the West Indian illegitimate son of a penniless Scottish lord. The ticket out of obscurity was enlightenment: their hunger for learning, ardor for ideas, and genius in linking those ideas to practical realities—in their case, a nation struggling to be born.

They were realistic about their accomplishments. When the Articles of Confederation government proved a failure, they reconstructed the American polity. But they understood, too, the imperfections and challenges of the new constitutional order and what was at stake in its fortunes. For Hamilton, the question was "whether societies of men are really capable or not, of establishing good government from reflection and choice, or whether they are forever destined to depend, for their political constitutions, on accident and force." The turbulence of the nation's first years made a skeptic of George Washington. A consummate man of action—and of inaction, as the moment required—he was steeped in the ideas bound into the republic's founding, an "Epocha" when, as he had written in 1783, the "collected wisdom" of enlightened "Philosophers, Sages, and Legislators" could be "happily applied in the Establishment of our forms of Government." But the violent partisanship of the 1790s led him to fear that such wisdom would collapse into an "endless variety of hypothesis and opinion," and that the "alternate domination of one faction over another," with all the attendant "disorders and miseries," would give rise to a "permanent despotism"—a dictatorship—built on "the ruins of Public Liberty."

Two hundred years later, Peter Gay wrote that enlightenment was being tested as never before. Even for America, "the hope of civilized men everywhere in the eighteenth century," he wrote, ". . . . [t]he world has not turned out the way the *philosophes* wished and half expected that it would." In fact, the United States faces problems the Founders would sadly have recognized: irrational political extremism; the push of religion into government even as public involvement in politics has declined; foreign entanglements that tempt Americans to sacrifice their own values; and persisting conflicts over race and gender and class and immigration, all too reminiscent of dark episodes in the past. The recognition of corporations, those artificial creatures of the enlightened economy, with the proud title of "citizen," along with their domination of public policy through vast political expenditures at the expense of actual—that is to say, human—citizens, would have staggered even Alexander Hamilton, the evangel of American manufacturing.

These are profound challenges to a nation that still claims to be based on Enlightenment principles. One answer to them was embraced by the Founders themselves. "In proportion as the structure of a government gives force to public opinion," George Washington said, "it is essential that public opinion should be enlightened." The long-run future of the American polity depends on elevated leadership, which in turn depends on an enlightened and engaged public. Modern science has complicated Locke's image of the mind as a tabula rasa, while modern society has eliminated Jefferson's enlightened yeomanry, noble backbone of the republic. Still, education's role in shaping minds, lives, and democratic government remains crucial. And that, in turn, calls for a renewed and unshakeable commitment to what Washington in his Farewell Address termed "Institutions for the general diffusion of knowledge," public schools. The proposal may appear commonplace. It was not only woven into the Founding, with Jefferson, Adams, and others joining Washington in calls for universal public education, but it has remained a staple of American political rhetoric ever since. What politician has not earnestly held forth on the topic of education? Some have even striven to reform it.

Perhaps such commonplaces encourage Americans to take education for granted and threats to it too lightly. I have been steeped in it my entire life as student and teacher—from third grade in a Paris public school to a long career in several American and foreign colleges and universities—and I have witnessed the transformations education can achieve. Consider those leaders of the American Enlightenment: While Franklin and Paine were largely self-taught, Adams and Hamilton scrambled up from local schools and tutors to Harvard and Columbia. Education, in fact, has been one of America's great successes despite endless obstacles, controversies, and setbacks. It has been crucial to the rise of the world's most powerful economy, and, even more, it has kept lit the beacon that has drawn the world to the United States for its freedoms. It has been proof of the value of widespread enlightenment.

But now more than ever, schools and their curricula are under attack on narrow religious and ideological grounds. Textbooks are being rewritten to undermine science or promote a partisan view of American history. The charter school movement, under the banner of school choice, draws parents discouraged by inferior public schools, but it risks hollowing out public schools financially and educationally, abandoning them to those who have no choice. Increasingly, the movement is driven by for-profit entrepreneurs who see primary and secondary education as a great untapped market or by anti-government zealots who detest public schools simply because they are *public*. We can't allow the education of children to divide us along class or ideological or religious lines. We can't afford the decimation of public schools. Let us recall that they are the fruit of many centuries of strife and striving against the forces of blind authority and obscurantism. Only if we build on their remarkable successes, if we improve and expand public education, will we be able together, as one people, to think our way out of the dilemmas and crises we face now and those that lie ahead.

In particular, I believe that for the growing numbers of American poor, only education will enable them to achieve both power and justice—or justice through power. Through education, equality can be reached not by revolutionary violence, but by the spread of enlightenment. Horace Mann, champion of public schooling, wrote in 1848 that education, "the great equalizer of the conditions of men," did better than to "disarm the poor of their hostility towards the rich; it prevents being poor." American public schools have been under political attack from their first days. Yet as a wholly socialistic enterprise, they have been among the most benign, most successful on earth, and are still the most promising. They are historically tested keys to self-improvement and national progress. Governments build and own the classrooms and fund what happens inside them. But where dictators might use this to control teachers and their teachings, democracies leave control in the hands of teachers, administrators, and local school board members, who can be held responsible. The democratic aim is not to indoctrinate and repress but to enlighten and empower.

Russian tsars and courtiers taught princes how to rule and win wars. Eton for centuries has been the training field for Britain's governing class. Confucian China closely controlled education as the way to power. Is it expecting too much of Americans, in the spirit of their own fundamental values of democracy and enlightenment, to ensure the broadest access to the best education possible, education that would in turn foster effective leadership and followership for the poor and the less privileged?

* * *

The peak of the Enlightenment impact, from the seventeenth century to the mid-1800s, was one of the most creative eras in Western history, rivaling the golden ages of Periclean Athens, Augustan Rome, and Renaissance Italy. Historians have uncovered a host of intellectual, political, economic, cultural, and other intertwined forces, but paramount among these was the role of leadership that mobilized—and was spurred by—enlightened and engaged followers. In this transformational epoch, creative leadership broadened and enriched human life and thought, fighting wars of intellectual liberation across the broadest domains, from philosophy to politics, from the sciences to poetry, from labor to religion. Leadership brought forth fresh torrents of thought, fresh expectations, that unsettled traditions, established and questioned new orders, in a heated, ceaseless dialectic of challenge and response. The more educated the populace, the more likely and deeper the questioning and opposing.

At its acme, as education, formal and informal, spread, the Enlightenment was producing thousands of grassroots and cobblestone activists in worker and student protests, in popular movements, and ultimately in steadily democratizing political parties. At first in the West but ultimately around the world, the Enlightenment penetrated the lives of working people, of the poor and dispossessed, and armed them to challenge rulerships that for centuries had protected their power through harsh repression and naked might.

* * *

The force of Enlightenment ideas was tested not only by their immediate impact on creative leaders and followers but by their persistence across generations, an extraordinary process of transmission as new generations of leaders mobilized people around the great values, and followers in turn became leaders themselves.

The Enlightenment, of course, supplied no rigid or detailed program to political leaders. Rather, philosophers offered a set of transcending ideas and—equally significant—a structure of conflict. Some conflicts, as between authority and liberty and between liberty and equality, are fundamental, everlasting across a host of dimensions. Others, like that between sectarianism and secularism, ebb and flow in intensity. Still others originate through new circumstances, as between liberalism and socialism, a conflict which, because the terms of debate have themselves undergone changes without losing their Enlightenment roots, remains highly relevant today.

Conflicts among values—order versus freedom, liberty versus equality, individual rights versus communal solidarity—ensure that the Enlightenment remains a work in progress. It suggests no finished state, no resting point, no culmination, no end to history. It was born in conflict and conflict renews its transformational energy.

Still, the Enlightenment has been far more than an engine of conflict. It has been the realization that human beings are not slaves of the past or present and that the future is theirs to make. It has opened the minds of men and women to do the most brilliant work transforming nearly all the old ideas and assumptions about human beings, about government and economic life, about religion and nature. No field that human understanding can reach has been left untouched, and entirely new ones, like sociology, anthropology, and many of the sciences, have been invented to give wing to the hunger for knowledge. The Enlightenment has created the opportunity and freedom to take part in a mighty intellectual revolution that has changed the lives of whole peoples. Indeed, the Enlightenment has taught that change is the constant, and that the opportunity and burden for human beings is to harness it for their common benefit.

Hope and striving have been at the heart of the Enlightenment, and in the end perhaps it is the poets who have best expressed that spirit. Tennyson in 1833 wrote of the aged traveler Ulysses and his men of "free hearts, free foreheads," of the desire

> To follow knowledge like a sinking star,
> Beyond the utmost bound of human thought. . . .
> The lights begin to twinkle from the rocks;
> The long day wanes; the slow moon climbs; the deep
> Moans round with many voices. Come, my friends.
> 'Tis not too late to seek a newer world.
> Push off, and sitting well in order smite
> The sounding furrows; for my purpose holds
> To sail beyond the sunset, and the baths
> Of all the western stars, until I die.

Notes

INTRODUCTION: *Enlightenment as Revolution*

1 ["stripped of everything"]: Peter Chelčický, quoted in Margaret Aston, *The Fifteenth Century: The Prospect of Europe* (New York: Harcourt, Brace, 1968), p. 145.

1 ["sombre melancholy"]: Huizinga, *The Waning of the Middle Ages* (Garden City, NY: Anchor, 1954), p. 31.

1 ["Time of mourning"]: quoted in ibid., p. 33, translation at fn. 2.

2 ["human mind becomes"]: quoted in Haydn Mason, "Optimism, Progress, and Philosophical History," in Mark Goldie and Robert Wokler, eds., *The Cambridge History of Eighteenth-Century Political Thought* (Cambridge: Cambridge University Press, 2006), p. 203.

3 ["proper study"]: Pope, *An Essay on Man*, in Pope, *Poems*, John Everett Butt, ed. (New Haven: Yale University Press, 1963), p. 516 (epistle 2, line 2).

3 ["Man, being the servant"]: Bacon, *The New Organon: Or, True Directions Concerning the Interpretation of Nature*, in Bacon, *Selected Philosophical Works*, Rose-Mary Sargent, ed. (Indianapolis: Hackett, 1999), pp. 89, 93 (bk. 1, aphorisms 1, 26).

3 ["received doctrine"]: Locke, *An Essay Concerning Human Understanding*, Peter Nidditch, ed. (New York: Oxford University Press, 1979), p. 105 (bk. 2, ch. 1, §1, 2).

3 ["difference to be found"]: Locke, *Some Thoughts Concerning Education*, John W. Yolton and Jean S. Yolton, eds. (Oxford: Clarendon Press, 1989), p. 103 (§32).

3 ["motto of enlightenment"]: Kant, "What Is Enlightenment?," Lewis White Beck, trans., in Kant, *Philosophical Writings*, Ernst Behler, ed. (New York: Continuum, 1986), pp. 263–69, quoted at p. 263.

4 ["carried their temerity"]: Brooke Boothby, quoted in Don Herzog, *Poisoning the Minds of the Lower Orders* (Princeton: Princeton University Press, 1998), p. 47.

4 ["solitary, poore"]: Hobbes, *Leviathan*, Richard Tuck, ed. (Cambridge: Cambridge University Press, 1996), p. 89 (ch. 13).

4 ["*Ordinance of God*"]: Locke, *Two Treatises of Government*, Peter Laslett, ed. (Cambridge: Cambridge University Press, 1988), pp. 233, 227, respectively (*First Treatise*, §126, 113, respectively).

4 ["sets up his own"]: ibid., p. 408 (*Second Treatise*, §214).

4 ["*Dissolution of the Government*"]: ibid., p. 406 (*Second Treatise*, §211).

5 ["as the king wills"]: quoted in Keith Michael Baker, "Enlightenment Idioms, Old Regime Discourses, and Revolutionary Improvisation," in Thomas E. Kaiser and Dale K. Van Kley, eds., *From Deficit to Deluge: The Origins of the French Revolution* (Palo Alto: Stanford University Press, 2011), p.183.

5 ["with all the force"]: Tackett, *Becoming a Revolutionary: The Deputies of the French National Assembly and the Emergence of a Revolutionary Culture (1789–1790)* (Princeton: Princeton University Press, 1996), p. 308.

5 ["laws and institutions"]: letter to Samuel Kercheval, July 12, 1816, in Jefferson, *Writings,* Merrill D. Peterson, ed. (New York: Library of America, 1984), pp. 1395–1403, quoted at p. 1401.

6 ["enlightened economy"]: see Mokyr, *The Enlightened Economy: An Economic History of Britain, 1700–1850* (New Haven: Yale University Press, 2009).

6 [Working class reading]: see E. P. Thompson, *The Making of the English Working Class* (London: Victor Gollancz, 1963), ch. 16, esp. p. 712; Roger Magraw, *A History of the French Working Class* (Oxford: Blackwell, 1992), vol. 1, pp. 58–90, esp. pp. 72–73.

6 ["two classes"]: quoted in Thompson, p. 759.

6 [Bolívar as enlightened general]: see John Lynch, *Simón Bolívar* (New Haven: Yale University Press, 2007), pp. 31–38, esp. pp. 33, 36.

7 ["immortal statement"]: "Vietnam Declaration of Independence (September 2, 1945)," reprinted in Marvin E. Gettleman, ed., *Vietnam and America,* 2nd ed. (New York: Grove Press, 1995), pp. 26–28, quoted at p. 26.

7 ["rainbow nation"]: from Mandela's inaugural address as president of South Africa, May 10, 1994, quoted in Martin Meredith, *Mandela* (New York: PublicAffairs, 2010), p. 515.

8 ["perfectibility of man"]: see Mason; and Peter Gay, *The Enlightenment: An Interpretation* (New York: Alfred A. Knopf, 1966–69), vol. 2, ch. 2. The phrase, used by Condorcet, is quoted in Gay, vol. 2, pp. 119–20.

8 ["Know then thyself"]: Pope, *An Essay on Man,* p. 516 (epistle 2, line 1).

1. *The Revolution in Ideas*

Hans Aarsleff, "Locke's Influence," in Chappell, pp. 252–89.

Henry E. Allison, *Benedict de Spinoza: An Introduction,* rev. ed. (New Haven: Yale University Press, 1987).

John Aubrey, "The Life of Mr Thomas Hobbes of Malmesbury," in Aubrey, *Brief Lives,* John Buchanan-Brown, ed. (London: Penguin, 2000), pp. 413–56.

Etienne Balibar, *Spinoza and Politics,* Peter Snowdon, trans. (London: Verso, 1998).

Stewart J. Brown and Timothy Tackett, eds., *Enlightenment, Reawakening, and Revolution, 1660–1815,* vol. 7 of *The Cambridge History of Christianity* (Cambridge: Cambridge University Press, 2006).

Stuart Brown, ed., *British Philosophy and the Age of Enlightenment* (London: Routledge, 1996).

Wiep van Bunge, "Censorship of Philosophers in the Seventeenth-Century Dutch Republic," in Laerke, pp. 95–117.

Ernst Cassirer, *The Philosophy of the Enlightenment,* Fritz C. A. Koelln and James P. Pettegrove, trans. (Princeton: Princeton University Press, 1951).

Vere Chappell, ed., *The Cambridge Companion to Locke* (Cambridge: Cambridge University Press, 1994).

Gale E. Christianson, *In the Presence of the Creator: Isaac Newton and His Times* (New York: Free Press, 1984).

Desmond M. Clarke, *Descartes* (Cambridge: Cambridge University Press, 2006).

I. Bernard Cohen and George E. Smith, eds., *The Cambridge Companion to Newton* (Cambridge: Cambridge University Press, 2002).

Conal Condren et al., eds., *The Philosopher in Early Modern Europe: The Nature of a Contested Identity* (Cambridge: Cambridge University Press, 2006).

John Cottingham, *Descartes* (London: Blackwell, 1986).

John Cottingham, ed., *The Cambridge Companion to Descartes* (Cambridge: Cambridge University Press, 1992).

Gerald R. Cragg, *Reason and Authority in the Eighteenth Century* (Cambridge: Cambridge University Press, 1964).

Edwin Curley, "The State of Nature and Its Law in Hobbes and Spinoza," in Lloyd, vol. 3, pp. 122–42.

René Descartes, *Philosophical Writings,* John Cottingham et al., trans., 3 vols. (Cambridge: Cambridge University Press, 1984–91).

Stillman Drake, *Galileo at Work* (Chicago: University of Chicago Press, 1978).

John Dunn, *Locke* (New York: Oxford University Press, 1984).

Louis Dupré, *The Enlightenment and the Intellectual Foundations of Modern Culture* (New Haven: Yale University Press, 2004).

Mordechai Feingold, "Mathematicians and Naturalists: Sir Isaac Newton and the Royal Society," in Jed Z. Buchwald and I. Bernard Cohen, eds., *Isaac Newton's Natural Philosophy* (Cambridge, MA: MIT Press, 2001).

Lewis S. Feuer, *Spinoza and the Rise of Liberalism* (Boston: Beacon Press, 1958).

Daniel Garber and Michael Ayers, eds., *The Cambridge History of Seventeenth-Century Philosophy,* 2 vols. (Cambridge: Cambridge University Press, 1998).

Don Garrett, ed., *The Cambridge Companion to Spinoza* (Cambridge: Cambridge University Press, 1996).

Stephen Gaukroger, *Descartes: An Intellectual Biography* (Oxford: Clarendon Press, 1995).

——, *Francis Bacon and the Transformation of Early-Modern Philosophy* (Cambridge: Cambridge University Press, 2001).

Stephen Gaukroger et al., eds., *Descartes' Natural Philosophy* (London: Routledge, 2000).

Peter Gay, *The Enlightenment: An Interpretation*, 2 vols. (New York: Alfred A. Knopf, 1966–69).

Mark Goldie and Robert Wokler, eds., *The Cambridge History of Eighteenth-Century Political Thought* (Cambridge: Cambridge University Press, 2006).

Margaret Gullan-Whur, *Within Reason: A Life of Spinoza* (New York: St. Martin's Press, 2000).

Knut Haakonssen, ed., *The Cambridge History of Eighteenth-Century Philosophy*, 2 vols. (Cambridge: Cambridge University Press, 2006).

Stuart Hampshire, *Spinoza and Spinozism* (Oxford: Clarendon Press, 2005).

Ian Harris, "Locke's Political Theory," in Brown, *British Philosophy and the Age of Enlightenment*, pp. 96–122.

John Henry, *The Scientific Revolution and the Origins of Modern Science*, 2nd ed. (New York: Palgrave, 2002).

Thomas Hobbes, *Leviathan*, Richard Tuck, ed. (Cambridge: Cambridge University Press, 1996).

Michael Hunter, *Robert Boyle: Between God and Science* (New Haven: Yale University Press, 2009).

Jonathan Israel, *Enlightenment Contested: Philosophy, Modernity, and the Emancipation of Man, 1670–1752* (New York: Oxford University Press, 2006).

——, *Radical Enlightenment: Philosophy and the Making of Modernity, 1650–1750* (New York: Oxford University Press, 2001).

——, *A Revolution of the Mind: Radical Enlightenment and the Intellectual Origins of Modern Democracy* (Princeton: Princeton University Press, 2010).

Margaret C. Jacob, "The Enlightenment Critique of Christianity," in Brown and Tackett, pp. 265–82.

Andrew Janiak, *Newton as Philosopher* (Cambridge: Cambridge University Press, 2008).

Diana M. Judd, *Questioning Authority: Political Resistance and the Ethic of Natural Science* (New Brunswick, NJ: Transaction, 2009).

Mogens Laerke, ed., *The Use of Censorship in the Enlightenment* (Leiden: Brill, 2009).

Genevieve Lloyd, ed., *Spinoza: Critical Assessments*, 4 vols. (London: Routledge, 2001).

John Locke, *An Essay Concerning Human Understanding,* Peter H. Nidditch, ed. (New York: Oxford University Press, 1979).

———, *Some Thoughts Concerning Education,* John W. Yolton and Jean S. Yolton, eds. (Oxford: Clarendon Press, 1989).

———, *Two Treatises of Government,* Peter Laslett, ed. (Cambridge: Cambridge University Press, 1988).

Michael Losonsky, *Enlightenment and Action from Descartes to Kant: Passionate Thought* (Cambridge: Cambridge University Press, 2001).

J. D. Mabbott, *John Locke* (Cambridge, MA: Schenkman, 1973).

Noel Malcolm, *Aspects of Hobbes* (Oxford: Clarendon Press, 2002).

John Marshall, *John Locke: Resistance, Religion and Responsibility* (Cambridge: Cambridge University Press, 1994).

A. P. Martinich, *Hobbes: A Biography* (Cambridge: Cambridge University Press, 1999).

———, *Thomas Hobbes* (New York: St. Martin's Press, 1997).

Trevor McClaughlin, "Censorship and Defenders of the Cartesian Faith in Mid-Seventeenth Century France," *Journal of the History of Ideas,* vol. 40, no. 4 (October–December 1979), pp. 563–81.

Darrin M. McMahon, *Happiness: A History* (New York: Atlantic Monthly Press, 2006), ch. 3.

Ernan McMullin, ed., *The Church and Galileo* (Notre Dame, IN: University of Notre Dame Press, 2005).

Robert J. McShea, *The Political Philosophy of Spinoza* (New York: Columbia University Press, 1968).

Ted H. Miller, *Mortal Gods: Science, Politics, and the Humanist Ambitions of Thomas Hobbes* (University Park: Pennsylvania State University Press, 2011).

Warren Montag, *Bodies, Masses, Power: Spinoza and His Contemporaries* (London: Verso, 1999).

Steven Nadler, "Baruch Spinoza," in Nadler, *Companion,* pp. 225–46.

———, *Spinoza: A Life* (Cambridge: Cambridge University Press, 1999).

Steven Nadler, ed., *A Companion to Early Modern Philosophy* (London: Blackwell, 2002).

Isaac Newton, *The Principia: Mathematical Principles of Natural Philosophy,* I. Bernard Cohen and Anne Whitman, trans. (Berkeley: University of California Press, 1999).

Robert Nisbet, *The Social Philosophers: Community and Conflict in Western Thought* (New York: Thomas Y. Crowell, 1973).

G. H. R. Parkinson, ed., *The Renaissance and Seventeenth-Century Rationalism* (London: Routledge, 1993).

J. A. Passmore, "The Malleability of Man in Eighteenth-Century Thought," in Earl R. Wasserman, ed., *Aspects of the Eighteenth Century* (Baltimore: Johns Hopkins Press, 1965), pp. 21–46.

Markku Peltonen, *The Cambridge Companion to Bacon* (Cambridge: Cambridge University Press, 1996).

Pauline Phemister, *The Rationalists: Descartes, Spinoza, and Leibniz* (Cambridge: Polity, 2006).

Roy Porter, *The Creation of the Modern World: The Untold Story of the British Enlightenment* (New York: W. W. Norton, 2000).

J. Samuel Preus, *Spinoza and the Irrelevance of Biblical Authority* (Cambridge: Cambridge University Press, 2001).

Raia Prokhovnik, *Spinoza and Republicanism* (New York: Palgrave Macmillan, 2004).

G. A. J. Rogers, *Locke's Enlightenment: Aspects of the Origin, Nature and Impact of His Philosophy* (Hildesheim: Georg Olms Verlag, 1998).

——, "Locke's *Essay* and Newton's *Principia*," *Journal of the History of Ideas,* vol. 39, no. 2 (April–June 1978), pp. 217–32.

G. A. J. Rogers and Alan Ryan, eds., *Perspectives on Thomas Hobbes* (New York: Oxford University Press, 1988).

G. A. J. Rogers et al., eds., *Insiders and Outsiders in Seventeenth-Century Philosophy* (London: Routledge, 2010).

Herbert H. Rowen, *John de Witt, Grand Pensionary of Holland, 1625–1672* (Princeton: Princeton University Press, 1978).

Donald Rutherford, ed., *The Cambridge Companion to Early Modern Philosophy* (Cambridge: Cambridge University Press, 2006).

William Sacksteder, "How Much of Hobbes Might Spinoza Have Read?," in Lloyd, vol. 1, pp. 222–35.

Rose-Mary Sargent, "Learning from Experience: Boyle's Construction of an Experimental Philosophy," in Michael Hunter, ed., *Robert Boyle Reconsidered* (Cambridge: Cambridge University Press, 1994), pp. 57–78.

Peter A. Schouls, *Descartes and the Enlightenment* (Kingston, ON: McGill-Queen's University Press, 1989).

——, *Reasoned Freedom: John Locke and Enlightenment* (Ithaca: Cornell University Press, 1992).

Martin Seliger, "Locke's Theory of Revolutionary Action," *Western Political Quarterly,* vol. 16, no. 3 (September 1963), pp. 548–68.

Russell Shorto, *Descartes' Bones* (New York: Doubleday, 2008).

H. J. Siebrand, *Spinoza and the Netherlanders: An Inquiry into the Early Reception of His Philosophy of Religion* (Assen, NL: Van Gorcum, 1988).

Quentin Skinner, *Hobbes and Civil Science,* vol. 3 of *Visions of Politics* (Cambridge: Cambridge University Press, 2002).

Steven B. Smith, *Spinoza's Book of Life: Freedom and Redemption in the* Ethics (New Haven: Yale University Press, 2003).

Tom Sorell, ed., *The Cambridge Companion to Hobbes* (Cambridge: Cambridge University Press, 1996).

Baruch de Spinoza, *Collected Works,* Edwin Curley, ed. and trans. (Princeton: Princeton University Press, 1985–), vol. 1.

——, *The Political Works,* A. G. Wernham, ed. and trans. (Oxford: Clarendon Press, 1958).

——, *The Theological-Political Treatise,* Samuel Shirley, trans. (Leiden: Brill, 1991; reprinted by Hackett, 1998).

Matthew Stewart, *The Courtier and the Heretic: Leibniz, Spinoza, and the Fate of God in the Modern World* (New York: W. W. Norton, 2006).

Theo Verbeek, *Spinoza's Theologico-Political Treatise: Exploring the 'Will of God'* (Aldershot: Ashgate, 2003).

Stephen Voss, ed., *Essays on the Philosophy and Science of René Descartes* (New York: Oxford University Press, 1993).

Manfred Walther, "Suppress or Refute? Reactions to Spinoza in Germany around 1700," in Laerke, pp. 25–40.

Roger Woolhouse, *Locke: A Biography* (Cambridge: Cambridge University Press, 2007).

John W. Yolton, ed., *John Locke: Problems and Perspectives* (Cambridge: Cambridge University Press, 1969).

Perez Zagorin, *Francis Bacon* (Princeton: Princeton University Press, 1998).

* * *

11 ["polis belongs"]: Aristotle, *Politics,* Ernest Barker, trans. (New York: Galaxy/Oxford University Press, 1962), p. 5 (I.ii.9). For this treatment of Hobbes, in addition to Martinich, *Hobbes: A Biography,* I have found two essays in Sorell exceptionally helpful: Alan Ryan, "Hobbes's Political Philosophy," pp. 208–45; and Bernard Gert, "Hobbes's Psychology," pp. 157–74.

11 ["perpetuall and restlesse"]: Hobbes, *Leviathan,* pp. 70 (ch. 11), 136 (ch. 19), 89 (ch. 13), respectively.

11 ["Confederacy of Deceivers"]: ibid., pp. 333, 334 (ch. 44).

11 ["common name"]: Hobbes, *De Homine,* Charles T. Wood et al., trans., in Bernard Gert, ed., *Man and Citizen* (London: Peter Smith, 1978), p. 47 (XI, §4).

12 ["procuration of *the safety*"]: Hobbes, *Leviathan,* pp. 231 (ch. 30), 117 (ch. 17), respectively.

12 ["sovereign in effect"]: Ryan, p. 232.

12 ["*Supremacy* against"]: Hobbes, *Leviathan,* p. 226 (ch. 29).

12 ["profess what is commanded"]: Springborg, "Hobbes and Religion," in Sorell, pp. 346–80, quoted at p. 353.

12 ["tongue of man"]: Hobbes, *De Cive,* Howard Warrender, ed. (New York: Oxford University Press, 1983), p. 88 (ch. 5, §5).

13 [Hobbes as Bacon's secretary]: Aubrey, pp. 34–35.

13 ["In the manner of spiders"]: Bacon, *Novum Organum,* in *The* Instauratio Magna, *Part II*: Novum Organum *and Associated Texts,* Graham Rees and Maria Wakely, eds. (Oxford: Clarendon Press, 2004), pp. 153, 129, 161, respectively (bk. 1, aphorisms 95, 82, 104, respectively).

13 ["sovereignty of Man"]: Bacon, "In Praise of Knowledge," in Bacon, *Essays,* Richard Whately, ed. (New York: C.S. Francis, 1857), pp. 529–32, quoted at p. 532.

13 [Bacon's experiment and death]: Aubrey, quoted at pp. 29–30; Martinich, *Hobbes: A Biography,* p. 66.

14 ["prerogative of the king"]: letter to John Scudamore, from Paris, April 12, 1641, in Hobbes, *The Correspondence,* Noel Malcolm, ed. (Oxford: Clarendon Press, 1994–97), vol. 2, pp. 114–15, quoted at p. 115.

14 ["Kingdome of Darknesse"]: Hobbes, *Leviathan,* pp. 417, 419 (ch. 44).

14 ["expense of machines"]: Hobbes, "Dialogus Physicus" (1661), Simon Schaffer, trans., in Steven Shapin and Schaffer, *Leviathan and the Air-Pump: Hobbes, Boyle, and the Experimental Life* (Princeton: Princeton University Press, 1985), pp. 345–91 (appendix), quoted at p. 379.

15 ["Successour to a Crown"]: quoted in Skinner, pp. 34, 35; for the echo in *Leviathan,* see Hobbes, *Leviathan,* p. 136 (ch. 19).

15 ["suddainly striken"]: Justinian Morse, secretary to the Earl of Devonshire, quoted in Skinner, p. 35.

15 ["nothing remarkable"]: quoted in Martinich, *Hobbes: A Biography,* p. 356.

15 [*Bene vixit*]: letter to Mersenne, April 1634, in Descartes, *Philosophical Writings,* vol. 3, pp. 42–44, quoted at p. 43 fn.1. For this treatment of Descartes, I have found Gaukroger's *Descartes: An Intellectual Biography* exceptionally useful.

15 ["good thing"]: letter to [Mesland], February 9, 1645, in Descartes, *Philosophical Writings,* vol. 3, pp. 244–46, quoted at p. 245.

16 ["greatest sorrow"]: Adrien Baillet, Descartes' first biographer, quoted in Gaukroger, *Descartes: An Intellectual Biography,* p. 353.

16 ["many errors"]: Descartes, *Discourse on the Method,* in Descartes, *Philosophical Writings,* vol. 2, p. 116 (pt. 1).

17 [Descartes' dreams]: Gaukroger, *Descartes: An Intellectual Biography,* pp. 106–11; Clarke, pp. 59–62.

17 ["libertines"]: Gaukroger, *Descartes: An Intellectual Biography,* pp. 135–39.

18 ["this machine"]: Descartes, *Treatise of Man,* Thomas Steele Hall, trans. (Cambridge, MA: Harvard University Press, 1972), pp. 113, 33, respectively.

18 ["control petulant minds"]: quoted in Clarke, p. 111.

19 ["so closely"]: letter to Mersenne, end of November 1633, in Descartes, *Philosophical Writings,* vol. 3, pp. 40–41, quoted at p. 41.

19 ["for anything"]: letter to Mersenne, April 1634, in ibid., vol. 3, pp. 42–44, quoted at p. 42.

19 ["forfeit almost all"]: letter to Mersenne, February 1634, in ibid., vol. 3, pp. 41–42, quoted at p. 42.

19 ["fear of God"]: quoted in Geneviève Rodis-Lewis, "Descartes' Life and the Development of His Philosophy," in Cottingham, *Cambridge Companion to Descartes,* pp. 21–57, at p. 30.

19 ["any proposition"]: letter to Mersenne, November 25, 1630, in Descartes, *Philosophical Writings,* vol. 3, pp. 28–29, quoted at p. 29.

19 ["as if absolutely false"]: Descartes, *Discourse on the Method,* in ibid., vol. 2, p. 127 (pt. 4).

20 ["that is—to explain"]: ibid., p. 128 (pt. 4).

20 ["Descartes must use"]: Gaukroger, *Descartes: An Intellectual Biography,* p. 343.

20 ["uncreated and independent"]: Descartes, *Principles of Philosophy,* in Descartes, *Philosophical Writings,* vol. 2, p. 211 (pt. 1, §54).

20 ["troop of theologians"]: letter to Princess Elizabeth of Bohemia, May 10, 1647, in ibid., vol. 3, pp. 317–19, quoted at p. 317.

20 ["bold, persistent"]: Gay, vol. 2, p. 146.

21 ["true substantial union"]: letter to Regius, January 1642, in Descartes, *Philosophical Writings,* vol. 3, pp. 205–9, quoted at p. 209.

21 ["thinking thing"]: Hobbes and Descartes, "Third Set of Objections [to Descartes' *Meditations*] with the Author's Replies," in ibid., vol. 2, pp. 122–23 (Second Objection), quoted at pp. 122, 123.

21 ["We do not have"]: ibid., p. 129 (Seventh Objection); see also Martinich, pp. 163–71; Richard Tuck, "Hobbes and Descartes," in Roger and Ryan, pp. 11–41.

21 ["head did not lye"]: Aubrey, p. 448.

22 ["topic where it is"]: letter to Father Dinet [1642], in Descartes, *Philosophical Writings,* vol. 3, pp. 384–97, quoted at p. 392.

22 ["was absolutely against"]: Aubrey, p. 448.

22 ["injurious to Faith"]: quoted in McClaughlin, p. 567.

22 [*donec corrigantur*]: quoted in Nicholas Jolley, "The Reception of Descartes' Philosophy," in Cottingham, *Cambridge Companion to Descartes,* pp. 393–423, at p. 398.

23 [*la précieuse relique*]: quoted in Shorto, p. 213.

23 ["abominable heresies"]: Asa Kasher and Shlomo Biderman, "Why Was Baruch De Spinoza

Excommunicated?," in Lloyd, vol. 1, pp. 58–99, quoted at p. 60. For this treatment of Spinoza, I found Nadler's *Spinoza* as well as Allison to be exceptionally helpful.

23 ["union that the mind"]: Spinoza, *Treatise on the Emendation of the Intellect,* in Spinoza, *Collected Works,* vol. 1, p. 11 (§13).

24 ["superseded Descartes"]: Oluf Borch, quoted in Gullan-Whur, p. 138.

24 ["dominion within"]: Spinoza, *Ethics,* in Spinoza, *Collected Works,* vol. 1, p. 491 (preface to pt. 3).

24 ["seat of the soul"]: Descartes, *Treatise of Man,* pp. 86 et seq.; letter to Meyssonnier, January 29, 1640, in Descartes, *Philosophical Letters,* Anthony Kenny, ed. and trans. (Oxford: Clarendon Press, 1970), pp. 69–70; letter to Mersenne, April 1, 1640, in ibid., pp. 71–72; letter to Mersenne, July 30, 1640, in ibid., p. 75; Stephen Voss, "Simplicity and the Seat of the Soul," in Voss, *Essays,* pp. 128–41.

24 ["say what we think"]: letter to Henry Oldenburg, [autumn 1665?], in Spinoza, *The Letters,* Samuel Shirley, trans. (Indianapolis: Hackett, 1995), pp. 185–86 (letter 30), quoted at p. 186.

24 ["spreading contention"]: Spinoza, *Theological-Political Treatise,* p. 88 (ch. 7).

25 ["straightforward study"]: ibid., p. 89 (ch. 7).

25 ["Nothing happens"]: ibid., pp. 74 (ch. 6), 18 (ch. 1), respectively.

25 ["instead of God's Word"]: ibid., p. 150 (ch. 12).

25 [Descartes' dissections]: Gaukroger, *Descartes: An Intellectual Biography,* p. 334.

25 ["To love God"]: Spinoza, *Theological-Political Treatise,* pp. 155 (ch. 12), 157 (ch. 13), 107 (ch. 7), 68 (ch. 5), respectively.

26 ["Except God"]: Spinoza, *Ethics,* pp. 420 (pt. 1, proposition 14), 436 (pt. 1, proposition 33).

26 ["laws and rules"]: ibid., p. 492 (preface to pt. 3).

26 ["Bondage"]: ibid., p. 543 (preface to pt. 4).

27 ["part of the whole"]: ibid., pp. 594 (appendix to pt. 4, §32), 611 (pt. 5, propositions 31 and 32).

27 [Collegiants]: Nadler, *Spinoza,* pp. 139–41.

27 [Oldenburg]: Allison, pp. 13–14.

28 ["by any means"]: Spinoza, *Theological-Political Treatise,* p. 180 (ch. 16).

28 ["decides to be just"]: Spinoza, *Treatise on Politics,* in Spinoza, *Political Works,* p. 287 (ch. 3, §5).

28 ["freedom of judgment"]: Spinoza, *Theological-Political Treatise,* p. 234 (ch. 20).

28 ["may more properly"]: Spinoza, *Treatise on Politics,* p. 311 (ch. 5, §4).

29 ["truly human"]: ibid., p. 311 (ch. 5, §5).

29 ["most closely"]: Spinoza, *Theological-Political Treatise*, p. 185 (ch. 16).

29 ["more than any other"]: Allison, p. 192.

29 ["no right"]: Spinoza, *Treatise on Politics*, p. 287 (ch. 3, §5).

29 ["should rational subjects"]: Allison, p. 194.

29 ["as vile"]: quoted in Nadler, *Spinoza*, p. 296.

30 ["idolatry and superstition"]: quoted in W. N. A. Klever, "Spinoza: Life and Works," in Garrett, pp. 13–60, at p. 40.

30 ["cut through him"]: Aubrey, p. 441.

30 ["fallen Jew"]: quoted in Nadler, *Spinoza*, p. 306.

30 ["his excellency"]: quoted in ibid., p. 256.

30 ["disaster year"]: quoted in Klever, p. 40.

30 [*radeloos*]: ibid.

31 ["thinks of nothing less"]: Spinoza, *Ethics*, p. 584 (pt. 4, proposition 67).

31 ["trifling quarrels"]: see letter to William Molyneux, September 11, 1697, in Locke, *Correspondence*, E. S. de Beer, ed. (Oxford: Clarendon Press, 1976–89), vol. 3, pp. 189–91, esp. p. 190.

31 ["unmedleing temper"]: letter to Thomas Herbert, Earl of Pembroke, November 28/December 8, 1684, in ibid., vol. 2, pp. 661–66, quoted at p. 663.

32 ["perplex'd with obscure"]: Mr. Le Clerc, "The Life and Character of Mr. John Locke," T. F. P. Gent, trans., in *Locke's Essay Concerning Human Understanding: Books II and IV (With Omissions)* (Chicago: Open Court, 1905), pp. xx–liii, quoted at p. xi.

32 ["there is no one"]: Locke, *Two Tracts on Government*, Philip Abrams, ed. (Cambridge: Cambridge University Press, 1967), pp. 119, 121 (preface to First Tract).

32 ["Conjurers"]: letter to Robert Boyle, May 5, 1666, in Locke, *Correspondence*, vol. 1, pp. 273–76, quoted at p. 274.

32 ["very often differed"]: quoted in Woolhouse, p. 35.

33 [*must teach*]: Locke, *Essay Concerning Human Understanding*, Nidditch, ed., pp. 644 (bk. 4, ch. 12, §9), 104 (bk. 2, ch. 1, §2), respectively.

33 ["Our Business"]: ibid., p. 46 (bk. 1, ch. 1, §6).

33 ["principles of metaphysics"]: Jean Le Rond d'Alembert, *Preliminary Discourse to the Encyclopedia of Diderot*, Richard N. Schwab, trans. (1751; Bobbs-Merrill, 1963), p. 84.

34 [*hypotheses non fingo*]: Newton, *Principia*, pp. 943 and 943 fn. oo (General Scholium); see also Janiak, p. 17.

34 ["it is enough"]: Newton, *Principia*, p. 943 (General Scholium).

34 ["voyaging through"]: Wordsworth, *The Prelude: The Four Texts (1798, 1799, 1805, 1850),* Jonathan Wordsworth, ed. (London: Penguin, 1995), p. 105 (1850 text, bk. 3, line 63.)

34 ["Nature, and Nature's Laws"]: Pope, "Epitaph. Intended for Sir Isaac Newton, Westminster-Abbey," in Pope, *Poems,* John Butt, ed. (New Haven: Yale University Press, 1963), p. 808.

34 [D'Alembert on Locke and Newton]: d'Alembert, p. 83.

34 ["Dictators of Principles"]: see Locke, *Essay Concerning Human Understanding,* Nidditch, ed., p. 102 (bk. 1, ch. 4, §24).

35 ["white Paper"]: Locke, *Some Thoughts Concerning Education,* p. 265 (§217).

35 ["We are born"]: Locke, "Of the Conduct of the Understanding," in Locke, *Philosophical Works,* J. A. St. John, ed. (London: George Bell and Sons, 1901), vol. 1, p. 41 (§6).

35 ["Ancient savage"]: Locke, *Essay Concerning Human Understanding,* Nidditch, ed., p. 646 (bk. 4, ch. 12, §11).

35 ["natural parts"]: Locke, "Of the Conduct of the Understanding," p. 32 (§3).

35 ["of all the Men"]: Locke, *Some Thoughts Concerning Education,* p. 83 (§1).

35 ["freer fortune"]: Locke, "Of the Conduct of the Understanding," p. 48 (§8).

36 ["State of Peace"]: Locke, *Second Treatise,* in Locke, *Two Treatises,* pp. 280 (ch. 3, §19), 301 (ch. 5, §49).

36 ["unquestionable Property"]: ibid., p. 288 (ch. 5, §27).

36 ["for the Regulating"]: ibid., p. 268 (ch. 1, §3).

36 ["*Invention of Money*"]: ibid., p. 301 (ch. 5, §48).

37 ["Rule of Propriety"]: ibid., p. 293 (ch. 5, §36).

37 ["Whatsoever may be"]: Locke, *A Letter Concerning Toleration,* William Popple, trans., in Locke, *Political Writings,* David Wootton, ed. (Indianapolis: Hackett, 2003), pp. 390–436, quoted at pp. 410, 423.

37 ["businesse of men"]: entry of February 8, 1677, in Locke, *An Early Draft of Locke's Essay, Together with Excerpts from His Journals,* R. I. Aaron and Jocelyn Gibb, eds. (Oxford: Clarendon Press, 1936), pp. 84–90, quoted at p. 88.

38 ["constant succession"]: Locke, *Essay Concerning Human Understanding,* Nidditch, ed., pp. 262 (bk. 2, ch. 21, §45), 266 (bk. 2, ch. 21, §51).

38 ["John Locke, previously"]: quoted in Woolhouse, p. 218.

38 ["lay the foundations"]: ibid., p. 263.

2. *Rule Britannia?*

Thomas Ahnert and Susan Manning, eds., *Character, Self, and Sociability in the Scottish Enlightenment* (New York: Palgrave Macmillan, 2011).

Stuart Andrews, *The Rediscovery of America: Transatlantic Crosscurrents in an Age of Revolution* (New York: St. Martin's Press, 1998).

David Armitage and Michael J. Braddick, eds., *The British Atlantic World, 1500–1800* (New York: Palgrave, 2002).

David Barnett, *London, Hub of the Industrial Revolution: A Revisionary History, 1775–1825* (London: Tauris Academic Studies, 1998).

W. Jackson Bate, *Samuel Johnson* (New York: Harcourt Brace Jovanovich, 1977).

George Louis Beer, *British Colonial Policy, 1754–1765* (New York: Macmillan, 1907).

Troy Bickham, *Making Headlines: The American Revolution as Seen through the British Press* (DeKalb: Northern Illinois University Press, 2009).

Jeremy Black, *George III: America's Last King* (New Haven: Yale University Press, 2006).

———, *Pitt the Elder* (Cambridge: Cambridge University Press, 1992).

Colin Bonwick, *English Radicals and the American Revolution* (Chapel Hill: University of North Carolina Press, 1977).

James Boswell, *Journal of a Tour to the Hebrides with Samuel Johnson, LL.D., 1773*, Frederick A. Pottle and Charles H. Bennett, eds. (New York: McGraw-Hill, 1961).

———, *The Life of Samuel Johnson L.L.D.* (New York: Modern Library, 1931).

John Bowle, *The Imperial Achievement: The Rise and Transformation of the British Empire* (Boston: Little, Brown, 1974), books 1–2.

James E. Bradley, *Popular Politics and the American Revolution in England: Petitions, the Crown, and Public Opinion* (Macon, GA: Mercer University Press, 1986).

John Brewer, *Party Ideology and Popular Politics at the Accession of George III* (Cambridge: Cambridge University Press, 1976).

Alexander Broadie, ed., *The Cambridge Companion to the Scottish Enlightenment* (Cambridge: Cambridge University Press, 2003).

Michael Brown, *Francis Hutcheson in Dublin, 1719–30: The Crucible of His Thought* (Dublin: Four Courts, 2002).

Peter Douglas Brown, *William Pitt Earl of Chatham, the Great Commoner* (London: George Allen & Unwin, 1978).

Stuart Brown, ed., *British Philosophy and the Age of Enlightenment* (London: Routledge, 1996).

Gladys Bryson, *Man and Society: The Scottish Inquiry of the Eighteenth Century* (Princeton: Princeton University Press, 1945).

James Buchan, *The Authentic Adam Smith* (New York: W. W. Norton, 2006).

——, *Crowded with Genius: The Scottish Enlightenment: Edinburgh's Moment of the Mind* (New York: HarperCollins, 2003).

Angus Calder, *Revolutionary Empire*, rev. ed. (London: Pimlico, 1998).

John Cannon, *Samuel Johnson and the Politics of Hanoverian England* (New York: Oxford University Press, 1994).

Nicholas Canny, ed., *The Origins of Empire: British Overseas Enterprise to the Close of the Seventeenth Century,* vol. 1 of *The Oxford History of the British Empire* (New York: Oxford University Press, 1998).

Ian R. Christie and Benjamin W. Labaree, *Empire or Independence, 1760–1776* (New York: W. W. Norton, 1976).

Linda Colley, *Britons: Forging the Nation, 1707–1837* (New Haven: Yale University Press, 1992).

Stephen Conway, *The British Isles and the War of American Independence* (New York: Oxford University Press, 2000).

Don Cook, *The Long Fuse: How England Lost the American Colonies, 1760–1785* (New York: Atlantic Monthly Press, 1995).

Mary Cosh, *Edinburgh: The Golden Age* (Edinburgh: John Donald, 2003).

David Daiches et al., eds., *A Hotbed of Genius: The Scottish Enlightenment, 1730–1790* (Edinburgh: Edinburgh University Press, 1986).

T. M. Devine, *Scotland's Empire and the Shaping of the Americas, 1600–1815* (Washington, D.C.: Smithsonian Books, 2004).

T. M. Devine and Gordon Jackson, eds., *Glasgow* (Manchester: Manchester University Press, 1994–), vol. 1.

H. T. Dickinson, ed., *Britain and the American Revolution* (London: Longman, 1998).

——, *A Companion to Eighteenth-Century Britain* (Oxford: Blackwell, 2002).

G. M. Ditchfield, *George III: An Essay in Monarchy* (New York: Palgrave, 2002).

Roger L. Emerson, *Essays on David Hume, Medical Men and the Scottish Enlightenment* (Burlington, VT: Ashgate, 2009).

Athol Fitzgibbons, *Adam Smith's System of Liberty, Wealth, and Virtue: The Moral and Political Foundations of* The Wealth of Nations (Oxford: Clarendon Press, 1995).

Samuel Fleischacker, *On Adam Smith's* Wealth of Nations: *A Philosophical Companion* (Princeton: Princeton University Press, 2004).

Archibald S. Foord, *His Majesty's Opposition, 1714–1830* (Oxford: Clarendon Press, 1964).

Julian H. Franklin, *John Locke and the Theory of Sovereignty: Mixed Monarchy and the Right of Resistance in the Political Thought of the English Revolution* (Cambridge: Cambridge University Press, 1978).

Alan Frost, "The Pacific Ocean: The Eighteenth Century's 'New World,'" *Studies on Voltaire and the Eighteenth Century,* vol. 152 (1976), pp. 779–822.

Brian Gardner, *The East India Company* (London: Rupert Hart-Davis, 1971).

Ian Gilmour, *Riot, Risings, and Revolution: Governance and Violence in Eighteenth-Century England* (London: Pimlico, 1993).

Mark Goldie, "The English System of Liberty," in Goldie and Robert Wokler, eds., *The Cambridge History of Eighteenth-Century Political Thought* (Cambridge: Cambridge University Press, 2006), pp. 40–78.

Eliga H. Gould, *The Persistence of Empire: British Political Culture in the Age of the American Revolution* (Chapel Hill: University of North Carolina Press, 2000).

Donald Greene, *The Politics of Samuel Johnson,* 2nd ed. (Athens: University of Georgia Press, 1990).

Jack P. Greene, *Peripheries and Center: Constitutional Development in the Extended Polities of the British Empire and the United States, 1607–1788* (Athens: University of Georgia Press, 1986).

Charles L. Griswold Jr., *Adam Smith and the Virtues of Enlightenment* (Cambridge: Cambridge University Press, 1999).

J. L. Hammond and Barbara Hammond, *The Village Labourer, 1760–1832: A Study in the Government of England before the Reform Bill* (London: Longmans, Green, 1912).

Vincent T. Harlow, *The Founding of the Second British Empire, 1763–1793,* 2 vols. (London: Longmans, Green, 1952–64).

Arthur Herman, *How the Scots Invented the Modern World* (New York: Crown, 2001).

Christopher Hibbert, *George III* (New York: Basic Books, 1998).

B. W. Hill, *British Parliamentary Parties, 1742–1832* (London: George Allen & Unwin, 1985).

———, *The Growth of Parliamentary Parties, 1689–1742* (London: George Allen & Unwin, 1976).

Andrew Hook, *Scotland and America: A Study of Cultural Relations, 1750–1835* (Glasgow: Blackie, 1975).

Nicholas Hudson, *Samuel Johnson and the Making of Modern England* (Cambridge: Cambridge University Press, 2003).

Lawrence James, *The Rise and Fall of the British Empire* (New York: St. Martin's Press, 1996), parts 1–2.

Samuel Johnson, *A Journey to the Western Islands of Scotland,* Mary Lascelles, ed., vol. 9 of Johnson, *Works* (New Haven: Yale University Press, 1971).

Brad A. Jones, "The American Revolution, Glasgow, and the Making of the Second City of the Empire," in Simon P. Newman, ed., *Europe's American Revolution* (New York: Palgrave, 2006), pp. 1–25.

Clyve Jones, ed., *Britain in the First Age of Party, 1680–1750* (London: Hambledon Press, 1987).

Klaus E. Knorr, *British Colonial Theories, 1570–1850* (Toronto: University of Toronto Press, 1944).

Paul Langford, "The Eighteenth Century (1688–1789)," in Kenneth O. Morgan, ed., *The Oxford History of Britain,* rev. ed. (New York: Oxford University Press, 1999), pp. 399–469.

———, "London and the American Revolution," in John Stevenson, ed., *London in the Age of Reform* (London: Basil Blackwell, 1977), pp. 55–78.

———, *A Polite and Commercial People: England, 1727–1783* (Oxford: Clarendon Press, 1989).

T. O. Lloyd, *The British Empire, 1558–1983* (Oxford: Oxford University Press, 1984).

Dorothy Marshall, *Dr. Johnson's London* (New York: John Wiley & Sons, 1968).

P. J. Marshall, "Europe and the Rest of the World," in T. C. W. Blanning, ed., *The Eighteenth Century: Europe, 1688–1815* (New York: Oxford University Press, 2000), pp. 218–46.

———, *The Making and Unmaking of Empires: Britain, India, and America, c. 1750–1783* (Oxford: Oxford University Press, 2005).

P. J. Marshall, ed., *The Eighteenth Century,* vol. 2 of *The Oxford History of the British Empire* (Oxford: Oxford University Press, 1998).

Peter Martin, *Samuel Johnson* (Cambridge, MA: Belknap Press, 2008).

Frank McLynn, *1759: The Year Britain Became Master of the World* (New York: Atlantic Monthly Press, 2004).

James Van Horn Melton, *The Rise of the Public in Enlightenment Europe* (Cambridge: Cambridge University Press, 2001).

Joel Mokyr, *The Enlightened Economy: An Economic History of Britain, 1700–1850* (New Haven: Yale University Press, 2009).

James Moore, "Natural Rights in the Scottish Enlightenment," in Goldie and Wokler, pp. 291–316.

Ernest Campbell Mossner, *The Life of David Hume* (Austin: University of Texas Press, 1954).

David Fate Norton and Jacqueline Taylor, eds., *The Cambridge Companion to Hume,* 2nd ed. (Cambridge: Cambridge University Press, 2009).

Frank O'Gorman, *The Long Eighteenth Century: British Political and Social History, 1688–1832* (London: Arnold, 1997).

Nicholas Phillipson, "The Scottish Enlightenment," in Roy Porter and Mikuláš Teich, eds., *The Enlightenment in National Context* (Cambridge: Cambridge University Press, 1981), pp. 19–40.

Liza Picard, *Dr. Johnson's London: Life in London, 1740–1770* (London: Weidenfeld & Nicolson, 2000).

Roy Porter, *The Creation of the Modern World: The Untold Story of the British Enlightenment* (New York: W. W. Norton, 2000).

———, *English Society in the Eighteenth Century,* rev. ed. (New York: Penguin, 1990).

———, *London: A Social History* (Cambridge, MA: Harvard University Press, 1995).

Adam Potkay, *The Passion for Happiness: Samuel Johnson and David Hume* (Ithaca, NY: Cornell University Press, 2000).

Jacob M. Price, "Who Cared about the Colonies? The Impact of the Thirteen Colonies on British Society and Politics, circa 1714–1775," in Bernard Bailyn and Philip D. Morgan, eds., *Strangers Within the Realm: Cultural Margins of the First British Empire* (Chapel Hill: University of North Carolina Press, 1991), pp. 395–436.

John Rae, *Adam Smith* (London: Macmillan, 1895).

Eric Richards, "Scotland and the Uses of the Atlantic Empire," in Bailyn and Morgan, pp. 67–114.

Brian W. Richardson, *Longitude and Empire: How Captain Cook's Voyages Changed the World* (Vancouver: UBC Press, 2005).

Charles R. Ritcheson, *British Politics and the American Revolution* (Norman: University of Oklahoma Press, 1954).

Pat Rogers, *Johnson and Boswell: The Transit of Caledonia* (Oxford: Clarendon Press, 1995).

J. Holland Rose et al., eds., *The Cambridge History of the British Empire* (New York: Macmillan, 1929–59), vols. 1–2, 4.

Jonathan Rose, *The Intellectual Life of the British Working Classes* (New Haven: Yale University Press, 2001).

Ian Simpson Ross, *The Life of Adam Smith* (Oxford: Clarendon Press, 1995).

George Rudé, *Hanoverian London, 1714–1808* (Berkeley: University of California Press, 1971).

———, *Wilkes and Liberty: A Social Study of 1763 to 1774* (Oxford: Clarendon Press, 1962).

John Sainsbury, *Disaffected Patriots: London Supporters of Revolutionary America, 1769–1782* (Kingston, ON: McGill-Queen's University Press, 1987).

Richard B. Schwartz, *Daily Life in Johnson's London* (Madison: University of Wisconsin Press, 1983).

Lois G. Schwoerer, *The Declaration of Rights, 1689* (Baltimore: Johns Hopkins University Press, 1981).

William Robert Scott, *Francis Hutcheson* (Cambridge: Cambridge University Press, 1900).

Robert Shackleton, "Johnson and the Enlightenment," in Mary M. Lascelles et al., eds., *Johnson, Boswell, and Their Circle* (Oxford: Clarendon Press, 1965), pp. 76–92.

Richard B. Sher, *The Enlightenment & the Book: Scottish Authors & Their Publishers in Eighteenth-Century Britain, Ireland, & America* (Chicago: University of Chicago Press, 2006).

Richard B. Sher and Jeffrey R. Smitten, eds., *Scotland and America in the Age of the Enlightenment* (Princeton: Princeton University Press, 1990).

Adam Smith, *An Inquiry into the Nature and Causes of the Wealth of Nations*, R. H. Campbell and A. S. Skinner, eds., 2 vols. (New York: Oxford University Press, 1976).

David Spadafora, *The Idea of Progress in Eighteenth-Century Britain* (New Haven: Yale University Press, 1990).

W. A. Speck, *Stability and Strife: England, 1714–1760* (Cambridge, MA: Harvard University Press, 1977).

Paul Stanistreet, *Hume's Skepticism and the Science of Human Nature* (Burlington, VT: Ashgate, 2002).

M. A. Stewart, ed., *Studies in the Philosophy of the Scottish Enlightenment* (Oxford: Clarendon Press, 1990).

W. L. Taylor, *Francis Hutcheson and David Hume as Predecessors of Adam Smith* (Durham, NC: Duke University Press, 1965).

Peter D. G. Thomas, *George III: King and Politicians, 1760–1770* (Manchester: Manchester University Press, 2002).

———, *John Wilkes: A Friend to Liberty* (Oxford: Clarendon Press, 1996).

E. P. Thompson, *The Making of the English Working Class* (London: Victor Gollancz, 1963).

Hugh Trevor-Roper, "The Scottish Enlightenment," in *Studies on Voltaire and the Eighteenth Century*, vol. 58 (1967), pp. 1635–58.

A. S. Turberville, ed., *Johnson's England: An Account of the Life & Manners of His Age*, 2 vols. (Oxford: Clarendon Press, 1933).

E. G. West, "Adam Smith and Alienation: Wealth Increases, Men Decay?," in Andrew S. Skinner and Thomas Wilson, eds., *Essays on Adam Smith* (Oxford: Clarendon Press, 1975), pp. 540–52.

Kathleen Wilson, *The Sense of the People: Politics, Culture, and Imperialism in England, 1715–1785* (Cambridge: Cambridge University Press, 1995).

Donald Winch, "Scottish Political Economy," in Goldie and Wokler, pp. 443–64.

* * *

39 ["establishment of equal liberty"]: letter to Philippus van Limbroch, September 10, 1689, in Locke, *Correspondence*, E. S. de Beer, ed. (Oxford: Clarendon Press, 1976–89), vol. 3, pp. 689–91, quoted at p. 689.

39 ["fit for nothing"]: quoted in Goldie, p. 49.

40 ["*Who shall be Judge*"]: Locke, *The Second Treatise of Government*, in Locke, *Two Treatises of Government*, Peter Laslett, ed. (Cambridge: Cambridge University Press, 1988), pp. 426–27 (§240).

40 ["antient rights"]: reprinted in Schwoerer, pp. 295–98, quoted at p. 296.

40 ["Power absolute"]: Edward Chamberlayne, *Angliae Notitia: Or, the Present State of England* (1700), p. 154.

41 [British population, 1730–90]: see Langford, "Eighteenth Century," pp. 415, 427; and Langford, *Polite and Commercial People*, p. 418.

41 ["But now!"]: Arthur Young, quoted in Porter, *London*, p. 133.

42 ["no sooner begin"]: Addison, *The Freeholder*, no. 53 (June 22, 1716), in Addison, *Works*, Richard Hurd, ed. (London: Henry G. Bohn, 1854–56), vol. 5, pp. 92–95, quoted at p. 95.

42 ["best parliament-man"]: Romney Sedgwick, "Robert Walpole," in Sedgwick, ed., *The House of Commons, 1715–1754* (Oxford: Oxford University Press, 1970), vol. 2, pp. 513–17, quoted at p. 516.

43 [Churchill on "First World War"]: see Churchill, *The Age of Revolution*, vol. 2 of *A History of the English-Speaking Peoples* (New York: Dodd, Mead, 1957), ch. 11.

43 ["assumed for themselves"]: Colley, p. 101.

43 ["Born and educated"]: quoted in Ditchfield, p. 23.

44 ["fixed plan"]: letter of the duc de Nivernais to the duc de Praslin, French foreign minister, May 11, 1763, quoted in Black, *George III*, p. 71.

44 ["put an end"]: quoted in Brewer, p. 47.

44 ["Gentlemen of landed property"]: letter to Lord North, August 24, 1774, in George III, *Correspondence, from 1760 to December 1783*, John Fortescue, ed. (London: Macmillan, 1927–28), vol. 3, pp. 125–26, quoted at p. 125.

44 ["ignorance in business"]: letter of George III to Bute, May 19, 1762, in Romney Sedgwick, ed., *Letters from George III to Lord Bute, 1756–1766* (London: Macmillan, 1939), p. 109.

44 ["At every level"]: Porter, *London*, p. 147.

44 [Wages]: see Picard, pp. 293–98 (appendix); and Schwartz, pp. 51–52.

45 ["dirty, bedraggled"]: Marshall, *Dr. Johnson's London*, p. 220.

45 ["under-rated the number"]: quoted in Boswell, *Life*, p. 876.

45 [Fielding on gin]: Fielding, *An Enquiry into the Causes of the Late Increase of Robbers* (1751), in Fielding, *Complete Works* (New York: Barnes & Noble, 1967), vol. 13, p. 34.

46 [Langford on combinations]: Langford, "Eighteenth Century," p. 433.

47 ["increase of reading"]: quoted in David Vincent, *Literacy and Popular Culture: England, 1750–1914* (Cambridge: Cambridge University Press, 1989), p. 228.

47 ["reason was too strong"]: Place, *Autobiography (1771–1854)*, Mary Thale, ed. (Cambridge: Cambridge University Press, 1972), p. 46.

47 [Provincial press and newspaper sales]: Porter, *Creation*, pp. 86, 78, respectively.

48 ["boundless liberty"]: Johnson, "Introduction to the *Harleian Miscellany*: An Essay on the Origin and Importance of Small Tracts and Fugitive Pieces" (1744), in Johnson, *The Major Works,* Donald Greene, ed. (New York: Oxford University Press, 2000), pp. 122–27, quoted at p. 123.

48 ["every man"]: Alexander Catcott, quoted in Porter, *Creation,* p. 79.

48 ["After smoke"]: from the epigraph to *The Spectator* No. 1, March 1, 1711, in Addison and Steele, *The Spectator* (London: J. M. Dent, 1907), vol. 1, p. 3.

48 ["Philosophy out of Closets"]: *The Spectator* No. 10, March 12, 1711, in ibid., vol. 1, pp. 38–41, quoted at pp. 39, 38, respectively.

48 ["the new play"]: Thomas Beddoes, quoted in Porter, *Creation,* pp. 93, 94.

48 [Sales of Richardson, Defoe, Fielding]: ibid., p. 73.

48 ["All Englishmen"]: César de Saussure, *A Foreign View of England in 1725–1729,* Madame Van Muyden, ed. and trans. (1902; reprinted by Caliban Books, 1995), p. 101.

49 [Robin Hood]: Picard, pp. 130–31.

50 ["Were not the law"]: Johnson, Sermon No. 24, in Johnson, *Sermons,* Jean Hagstrum and James Gray, eds. (New Haven: Yale University Press, 1978), pp. 249–59, quoted at pp. 258, 259.

50 ["not absolute"]: Johnson, "The False Alarm" (1770), in Johnson, *Political Writings,* Donald J. Greene, ed. (New Haven: Yale University Press, 1977), pp. 317–45, quoted at pp. 327, 341.

50 [Wilkes-Johnson encounter]: Boswell, *Life,* pp. 651–61.

51 ["Enlightenment's 'New World'"]: Blanning, *The Pursuit of Glory: Europe, 1648–1815* (New York: Viking, 2007), p. 496.

51 ["smallest characteristics"]: George Forster, quoted in Frost, p. 798.

52 ["better classes"]: Rajat Kanta Ray, "Indian Society and the Establishment of British Supremacy, 1765–1818," in Marshall, *The Eighteenth Century,* pp. 508–29, quoted at pp. 524, 525.

53 ["we introduce"]: quoted in Blanning, p. 496.

53 ["East is East"]: Kipling, "The Ballad of East and West," in Kipling, *Rudyard Kipling's Verse: Inclusive Edition, 1885–1918* (Garden City, NY: Doubleday, Page, 1921), pp. 268–72, quoted at p. 268 (line 1).

53 ["Within parliament"]: Dickinson, Introduction, in Dickinson, *Britain and the American Revolution,* pp. 1–20, quoted at p. 8.

54 ["in all cases"]: quoted in Marshall, *Making and Unmaking of Empires,* p. 297.

55 [Parliamentary opposition to North's policies]: see Frank O'Gorman, "The Parliamentary Opposition to the Government's American Policy, 1760–1782," in Dickinson, *Britain and the American Revolution,* pp. 97–123.

55 ["former unsuspecting confidence"]: Burke, Speech on Moving His Resolutions for Conciliation

with the Colonies, March 22, 1775, in Burke, *Selected Writings*, W. J. Bate, ed. (New York: Modern Library, 1960), pp. 107–76, quoted at p. 111.

56 ["conducting head"]: quoted in Black, *Pitt the Elder*, p. 259.

56 ["long train"]: Locke, *Second Treatise*, pp. 415 (§225), 370 (§155), respectively.

56 ["almost universal"]: speaking before the Commons, May 7, 1783, quoted in James E. Bradley, "The British Public and the American Revolution: Ideology, Interest, and Opinion," in Dickinson, *Britain and the American Revolution*, pp. 124–54, at p. 126.

56 ["cause of Great Britain"]: letter of August 25, 1775, in George III, *Correspondence*, vol. 3, p. 249.

57 ["a Sanctuary"]: Daniel Neal, *The History of New-England*, 2nd ed. (1742), vol. 2, p. 254.

57 ["new opening"]: Price, "Two Tracts on Civil Liberty" (1778), in Price, *Political Writings*, D. O. Thomas, ed. (Cambridge: Cambridge University Press, 1991), pp. 14–100, quoted at p. 19.

57 ["wise and political"]: quoted in Bonwick, p. 102.

57 ["nobly contending"]: quoted in Sainsbury, p. 94.

57 ["BELOVED American"]: ibid., p. 90.

57 ["vile incendiaries"]: Society for Constitutional Information, "A Second Address to the Public" (1780), quoted at pp. 11, 12, 11, 14–15, respectively.

58 [Scottish franchise]: Hook, p. 64.

59 ["howling Wilderness"]: quoted in Richards, p. 88.

59 ["rapid and uniform"]: Johnson, pp. 28, 138.

59 ["persevering in the old jokes"]: Boswell, *Life*, p. 659.

59 ["Am I, or are you"]: letter to Gilbert Elliot, September 22, 1764, in Hume, *Letters*, J. Y. T. Greig, ed. (Oxford: Clarendon Press, 1932), vol. 1, pp. 467–71, quoted at p. 470.

59 ["alliance for improvement"]: Richards, p. 104.

59 [Hume and the old woman in the bog]: Mossner, p. 563.

59 ["Scotch knowledge"]: Richards, p. 86.

60 ["outsiders as diverse"]: Herman, pp. 161–62.

60 ["love, serve"]: quoted in ibid., p. 63.

61 ["enjoyment of the things"]: Locke, "Understanding" (1677), in Locke, *Political Essays*, Mark Goldie, ed. (Cambridge: Cambridge University Press, 1997), pp. 260–65, quoted at p. 264.

61 ["faithfully pursue"]: Locke, "Thus I Think," in ibid., pp. 296–97, quoted at p. 297.

61 ["two Forces"]: Hutcheson, *An Inquiry into the Original of Our Ideas of Beauty and Virtue* (1725),

in Hutcheson, *Collected Works* (Hildesheim: Georg Olms Verlag, 1990), vol. 1, p. 130 (Treatise II, sect. 2.3).

61 ["Thus God and Nature"]: Pope, *An Essay on Man,* in Pope, *Poems,* John Butt, ed. (New Haven: Yale University Press, 1963), p. 535 (Epistle III, lines 317–18).

61 ["delight in the Good"]: Hutcheson, *Inquiry* (1725), pp. 129, 110, respectively (Treatise II, sects. 2.3 and 1.2, respectively).

61 [*"greatest happiness"*]: Hutcheson, *An Inquiry into the Original of Our Ideas of Beauty and Virtue,* 4th rev. ed. (1738), excerpted in Hutcheson, *Philosophical Writings,* R. S. Downie, ed. (London: J. M. Dent, 1994), p. 90.

62 ["called new light"]: letter to Thomas Drennan, c. 1743, quoted in Brown, *Francis Hutcheson in Dublin,* p. 89.

62 ["science of man"]: Hume, *A Treatise of Human Nature,* in Hume, *Philosophical Works,* T. H. Green and T. H. Grose, eds. (1882–86; reprinted by Scientia Verlag Aalen, 1964), vol. 1, pp. 307, 308 (Introduction).

62 ["no rational principle"]: quoted in Boswell, *Journal,* p. 155.

62 ["From my earliest"]: "A Kind of History of My Life" (1734), reprinted in Norton and Taylor, pp. 515–22 (appendix), quoted at p. 516.

63 ["endless Disputes"]: ibid.

63 ["Reason is"]: Hume, *Treatise,* vol. 2, p. 195 (bk. 2, pt. 3, sect. 3).

63 ["ambition, avarice"]: Hume, *An Enquiry Concerning Human Understanding,* in Hume, *Philosophical Works,* vol. 4, pp. 3–135, quoted at p. 68 (sect. 8, pt. 1).

63 [Hume to Hutcheson on utility]: letter of September 17, 1739, in Hume, *Letters,* vol. 1, pp. 32–34, esp. p. 33.

63 ["most entire system"]: Hume, *The History of England* (1778; Liberty Fund, 1983), vol. 6, p. 531.

64 ["commonly to be subordinate"]: ibid., vol. 6, p. 533.

64 ["Abuse of Liberty"]: letter to Anne-Robert-Jacques Turgot, June 16, 1768, in Hume, *Letters,* vol. 2, pp. 179–81, quoted at p. 180.

64 ["no party"]: Hume, "Of the Original Contract," in Hume, *Essays, Moral, Political, and Literary,* Eugene F. Miller, ed. (Indianapolis: Liberty Fund, 1987), pp. 465–87, quoted at p. 465.

64 ["I am an American"]: letter to Baron Mure of Caldwell, October 27, 1775, in Hume, *Letters,* vol. 2, pp. 302–3, quoted at p. 302.

64 ["spirit of independency"]: Hume, *History of England,* vol. 5, p. 147.

64 ["govern or misgovern"]: letter to Baron Mure, p. 303.

65 ["certainly tend"]: Smith, "Thoughts on the Contest with America" (February 1778), in Smith,

Correspondence, Ernest C. Mossner and Ian S. Ross, eds., 2nd ed. (Oxford: Clarendon Press, 1987), pp. 380–85 (Appendix B), quoted at pp. 382, 381, 380, 381, respectively.

65 ["never to be forgotten"]: letter to Dr. Archibald Davidson, November 16, 1787, in ibid., pp. 308–9, quoted at p. 309.

65 ["immense and connected"]: Smith, *The Theory of Moral Sentiments,* D. D. Raphael and A. L. Macfie, eds. (Oxford: Clarendon Press, 1976), p. 289.

65 ["essential principles"]: Pierre Samuel Du Pont, quoted in Thomas P. Neill, "Quesnay and Physiocracy," *Journal of the History of Ideas,* vol. 9, no. 2 (April 1948), pp. 153–73, quoted at p. 165.

66 ["enlightened economy"]: see Mokyr.

66 [Smith on government role]: see Smith, *An Inquiry into the Nature and Causes of the Wealth of Nations,* R. H. Campbell and A. S. Skinner, eds. (New York: Oxford University Press, 1976), vol. 2, pp. 687–88 (pt. 4, bk. 9); and pt. 5 passim.

66 ["in proportion to"]: ibid., vol. 2, p. 825 (pt. 5, bk. 2, sect. b).

66 ["All systems"]: ibid., p. 687 (pt. 4, bk. 2).

66 ["desire of bettering"]: ibid., vol. 1, pp. 341 (pt. 2, bk. 3), 456 (pt. 4, bk. 2).

66 ["universal opulence"]: ibid., vol. 1, p. 22 (pt. 1, bk. 1).

66 ["from the heap"]: Smith, *Theory of Moral Sentiments,* pp. 184–85.

67 ["selfishness and rapacity"]: ibid., p. 184.

67 ["as stupid"]: Smith, *Wealth of Nations,* vol. 2, p. 782 (pt. 5, bk. 1, sect. f)

67 ["mental mutilation"]: ibid., vol. 2, p. 787 (pt. 5, bk. 1, sect. f).

67 ["most serious attention"]: ibid.

67 ["beggar, who suns himself"]: Smith, *Theory of Moral Sentiments,* p. 185.

3. *Revolutionary Americans*

Willi P. Adams, *The First American Constitutions: Republican Ideology and the Making of the State Constitutions in the Revolutionary Era,* Rita and Robert Kimber, trans. (Lanham, MD: Rowman & Littlefield, 2001).

Douglas Anderson, *The Radical Enlightenments of Benjamin Franklin* (Baltimore: Johns Hopkins University Press, 1997).

Bernard Bailyn, *The Ideological Origins of the American Revolution* (Cambridge, MA: Belknap Press, 1967).

———, *The Ordeal of Thomas Hutchinson* (Cambridge, MA: Harvard University Press, 1974).

E. Digby Baltzell, *Puritan Boston and Quaker Philadelphia: Two Protestant Ethics and the Spirit of Class Authority and Leadership* (New York: Free Press, 1979), esp. parts 3–4.

Benson Bobrick, *Angel in the Whirlwind: The Triumph of the American Revolution* (New York: Simon & Schuster, 1997).

Colin Bonwick, *The American Revolution* (Charlottesville: University Press of Virginia, 1991).

Daniel J. Boorstin, *The Lost World of Thomas Jefferson* (Boston: Beacon Press, 1960).

Carl Bridenbaugh, *Cities in Revolt: Urban Life in America, 1743–1776* (New York: Alfred A. Knopf, 1955).

Carl Bridenbaugh and Jessica Bridenbaugh, *Rebels and Gentlemen: Philadelphia in the Age of Franklin* (New York: Reynal & Hitchcock, 1942).

Richard D. Brown, *Revolutionary Politics in Massachusetts: The Boston Committee of Correspondence and the Towns, 1772–1774* (Cambridge, MA: Harvard University Press, 1970).

Robert E. Brown, *Middle-Class Democracy and the Revolution in Massachusetts, 1691–1780* (Ithaca, NY: Cornell University Press, 1955).

James MacGregor Burns and Stewart Burns, *A People's Charter: The Pursuit of Rights in America* (New York: Alfred A. Knopf, 1991), ch. 2.

Richard L. Bushman, *King and People in Provincial Massachusetts* (Chapel Hill: University of North Carolina Press, 1985), esp. part 1.

Jon Butler, *Becoming America: The Revolution before 1776* (Cambridge, MA: Harvard University Press, 2000).

John Clive and Bernard Bailyn, "England's Cultural Provinces: Scotland and America," *William and Mary Quarterly,* 3rd series, vol. 11, no. 2 (April 1954), pp. 200–13.

Francis D. Cogliano, *Revolutionary America, 1763–1815* (London: Routledge, 2000).

I. Bernard Cohen, *Science and the Founding Fathers: Science in the Political Thought of Jefferson, Franklin, Adams, and Madison* (New York: W. W. Norton, 1995).

Henry Steele Commager, *The Empire of Reason: How Europe Imagined and America Realized the Enlightenment* (Garden City, NY: Anchor/Doubleday, 1977).

Paul K. Conkin, *Puritans and Pragmatists: Eight Eminent American Thinkers* (New York: Dodd, Mead, 1968), chs. 3–4.

Edward Countryman, *The American Revolution* (New York: Hill and Wang, 1985).

James Delbourgo, *A Most Amazing Scene of Wonders: Electricity and Enlightenment in Early America* (Cambridge, MA: Harvard University Press, 2006).

Frank L. Dewey, *Thomas Jefferson, Lawyer* (Charlottesville: University Press of Virginia, 1986).

Oliver Morton Dickerson, comp., *Boston under Military Rule, 1768–1769* (Boston: Chapman & Grimes, 1936).

Joseph J. Ellis, *Passionate Sage: The Character and Legacy of John Adams* (New York: W. W. Norton, 1993).

John Ferling, *John Adams* (Knoxville: University of Tennessee Press, 1992).

———, *A Leap in the Dark: The Struggle to Create the American Republic* (New York: Oxford University Press, 2003).

———, *Setting the World Ablaze: Washington, Adams, Jefferson, and the American Revolution* (New York: Oxford University Press, 2000).

Samuel Fleischacker, "The Impact on America: Scottish Philosophy and the American Founding," in Alexander Broadie, ed., *The Cambridge Companion to the Scottish Enlightenment* (Cambridge: Cambridge University Press, 2003), pp. 316–37.

Eric Foner, *Tom Paine and Revolutionary America* (New York: Oxford University Press, 1976).

———, "Tom Paine's Republic: Radical Ideology and Social Change," in Young, *The American Revolution*, pp. 187–232.

Philip S. Foner, *Labor and the American Revolution* (Westport, CT: Greenwood Press, 1976).

Scott D. Gerber, ed., *The Declaration of Independence: Origins and Impact* (Washington, D.C.: CQ Press, 2002).

James Gilreath, ed., *Thomas Jefferson and the Education of a Citizen* (Washington, D.C.: Library of Congress, 1999).

Eliga H. Gould and Peter S. Onuf, eds., *Empire and Nation: The American Revolution in the Atlantic World* (Baltimore: Johns Hopkins University Press, 2005), esp. part 1.

James Grant, *John Adams: Party of One* (New York: Farrar, Straus and Giroux, 2005).

Jack P. Greene, ed., *The American Revolution: Its Character and Limits* (New York: New York University Press, 1987).

Jack P. Greene and J. R. Pole, eds., *The Blackwell Encyclopedia of the American Revolution* (Cambridge, MA: Blackwell, 1991).

Ronald Hamowy, "Jefferson and the Scottish Enlightenment: A Critique of Garry Wills's *Inventing America*," *William and Mary Quarterly*, 3rd ser., vol. 36, no. 4 (October 1979), pp. 503–23.

Dirk Hoerder, "Boston Leaders and Boston Crowds, 1765–1776," in Young, *The American Revolution*, pp. 233–71.

Andrew Hook, *Scotland and America: A Study of Cultural Relations, 1750–1835* (Glasgow: Blackie, 1975).

Thomas Hutchinson, *The History of the Colony and Province of Massachusetts-Bay*, Lawrence Shaw Mayo, ed., 3 vols. (Cambridge, MA: Harvard University Press, 1936).

Walter Isaacson, *Benjamin Franklin: An American Life* (New York: Simon & Schuster, 2003).

Harvey J. Kaye, *Thomas Paine and the Promise of America* (New York: Hill and Wang, 2005).

John Keane, *Tom Paine: A Political Life* (Boston: Little, Brown, 1995), ch. 11.

Adrienne Koch, ed., *The American Enlightenment: The Shaping of the American Experiment and a Free Society* (New York: George Braziller, 1965).

Marc W. Kruman, *Between Authority & Liberty: State Constitution Making in Revolutionary America* (Chapel Hill: University of North Carolina Press, 1997).

Benjamin W. Labaree, *Colonial Massachusetts* (Millwood, NY: KTO Press, 1979).

J. A. Leo Lemay, ed., *Reappraising Benjamin Franklin* (Newark: University of Delaware Press, 1993).

Scott Liell, *46 Pages: Thomas Paine,* Common Sense, *and the Turning Point to American Independence* (Philadelphia: Running Press, 2003).

Kenneth A. Lockridge, *Literacy in Colonial New England: An Enquiry into the Social Context of Literacy in the Early Modern West* (New York: W. W. Norton, 1974).

David Lundberg and Henry F. May, "The Enlightened Reader in America," *American Quarterly,* vol. 28, no. 2 (Summer 1976), pp. 262–93.

Donald S. Lutz, "The Relative Influence of European Writers on Late Eighteenth-Century American Political Thought," *American Political Science Review,* vol. 78, no. 1 (March 1984), pp. 189–97.

Pauline Maier, *American Scripture: Making the Declaration of Independence* (New York: Alfred A. Knopf, 1997).

———, "Boston and New York in the Eighteenth Century," *Proceedings of the American Antiquarian Society,* vol. 91 (October 1981), pp. 177–95.

———, *From Resistance to Revolution: Colonial Radicals and the Development of American Opposition to Britain, 1765–1776* (New York: Alfred A. Knopf, 1972).

Jackson Turner Main, *The Sovereign States, 1775–1783* (New York: New Viewpoints, 1973).

Dumas Malone, *Jefferson the Virginian,* vol. 1 of *Jefferson and His Time* (Boston: Little, Brown, 1948).

Richard K. Matthews, *The Radical Politics of Thomas Jefferson* (Lawrence: University Press of Kansas, 1986).

Henry F. May, *The Enlightenment in America* (New York: Oxford University Press, 1976).

Forrest McDonald, *E Pluribus Unum: The Formation of the American Republic, 1776–1790,* 2nd ed. (Indianapolis: Liberty Press, 1979).

Philip McFarland, *The Brave Bostonians: Hutchinson, Quincy, Franklin, and the Coming of the American Revolution* (Boulder, CO: Westview Press, 1998).

Donald H. Meyer, *The Democratic Enlightenment* (New York: G. P. Putnam's Sons, 1976).

———, "The Uniqueness of the American Enlightenment," *American Quarterly,* vol. 28, no. 2 (Summer 1976), pp. 165–86.

Robert Middlekauff, "Why Men Fought in the American Revolution," in David D. Hall et al., eds., *Saints and Revolutionaries* (New York: W. W. Norton, 1984), pp. 318–31.

Broadus Mitchell, *The Price of Independence* (New York: Oxford University Press, 1974).

Robert J. Morgan, "'Time Hath Found Us': The Jeffersonian Revolutionary Vision," *Journal of Politics*, vol. 38, no. 3 (August 1976), pp. 20–36.

Carla Mulford, ed., *The Cambridge Companion to Benjamin Franklin* (Cambridge: Cambridge University Press, 2008).

Gary B. Nash, "Social Change and the Growth of Prerevolutionary Urban Radicalism," in Young, *American Revolution*, pp. 3–36.

———, *The Urban Crucible: Social Change, Political Consciousness, and the Origins of the American Revolution* (Cambridge, MA: Harvard University Press, 1979).

Eric G. Nellis, "Misreading the Signs: Industrial Imitation, Poverty, and the Social Order in Colonial Boston," *New England Quarterly*, vol. 59, no. 4 (December 1986), pp. 486–507.

Craig Nelson, *Thomas Paine: Enlightenment, Revolution, and the Birth of Modern Nations* (New York: Viking, 2006).

H. G. Nicholas, "The American Revolution," in Noel O'Sullivan, ed., *Revolutionary Theory and Political Reality* (New York: St. Martin's Press, 1983), pp. 43–55.

David Fate Norton, "Francis Hutcheson in America," *Studies on Voltaire and the Eighteenth Century*, vol. 154 (1976), pp. 1547–68.

Gilman M. Ostrander, *Republic of Letters: The American Intellectual Community, 1776–1865* (Madison, WI: Madison House, 1999).

William Pencak, *War, Politics & Revolution in Provincial Massachusetts* (Boston: Northeastern University Press, 1981).

Merrill D. Peterson, "Thomas Jefferson and the Enlightenment: Reflections on Literary Influence," in William G. Shade, ed., *Revisioning the British Empire in the Eighteenth Century* (Bethlehem, PA: Lehigh University Press, 1998), pp. 102–42.

J. R. Pole, "Enlightenment and the Politics of American Nature," in Roy Porter and Mikuláš Teich, eds., *The Enlightenment in National Context* (Cambridge: Cambridge University Press, 1981), pp. 196–214.

———, *The Pursuit of Equality in American History*, rev. ed. (Berkeley: University of California Press, 1993), esp. ch. 2.

David M. Post, "Jeffersonian Revisions of Locke: Education, Property-Rights, and Liberty," *Journal of the History of Ideas*, vol. 47, no. 1 (January–March 1986), pp. 147–57.

Jack N. Rakove, *The Beginnings of National Politics: An Interpretive History of the Continental Congress* (New York: Alfred A. Knopf, 1979).

Ray Raphael, *The First American Revolution: Before Lexington and Concord* (New York: New Press, 2002).

———, *A People's History of the American Revolution* (New York: New Press, 2001).

Marjorie Drake Ross, *The Book of Boston: The Colonial Period, 1630–1775* (New York: Hastings House, 1960).

Charles Royster, *A Revolutionary People at War: The Continental Army and the American Character, 1775–1783* (Chapel Hill: University of North Carolina Press, 1979).

Richard A. Ryerson, ed., *John Adams and the Founding of the Republic* (Boston: Massachusetts Historical Society, 2001).

Horace E. Scudder, "Life in Boston in the Provincial Period," in Justin Winsor, ed., *The Memorial History of Boston, 1630–1880* (Boston: Ticknor, 1886), vol. 2, pp. 437–90.

———, "Life in Boston in the Revolutionary Period," in ibid., vol. 3, pp. 149–87.

Robert E. Shalhope, *The Roots of Democracy: American Thought and Culture, 1760–1800* (Boston: Twayne, 1990).

Richard B. Sher, *The Enlightenment & the Book: Scottish Authors & Their Publishers in Eighteenth-Century Britain, Ireland, & America* (Chicago: University of Chicago Press, 2006), ch. 8.

Richard B. Sher and Jeffrey R. Smitten, eds., *Scotland and America in the Age of the Enlightenment* (Princeton: Princeton University Press, 1990).

Page Smith, *John Adams* (Garden City, NY: Doubleday, 1962–63), vol. 1.

Paul Merrill Spurlin, *The French Enlightenment in America* (Athens: University of Georgia Press, 1984).

Darren Staloff, *Hamilton, Adams, Jefferson: The Politics of Enlightenment and the American Founding* (New York: Hill and Wang, 2005).

Peter D. G. Thomas, *Tea Party to Independence: The Third Phase of the American Revolution, 1773–1776* (Oxford: Clarendon Press, 1991).

Keith Thomson, *Jefferson's Shadow: The Story of His Science* (New Haven: Yale University Press, 2012).

Maurizio Valsania, *The Limits of Optimism: Thomas Jefferson's Dualistic Enlightenment* (Charlottesville: University of Virginia Press, 2011).

Carl Van Doren, *Benjamin Franklin* (New York: Viking Press, 1938).

Harry M. Ward, *The American Revolution: Nationhood Achieved, 1763–1788* (New York: St. Martin's Press, 1995).

———, *The War for Independence and the Transformation of American Society* (London: UCL Press, 1999).

Lee Ward, *The Politics of Liberty in England and Revolutionary America* (Cambridge: Cambridge University Press, 2004).

G. B. Warden, *Boston, 1689–1776* (Boston: Little, Brown, 1970).

Michael Warner, *The Letters of the Republic: Publication and the Public Sphere in Eighteenth-Century America* (Cambridge, MA: Harvard University Press, 1990).

William Warner, "Transmitting Liberty: The Boston Committee of Correspondence's Revolutionary Experiments in Enlightenment Mediation," in Clifford Siskin and William Warner, eds., *This Is Enlightenment* (Chicago: University of Chicago Press, 2010), pp. 102–119.

Robert H. Webking, *The American Revolution and the Politics of Liberty* (Baton Rouge: Louisiana State University Press, 1988).

Jerry Weinberger, *Benjamin Franklin Unmasked: On the Unity of His Moral, Religious, and Political Thought* (Lawrence: University Press of Kansas, 2005).

Walter Muir Whitehill and Lawrence W. Kennedy, *Boston: A Topographical History,* 3rd ed. (Cambridge, MA: Belknap Press, 2000), esp. ch. 2.

Sean Wilentz, "America's Lost Egalitarian Tradition," *Daedalus,* vol. 131, no. 1 (Winter 2002), pp. 66–80.

Garry Wills, *Inventing America: Jefferson's Declaration of Independence* (Garden City, NY: Doubleday, 1978).

Douglas L. Wilson, "Jefferson and the Republic of Letters," in Peter S. Onuf, ed., *Jeffersonian Legacies* (Charlottesville: University Press of Virginia, 1993), pp. 50–76.

Bernard Wishy, "John Locke and the Spirit of '76," *Political Science Quarterly,* vol. 73, no. 3 (September 1958), pp. 413–25.

Gordon S. Wood, *The Creation of the American Republic, 1776–1787* (Chapel Hill: University of North Carolina Press, 1969).

———, *The Idea of America: Reflections on the Birth of the United States* (New York: Penguin Press, 2011).

———, *The Radicalism of the American Revolution* (New York: Alfred A. Knopf, 1992).

———, *Revolutionary Characters: What Made the Founders Different* (New York: Penguin Press, 2006).

Esmond Wright, *Fabric of Freedom, 1763–1800,* rev. ed. (New York: Hill and Wang, 1978).

———, *Franklin of Philadelphia* (Cambridge, MA: Belknap Press, 1986).

Alfred F. Young, ed., *The American Revolution: Explorations in the History of American Radicalism* (DeKalb: Northern Illinois University Press, 1976).

Alfred F. Young and Gregory H. Nobles, eds., *Whose American Revolution Was It? Historians Interpret the Founding* (New York: New York University Press, 2011).

* * *

69 ["amazing ascendancy"]: entry of August 15, 1765, in Adams, *Diary and Autobiography,* L. H. Butterfield, ed. (Cambridge, MA: Belknap Press, 1961), vol. 1, p. 260.

70 [Male literacy in the colonies]: Lockridge, pp. 17–18, 76–77.

70 [Master printers in the colonies]: Warner, p. 32.

71 [May on time lag]: May, p. 41.

71 [Meyer on literati]: Meyer, "Uniqueness of the American Enlightenment," p. 175.

72 ["polemic Divinity"]: Franklin, *The Autobiography,* in Franklin, *Writings,* J. A. Leo Lemay, ed. (New York: Library of America, 1987), pp. 1307–1469, quoted at p. 1317.

72 ["All the little Money"]: ibid.

72 ["word for word"]: Schlesinger, *The Birth of the Nation: A Portrait of the American People on the Eve of Independence* (New York: Alfred A. Knopf, 1968), p. 158.

72 ["I now had Access"]: Franklin, *The Autobiography,* p. 1318.

72 ["*most useful*"]: Franklin, "Proposals Relating to the Education of Youth in Pensilvania" (1749), in Franklin, *Writings,* pp. 323–44, quoted at pp. 329, 337, 341.

73 ["first great fighter"]: Isaacson, p. 34.

73 ["Printers are educated"]: Franklin, "Apology for Printers," *Pennsylvania Gazette,* June 10, 1731, in Franklin, *Writings,* pp. 171–77, quoted at p. 172.

73 ["intercolonial Junto"]: Isaacson, p. 122.

74 ["Promoting Useful"]: Franklin, *Writings,* pp. 295–97.

74 ["America has sent"]: letter of May 10, 1762, in Franklin, *Papers,* Leonard W. Labaree, ed. (New Haven: Yale University Press, 1959–), vol. 10, pp. 80–82, quoted at pp. 81–82.

74 ["Dirty, dusty"]: entry of August 29, 1774, in Adams, *Diary and Autobiography,* vol. 2, p. 114.

74 ["his conversation"]: Rush, *Autobiography,* George W. Corner, ed. (Princeton: Princeton University Press, 1948), p. 110.

74 ["passed the Rubicon"]: letter to Abigail Adams, July 9, 1774, in *Adams Family Correspondence,* L. H. Butterfield, ed. (Cambridge, MA: Belknap Press, 1963–), vol. 1, pp. 134–35; Adams's words are from his account of parting from a loyalist friend given at p. 136 fn. 5; see also Carol Berkin, *Jonathan Sewall: Odyssey of an American Loyalist* (New York: Columbia University Press, 1974), pp. 104–5.

74 ["most genteel"]: entry of August 29, 1774, in Adams, *Diary and Autobiography,* vol. 2, p. 114.

75 ["torrent of virulent abuse"]: quoted in Isaacson, p. 277.

75 ["bull baiting"]: ibid.

75 [Franklin's lightning rod in Boston]: Cohen, pp. 212–15, Adams quoted at p. 215.

75 ["Society of females"]: Adams, *Autobiography,* in Adams, *Diary and Autobiography,* vol. 3, p. 260.

75 ["Admiration of Learning"]: ibid., vol. 3, p. 257.

76 ["ignorant, obscure"]: diary entry of April 23 [i.e., 24], 1756, in ibid., vol. 1, p. 22.

76 ["find my self"]: letter to John Wentworth, October–November 1758, in Adams, *Earliest Diary*, L. H. Butterfield, ed. (Cambridge, MA: Belknap Press, 1966), pp. 64–65, quoted at p. 65.

76 ["spread my Fame"]: diary entry, October–December 1758, in ibid., p. 77.

76 ["dreary Ramble"]: Adams, *Autobiography*, in Adams, *Diary and Autobiography*, vol. 3, p. 273.

76 ["Observation and Experiment"]: Adams, "Notes for an Oration at Braintree," Spring 1772, in ibid., vol. 2, pp. 56–61, quoted at p. 56.

76 ["State of Ignorance"]: ibid., vol. 2, quoted at pp. 56–57.

76 ["monopolized, or"]: Adams, "Fragmentary Notes for 'A Dissertation on the Canon and the Feudal Law,'" March–August 1765, in Adams, *Papers*, Robert J. Taylor, ed. (Cambridge, MA: Belknap Press, 1977–), vol. 1, pp. 106–7, quoted at p. 106.

76 ["whenever a general"]: Adams, "A Dissertation on the Canon and the Feudal Law," No. 1, August 12, 1765, in ibid., vol. 1, pp. 111–14, quoted at p. 111.

76 ["easy and cheap"]: Adams, "A Dissertation on the Canon and the Feudal Law," No. 3, September 30, 1765, in ibid., vol. 1, pp. 118–22, quoted at p. 121.

76 ["dare to read"]: Adams, "A Dissertation on the Canon and the Feudal Law," No. 4, October 21, 1765, in ibid., vol. 1, pp. 123–28, quoted at pp. 126, 127.

77 ["as Free men"]: quoted in Rakove, *Beginnings*, p. 32.

77 ["powerful corpus"]: ibid., p. 31.

77 ["life, liberty, & property"]: resolutions of Congress, October 14, 1774, in *Journals of the Continental Congress, 1774–1789*, Worthington Chauncey Ford, ed. (Washington, D.C.: U.S. Government Printing Office, 1904–37), vol. 1, pp. 63–73, quoted at pp. 67, 68, 73.

78 ["That he was a Virginian"]: Adams, *Autobiography*, in Adams, *Diary and Autobiography*, vol. 3, p. 336.

78 [Jefferson and "mutilation" of his draft]: see enclosure of "anecdotes of Dr. Franklin," with letter to Robert Walsh, December 4, 1818, in Jefferson, *Writings*, Paul Leicester Ford, ed. (New York: G. P. Putnam's Sons, 1892–99), vol. 10, p. 120 fn. 1.

79 ["what had been hackneyed"]: letter to Timothy Pickering, August 6, 1822, in Adams, *Works* (Boston: Little, Brown, 1850–56), vol. 2, pp. 512–14 fn. 1, quoted at p. 514.

79 ["complete philosophe"]: Commager, p. 19.

79 ["The young ascended"]: quoted in Malone, p. 184.

79 [Jefferson's book list]: letter to Skipwith, August 3, 1771, in Jefferson, *Papers*, Julian P. Boyd, ed. (Princeton: Princeton University Press, 1950–), vol. 1, pp. 76–81.

80 ["sacred deposit"]: Jefferson, "A Bill for the More General Diffusion of Knowledge" (1778), in ibid., vol. 2, pp. 526–27, quoted at p. 527.

80 ["in pursuit"]: letter to Thomas Cooper, February 10, 1814, in Jefferson, *Papers: Retirement*

Series, J. Jefferson Looney, ed. (Princeton: Princeton University Press, 2004–), vol. 7, pp. 190–91, quoted at p. 191.

80 ["canine appetite"]: letter to John Adams, May 17, 1818, in Jefferson, *Writings,* vol. 10, pp. 107–9, quoted at p. 108.

80 ["It is wonderful"]: letter to his daughter Martha Jefferson, May 5, 1787, in Jefferson, *Papers,* vol. 11, pp. 348–49, quoted at p. 349.

80 ["force and elegance"]: Rev. Jonathan Boucher, quoted in Randall, p. 22.

80 ["probably fixed"]: Jefferson, *Autobiography,* Paul Leicester Ford, ed. (1914; reprinted by University of Pennsylvania Press, 2005), pp. 5–6.

80 [Jefferson's divorce appeal]: Dewey, ch. 7.

81 [Advice to law students]: letter to Thomas Mann Randolph Jr., August 27, 1786, in Jefferson, *Papers,* vol. 10, pp. 305–9, quoted at p. 306; see also letter to John Minor, August 30, 1814, in Jefferson, *Papers: Retirement Series,* vol. 7, pp. 625–31.

81 ["Every science"]: letter to Randolph, August 27, 1786, p. 306.

81 ["any information"]: Jefferson, *Autobiography,* p. 94.

81 ["ideas of those"]: letter to John Adams, October 28, 1813, in Jefferson, *Papers: Retirement Series,* vol. 6, pp. 562–67, quoted at p. 566.

81 ["to illuminate"]: Jefferson, "Bill for the More General Diffusion of Knowledge," p. 526.

81 ["It is an axiom"]: letter of January 4, 1785 [i.e., 1786], in Jefferson, *Papers,* vol. 9, pp. 150–52, quoted at p. 151.

82 ["best geniuses"]: Jefferson, *Notes on the State of Virginia* (New York: Harper Torchbooks, 1964), pp. 140, 142.

82 ["not to find out"]: letter to Henry Lee, May 8, 1825, in Jefferson, *Writings,* vol. 10, pp. 342–43, quoted at p. 343.

83 ["Lives, Liberties"]: Locke, *Second Treatise,* in Locke, *Two Treatises of Government,* Peter Laslett, ed. (Cambridge: Cambridge University Press, 1988), p. 350 (ch. 9, §123).

83 ["State of War"]: ibid., p. 282 (ch. 3, §21).

84 [Bonwick on inequality]: Bonwick, p. 31.

85 ["Few opportunities"]: quoted in Ward, *War for Independence,* p. 20.

85 ["Government founded in Compact"]: letter to Samuel Wyman, May 16, 1776, in Paul H. Smith, ed., *Letters of Delegates to Congress, 1774–1789* (Washington, D.C.: Library of Congress, 1976–2000), vol. 4, pp. 16–17.

86 ["general want"]: quoted in Foner, *Tom Paine and Revolutionary America,* pp. 14, 12, respectively.

86 ["rescue man from tyranny"]: letter to John Inskeep, Mayor of the City of Philadelphia, February

1806, in Paine, *Complete Writings,* Philip S. Foner, ed. (New York: Citadel Press, 1945), vol. 2, pp. 1479–80, quoted at p. 1480.

86 ["so much boasted Constitution"]: Paine, *Common Sense,* in ibid., vol. 1, quoted at pp. 6, 13.

86 ["Crack Brain Zealot"]: Elias Boudinot, quoted in Kaye, p. 51.

86 [Audience for *Common Sense*]: see Foner, *Tom Paine and Revolutionary America,* p. 79.

86 ["government of our own"]: Paine, *Common Sense,* in Paine, *Complete Writings,* vol. 1, p. 29.

86 ["vital part"]: William G. McLoughlin, "The American Revolution as Religious Revival: 'The Millennium in One Country,'" *New England Quarterly,* vol. 40, no. 1 (March 1967), pp. 99–110, quoted at p. 102.

86 ["have it in our power"]: Paine, *Common Sense,* p. 45.

87 ["dead have neither powers"]: letter to James Madison, September 6, 1789, in Jefferson, *Papers,* vol. 15, pp. 392–97, quoted at p. 392.

87 ["misery to the bulk"]: letter to Madison, October 28, 1785, in ibid., vol. 8, pp. 681–83, quoted at p. 682.

87 ["human happiness proceeds"]: Lewis, "Happiness," in Greene and Pole, pp. 641–47, quoted at p. 642.

87 ["*greatest happiness*"]: Hutcheson, *An Inquiry into the Original of Our Ideas of Beauty and Virtue,* 4th rev. ed. (1738), excerpted in Hutcheson, *Philosophical Writings,* R. S. Downie, ed. (London: J. M. Dent, 1994), p. 90.

87 [Matthews on Jefferson]: Matthews, p. 28.

88 [Franchise in Pennsylvania]: Alexander Keyssar, *The Right to Vote: The Contested History of Democracy in the United States,* rev. ed. (New York: Basic Books, 2009), pp. 13–14.

88 ["gone all summer"]: quoted in Ward, *War for Independence,* p. 167.

89 [Women's suffrage in New Jersey]: see Keyssar, p. 54.

89 ["remember the Ladies"]: letter of March 31, 1776, in *Adams Family Correspondence,* vol. 1, pp. 369–71, quoted at p. 370.

4 . *France: Rule or Ruin?*

Thomas McStay Adams, *Bureaucrats and Beggars: French Social Policy in the Age of the Enlightenment* (New York: Oxford University Press, 1990).

Alfred Owen Aldridge, *Franklin and His French Contemporaries* (New York: New York University Press, 1957).

———, *Voltaire and the Century of Light* (Princeton: Princeton University Press, 1975).

David Andress, *The French Revolution and the People* (London: Hambledon, 2004).

———, *French Society in Revolution, 1789–1799* (Manchester: Manchester University Press, 1999).

Nigel Aston, *The French Revolution, 1789–1804: Authority, Liberty, and the Search for Stability* (Basingstoke: Palgrave, 2004).

Keith Michael Baker, *Condorcet: From Natural Philosophy to Social Mathematics* (Chicago: University of Chicago Press, 1975).

———, *Inventing the French Revolution* (Cambridge: Cambridge University Press, 1990).

Keith Michael Baker et al., eds., *The French Revolution and the Creation of Modern Political Culture*, 4 vols. (Oxford: Pergamon Press, 1987–94).

Archibald Ballantyne, *Voltaire's Visit to England, 1726–1729* (1893; reprinted by Slatkine Reprints, 1970).

David W. Bates, *Enlightenment Aberrations: Error and Revolution in France* (Ithaca, NY: Cornell University Press, 2002).

Carl L. Becker, *The Heavenly City of the Eighteenth-Century Philosophers* (New Haven: Yale University Press, 1932).

C. B. A. Behrens, *The Ancien Régime* (New York: Harcourt, Brace & World, 1967).

———, *Society, Government, and the Enlightenment: The Experiences of Eighteenth-Century France and Prussia* (New York: Harper & Row, 1985).

Philip Benedict, "French Cities from the Sixteenth Century to the Revolution," in Benedict, ed., *Cities and Social Change in Early Modern France* (London: Routledge, 1992), pp. 7–68.

Philipp Blom, *Enlightening the World: Encyclopédie, the Book that Changed the Course of History* (New York: Palgrave, 2005).

———, *A Wicked Company: The Forgotten Radicalism of the European Enlightenment* (New York: Basic Books, 2010).

Allan Bloom, "Jean-Jacques Rousseau," in Leo Strauss and Joseph Cropsey, eds., *History of Political Philosophy*, 3rd ed. (Chicago: University of Chicago Press, 1987), pp. 559–80.

Daniel Brewer, *The Enlightenment Past: Reconstructing Eighteenth-Century French Thought* (Cambridge: Cambridge University Press, 2008).

Peter R. Campbell, ed., *The Origins of the French Revolution* (New York: Palgrave, 2006).

David W. Carrithers et al., eds., *Montesquieu's Science of Politics: Essays on* The Spirit of Laws (Lanham, MD: Rowman & Littlefield, 2001).

Jack R. Censer and Jeremy D. Popkin, eds., *Press and Politics in Pre-Revolutionary France* (Berkeley: University of California Press, 1987).

Roger Chartier, *The Cultural Origins of the French Revolution*, Lydia G. Cochrane, trans. (Durham, NC: Duke University Press, 1991).

Guy Chaussinand-Nogaret, *The French Nobility in the Eighteenth Century: From Feudalism to Enlightenment*, William Doyle, trans. (Cambridge: Cambridge University Press, 1985).

Harvey Chisick, *The Limits of Reform in the Enlightenment: Attitudes Toward the Education of the Lower Classes in Eighteenth-Century France* (Princeton: Princeton University Press, 1981).

Maurice Cranston, *Jean-Jacques Rousseau*, 3 vols. (New York: W. W. Norton/University of Chicago Press, 1983–97).

Lester G. Crocker, *An Age of Crisis: Man and World in Eighteenth Century French Thought* (Baltimore: Johns Hopkins Press, 1959).

Robert Darnton, *The Literary Underground of the Old Regime* (Cambridge, MA: Harvard University Press, 1982).

Ian Davidson, *Voltaire in Exile: The Last Years, 1753–78* (New York: Grove Press, 2004).

Clorinda Donato and Robert M. Maniquis, eds., *The Encyclopédie and the Age of Revolution* (Boston: G. K. Hall, 1992).

William Doyle, *The Ancien Regime* (Basingstoke: Macmillan, 1986).

———, *Origins of the French Revolution*, 3rd ed. (New York: Oxford University Press, 1999).

———, *The Oxford History of the French Revolution* (Oxford: Clarendon Press, 1989).

Susan Dunn, *Sister Revolutions: French Lightning, American Light* (New York: Faber and Faber, 1999).

Durand Echeverria, *Mirage in the West: A History of the French Image of American Society to 1815* (Princeton: Princeton University Press, 1957).

Dan Edelstein, *The Terror of Natural Right: Republicanism, the Cult of Nature, and the French Revolution* (Chicago: University of Chicago Press, 2009).

Arlette Farge, *Fragile Lives: Violence, Power and Solidarity in Eighteenth-Century Paris*, Carol Shelton, trans. (Cambridge, MA: Harvard University Press, 1993).

———, *Subversive Words: Public Opinion in Eighteenth-Century France*, Rosemary Morris, trans. (University Park: Pennsylvania State University Press, 1995).

Arlette Farge and Jacques Revel, *The Vanishing Children of Paris: Rumor and Politics before the French Revolution*, Claudia Miéville, trans. (Cambridge, MA: Harvard University Press, 1991).

Bernard Faÿ, *The Revolutionary Spirit in France and America*, Ramon Guthrie, trans. (New York: Harcourt, Brace, 1927).

Graeme Fife, *The Terror: The Shadow of the Guillotine: France 1792–1794* (New York: St. Martin's Press, 2004).

Michael P. Fitzsimmons, *The Night the Old Regime Ended: August 4, 1789, and the French Revolution* (University Park: Pennsylvania State University Press, 2003).

———, *The Remaking of France: The National Assembly and the Constitution of 1791* (Cambridge: Cambridge University Press, 1994).

Alan Forrest, *Paris, the Provinces, and the French Revolution* (London: Arnold, 2004).

François Furet, *Revolutionary France, 1770–1880,* Antonia Nevill, trans. (Oxford: Blackwell, 1992), part 1.

François Furet and Mona Ozouf, eds., *A Critical Dictionary of the French Revolution,* Arthur Goldhammer, trans. (Cambridge, MA: Belknap Press, 1989).

Graeme Garrard, *Rousseau's Counter-Enlightenment: A Republican Critique of the* Philosophes (Albany: State University of New York Press, 2003).

David Garrioch, *The Making of Revolutionary Paris* (Berkeley: University of California Press, 2002).

Peter Gay, *The Enlightenment: An Interpretation,* 2 vols. (New York: Alfred A. Knopf, 1966–69).

———, *The Party of Humanity: Essays in the French Enlightenment* (New York: Alfred A. Knopf, 1964).

David P. Geggus, "The Effects of the American Revolution on France and Its Empire," in Jack P. Greene and J. R. Pole, eds., *The Blackwell Encyclopedia of the American Revolution* (Cambridge, MA: Blackwell, 1991), pp. 518–27.

Jacques Godechot, *The Counter-Revolution: Doctrine and Action, 1789–1804,* Salvator Attanasio, trans. (New York: Howard Fertig, 1971).

Dominique Godineau, *The Women of Paris and Their French Revolution* (Berkeley: University of California Press, 1998).

Dena Goodman, *The Republic of Letters: A Cultural History of the French Enlightenment* (Ithaca, NY: Cornell University Press, 1994).

Daniel Gordon, *Citizens Without Sovereignty: Equality and Sociability in French Thought, 1670–1789* (Princeton: Princeton University Press, 1994).

Louis Gottschalk, *Lafayette and the Close of the American Revolution* (Chicago: University of Chicago Press, 1942).

———, *Lafayette Comes to America* (Chicago: University of Chicago Press, 1935).

———, *Lafayette Joins the American Army* (Chicago: University of Chicago Press, 1937).

———, "The Place of the American Revolution in the Causal Pattern of the French Revolution," in Peter Amann, ed., *The Eighteenth-Century Revolution: French or Western?* (Boston: D. C. Heath, 1963), pp. 56–65.

Louis Gottschalk and Margaret Maddox, *Lafayette in the French Revolution: Through the October Days* (Chicago: University of Chicago Press, 1969).

Pierre Goubert, *The Ancien Régime: French Society, 1600–1750,* Steve Cox, trans. (New York: Harper & Row, 1973).

Vivian R. Gruder, *The Notables and the Nation: The Political Schooling of the French, 1787–1788* (Cambridge, MA: Harvard University Press, 2007).

Norman Hampson, *Prelude to Terror: The Constituent Assembly and the Failure of Consensus, 1789–1791* (Oxford: Basil Blackwell, 1988).

Paul R. Hanson, *The Jacobin Republic Under Fire: The Federalist Revolt in the French Revolution* (University Park: Pennsylvania State University Press, 2003).

John Hardman, *French Politics, 1774–1789* (London: Longman, 1995).

———, *Louis XVI* (New Haven: Yale University Press, 1993).

Ursula Haskins Gonthier, *Montesquieu and England: Enlightened Exchanges, 1689–1755* (London: Pickering & Chatto, 2010).

Patrice Higonnet, *Goodness Beyond Virtue: Jacobins during the French Revolution* (Cambridge, MA: Harvard University Press, 1998).

———, *Sister Republics: The Origins of French and American Republicanism* (Cambridge, MA: Harvard University Press, 1988).

Alistair Horne, *Seven Ages of Paris* (New York: Alfred A. Knopf, 2002), chs. 7–9 passim.

Olwen H. Hufton, *The Poor of Eighteenth-Century France, 1750–1789* (Oxford: Clarendon Press, 1974).

Stanley J. Idzerda et al., eds., *Lafayette in the Age of the American Revolution: Selected Letters and Papers, 1776–1790*, 5 vols. (Ithaca, NY: Cornell University Press, 1977–).

P. M. Jones, *The Peasantry in the French Revolution* (Cambridge: Cambridge University Press, 1988).

Thomas E. Kaiser and Dale K. Van Kley, eds., *From Deficit to Deluge: The Origins of the French Revolution* (Palo Alto: Stanford University Press, 2011).

Jeffry Kaplow, *The Names of Kings: The Parisian Laboring Poor in the Eighteenth Century* (New York: Basic Books, 1972).

John Keane, *Tom Paine: A Political Life* (Boston: Little, Brown, 1995), part 3.

Emmet Kennedy, *A Cultural History of the French Revolution* (New Haven: Yale University Press, 1989).

Georges Lefebvre, *The Great Fear of 1789: Rural Panic in Revolutionary France,* Joan White, trans. (New York: Pantheon, 1973).

Evelyne Lever, *Marie Antoinette: The Last Queen of France,* Catherine Temerson, trans. (New York: Farrar, Straus and Giroux, 2000).

James Livesey, *Making Democracy in the French Revolution* (Cambridge, MA: Harvard University Press, 2001).

Colin Lucas, ed., *Rewriting the French Revolution* (Oxford: Clarendon Press, 1991).

Philip Mansel, *The Court of France, 1789–1830* (Cambridge: Cambridge University Press, 1988), chs. 1–2.

Frank E. Manuel, *The Prophets of Paris* (Cambridge, MA: Harvard University Press, 1962), ch. 2.

Jonathan Marks, *Perfection and Disharmony in the Thought of Jean-Jacques Rousseau* (Cambridge: Cambridge University Press, 2005).

Kingsley Martin, *The Rise of French Liberal Thought*, J. P. Mayer, ed. (New York: New York University Press, 1956).

Peter McPhee, *Living the French Revolution, 1789–99* (New York: Palgrave, 2006).

———, *Robespierre: A Revolutionary Life* (New Haven: Yale University Press, 2012).

James Van Horn Melton, *The Rise of the Public in Enlightenment Europe* (Cambridge: Cambridge University Press, 2001).

Louis-Sébastien Mercier, *Panorama of Paris*, Helen Simpson, trans., and Jeremy D. Popkin, ed. and trans. (University Park: Pennsylvania State University Press, 1999).

———, *The Waiting City: Paris, 1782–88*, Helen Simpson, ed. and trans. (London: George G. Harrap, 1933).

R. R. Palmer, *The Age of the Democratic Revolution: A Political History of Europe and America, 1760–1800*, 2 vols. (Princeton: Princeton University Press, 1959–64).

———, "The Declaration of Independence in France," *Studies on Voltaire and the Eighteenth Century*, vol. 154 (1976), pp. 1569–79.

———, *Twelve Who Ruled: The Year of the Terror in the French Revolution* (Princeton: Princeton University Press, 1969).

Harry C. Payne, "*Pauvreté, Misère*, and the Aims of Enlightened Economics," *Studies on Voltaire and the Eighteenth Century*, vol. 154 (1976), pp. 1581–92.

———, *The Philosophes and the People* (New Haven: Yale University Press, 1976).

Roger Pearson, *Voltaire Almighty: A Life in Pursuit of Freedom* (London: Bloomsbury, 2005).

Munro Price, *The Road from Versailles: Louis XVI, Marie Antoinette, and the Fall of the French Monarchy* (New York: St. Martin's Press, 2003).

Orest Ranum, *Paris in the Age of Absolutism* (New York: John Wiley & Sons, 1968).

Nicolas-Edme Restif de la Bretonne, *Les Nuits de Paris; or, The Nocturnal Spectator*, Linda Asher and Ellen Fertig, trans. (New York: Random House, 1964).

Patrick Riley, ed., *The Cambridge Companion to Rousseau* (Cambridge: Cambridge University Press, 2001).

Daniel Roche, *France in the Enlightenment*, Arthur Goldhammer, trans. (Cambridge, MA: Harvard University Press, 1998).

———, *The People of Paris*, Marie Evans and Gwynne Lewis, trans. (Berkeley: University of California Press, 1987).

George Rudé, *The Crowd in the French Revolution* (Oxford: Clarendon Press, 1959).

———, *Paris and London in the Eighteenth Century: Studies in Popular Protest* (New York: Viking, 1971).

Anne Sa'adah, *The Shaping of Liberal Politics in Revolutionary France* (Princeton: Princeton University Press, 1990).

Rémy G. Saisselin, *The Literary Enterprise in Eighteenth-Century France* (Detroit: Wayne State University Press, 1979).

Simon Schama, *Citizens* (New York: Alfred A. Knopf, 1989).

Florian Schui, *Early Debates about Industry: Voltaire and His Contemporaries* (Basingstoke: Palgrave, 2005).

Robert Shackleton, *Montesquieu* (New York: Oxford University Press, 1961).

J. B. Shank, *The Newton Wars and the Beginning of the French Enlightenment* (Chicago: University of Chicago Press, 2008).

Gilbert Shapiro and John Markoff, *Revolutionary Demands: A Content Analysis of the Cahiers de Doléances of 1789* (Palo Alto: Stanford University Press, 1998).

John Shovlin, *The Political Economy of Virtue: Luxury, Patriotism, and the Origins of the French Revolution* (Ithaca, NY: Cornell University Press, 2006).

Albert Soboul, *The Sans-Culottes: The Popular Movement and Revolutionary Government, 1793–1794,* Rémy Inglis Hall, trans. (Garden City, NY: Anchor Books, 1972).

Bailey Stone, *The Genesis of the French Revolution: A Global-Historical Interpretation* (Cambridge: Cambridge University Press, 1994).

Timothy Tackett, *Becoming a Revolutionary: The Deputies of the French National Assembly and the Emergence of a Revolutionary Culture (1789–1790)* (Princeton: Princeton University Press, 1996).

———, *When the King Took Flight* (Cambridge, MA: Harvard University Press, 2003).

Michel Vovelle, *The Fall of the French Monarchy, 1787–1792,* Susan Burke, trans. (Cambridge: Cambridge University Press, 1984).

Henry Vyverberg, *Human Nature, Cultural Diversity, and the French Enlightenment* (New York: Oxford University Press, 1989).

Ira O. Wade, *The Intellectual Development of Voltaire* (Princeton: Princeton University Press, 1969).

G. Charles Walton, *Policing Public Opinion in the French Revolution: The Culture of Calumny and the Problem of Free Speech* (New York: Oxford University Press, 2009).

R. J. White, *The Anti-Philosophers: A Study of the Philosophes in Eighteenth-Century France* (New York: Macmillan, 1970).

David Williams, *Condorcet and Modernity* (Cambridge: Cambridge University Press, 2004).

Johannes Willms, *Paris, Capital of Europe: From the Revolution to the Belle Epoque*, Eveline L. Kanes, trans. (New York: Holmes & Meier, 1997), pp. 37–87.

Arthur M. Wilson, *Diderot* (New York: Oxford University Press, 1972).

Robert Wokler and Bryan Garsten, *Rousseau, the Age of Enlightenment, and Their Legacies* (Princeton: Princeton University Press, 2012).

Robert Zaretsky and John T. Scott, *The Philosophers' Quarrel: Rousseau, Hume, and the Limits of Human Understanding* (New Haven: Yale University Press, 2009).

* * *

90 ["I am writing you"]: letter of May 30–June 15, 1777, in Idzerda et al., vol. 1, pp. 56–60, quoted at pp. 56, 58–59.

91 ["personal dignity"]: Ségur, *Memoirs and Recollections* (1825–27; reprinted by Arno Press, 1970), vol. 1, p. 349.

91 ["ameliorate the lot"]: quoted in Echeverria, pp. 153, 154.

91 ["Mobbed"]: Schama, p. 43.

92 ["no Satisfaction"]: entry of April 29, 1778, in Adams, *Diary and Autobiography*, L. H. Butterfield, ed. (Cambridge, MA: Belknap Press, 1961), vol. 4, pp. 80–81; see also Aldridge, *Voltaire*, pp. 399–401.

92 ["one of the most beautiful"]: quoted in Kaplow, p. 3.

92 [Rousseau on Paris]: Rousseau, *The Confessions*, Christopher Kelly, trans., in Rousseau, *Collected Writings*, Kelly et al., eds. (Hanover, NH: University Press of New England, 1990–), vol. 5, p. 133 (bk. 4).

93 [Mercier on Parisian classes]: Mercier, "The Eight Social Classes," in Mercier, *Panorama*, pp. 215–17.

93 ["elongated cage"]: Mercier, "Carrabas; and Pots-de-Chambre," in Mercier, *Waiting City*, pp. 235–38, quoted at p. 235.

94 ["No other court"]: Mansel, p. 6.

94 ["impoverished man"]: quoted in Willms, p. 27.

95 ["stoppage of the bowels"]: Joseph-Marie Audin-Rouvière, quoted in Kaplow, pp. 86–87.

96 ["This evening's ball"]: quoted in Mansel, p. 5, whose comment is at ibid.

96 ["small bookshops"]: quoted in Roche, *France in the Enlightenment*, p. 662.

96 [Literacy in Paris]: ibid., p. 659.

96 [Elementary education in Paris]: Garrioch, pp. 135–36.

96 ["Gone are the days"]: quoted in Doyle, *Origins*, p. 77.

96 [*Le Libertin*]: Darnton, p. 129.

96 ["trade in books today"]: quoted in Doyle, *Origins,* p. 78.

96 ["would be behind"]: quoted in Wilson, p. 163.

96 [*Permissions de police*]: Darnton, p. 17.

98 ["one nation"]: Montesquieu, *The Spirit of the Laws,* Anne M. Cohler et al., eds. and trans. (Cambridge: Cambridge University Press, 1989), p. 156 (pt. 2, bk. 11, ch. 5).

98 ["tranquility of spirit"]: ibid., p. 157 (pt. 2, bk. 11, ch. 6).

98 ["Latin and nonsense"]: quoted in Aldridge, *Voltaire,* p. 10.

99 ["candid liberalism"]: Gay, *Enlightenment,* vol. 2, p. 526.

99 ["representatives of all nations"]: Voltaire, "The Presbyterians" (Philosophical Letter VI), in Voltaire, *Works,* William F. Fleming, trans. (Paris: E. R. DuMont, 1901), vol. 39, pp. 216–19, quoted at p. 218; see also Margaret C. Jacob, *Strangers Nowhere in the World: The Rise of Cosmopolitanism in Early Modern Europe* (Philadelphia: University of Pennsylvania Press, 2006), ch. 3.

99 ["most numerous"]: Voltaire, "The English Constitution" (Philosophical Letter IX), in ibid., vol. 39, pp. 9–16, quoted at p. 12.

99 [Voltaire on slavery]: see Gay, *Enlightenment,* vol. 2, pp. 413–15.

100 ["In the human understanding"]: quoted in ibid., vol. 2, pp. 25–26.

100 ["contrary to Religion"]: quoted in Wilson, p. 103.

100 ["spirit of independence"]: quoted in White, p. 106.

100 ["deliberate plan"]: quoted in Gay, *Enlightenment,* vol. 2, p. 76.

100 [*Encyclopédie* subscriptions]: Wilson, p. 168.

100 ["Our Encyclopedia"]: Diderot, quoted in White, p. 92.

100 ["man in all the truth"]: Rousseau, *Confessions,* p. 5.

101 ["Man is born free"]: Rousseau, *The Social Contract,* in Rousseau, *The Social Contract/Discourses* (London: J. M. Dent, 1913), p. 3 (bk. 1, ch. 1).

101 ["long debates"]; ibid., p. 87 (bk. 4, ch. 2).

101 ["sweet and precious"]: Rousseau, "Observations by Jean-Jacques Rousseau of Geneva on the Reply Made to His Discourse," in Rousseau, *Collected Writings,* vol. 2, quoted at p. 52.

102 ["Day labourers"]: quoted in Doyle, *History,* p. 14.

103 ["no self-respecting"]: ibid., p. 46.

105 ["until the constitution"]: "The Tennis Court Oath," June 20, 1789, in John Hall Stewart, ed., *A Documentary Survey of the French Revolution* (New York: Macmillan, 1951), p. 88.

107 ["abolishes the feudal regime"]: "The August 4th Decrees," August 4–11, 1789, in ibid., pp. 106–10, quoted at pp. 107, 108, 109.

107 ["will of the community"]: reprinted in Thomas Paine, *The Rights of Man,* in Paine, *Collected Writings,* Eric Foner, ed. (New York: Library of America, 1995), pp. 506–8, quoted at p. 507.

107 ["Citizens in common"]: Marcel Gauchet, "Rights of Man," in Furet and Ozouf, pp. 818–28, quoted at p. 825.

108 ["more like prisoners"]: quoted in Doyle, p. 123.

109 ["shall be burned"]: "Decree Abolishing Hereditary Nobility and Titles," June 19, 1790, in Stewart, pp. 142–43.

109 ["assemblage of so many"]: Tackett, *Becoming a Revolutionary,* p. 307. The title of this section is adapted from the title of Tackett's excellent study.

110 ["between candidates"]: ibid., p. 264.

112 ["He has gone"]: *L'Orateur du Peuple,* quoted in Schama, p. 555.

113 ["*patrie est en danger*"]: ibid., p. 610.

114 ["Laws are simply"]: quoted in McPhee, *Robespierre,* p. 72.

114 [1793 Constitution]: Doyle, *History,* p. 244.

114 [Danton on terror]: quoted in Dunn, p. 113.

114 ["A people does not judge"]: speeches at the trial of Louis XVI, December 3 and December 28, 1792, in Michael Walzer, ed., *Regicide and Revolution,* Marian Rothstein, trans. (New York: Columbia University Press, 1992), pp. 131–38 and 178–94, quoted at p. 133.

115 ["all their talk"]: Dunn, p. 135.

116 ["slow but lasting"]: quoted in Aldridge, *Franklin,* p. 225.

116 ["appreciate their true title"]: quoted in Baker, *Condorcet,* pp. 355, 350, respectively.

5. *Transforming American Politics*

Willi P. Adams, *The First American Constitutions: Republican Ideology and the Making of the State Constitutions in the Revolutionary Era,* Rita and Robert Kimber, trans. (Lanham, MD: Rowman & Littlefield, 2001).

Thornton Anderson, *Creating the Constitution: The Convention of 1787 and the First Congress* (University Park: Pennsylvania State University Press, 1993).

Joyce Appleby, *Capitalism and a New Social Order: The Republican Vision of the 1790s* (New York: New York University Press, 1984).

———, *Liberalism and Republicanism in the Historical Imagination* (Cambridge, MA: Harvard University Press, 1992).

Bernard Bailyn, *To Begin the World Anew: The Genius and Ambiguities of the American Founders* (New York: Alfred A. Knopf, 2003).

Lance Banning, "Jeffersonian Ideology Revisited: Liberal and Classical Ideas in the New American Republic," *William and Mary Quarterly*, 3rd series, vol. 43, no. 1 (January 1986), pp. 3–19.

———, *The Jeffersonian Persuasion: Evolution of a Party Ideology* (Ithaca, NY: Cornell University Press, 1978).

———, "The Problem of Power: Parties, Aristocracy, and Democracy in Revolutionary Thought," in Jack P. Greene, ed., *The American Revolution: Its Character and Limits* (New York: New York University Press, 1987), pp. 104–23.

———, *The Sacred Fire of Liberty: James Madison and the Founding of the Federal Republic* (Ithaca, NY: Cornell University Press, 1995).

Lance Banning, ed., *Liberty and Order: The First American Party Struggle* (Indianapolis: Liberty Fund, 2004).

Richard Beeman, *Plain, Honest Men: The Making of the American Constitution* (New York: Random House, 2009).

Richard Beeman et al., eds., *Beyond Confederation: Origins of the Constitution and American National Identity* (Chapel Hill: University of North Carolina Press, 1987).

Herman Belz et al., eds., *To Form a More Perfect Union: The Critical Ideas of the Constitution* (Charlottesville: University Press of Virginia, 1992).

Doron Ben-Atar and Barbara B. Oberg, eds., *Federalists Reconsidered* (Charlottesville: University Press of Virginia, 1998).

Ruth H. Bloch, *Visionary Republic: Millennial Themes in American Thought, 1756–1800* (Cambridge: Cambridge University Press, 1985), part 3.

Morton Borden, *Parties and Politics in the Early Republic, 1789–1815* (New York: Thomas Y. Crowell, 1967).

Kenneth R. Bowling and Donald R. Kennon, eds., *Neither Separate Nor Equal: Congress in the 1790s* (Athens: Ohio University Press, 2000).

Steven R. Boyd, ed., *The Whiskey Rebellion: Past and Present Perspectives* (Westport, CT: Greenwood Press, 1985).

Richard Buel Jr., *Securing the Revolution: Ideology in American Politics, 1789–1815* (Ithaca, NY: Cornell University Press, 1972).

James MacGregor Burns, *The Vineyard of Liberty* (New York: Alfred A. Knopf, 1982), part 1.

James MacGregor Burns and Stewart Burns, *A People's Charter: The Pursuit of Rights in America* (New York: Alfred A. Knopf, 1991), ch. 2.

James MacGregor Burns and Susan Dunn, *George Washington* (New York: Times Books/Henry Holt, 2004).

William Nisbet Chambers, *Political Parties in a New Nation: The American Experience, 1776–1809* (New York: Oxford University Press, 1963).

Ron Chernow, *Alexander Hamilton* (New York: Penguin, 2004).

James Conniff, "The Enlightenment and American Political Thought: A Study of the Origins of Madison's *Federalist Number 10*," *Political Theory*, vol. 8, no. 3 (August 1980), pp. 381–402.

Saul Cornell, *The Other Founders: Anti-Federalism and the Dissenting Tradition in America, 1788–1828* (Chapel Hill: University of North Carolina Press, 1999).

Noble E. Cunningham Jr., *The Jeffersonian Republicans: The Formation of Party Organization, 1789–1801* (Chapel Hill: University of North Carolina Press, 1957).

Matthew Q. Dawson, *Partisanship and the Birth of America's Second Party, 1796–1800: "Stop the Wheels of Government"* (Westport, CT: Greenwood Press, 2000).

Alexander DeConde, *Entangling Alliance: Politics & Diplomacy under George Washington* (Durham, NC: Duke University Press, 1958).

Horst Dippel, "The Changing Idea of Popular Sovereignty in Early American Constitutionalism: Breaking Away from European Patterns," *Journal of the Early Republic*, vol. 16, no. 1 (Spring 1996), pp. 21–45.

Keith L. Dougherty, *Collective Action under the Articles of Confederation* (Cambridge: Cambridge University Press, 2001).

Susan Dunn, *Jefferson's Second Revolution: The Election of 1800 and the Triumph of Republicanism* (Boston: Houghton Mifflin, 2004).

———, *Sister Revolutions: French Lightning, American Light* (New York: Faber and Faber, 1999).

Max M. Edling, *A Revolution in Favor of Government: Origins of the U. S. Constitution and the Making of the American State* (New York: Oxford University Press, 2003).

Stanley Elkins and Eric McKitrick, *The Age of Federalism* (New York: Oxford University Press, 1993).

John Ferling, *Adams vs. Jefferson: The Tumultuous Election of 1800* (New York: Oxford University Press, 2004).

Samuel Fleischacker, "The Impact on America: Scottish Philosophy and the American Founding," in Alexander Broadie, ed., *The Cambridge Companion to the Scottish Enlightenment* (Cambridge: Cambridge University Press, 2003), pp. 316–37.

Philip S. Foner, ed., *The Democratic-Republican Societies, 1790–1800* (Westport, CT: Greenwood Press, 1976).

Jack P. Greene and J. R. Pole, eds., *The Blackwell Encyclopedia of the American Revolution* (Cambridge, MA: Blackwell, 1991).

Morton Grodzins, "Political Parties and the Crisis of Succession in the United States: The Case of 1800," in Joseph LaPalombara and Myron Weiner, eds., *Political Parties and Political Development* (Princeton: Princeton University Press, 1966), pp. 303–27.

David C. Hendrickson, *Peace Pact: The Lost World of the American Founding* (Lawrence: University Press of Kansas, 2003).

Ronald Hoffman and Peter J. Albert, eds., *The Bill of Rights: Government Proscribed* (Charlottesville: University Press of Virginia, 1997).

James Horn et al., eds., *The Revolution of 1800: Democracy, Race, and the New Republic* (Charlottesville: University of Virginia Press, 2002).

John R. Howe Jr., "Republican Thought and the Political Violence of the 1790s," *American Quarterly*, vol. 19, no. 2 (Summer 1967), pp. 147–65.

Merrill Jensen, *The Articles of Confederation: An Interpretation of the Social-Constitutional History of the American Revolution, 1774–1781* (Madison: University of Wisconsin Press, 1940).

Calvin C. Jillson, *Constitution Making: Conflict and Consensus in the Federal Convention of 1787* (New York: Agathon Press, 1988).

Calvin H. Johnson, *Righteous Anger at the Wicked States: The Meaning of the Founders' Constitution* (Cambridge: Cambridge University Press, 2005).

Samuel Kernell, ed., *James Madison: The Theory and Practice of Republican Government* (Palo Alto: Stanford University Press, 2003).

Rogan Kersh, *Dreams of a More Perfect Union* (Ithaca, NY: Cornell University Press, 2001).

Larry D. Kramer, "Madison's Audience," *Harvard Law Review*, vol. 112, no. 3 (January 1999), pp. 611–79.

Lloyd S. Kramer, "The French Revolution and the Creation of American Political Culture," in Joseph Klaits and Michael H. Haltzel, eds., *The Global Ramifications of the French Revolution* (Washington, D.C.: Woodrow Wilson Center Press/Cambridge University Press, 1994), pp. 26–54.

Isaac Kramnick, *Republicanism and Bourgeois Radicalism: Political Ideology in Late Eighteenth-Century England and America* (Ithaca, NY: Cornell University Press, 1990).

Marc W. Kruman, *Between Authority & Liberty: State Constitution Making in Revolutionary America* (Chapel Hill: University of North Carolina Press, 1997).

Michael Lienesch, *New Order of the Ages: Time, the Constitution, and the Making of Modern American Political Thought* (Princeton: Princeton University Press, 1988).

———, "Thomas Jefferson and the American Democratic Experiment: The Origins of the Partisan Press, Popular Political Parties, and Public Opinion," in Peter S. Onuf, ed., *Jeffersonian Legacies* (Charlottesville: University Press of Virginia, 1993), pp. 316–39.

Eugene Perry Link, *Democratic-Republican Societies, 1790–1800* (1942; reprinted by Octagon Books, 1965).

Donald S. Lutz, *The Origins of American Constitutionalism* (Baton Rouge: Louisiana State University Press, 1988).

Jackson Turner Main, *The Antifederalists: Critics of the Constitution, 1781–1788* (Chapel Hill: University of North Carolina Press, 1961).

Drew R. McCoy, *The Elusive Republic: Political Economy in Jeffersonian America* (Chapel Hill: University of North Carolina Press, 1980).

Forrest McDonald, *Novus Ordo Seclorum: The Intellectual Origins of the Constitution* (Lawrence: University Press of Kansas, 1985).

———, *E Pluribus Unum: The Formation of the American Republic, 1776–1790*, 2nd ed. (Indianapolis: Liberty Press, 1979).

Gary L. McDowell and Johnathan O'Neill, eds., *America and Enlightenment Constitutionalism* (New York: Palgrave, 2006).

Robert J. Morgan, "Madison's Analysis of the Sources of Political Authority," *American Political Science Review*, vol. 75, no. 3 (September 1981), pp. 613–25.

Richard B. Morris, *The Forging of the Union, 1781–1789* (New York: Harper & Row, 1987), chs. 10–12.

Jeffry H. Morrison, *The Political Philosophy of George Washington* (Baltimore: Johns Hopkins University Press, 2009).

John M. Murrin, "Fundamental Values, the Founding Fathers, and the Constitution," in Belz et al., pp. 1–37.

Simon P. Newman, *Parades and the Politics of the Street: Festive Culture in the Early American Republic* (Philadelphia: University of Pennsylvania Press, 1997).

Roy F. Nichols, *The Invention of the American Political Parties* (New York: Macmillan, 1967).

David Fate Norton, "Francis Hutcheson in America," *Studies on Voltaire and the Eighteenth Century*, vol. 154 (1976), pp. 1547–68.

Jeffrey L. Pasley et al., eds., *Beyond the Founders* (Chapel Hill: University of North Carolina Press, 2004).

J. R. Pole, *The Pursuit of Equality in American History*, rev. ed. (Berkeley: University of California Press, 1993), esp. ch. 3.

Jack N. Rakove, *The Beginnings of National Politics: An Interpretive History of the Continental Congress* (New York: Alfred A. Knopf, 1979).

———, *Original Meanings: Politics and Ideas in the Making of the Constitution* (New York: Alfred A. Knopf, 1996).

James H. Read, *Power Versus Liberty: Madison, Hamilton, Wilson, and Jefferson* (Charlottesville: University Press of Virginia, 2000).

Norman K. Risjord, ed., *The Early American Party System* (New York: Harper & Row, 1969).

David B. Robertson, *The Constitution and America's Destiny* (Cambridge: Cambridge University Press, 2005).

Matthew Schoenbachler, "Republicanism in the Age of Democratic Revolution: The Democratic-Republican Societies of the 1790s," *Journal of the Early Republic,* vol. 18, no. 2 (Spring 1998), pp. 237–61.

Bernard Schwartz, *The Great Rights of Mankind: A History of the American Bill of Rights* (New York: Oxford University Press, 1977).

Robert E. Shalhope, *The Roots of Democracy: American Thought and Culture, 1760–1800* (Boston: Twayne, 1990).

James Roger Sharp, *American Politics in the Early Republic: The New Nation in Crisis* (New Haven: Yale University Press, 1993).

Garrett W. Sheldon, *The Political Philosophy of James Madison* (Baltimore: Johns Hopkins University Press, 2001).

David J. Siemers, *Ratifying the Republic: Antifederalists and Federalists in Constitutional Time* (Palo Alto: Stanford University Press, 2002).

Eric Slauter, *The State as a Work of Art: The Cultural Origins of the Constitution* (Chicago: University of Chicago Press, 2009).

Marshall Smelser, "The Jacobin Phrenzy: Federalism and the Menace of Liberty, Equality, and Fraternity," *Review of Politics,* vol. 13, no. 4 (October 1951), pp. 457–82.

———, "The Jacobin Phrenzy: The Menace of Monarchy, Plutocracy, and Anglophilia, 1789–1798," *Review of Politics,* vol. 21, no. 1 (January 1959), pp. 239–58.

James Morton Smith, *Freedom's Fetters: The Alien and Sedition Laws and American Civil Liberties* (Ithaca, NY: Cornell University Press, 1956).

James Morton Smith, ed., *The Republic of Letters: The Correspondence between Thomas Jefferson and James Madison, 1776–1826,* 3 vols. (New York: W. W. Norton, 1995).

Darren Staloff, *Hamilton, Adams, Jefferson: The Politics of Enlightenment and the American Founding* (New York: Hill and Wang, 2005).

Sarah Baumgartner Thurow, ed., *To Secure the Blessings of Liberty: First Principles of the Constitution* (Lanham, MD: University Press of America, 1988).

John R. Vile et al., eds., *James Madison: Philosopher, Founder, and Statesman* (Athens: Ohio University Press, 2008).

Bernard A. Weisberger, *America Afire: Jefferson, Adams, and the Revolutionary Election of 1800* (New York: William Morrow, 2000).

Gordon S. Wood, *The Creation of the American Republic, 1776–1787* (Chapel Hill: University of North Carolina Press, 1969).

———, *The Radicalism of the American Revolution* (New York: Alfred A. Knopf, 1992).

Melvin Yazawa, "Creating a Republican Citizenry," in Greene, *American Revolution,* pp. 282–308.

Alfred F. Young, *The Democratic Republicans of New York: The Origins, 1763–1797* (Chapel Hill: University of North Carolina Press, 1967).

John Zvesper, *Political Philosophy and Rhetoric: A Study of the Origins of American Party Politics* (Cambridge: Cambridge University Press, 1977).

* * *

120 [*"Self-Interest"*]: quoted in Wood, *Radicalism,* p. 246.

121 ["a little rebellion"]: letter of January 30, 1787, in Jefferson, *Papers,* Julian P. Boyd, ed. (Princeton: Princeton University Press, 1950–), vol. 11, pp. 92–97, quoted at p. 93.

121 ["latent causes"]: Madison, Federalist No. 10, in Jacob E. Cooke, ed., *The Federalist* (Middletown, CT: Wesleyan University Press, 1961), pp. 56–65, quoted at pp. 58–59, 64; see also David Hume, "Idea of a Perfect Commonwealth," in Hume, *Philosophical Works,* T. H. Green and T. H. Grose, eds. (1882–86; reprinted by Scientia Verlag Aalen, 1964), vol. 3, pp. 480–93; Elkins and McKitrick, pp. 86–87.

123 ["despising what he calls"]: Cornell, pp. 40–42, "An Officer of the Late Continental Army" quoted at p. 41.

124 ["I will now add"]: letter of December 20, 1787, in Smith, *Republic of Letters,* vol. 1, pp. 511–15, quoted at p. 512; for Madison's letter, dated October 24 and November 1, 1787, see ibid., vol. 1, pp. 495–507.

124 ["Half a loaf"]: letter of March 5, 1789, in ibid., vol. 1, pp. 586–89, quoted at pp. 587, 588; Madison's letter, dated October 17, 1788, in ibid., vol. 1, pp. 562–66.

125 ["parchment barriers"]: letter to Jefferson, October 17, 1788, in ibid., vol. 1, pp. 562–66, quoted at p. 564.

125 ["Constitution ought"]: letter to George Eve, January 2, 1789, in Madison, *Writings,* Jack N. Rakove, ed. (New York: Library of America, 1999), pp. 427–29, quoted at p. 428.

125 ["great rights"]: *Congressional Register,* June 8, 1789, in Helen E. Veit et al., eds., *Creating the Bill of Rights: The Documentary Record from the First Federal Congress* (Baltimore: Johns Hopkins University Press, 1991), quoted at p. 78.

126 [Madison on "property" at the Virginia convention]: see excerpts from debates at the Virginia convention, June 17, 1788, in Bernard Bailyn, ed., *The Debate on the Constitution* (New York: Library of America, 1993–), pt. 2, pp. 706–8.

127 ["hellish school"]: "Xantippe," in *Virginia Chronicle,* July 17, 1794, quoted in Link, p. 175.

128 ["Behold the Chief"]: Smith, *Freedom's Fetters,* pp. 270, 271.

128 [*"aggregate happiness"*]: Washington, *Maxims,* John F. Schroeder, ed., 3rd ed. (New York: D. Appleton, 1855), p. 17.

128 ["rioters and delinquent distillers"]: Washington, "Sixth Annual Address to Congress," November 19, 1794, in Washington, *Writings,* John C. Fitzpatrick, ed. (Washington, D.C.: U.S. Government Printing Office, 1931–44), vol. 34, pp. 28–37, quoted at p. 29.

128 [Pole on the Revolution]: Pole, "Equality," in Greene and Pole, pp. 616–19, esp. p. 619.

129 ["establishing a political equality"]: Madison, "Parties," *National Gazette,* January 23, 1792, in Madison, *Writings,* pp. 504–5, quoted at p. 504.

129 ["contemplative statesman"]: Madison, "A Candid State of Parties," *National Gazette,* September 26, 1792, in ibid., pp. 530–32, quoted at pp. 530, 531, 532.

129 ["Principles of the Revolution"]: Philadelphia *Aurora,* October 14, 1800, in Arthur M. Schlesinger Jr., *History of American Presidential Elections* (New York: Chelsea House, 1971), vol. 1, pp. 138–39, quoted at p. 138.

129 ["sincere and enlightened"]: "To the Citizens of Virginia," Richmond *Virginia Argus,* July 11, 1800, in ibid., vol. 1, pp. 144–46, quoted at p. 146.

130 ["critical and turbulent"]: "A Candid Address to the Freemen of the State of Rhode-Island," in ibid., vol. 1, pp. 140–43, quoted at p. 140.

130 [American population, 1790s]: U.S. Bureau of the Census, *Historical Statistics of the United States: From Colonial Times to 1970* (Washington, D.C.: U.S. Government Printing Office, 1975), pt. 1, pp. 8 (A-7) and 22 (A-72).

131 ["For Americans"]: Shalhope, "Republicanism," in Greene and Pole, pp. 654–60, quoted at p. 656.

131 ["people grow less steady"]: Adams, writing as "Novanglus," "To the Inhabitants of the Colony of Massachusetts Bay," February 6, 1775, in Adams, *Papers,* Robert J. Taylor, ed. (Cambridge, MA: Belknap Press, 1977–), vol. 2, pp. 243–55, quoted at p. 255.

132 [Kramnick on multiple "discourses"]: Kramnick, p. 261.

6. *Britain: The Rules of Rulership*

Stuart Andrews, *The British Periodical Press and the French Revolution, 1789–99* (Basingstoke: Palgrave, 2000).

Stanley Ayling, *George the Third* (London: Collins, 1972).

John Barrell, "London and the London Corresponding Societies," in James Chandler and Kevin Gilmartin, eds., *Romantic Metropolis: The Urban Scene of British Culture, 1780–1840* (Cambridge: Cambridge University Press, 2005), pp. 85–112.

David Bindman, *The Shadow of the Guillotine: Britain and the French Revolution* (London: British Museum Publications, 1989).

Jeremy Black, *George III: America's Last King* (New Haven: Yale University Press, 2006).

Edmund Burke, *Reflections on the Revolution in France* (London: J. M. Dent, 1971).

Marilyn Butler, ed., *Burke, Paine, Godwin, and the Revolution Controversy* (Cambridge: Cambridge University Press, 1984).

H. Butterfield, "Charles James Fox and the Whig Opposition in 1792," *Cambridge Historical Journal*, vol. 9, no. 3 (1949), pp. 293–330.

Francis P. Canavan, *The Political Reason of Edmund Burke* (Durham, NC: Duke University Press, 1960).

Ian R. Christie, *Stress and Stability in Late Eighteenth-Century Britain: Reflections on the British Avoidance of Revolution* (Oxford: Clarendon Press, 1984).

Gregory Claeys, *The French Revolution Debate in Britain: The Origins of Modern Politics* (Basingstoke: Palgrave, 2007).

Pamela Clemit, ed., *The Cambridge Companion to British Literature of the French Revolution in the 1790s* (Cambridge: Cambridge University Press, 2011).

Carl B. Cone, *Burke and the Nature of Politics: The Age of the French Revolution* (Lexington: University of Kentucky Press, 1964).

———, *Torchbearer of Freedom: The Influence of Richard Price on Eighteenth Century Thought* (Lexington: University of Kentucky Press, 1952).

Gerald R. Cragg, *Reason and Authority in the Eighteenth Century* (Cambridge: Cambridge University Press, 1964).

Michael T. Davis, ed., *Radicalism and Revolution in Britain, 1775–1848* (New York: St. Martin's Press, 2000).

John W. Derry, *Politics in the Age of Fox, Pitt, and Liverpool*, rev. ed. (Basingstoke: Palgrave, 2001).

H. T. Dickinson, "Popular Loyalism in Britain in the 1790s," in Eckhart Hellmuth, ed., *The Transformation of Political Culture: England and Germany in the Late Eighteenth Century* (New York: Oxford University Press, 1990), pp. 503–33.

H. T. Dickinson, ed., *Britain and the French Revolution, 1789–1815* (New York: St. Martin's Press, 1989).

John Dinwiddy, "Conceptions of Revolution in the English Radicalism of the 1790s," in Hellmuth, pp. 535–60.

Diana Donald, *The Age of Caricature: Satirical Prints in the Reign of George III* (New Haven: Yale University Press, 1996).

Robert R. Dozier, *For King, Constitution, and Country: The English Loyalists and the French Revolution* (Lexington: University Press of Kentucky, 1983).

David Dwan and Christopher J. Insole, eds., *The Cambridge Companion to Edmund Burke* (Cambridge: Cambridge University Press, 2012).

John Ehrman, *The Younger Pitt*, 3 vols. (Palo Alto: Stanford University Press, 1983–96).

Clive Emsley, *British Society and the French Wars, 1793–1815* (Lanham, MD: Rowman and Littlefield, 1979), chs. 1–4.

———, "The Impact of the French Revolution on British Politics and Society," in Ceri Crossley and Ian Small, eds., *The French Revolution and British Culture* (New York: Oxford University Press, 1989), pp. 31–62.

————, "Repression, 'Terror' and the Rule of Law in England during the Decade of the French Revolution," *English Historical Review*, vol. 100, no. 4 (October 1985), pp. 801–25.

Chris Evans, *Debating the Revolution: Britain in the 1790s* (London: I. B. Tauris, 2006).

Eric J. Evans, *William Pitt the Younger* (London: Routledge, 1999).

Archibald S. Foord, *His Majesty's Opposition, 1714–1830* (Oxford: Clarendon Press, 1964), chs. 7–8.

Iain Gilmour, *Riot, Risings, and Revolution: Governance and Violence in Eighteenth-Century England* (London: Pimlico, 1993), chs. 16–19.

Albert Goodwin, *The Friends of Liberty: The English Democratic Movement in the Age of the French Revolution* (Cambridge, MA: Harvard University Press, 1979).

Eliga H. Gould, *The Persistence of Empire: British Political Culture in the Age of the American Revolution* (Chapel Hill: University of North Carolina Press, 2000).

J. A. W. Gunn, *Factions No More: Attitudes to Party in Government and Opposition in Eighteenth-Century England* (London: Frank Cass, 1972).

Iain Hampsher-Monk, "John Thelwall and the Eighteenth-Century Radical Response to Political Economy," *Historical Journal*, vol. 34, no. 1 (March 1991), pp. 1–20.

Norman Hampson, *The Perfidy of Albion: French Perceptions of England during the French Revolution* (New York: St. Martin's Press, 1998).

Ray Hemmings, *Liberty or Death: The Story of Thomas Hardy, Shoemaker, and John Cartwright, Landowner, in the Early Struggles for Parliamentary Democracy* (London: Lawrence and Wishart, 2000).

Don Herzog, *Poisoning the Minds of the Lower Orders* (Princeton: Princeton University Press, 1998).

Christopher Hibbert, *George III* (New York: Basic Books, 1998).

B. W. Hill, *British Parliamentary Parties, 1742–1832* (London: George Allen & Unwin, 1985).

Christopher Hitchens, *Thomas Paine's* Rights of Man (Vancouver: Douglas & McIntyre, 2006).

J. Ann Hone, "Radicalism in London, 1796–1802: Convergences and Continuities," in John Stevenson, ed., *London in the Age of Reform* (Oxford: Basil Blackwell, 1977), pp. 79–95.

Derek Jarrett, *Pitt the Younger* (London: Weidenfeld and Nicolson, 1974).

Isaac Kramnick, *The Rage of Edmund Burke: Portrait of an Ambivalent Conservative* (New York: Basic Books, 1977).

L. G. Mitchell, *Charles James Fox* (New York: Oxford University Press, 1992).

————, *Charles James Fox and the Disintegration of the Whig Party, 1782–1794* (New York: Oxford University Press, 1971).

Jennifer Mori, "Languages of Loyalism: Patriotism, Nationhood, and the State in the 1790s," *English Historical Review*, vol. 118, no. 475 (2003), pp. 33–58.

———, *William Pitt and the French Revolution, 1785–1795* (New York: St. Martin's Press, 1997).

Marilyn Morris, *The British Monarchy and the French Revolution* (New Haven: Yale University Press, 1998).

Craig Nelson, *Thomas Paine: Enlightenment, Revolution, and the Birth of Modern Nations* (New York: Viking, 2006).

Frank O'Gorman, *The Whig Party and the French Revolution* (London: Macmillan, 1967).

Daniel I. O'Neill, *The Burke-Wollstonecraft Debate: Savagery, Civilization, and Democracy* (University Park: Pennsylvania State University Press, 2007).

Thomas Paine, *Collected Writings,* Eric Foner, ed. (New York: Library of America, 1995).

Charles Parkin, *The Moral Basis of Burke's Political Thought* (Cambridge: Cambridge University Press, 1956).

Mark Philp, ed., *The French Revolution and British Popular Politics* (Cambridge: Cambridge University Press, 1991).

Nicholas Rogers, *Crowds, Culture, and Politics in Georgian Britain* (Oxford: Clarendon Press, 1998).

James J. Sack, *From Jacobite to Conservative: Reaction and Orthodoxy in Britain, c. 1760–1832* (Cambridge: Cambridge University Press, 1993).

Philip Schofield, "British Politicians and French Arms: The Ideological War of 1793–1795," *History,* vol. 77, no. 250 (June 1992), pp. 183–201.

———, "Conservative Political Thought in Britain in Response to the French Revolution," *Historical Journal,* vol. 29, no. 3 (1986), pp. 601–22.

Peter J. Stanlis, *Edmund Burke: The Enlightenment and the Revolution* (New Brunswick, NJ: Transaction, 1991).

Mary Thale, "London Debating Societies in the 1790s," *Historical Journal,* vol. 32, no. 1 (March 1989), pp. 57–86.

John Thelwall, *The Politics of English Jacobinism: Writings of John Thelwall,* Gregory Claeys, ed. (University Park: Pennsylvania State University Press, 1995).

Roger Wells, *Wretched Faces: Famine in Wartime England, 1793–1801* (Gloucester, UK: Alan Sutton, 1988).

* * *

134 ["one of the most indulged"]: Mitchell, *Fox* (1992), pp. 3, 8.

134 ["most fixed Resolution"]: quoted in ibid., p. 13.

134 ["appeared more radical"]: Derry, p. 21.

135 ["seemingly tireless"]: ibid., p. 20.

138 ["I say nothing"]: letter to Thomas Grenville, August 1789, quoted in Mitchell, *Fox* (1992), p. 110.

138 ["consent to the correction"]: Price, *A Discourse on the Love of our Country,* delivered November 4, 1789, quoted in Cone, *Torchbearer,* p. 183.

139 ["nothing but human labour"]: Thelwall, *The Natural and Constitutional Right of Britons* (1795), in Thelwall, p. 31.

139 ["*property of the country*"]: Thelwall, *Rights of Nature, Against the Usurpations of the Establishments* (1796), in Thelwall, pp. 496, 463, 482, 478, respectively.

139 ["monopoly of knowledge"]: ibid., pp. 487, 486, 400, respectively.

140 ["vile democrat"]: said of George Cannt by Samuel Wettall, quoted in Emsley, "Repression," p. 803.

140 ["wicked and seditious"]: quoted in Hitchens, p. 52.

140 [Emsley on habeas corpus suspension]: Emsley, "Repression," pp. 807–8.

141 ["Peace and Bread!"]: quoted in Ayling, p. 363.

141 ["directed against working men"]: Emsley, "Repression," p. 820.

141 ["conspiracy to overthrow"]: quoted in Claeys, "Introduction," in Thelwall, p. xxii.

142 ["irrational, unprincipled"]: Burke, "Speech on the Army Estimates," February 9, 1790, in Burke, *Writings and Speeches* (Boston: Little, Brown, 1901), vol. 3, pp. 213–30, quoted at p. 218.

142 ["principle of improvement"]: Burke, *Reflections,* p. 31.

142 ["even when I changed"]: ibid., p. 243.

142 ["true principles"]: ibid., p. 23.

143 ["fresh ruins"]: ibid., p. 37.

143 ["greatest of all"]: ibid., p. 241.

144 ["pretended rights"]: ibid., pp. 59, 56, respectively.

144 [Burke on friendship and Western civilization]: see Cone, *Burke,* p. 304.

144 ["politician without a party"]: ibid., p. 430.

144 [Burke-Paine relationship]: ibid., pp. 293–94, 302.

145 ["neither deviseable"]: Paine, *Rights of Man,* in Paine, *Collected Writings,* pp. 518, 464, 536, 513, respectively.

145 ["firmly lodged"]: Philp, "The Fragmented Ideology of Reform," in Philp, *French Revolution,* pp. 50–77, quoted at p. 59.

146 ["invasion of the constitution"]: quoted in Mitchell, *Fox* (1992), p. 133.

7. *Napoleonic Rulership*

Peter Amann, ed., *The Eighteenth-Century Revolution: French or Western?* (Boston: D. C. Heath, 1963).

Frederick B. Artz, *Reaction and Revolution, 1814–1832* (New York: Harper & Brothers, 1934).

Robert B. Asprey, *The Reign of Napoleon Bonaparte* (New York: Basic Books, 2001).

———, *The Rise of Napoleon Bonaparte* (New York: Basic Books, 2000).

David A. Bell, *The First Total War* (Boston: Houghton Mifflin, 2007).

Robert M. Berdahl, *The Politics of the Prussian Nobility: The Development of a Conservative Ideology, 1770–1848* (Princeton: Princeton University Press, 1988).

Louis Bergeron, *France Under Napoleon*, R. R. Palmer, trans. (Princeton: Princeton University Press, 1981).

G. de Bertier de Sauvigny, *Metternich and His Times,* Peter Ryde, trans. (London: Darton, Longman & Todd, 1962).

Geoffrey Best, *War and Society in Revolutionary Europe, 1770–1870* (New York: Oxford University Press, 1986), chs. 1–14.

T. C. W. Blanning, *The French Revolutionary Wars, 1787–1802* (London: Arnold, 1996).

Jerome Blum, *Lord and Peasant in Russia: From the Ninth to the Nineteenth Century* (Princeton: Princeton University Press, 1961).

Michael Broers, *Europe After Napoleon: Revolution, Reaction, and Romanticism, 1814–1848* (Manchester: Manchester University Press, 1996).

———, *Europe Under Napoleon, 1799–1815* (London: Arnold, 1996).

———, *The Napoleonic Empire in Italy, 1796–1814: Cultural Imperialism in a European Context?* (New York: Palgrave, 2005).

Howard G. Brown, *Ending the French Revolution: Violence, Justice, and Repression from the Terror to Napoleon* (Charlottesville: University of Virginia Press, 2006).

Geoffrey Bruun, *Europe and the French Imperium, 1799–1814* (New York: Harper & Bros., 1938).

Nina Burleigh, *Mirage: Napoleon's Scientists and the Unveiling of Egypt* (New York: Harper, 2007).

David G. Chandler, *The Campaigns of Napoleon* (New York: Macmillan, 1966).

Tim Chapman, *The Congress of Vienna: Origins, Processes, and Results* (London: Routledge, 1998).

Michael Confino, *Russia Before the "Radiant Future"* (New York: Berghahn Books, 2011).

Owen Connelly, *The Wars of the French Revolution and Napoleon, 1792–1815* (London: Routledge, 2006).

C. W. Crawley, ed., *War and Peace in an Age of Upheaval, 1793–1830,* vol. 9 of *The New Cambridge Modern History* (Cambridge: Cambridge University Press, 1965).

W. P. Cresson, *The Holy Alliance: The European Background of the Monroe Doctrine* (New York: Oxford University Press, 1922).

Gregor Dallas, *The Final Act: The Roads to Waterloo* (New York: Henry Holt, 1997).

Isabel de Madariaga, *Catherine the Great* (New Haven: Yale University Press, 1990).

———, *Politics and Culture in Eighteenth-Century Russia* (London: Longman, 1998).

Spencer M. Di Scala, *Italy: From Revolution to Republic,* 2nd ed. (Boulder, CO: Westview Press, 1998), part 1.

William Doyle, *The Oxford History of the French Revolution* (Oxford: Clarendon Press, 1989).

Philip Dwyer, *Napoleon: The Path to Power* (New Haven: Yale University Press, 2008).

Geoffrey Ellis, *The Napoleonic Empire,* 2nd ed. (Basingstoke: Palgrave Macmillan, 2003).

Clive Emsley, *British Society and the French Wars, 1793–1815* (Lanham, MD: Rowman and Littlefield, 1979).

Charles J. Esdaile, *Fighting Napoleon: Guerrillas, Bandits, and Adventurers in Spain, 1808–1814* (New Haven: Yale University Press, 2004).

Alan Forrest, *Napoleon's Men: The Soldiers of the Revolution and Empire* (London: Hambledon and London, 2002).

François Furet and Mona Ozouf, eds., *A Critical Dictionary of the French Revolution,* Arthur Goldhammer, trans. (Cambridge, MA: Belknap Press, 1989).

John G. Garrard, ed., *The Eighteenth Century in Russia* (Oxford: Clarendon Press, 1973).

Pieter Geyl, *Napoleon: For and Against,* Olive Renier, trans. (London: Jonathan Cape, 1949).

Robert Gildea, *Barricades and Borders: Europe, 1800–1914,* 2nd ed. (New York: Oxford University Press, 1996), chs. 2–3.

Charles Coulston Gillispie, *Science and Polity in France: The Revolutionary and Napoleonic Years* (Princeton: Princeton University Press, 2004), ch. 8.

Jacques Godechot, *France and the Atlantic Revolution of the Eighteenth Century, 1770–1799,* Herbert H. Rowen, trans. (New York: Free Press, 1965).

Alexander Grab, *Napoleon and the Transformation of Europe* (New York: Palgrave, 2003).

Harry Hearder, *Italy in the Age of the Risorgimento, 1790–1870* (London: Longman, 1983), ch. 6.

J. Christopher Herold, *The Age of Napoleon* (1963; reprinted by Houghton Mifflin, 1987).

Alistair Horne, *The Age of Napoleon* (New York: Modern Library, 2004).

Charles W. Ingrao, *The Habsburg Monarchy, 1618–1815* (Cambridge: Cambridge University Press, 1994), chs. 6–7.

André Jardin and André-Jean Tudesq, *Restoration and Reaction, 1815–1848,* Elborg Forster, trans. (Cambridge: Cambridge University Press, 1983), chs. 1–4.

Robert A. Kann, *The Problem of Restoration* (Berkeley: University of California Press, 1968), ch. 16.

Henry A. Kissinger, *A World Restored: Europe After Napoleon* (New York: Grosset & Dunlap, 1964).

David Laven and Lucy Riall, eds., *Napoleon's Legacy: Problems of Government in Restoration Europe* (Oxford: Berg, 2000).

John A. Lynn, *The Bayonets of the Republic: Motivation and Tactics in the Army of Revolutionary France, 1791–94* (Urbana: University of Illinois Press, 1984).

———, "International Rivalry and Warfare," in T. C. W. Blanning, ed., *The Eighteenth Century: Europe 1688–1815* (New York: Oxford University Press, 2000), pp. 178–217.

Martyn Lyons, *Napoleon Bonaparte and the Legacy of the French Revolution* (New York: St. Martin's Press, 1994).

Andy Martin, "Napoleon on Happiness," *Raritan,* vol. 19, no. 4 (Spring 2000), pp. 80–105.

Derek McKay and H. M. Scott, *The Rise of the Great Powers, 1648–1815* (London: Longman, 1983).

Frank McLynn, *Napoleon* (New York: Arcade, 2002).

John McManners, *Lectures on European History, 1789–1914: Men, Machines, and Freedom* (Oxford: Basil Blackwell, 1966), ch. 6.

Stanley Mellon, *The Political Uses of History: A Study of Historians in the French Restoration* (Palo Alto: Stanford University Press, 1958).

Thomas Nipperdey, *Germany from Napoleon to Bismarck, 1800–1866,* Daniel Nolan, trans. (Princeton: Princeton University Press, 1996).

Alan Palmer, *Alexander I: Tsar of War and Peace* (London: Weidenfeld and Nicolson, 1974).

———, *Metternich: Councillor of Europe* (London: Phoenix Giant, 1997), esp. chs. 8–10.

R. R. Palmer, *The Age of the Democratic Revolution: A Political History of Europe and America, 1760–1800,* 2 vols. (Princeton: Princeton University Press, 1959–64).

Marc Raeff, "The Enlightenment in Russia and Russian Thought in the Enlightenment," in Garrard, pp. 25–47.

Gunther E. Rothenberg, *The Art of Warfare in the Age of Napoleon* (Bloomington: Indiana University Press, 1978).

Michael Rowe, ed., *Collaboration and Resistance in Napoleonic Europe: State Formation in an Age of Upheaval, c. 1800–1815* (Basingstoke: Palgrave, 2003).

George Rudé, *Revolutionary Europe, 1783–1815,* 2nd ed. (Oxford: Blackwell, 2000).

David Saunders, *Russia in the Age of Reaction and Reform, 1801–1881* (London: Longman, 1992).

Simon Schama, *Patriots and Liberators: Revolution in the Netherlands, 1780–1813* (New York: Alfred A. Knopf, 1977).

H. G. Schenk, *The Aftermath of the Napoleonic Wars: The Concert of Europe—An Experiment* (New York: Oxford University Press, 1947).

Alan Schom, *Napoleon Bonaparte* (New York: HarperCollins, 1997).

Paul W. Schroeder, *The Transformation of European Politics, 1763–1848* (Oxford: Clarendon Press, 1994).

H. M. Scott, ed., *Enlightened Absolutism: Reform and Reformers in Later Eighteenth-Century Europe* (Ann Arbor: University of Michigan Press, 1990).

Stuart Semmel, *Napoleon and the British* (New Haven: Yale University Press, 2004).

James J. Sheehan, *German History, 1770–1866* (Oxford: Clarendon Press, 1989), part 2.

Brendan Simms, *The Impact of Napoleon: Prussian High Politics, Foreign Policy, and the Crisis of the Executive, 1797–1806* (Cambridge: Cambridge University Press, 1997).

Jonathan Sperber, *Revolutionary Europe, 1780–1850* (London: Longman, 2000).

D. M. G. Sutherland, *The French Revolution and Empire: The Quest for a Civic Order* (Oxford: Blackwell, 2003).

Jean Tulard, *Napoleon: The Myth of the Saviour*, Teresa Waugh, trans. (London: Methuen, 1985).

Arthur Wilson, "Diderot in Russia, 1773–1774," in Garrard, pp. 166–97.

Isser Woloch, *Napoleon and His Collaborators: The Making of a Dictatorship* (New York: W. W. Norton, 2001).

———, *The New Regime: Transformations of the French Civic Order, 1789–1820s* (New York: W. W. Norton, 1994).

E. L. Woodward, *Three Studies in European Conservatism: Metternich, Guizot, the Catholic Church in the Nineteenth Century* (London: Frank Cass, 1963).

Stuart Woolf, *Napoleon's Integration of Europe* (London: Routledge, 1991).

D. G. Wright, *Napoleon and Europe* (London: Longman, 1984).

Adam Zamoyski, *Moscow 1812: Napoleon's Fatal March* (New York: HarperCollins, 2004).

———, *Rites of Peace: The Fall of Napoleon and the Congress of Vienna* (New York: HarperCollins, 2007).

✦   ✦   ✦

149 ["seven and a half million"]: Forrest, "Army," in Furet and Ozouf, pp. 417–25, quoted at p. 423.

150 ["Soldiers!"]: proclamation of June 22, 1798, reprinted in Lyons, p. 25.

152 ["constitutional jury"]: quoted in Doyle, p. 377.

152 [Corruption in constitution plebiscite]: Woloch, *New Regime,* p. 109.

152 ["established on the principles"]: quoted in Doyle, p. 378.

153 ["Political liberty"]: quoted in Woolf, p. 97.

153 ["repressed with impunity"]: quoted in Herold, p. 94.

153 ["fraternity and assistance"]: quoted in Blanning, p. 92.

154 [Rudé on Napoleon's army]: Rudé, p. 193.

155 ["all the peoples"]: quoted in Bell, p. 243.

155 [Herold on Civil Code]: Herold, p. 149.

155 ["They should stick"]: quoted in ibid.

155 ["as if the citizens"]: Jean-Louis Halpérin, quoted in Ellis, p. 49.

156 [Napoleon on church]: quoted in Horne, p. 17.

157 ["Kings, and Persons"]: Hobbes, *Leviathan* (London: J. M. Dent & Sons, 1914), p. 65 (ch. 13).

158 ["benefits of reform"]: quoted in Asprey, *Reign of Napoleon,* p. 109.

159 ["in addition to"]: Herold, p. 341.

159 ["prayer-book"]: Paul Dukes, "Introduction," in Paul Dukes, ed., *Russia Under Catherine the Great* (Newtonville, MA: Oriental Research Partners, 1977–78), vol. 2, quoted at p. 12.

159 ["produced a revolution"]: Catherine II, *Memoirs,* Mark Cruse and Hilde Hoogenboom, trans. (New York: Modern Library, 2005), p. 138.

159 ["erased more than half"]: quoted in Dukes, "Introduction," p. 11.

159 ["soul of everything"]: quoted in Blum, p. 537.

159 ["best sort"]: quoted in Saunders, p. 6.

160 ["war as a personal contest"]: Herold, p. 341.

160 ["the one thing"]: Rudé, p. 213.

161 ["his contempt"]: ibid., p. 217.

161 ["Come and range yourselves"]: quoted in Herold, p. 406.

162 ["men born in the upper classes"]: ibid., p. 409.

162 ["Emperor of the rabble"]: quoted in McLynn, p. 629.

164 ["course, formerly adopted"]: quoted in Kissinger, p. 188.

164 ["whose dreams"]: Palmer, *Alexander*, p. 333.

164 ["loud sounding nothing"]: quoted in Chapman, p. 61.

165 ["proclamation of a new era"]: Kissinger, p. 189.

8. *Britain: Industrializing Enlightenment*

T. S. Ashton, *The Industrial Revolution, 1760–1830* (New York: Oxford University Press, 1948).

A. Aspinall, ed., *The Early English Trade Unions* (London: Batchworth Press, 1949).

John Belchem, "Henry Hunt and the Evolution of the Mass Platform," *English Historical Review,* vol. 93, no. 369 (October 1978), pp. 739–73.

———, *"Orator" Hunt: Henry Hunt and English Working-Class Radicalism* (Oxford: Clarendon Press, 1985).

———, *Popular Radicalism in Nineteenth-Century Britain* (New York: St. Martin's Press, 1996), esp. chs. 2–4.

Maxine Berg, *The Age of Manufactures, 1700–1820: Industry, Innovation, and Work in Britain,* 2nd ed. (London: Routledge, 1994).

Leonard Billet, "Justice, Liberty, and Economy," in Fred R. Glahe, ed., *Adam Smith and the Wealth of Nations* (Boulder: Colorado Associated University Press, 1978), pp. 83–109.

Kevin Binfield, ed., *Writings of the Luddites* (Baltimore: Johns Hopkins University Press, 2004).

Eric Dorn Brose, *Technology and Science in the Industrializing Nations, 1500–1914* (Atlantic Highlands, NJ: Humanities Press, 1998).

D. S. L. Cardwell, *Technology, Science and History* (London: Heinemann, 1972), chs. 3–4.

Gregory Claeys, *Machinery, Money, and the Millennium: From Moral Economy to Socialism, 1815–1860* (Princeton: Princeton University Press, 1987).

———, "The Origins of the Rights of Labor: Republicanism, Commerce, and the Construction of Modern Social Theory in Britain, 1796–1805," *Journal of Modern History,* vol. 66, no. 2 (June 1994), pp. 249–90.

William Clark et al., eds., *The Sciences in Enlightened Europe* (Chicago: University of Chicago Press, 1999).

A. W. Coats, "The Classical Economists, Industrialisation, and Poverty," in R. M. Hartwell et al., *The Long Debate on Poverty* (London: Institute of Economic Affairs, 1972), pp. 141–68.

I. Bernard Cohen, *Revolution in Science* (Cambridge, MA: Belknap Press, 1985), esp. part 4.

Arthur Cole, "An Approach to the Study of Entrepreneurship," in Frederic C. Lane and Jelle C. Riemersma, eds., *Enterprise and Secular Change* (Homewood, IL: Richard D. Irwin, 1953), pp. 181–95.

G. D. H. Cole, *Robert Owen* (Boston: Little, Brown, 1925).

——, *Socialist Thought: The Forerunners, 1789–1850* (New York: Macmillan, 1953).

G. D. H. Cole and Raymond Postgate, *The British People, 1746–1946* (New York: Alfred A. Knopf, 1947), esp. chs. 14–17.

François Crouzet, *The First Industrialists: The Problem of Origins* (Cambridge: Cambridge University Press, 1985).

Frank O. Darvall, *Popular Disturbances and Public Order in Regency England* (1934; reprinted by Augustus M. Kelley, 1969).

M. J. Daunton, *Progress and Poverty: An Economic and Social History of Britain, 1700–1850* (New York: Oxford University Press, 1995).

Phyllis Deane, *The First Industrial Revolution,* 2nd ed. (Cambridge: Cambridge University Press, 1979).

John W. Derry, *The Radical Tradition: Tom Paine to Lloyd George* (New York: St. Martin's Press, 1967), chs. 2–4.

——, *Reaction and Reform, 1793–1868: England in the Early Nineteenth Century* (London: Blandford Press, 1963).

H. W. Dickinson, *Matthew Boulton* (Cambridge: Cambridge University Press, 1937).

J. R. Dinwiddy, *From Luddism to the First Reform Bill: Reform in England, 1810–1832* (Oxford: Basil Blackwell, 1986).

——, *Radicalism and Reform in Britain, 1780–1850* (London: Hambledon Press, 1992), esp. ch. 5.

James Epstein, "'Bred as a Mechanic': Plebeian Intellectuals and Popular Politics in Early Nineteenth-Century England," in Leon Fink et al., eds., *Intellectuals and Public Life: Between Radicalism and Reform* (Ithaca, NY: Cornell University Press, 1996), pp. 53–73.

Eric J. Evans, *The Forging of the Modern State: Early Industrial Britain, 1783–1870,* 2nd ed. (London: Longman, 1996), ch. 18.

Frank W. Fetter, *The Economist in Parliament, 1780–1868* (Durham, NC: Duke University Press, 1980).

Athol Fitzgibbons, *Adam Smith's System of Liberty, Wealth, and Virtue: The Moral and Political Foundations of* The Wealth of Nations (Oxford: Clarendon Press, 1995).

Roderick Floud and Donald McCloskey, eds., *The Economic History of Britain since 1700,* 2nd ed. (Cambridge: Cambridge University Press, 1994), vol. 1.

Jan Golinski, *Science as Public Culture: Chemistry and Enlightenment in Britain, 1760–1820* (Cambridge: Cambridge University Press, 1992).

Elie Halévy, *The Growth of Philosophic Radicalism,* Mary Morris, trans. (London: Faber & Gwyer, 1928).

A. R. Hall, *The Scientific Revolution, 1500–1800: The Formation of the Modern Scientific Attitude* (London: Longmans, Green, 1954).

———, "What Did the Industrial Revolution in Britain Owe to Science?," in Neil McKendrick, ed., *Historical Perspectives: Studies in English Thought and Society* (London: Europa, 1974), pp. 129–51.

Robert G. Hall, "Tyranny, Work and Politics: The 1818 Strike Wave in the English Cotton District," *International Review of Social History*, vol. 34, no. 3 (December 1989), pp. 433–70.

Joseph Hamburger, *Intellectuals in Politics: John Stuart Mill and the Philosophic Radicals* (New Haven: Yale University Press, 1965), chs. 1–2.

J. L. Hammond and Barbara Hammond, *The Rise of Modern Industry*, 9th ed. (London: Methuen, 1966).

———, *The Skilled Labourer, 1760–1832*, 2nd ed. (London: Longmans, Green, 1920).

———, *The Town Labourer, 1760–1832: The New Civilisation*, 2nd ed. (London: Longmans, Green, 1925).

———, *The Village Labourer, 1760–1832: A Study in the Government of England before the Reform Bill* (London: Longmans, Green, 1912).

J. F. C. Harrison, *Quest for the New Moral World: Robert Owen and the Owenites in Britain and America* (New York: Charles Scribner's Sons, 1969).

Mark Harrison, *Crowds and History: Mass Phenomena in English Towns, 1790–1835* (Cambridge: Cambridge University Press, 1988).

H. L. A. Hart, "Bentham and the United States of America," *Journal of Law & Economics*, vol. 19, no. 3 (October 1976), pp. 547–67.

Ivor B. Hart, *James Watt and the History of Steam Power* (New York: Henry Schuman, 1949).

R. M. Hartwell, ed., *The Causes of the Industrial Revolution in England* (London: Methuen, 1967).

Francis Hearn, *Domination, Legitimation, and Resistance: The Incorporation of the Nineteenth-Century English Working Class* (Westport, CT: Greenwood Press, 1978).

John Henry, "National Styles in Science: A Possible Factor in the Scientific Revolution?," in David N. Livingstone and Charles W. J. Withers, eds., *Geography and Revolution* (Chicago: University of Chicago Press, 2005), pp. 43–74.

J. Ann Hone, *For the Cause of Truth: Radicalism in London, 1796–1821* (Oxford: Clarendon Press, 1982).

Katrina Honeyman, *Origins of Enterprise: Business Leadership in the Industrial Revolution* (Manchester: Manchester University Press, 1982).

Thomas A. Horne, *Property Rights and Poverty: Political Argument in Britain, 1605–1834* (Chapel Hill: University of North Carolina Press, 1990).

Margaret C. Jacob, *Scientific Culture and the Making of the Industrial West* (New York: Oxford University Press, 1997).

Steven King and Geoffrey Timmins, *Making Sense of the Industrial Revolution* (Manchester: Manchester University, Press, 2001).

Melvin Kranzberg and Carroll W. Pursell Jr., eds., *Technology in Western Civilization* (New York: Oxford University Press, 1967), vol. 1, esp. parts 2–3.

David S. Landes, *The Unbound Prometheus: Technological Change and Industrial Development in Western Europe from 1750 to the Present* (Cambridge: Cambridge University Press, 1969).

D. J. Manning, *The Mind of Jeremy Bentham* (New York: Barnes & Noble, 1968).

Paul Mantoux, *The Industrial Revolution in the Eighteenth Century: An Outline of the Beginnings of the Modern Factory System in England*, Marjorie Vernon, trans., rev. ed. (London: Jonathan Cape, 1928).

Stephen A. Marglin, "What Do Bosses Do? The Origins and Functions of Hierarchy in Capitalist Production," *Review of Radical Political Economics,* vol. 6, no. 2 (July 1974), pp. 60–112.

Ben Marsden, *Watt's Perfect Engine: Steam and the Age of Invention* (New York: Columbia University Press, 2002).

Dorothy Marshall, *Industrial England, 1776–1851* (London: Routledge & Kegan Paul, 1973).

Peter Mathias, *The Transformation of England* (New York: Columbia University Press, 1979).

Peter Mathias and M. M. Postan, eds., *The Industrial Economies: Capital, Labour and Enterprise,* vol. 7 of *The Cambridge Economic History of Europe* (Cambridge: Cambridge University Press, 1978), part 1.

Iain McCalman, *Radical Underworld: Prophets, Revolutionaries, and Pornographers in London, 1795–1840* (Cambridge: Cambridge University Press, 1988).

Robert K. Merton, *Science, Technology & Society in Seventeenth Century England* (New York: Howard Fertig, 1970).

Naomi Churgin Miller, "John Cartwright and Radical Parliamentary Reform, 1808–1819," *English Historical Review,* vol. 83, no. 329 (October 1968), pp. 705–28.

Joel Mokyr, *The Enlightened Economy: An Economic History of Britain, 1700–1850* (New Haven: Yale University Press, 2009).

——, *The Lever of Riches: Technological Creativity and Economic Progress* (New York: Oxford University Press, 1990).

A. E. Musson, ed., *Science, Technology, and Economic Growth in the Eighteenth Century* (London: Methuen, 1972).

A. E. Musson and Eric Robinson, *Science and Technology in the Industrial Revolution* (New York: Gordon and Breach, 1989).

Patrick K. O'Brien and Roland Quinault, eds., *The Industrial Revolution and British Society* (Cambridge: Cambridge University Press, 1993).

Arnold Pacey, *The Maze of Ingenuity: Ideas and Idealism in the Development of Technology* (New York: Holmes & Meier, 1975).

Bhikhu Parekh, ed., *Bentham's Political Thought* (New York: Barnes & Noble, 1973).

Harold Perkin, *The Origins of Modern English Society, 1780–1880* (London: Routledge & Kegan Paul, 1969).

E. Royston Pike, ed., *"Hard Times": Human Documents of the Industrial Revolution* (New York: Praeger, 1966).

John Plamenatz, *The English Utilitarians* (Oxford: Basil Blackwell, 1966).

Sidney Pollard, *The Genesis of Modern Management: A Study of the Industrial Revolution in Great Britain* (Cambridge, MA: Harvard University Press, 1965).

Roy Porter, *The Creation of the Modern World: The Untold Story of the British Enlightenment* (New York: W. W. Norton, 2000).

Adrian Randall, *Before the Luddites: Custom, Community, and Machinery in the English Woollen Industry, 1776–1809* (Cambridge: Cambridge University Press, 1991).

D. D. Raphael, *Adam Smith* (New York: Oxford University Press, 1985).

Robert Reid, *The Peterloo Massacre* (London: Heinemann, 1989).

Kirkpatrick Sale, *Rebels Against the Future: The Luddites and Their War on the Industrial Revolution* (Reading, MA: Addison-Wesley, 1995).

Philip Schofield, *Utility and Democracy: The Political Thought of Jeremy Bentham* (New York: Oxford University Press, 2006).

Robert E. Schofield, *The Lunar Society of Birmingham: A Social History of Provincial Science and Industry in Eighteenth-Century England* (Oxford: Clarendon Press, 1963).

Andrew S. Skinner and Thomas Wilson, eds., *Essays on Adam Smith* (Oxford: Clarendon Press, 1975).

Neil J. Smelser, *Social Change in the Industrial Revolution: An Application of Theory to the Lancashire Cotton Industry, 1770–1840* (London: Routledge & Kegan Paul, 1959).

William Stafford, *Socialism, Radicalism, and Nostalgia: Social Criticism in Britain, 1775–1830* (Cambridge: Cambridge University Press, 1987).

Marc W. Steinberg, *Fighting Words: Working-Class Formation, Collective Action, and Discourse in Early Nineteenth-Century England* (Ithaca, NY: Cornell University Press, 1999).

John Stevenson, ed., *London in the Age of Reform* (Oxford: Basil Blackwell, 1977).

David Sunderland, *Social Capital, Trust and the Industrial Revolution, 1780–1880* (London: Routledge, 2007).

Malcolm I. Thomis, *The Luddites: Machine-Breaking in Regency England* (Hamden, CT: Archon Books, 1970).

Malcolm I. Thomis and Peter Holt, *Threats of Revolution in Britain, 1789–1848* (London: Macmillan, 1977), ch. 6.

Allan Thompson, *The Dynamics of the Industrial Revolution* (New York: St. Martin's Press, 1973).

E. P. Thompson, *The Making of the English Working Class* (London: Victor Gollancz, 1963).

Noel W. Thompson, *The People's Science: The Popular Political Economy of Exploitation and Crisis, 1816–34* (Cambridge: Cambridge University Press, 1984).

Charles Tilly, *Popular Contention in Great Britain, 1758–1834* (Cambridge, MA: Harvard University Press, 1995).

Jenny Uglow, *The Lunar Men: Five Friends Whose Curiosity Changed the World* (New York: Farrar, Straus and Giroux, 2002).

J. T. Ward, ed., *The Factory System* (New York: Barnes & Noble, 1970), vol. 1.

R. J. White, *Waterloo to Peterloo* (New York: Macmillan, 1957).

Charles Wilson, "The Entrepreneur in the Industrial Revolution in Britain," *History*, vol. 42 (1957), pp. 101–17.

Donald Winch, *Malthus* (New York: Oxford University Press, 1987).

D. G. Wright, *Popular Radicalism: The Working-Class Experience, 1780–1880* (London: Longman, 1988), esp. chs. 3–4.

E. A. Wrigley, *Poverty, Progress, and Population* (Cambridge: Cambridge University Press, 2004).

* * *

166 ["Suppose two shutters"]: quoted in Jacob, p. 204.

167 ["dishonour unto learning"]: Bacon, *The Advancement of Learning*, in Bacon, *The Advancement of Learning and New Atlantis* (New York: Oxford University Press, 1956), pp. 84, 85.

167 [John Watt]: A fine reconstruction of Watt, upon which this account is based, is at Jacob, pp. 99–105, quoted at p. 101.

170 ["among the fictions"]: Dickens, *Hard Times* (New York: W. W. Norton, 2001), p. 91.

170 ["fertile genius"]: letter of February 22, 1766, quoted in Dickinson, p. 76.

170 ["vase-maker general"]: quoted in Porter, p. 432.

171 ["see English liberty"]: quoted in Mantoux, p. 393.

172 ["Wedgwood supplied"]: Musson and Robinson, p. 143.

172 ["Am I not a man"]: quoted in Porter, p. 359.

172 ["nervous strain"]: Hammond and Hammond, *Town Labourer*, p. 21.

172 ["it is in the power of"]: J. C. Hippisley, quoted in ibid., p. 27.

173 [Mortality rates]: see William Farr, *Vital Statistics* (1837), excerpted in George Davey Smith et al., eds., *Poverty, Inequality and Health in Britain, 1800–2000* (Bristol: Policy Press, 2001), pp. 34–44.

173 ["permanent deterioration"]: "Factory Commission Report" (1833), excerpted in ibid., pp. 24–31, quoted at p. 31.

173 [Hammonds on Industrial Revolution and England's past]: see Hammond and Hammond, *Town Labourer,* p. 3.

173 ["deliberately sought"]: ibid., p. 325.

173 ["when ordered"]: John Blackner, an historian of Nottingham, quoted in Thomis, p. 11.

173 ["for workinge of tape"]: ibid., p. 14.

176 ["no society"]: Smith, *An Inquiry into the Nature and Causes of the Wealth of Nations,* R. H. Campbell and A. S. Skinner, eds. (New York: Oxford University Press, 1976), vol. 1, p. 96.

176 [McCulloch on workers]: quoted in Coats, p. 154.

176 [Ricardo on machines' impact]: see ibid., p. 152.

176 ["scientific impartiality"]: Marx, *Capital: A Critique of Political Economy,* Samuel Moore and Edward Aveling, trans. (New York: Modern Library, 1936), p. 478 fn. 2.

176 [Bentham and "greatest happiness"]: see Robert Shackleton, "The Greatest Happiness of the Greatest Number: The History of Bentham's Phrase," *Studies on Voltaire and the Eighteenth Century,* vol. 90 (1972), pp. 1461–82.

177 ["two sovereign masters"]: Bentham, *An Introduction to the Principles of Morals and Legislation,* J. H. Burns and H. L. A. Hart, eds. (London: University of London/Athlone Press, 1970), p. 11 and p. 11 fn. a.

177 ["under three heads"]: letter to Jacques Pierre Brissot de Warville, mid-August 1789, in Bentham, *Correspondence,* Timothy L. S. Sprigge et al., eds. (London: Athlone Press, 1968–), vol. 4, pp. 84–85, quoted at p. 84.

177 ["to talk of what the law"]: Bentham, *Nonsense Upon Stilts, or Pandora's Box Opened, or The French Declaration of Rights Prefixed to the 1791 Constitution Laid Open and Exposed* (also known as *Anarchical Follies*), in Bentham, *Rights, Representation, and Reform,* Philip Schofield et al., eds. (New York: Oxford University Press, 2002), pp. 319–75, quoted at p. 328.

177 ["lords of their own property"]: quoted in Horne, p. 147.

177 ["nonsense upon stilts"]: Bentham, *Nonsense Upon Stilts,* p. 330.

177 ["his utilitarianism took away"]: Horne, p. 160.

178 ["pauper management improvement"]: Bentham, "Outline of a Work Entitled Pauper Management Improved; Particularly by Means of an Application of the Panopticon Principle of Construction," *Young's Annals of Agriculture,* vol. 29, no. 167 (1797). This was reprinted as a pamphlet in 1812.

178 ["altogether premature"]: Bentham, *Plan of Parliamentary Reform* (London: R. Hunter, 1817), p. xcv.

178 ["freely chosen"]: ibid., pp. xxxix, xxxvii, respectively.

179 ["Old, Immoral World"]: quoted in Cole, *Socialist Thought,* p. 96.

180 ["habits of the individual system"]: quoted in Cole, *Owen,* p. 186.

180 [Warren on New Harmony]: quoted in Martin, p. 10.

180 ["perfect Liberty"]: quoted in Marshall, p. 145.

181 ["small manufacturers"]: Miller, p. 722.

181 ["Why not go forth"]: John Gast, quoted in Belchem, "Henry Hunt," p. 751.

181 ["cutting most indiscriminately"]: quoted in Reid, pp. 136, 138.

181 [Thompson on Peterloo]: Thompson, *Making,* pp. 687, 689.

182 ["Reform, Reform"]: Hone, *The Man in the Moon* (1820), reprinted in Edgell Rickword, ed., *Radical Squibs & Loyal Ripostes* (Bath: Adams & Dart, 1971), pp. 83–98, quoted at p. 90.

182 ["contempt and hatred"]: quoted in Samuel Bamford, *Passages in the Life of a Radical* (1839–41), in Bamford, *Autobiography,* W. H. Chaloner, ed. (London: Frank Cass, 1967), vol. 2, p. 93. Bamford was a codefendant of Hunt.

9. *France: The Crowds of July*

Anthony Arblaster, *The Rise and Decline of Western Liberalism* (Oxford: Basil Blackwell, 1984).

Frederick B. Artz, *France Under the Bourbon Restoration, 1814–1830* (Cambridge, MA: Harvard University Press, 1931).

———, *Reaction and Revolution, 1814–1832* (New York: Harper & Bros., 1934), chs. 7–9.

Jonathan Beecher, *Charles Fourier: The Visionary and His World* (Berkeley: University of California Press, 1986).

Edward Berenson, *Populist Religion and Left-Wing Politics in France, 1830–1852* (Princeton: Princeton University Press, 1984).

Robert J. Bezucha, *The Lyon Uprising of 1834: Social and Political Conflict in the Early July Monarchy* (Cambridge, MA: Harvard University Press, 1974).

———, "The Revolution of 1830 and the City of Lyon," in Merriman, *1830 in France,* pp. 119–38.

Ian H. Birchall, *The Spectre of Babeuf* (New York: St. Martin's Press, 1997).

Michael Broers, *Europe After Napoleon: Revolution, Reaction, and Romanticism, 1814–1848* (Manchester: Manchester University Press, 1996).

D. W. Brogan, *The French Nation: From Napoleon to Pétain, 1814–1940* (London: Hamish Hamilton, 1957).

D. G. Charlton, *Secular Religions in France, 1815–1870* (New York: Oxford University Press, 1963).

Louis Chevalier, *Laboring Classes and Dangerous Classes in Paris during the First Half of the Nineteenth Century*, Frank Jellinek, trans. (New York: Howard Fertig, 1973).

Clive H. Church, *Europe in 1830: Revolution and Political Change* (London: George Allen & Unwin, 1983).

G. D. H. Cole, *Socialist Thought: The Forerunners, 1789–1850* (London: Macmillan, 1953).

H. A. C. Collingham, *The July Monarchy: A Political History of France, 1830–1848* (London: Longman, 1988).

Irene Collins, "The Government and the Press in France during the Reign of Louis-Philippe," *English Historical Review*, vol. 69, no. 271 (April 1954), pp. 262–82.

Peter Davies, *The Extreme Right in France, 1789 to the Present: From de Maistre to Le Pen* (London: Routledge, 2002), ch. 2.

Anthony Esler, "Youth in Revolt: The French Generation of 1830," in Robert J. Bezucha, ed., *Modern European Social History* (Lexington, MA: D. C. Heath, 1972), pp. 301–34.

David Owen Evans, *Social Romanticism in France, 1830–1848* (Oxford: Clarendon Press, 1951).

Joseph V. Femia, *Against the Masses: Varieties of Anti-Democratic Thought since the French Revolution* (New York: Oxford University Press, 2001).

Biancamaria Fontana, *Benjamin Constant and the Post-Revolutionary Mind* (New Haven: Yale University Press, 1991).

Jill Harsin, *Barricades: The War of the Streets in Revolutionary Paris, 1830–1848* (New York: Palgrave, 2002).

W. O. Henderson, *Britain and Industrial Europe, 1750–1870*, 2nd ed. (Leicester: Leicester University Press, 1965).

Robert L. Hoffman, *Revolutionary Justice: The Social and Political Theory of P.-J. Proudhon* (Urbana: University of Illinois Press, 1972).

Jeff Horn, *The Path Not Taken: French Industrialization in the Age of Revolution, 1750–1830* (Cambridge, MA: MIT Press, 2006).

T. E. B. Howarth, *Citizen-King: The Life of Louis-Philippe, King of the French* (London: Eyre & Spottiswoode, 1961).

Margaret C. Jacob, *Scientific Culture and the Making of the Industrial West* (New York: Oxford University Press, 1997).

Andrew Jainchill, *Reimagining Politics after the Terror: The Republican Origins of French Liberalism* (Ithaca, NY: Cornell University Press, 2008).

André Jardin and André-Jean Tudesq, *Restoration and Reaction, 1815–1848*, Elborg Forster, trans. (Cambridge: Cambridge University Press, 1983).

Christopher H. Johnson, "The Revolution of 1830 in French Economic History," in Merriman, *1830 in France*, pp. 139–89.

Eugene Kamenka and F. B. Smith, eds., *Intellectuals and Revolution: Socialism and the Experience of 1848* (New York: St. Martin's Press, 1979).

Robert A. Kann, *The Problem of Restoration* (Berkeley: University of California Press, 1968), ch. 16.

George Armstrong Kelly, *The Humane Comedy: Constant, Tocqueville, and French Liberalism* (Cambridge: Cambridge University Press, 1992).

Lloyd Kramer, *Lafayette in Two Worlds: Public Cultures and Personal Identities in an Age of Revolutions* (Chapel Hill: University of North Carolina Press, 1996).

Carl Landauer, *European Socialism: A History of Ideas and Movements* (Berkeley: University of California Press, 1959), vol. 1, part 1.

David S. Landes, "French Entrepreneurship and Industrial Growth in the Nineteenth Century," *Journal of Economic History,* vol. 9, no. 1 (May 1949), pp. 45–61.

David Laven and Lucy Riall, eds., *Napoleon's Legacy: Problems of Government in Restoration Europe* (Oxford: Berg, 2000).

George Lichtheim, *The Origins of Socialism* (New York: Praeger, 1969).

Albert S. Lindemann, *A History of European Socialism* (New Haven: Yale University Press, 1983), chs. 1–2.

Roger Magraw, *France 1815–1914: The Bourgeois Century* (New York: Oxford University Press, 1986), ch. 1.

———, *A History of the French Working Class* (Oxford: Blackwell, 1992), vol. 1, esp. part 2, ch. 1.

Philip Mansel, *Paris Between Empires: Monarchy and Revolution, 1814–1852* (New York: St. Martin's Press, 2003).

Frank E. Manuel, "The Luddite Movement in France," *Journal of Modern History,* vol. 10, no. 2 (June 1938), pp. 180–211.

———, *The New World of Henri Saint-Simon* (Cambridge, MA: Harvard University Press, 1956).

———, *The Prophets of Paris* (Cambridge, MA: Harvard University Press, 1962).

Peter Mathias and M. M. Postan, eds., *The Industrial Economies: Capital, Labour and Enterprise,* vol. 7 of *The Cambridge Economic History of Europe* (Cambridge: Cambridge University Press, 1978), part 1.

Darrin M. McMahon, *Enemies of the Enlightenment: The French Counter-Enlightenment and the Making of Modernity* (New York: Oxford University Press, 2001).

Stanley Mellon, *The Political Uses of History: A Study of Historians in the French Restoration* (Palo Alto: Stanford University Press, 1958).

J. G. Merquior, *Liberalism: Old and New* (Boston: Twayne, 1991).

John M. Merriman, "Contested Freedoms in the French Revolutions, 1830–1871," in Isser Woloch, ed., *Revolution and the Meanings of Freedom in the Nineteenth Century* (Palo Alto: Stanford University Press, 1996), pp. 173–211.

———, *The Red City: Limoges and the French Nineteenth Century* (New York: Oxford University Press, 1985), esp. chs. 1–2.

John M. Merriman, ed., *1830 in France* (New York: New Viewpoints, 1975).

Bernard H. Moss, "Parisian Workers and the Origins of Republican Socialism, 1830–1833," in Merriman, *1830 in France,* pp. 203–21.

Sylvia Neely, *Lafayette and the Liberal Ideal, 1814–1824: Politics and Conspiracy in an Age of Reaction* (Carbondale: Southern Illinois University Press, 1991).

Edgar Leon Newman, "The Blouse and the Frock Coat: The Alliance of the Common People of Paris with the Liberal Leadership and the Middle Class during the Last Years of the Bourbon Restoration," *Journal of Modern History,* vol. 46, no. 1 (March 1974), pp. 26–59.

———, "What the Crowd Wanted in the French Revolution of 1830," in Merriman, *1830 in France,* pp. 17–40.

Harold T. Parker, "French Administrators and French Scientists during the Old Regime and the Early Years of the Revolution," in Richard Herr and Parker, eds., *Ideas in History* (Durham, NC: Duke University Press, 1965), pp. 85–109.

Zbigniew Pelczynski and John Gray, eds., *Conceptions of Liberty in Political Philosophy* (New York: St. Martin's Press, 1984).

Pamela M. Pilbeam, *The 1830 Revolution in France* (New York: St. Martin's Press, 1991).

———, "The Emergence of Opposition to the Orleanist Monarchy, August 1830–April 1831," *English Historical Review,* vol. 85, no. 334 (January 1970), pp. 12–28.

———, *French Socialists Before Marx: Workers, Women, and the Social Question in France* (Montreal: McGill-Queen's University Press, 2000).

———, *The Middle Classes in Europe, 1789–1914: France, Germany, Italy, and Russia* (Chicago: Lyceum, 1990), esp. ch. 9.

———, "Popular Violence in Provincial France after the 1830 Revolution," *English Historical Review,* vol. 91, no. 359 (April 1976), pp. 278–97.

———, *Republicanism in Nineteenth-Century France, 1814–1871* (New York: St. Martin's Press, 1995).

———, "The 'Three Glorious Days': The Revolution of 1830 in Provincial France," *Historical Journal,* vol. 26, no. 4 (December 1983), pp. 831–44.

David H. Pinkney, *Decisive Years in France, 1840–1847* (Princeton: Princeton University Press, 1986), ch. 1.

———, *The French Revolution of 1830* (Princeton: Princeton University Press, 1972).

———, "Laissez-Faire or Intervention? Labor Policy in the First Months of the July Monarchy," *French Historical Studies*, vol. 3, no. 1 (Spring 1963), pp. 123–28.

John Plamenatz, *The Revolutionary Movement in France, 1815–71* (London: Longmans, Green, 1952), esp. chs. 2–3.

Jacques Rancière, *The Nights of Labor: The Workers' Dream in Nineteenth-Century France,* John Drury, trans. (Philadelphia: Temple University Press, 1989).

René Rémond, *The Right Wing in France: From 1815 to de Gaulle,* James M. Laux, trans. (Philadelphia: University of Pennsylvania Press, 1966).

Daniel P. Resnick, *The White Terror and the Political Reaction After Waterloo* (Cambridge, MA: Harvard University Press, 1966).

Nicholas V. Riasanovsky, *The Teaching of Charles Fourier* (Berkeley: University of California Press, 1969).

Alan Ritter, *The Political Thought of Pierre-Joseph Proudhon* (Princeton: Princeton University Press, 1969).

Guido de Ruggiero, *The History of European Liberalism,* R. G. Collingwood, trans. (New York: Oxford University Press, 1927).

Steven Seidman, *Liberalism and the Origins of European Social Theory* (Berkeley: University of California Press, 1983), part 1.

William H. Sewell Jr., "Beyond 1793: Babeuf, Louis Blanc and the Genealogy of 'Social Revolution,'" in François Furet and Mona Ozouf, eds., *The Transformation of Political Culture, 1789–1848* (Oxford: Pergamon Press, 1989), pp. 509–26.

———, *Work and Revolution in France: The Language of Labor from the Old Regime to 1848* (Cambridge: Cambridge University Press, 1980), esp. ch. 9.

Alan B. Spitzer, *The French Generation of 1820* (Princeton: Princeton University Press, 1987).

———, *Old Hatreds and Young Hopes: The French Carbonari against the Bourbon Restoration* (Cambridge, MA: Harvard University Press, 1971).

Peter N. Stearns, "Patterns of Industrial Strike Activity in France during the July Monarchy," *American Historical Review*, vol. 70, no. 2 (January 1965), pp. 371–94.

Harlow Giles Unger, *Lafayette* (New York: John Wiley & Sons, 2002).

* * *

183 ["men are cowards"]: quoted in Manuel, "Luddite Movement," p. 200.

184 ["gentlemanly zeal"]: Jacob, p. 136.

184 ["enlightenment in the principles"]: Jean-Antoine Chaptal, Napoleon's minister of the interior, quoted in ibid., p. 181.

185 ["good king"]: quoted in Manuel, "Luddite Movement," p. 196.

185 ["fat, lame"]: Brogan, p. 3.

185 ["king of two peoples"]: quoted in Artz, *France Under the Bourbon Restoration,* p. 16.

185 [Suffrage in Charter]: see Pilbeam, *Republicanism,* p. 63; and Jardin and Tudesq, p. 12.

186 ["demand for self-determination"]: Palmer, "The World Revolution of the West: 1763–1801," *Political Science Quarterly,* vol. 69, no. 1 (March 1954), pp. 1–14, quoted at p. 5.

187 ["I have more experience"]: quoted in Pinkney, *French Revolution of 1830,* p. 39.

188 ["misled children"]: *Les Annales de la Haute-Vienne,* quoted in Merriman, *Red City,* p. 50.

189 [July casualties]: cited in Newman, "The Blouse and the Frock Coat," p. 30 fn. 17.

189 ["doctrine of individual self-help"]: ibid., p. 27.

190 ["serve only the interests"]: quoted in Magraw, *History of the French Working Class,* vol. 1, p. 53.

190 [Strikes in Paris, 1830–33]: ibid.

190 ["Without a tribune"]: quoted in Sewell, p. 197.

191 [Engels on Fourier]: Engels, "Socialism: Utopian and Scientific," in Karl Marx and Friedrich Engels, *Selected Works* (New York: International Publishers, 1968), p. 405.

191 [Riasanovsky on Fourier]: Riasanovsky, pp. 30–31, quoted at p. 31.

192 [Fourier's passions]: see Fourier, *The Theory of the Four Movements,* Gareth Stedman Jones and Ian Patterson, eds. (Cambridge: Cambridge University Press, 1996), esp. pp. 78–88; Beecher, ch. 11.

192 ["boundless philanthropy"]: Fourier, p. 82.

192 ["full development"]: ibid.

192 [Pilbeam on Utopian dream worlds]: see Pilbeam, *French Socialists Before Marx,* p. 107 (chapter title).

193 ["one bedroom for all"]: quoted in ibid., p. 24.

194 ["almost fully fledged"]: Cole, p. 17.

194 ["private property is the source"]: quoted in Pilbeam, *Republicanism,* p. 48.

194 ["French men shot"]: Robert Sutton, "Introduction," in Cabet, *Travels in Icaria,* Leslie J. Roberts, trans. (Syracuse, NY: Syracuse University Press, 2003), pp. vii–xlix, quoted at p. ix.

195 ["scarecrow spectre"]: quoted in Pilbeam, *French Socialists Before Marx,* p. 34.

195 ["most Jacobin"]: Philippe Vigier, quoted in ibid.

195 ["whole power"]: quoted in Magraw, *History of the French Working Class,* vol. 1, p. 73.

196 ["networks of opposition societies"]: Pilbeam, *Republicanism,* p. 97.

197 ["When a government violates"]: quoted in ibid., p. 109.

198 [Lafayette's conversation with Louis-Philippe]: quoted in Pinkney, *French Revolution in 1830,* p. 163.

10. *The American Experiment*

Joyce Appleby, *Inheriting the Revolution: The First Generation of Americans* (Cambridge, MA: Belknap Press, 2000).

——, *Thomas Jefferson* (New York: Times Books/Henry Holt, 2004).

John Ashworth, *"Agrarians" and "Aristocrats": Party Political Ideology in the United States, 1837–1846* (Atlantic Highlands, NJ: Humanities Press, 1983).

——, "The Jacksonian as Leveller," *Journal of American Studies,* vol. 14, no. 3 (December 1980), pp. 407–21.

Irving H. Bartlett, *John C. Calhoun* (New York: W. W. Norton, 1993).

Max Berger, *The British Traveller in America, 1836–1860* (New York: Columbia University Press, 1943).

Rowland Berthoff, "Independence and Attachment, Virtue and Interest: From Republican Citizen to Free Enterprise, 1787–1837," in Richard L. Bushman et al., eds., *Uprooted Americans* (Boston: Little, Brown, 1979), pp. 97–124.

Joseph L. Blau, ed., *Social Theories of Jacksonian Democracy* (New York: Hafner, 1947).

Irving Brant, *The Fourth President: A Life of James Madison* (Indianapolis: Bobbs-Merrill, 1970).

Hugh Brogan, "Tocqueville and the American Presidency," *Journal of American Studies,* vol. 15, no. 3 (December 1981), pp. 357–75.

David Brown, "Jeffersonian Ideology and the Second Party System," *Historian,* vol. 62, no. 1 (Fall 1999), pp. 17–30.

Thomas Brown, *Politics and Statesmanship: Essays on the American Whig Party* (New York: Columbia University Press, 1985).

Richard Buel Jr., *America on the Brink* (New York: Palgrave, 2005).

James MacGregor Burns, *The Vineyard of Liberty* (New York: Alfred A. Knopf, 1982), parts 2–4 passim.

Andrew Burstein, *The Passions of Andrew Jackson* (New York: Alfred A. Knopf, 2003).

Thomas C. Cochran, *Frontiers of Change: Early Industrialism in America* (New York: Oxford University Press, 1981).

Donald B. Cole, *Martin Van Buren and the American Political System* (Princeton: Princeton University Press, 1984).

——, *The Presidency of Andrew Jackson* (Lawrence: University Press of Kansas, 1993).

Henry Steele Commager, *Commager on Tocqueville* (Columbia: University of Missouri Press, 1993).

John R. Commons et al., *History of Labour in the United States* (New York: Macmillan, 1918–35), vol. 1.

William J. Cooper Jr., *The South and the Politics of Slavery, 1828–1856* (Baton Rouge: Louisiana State University Press, 1978)

Matthew A. Crenson, *The Federal Machine: Beginnings of Bureaucracy in Jacksonian America* (Baltimore: Johns Hopkins University Press, 1975).

Noble E. Cunningham Jr., *The Jeffersonian Republicans in Power: Party Operations, 1801–1809* (Chapel Hill: University of North Carolina Press, 1963).

Robert F. Dalzell Jr., *Enterprising Elite: The Boston Associates and the World They Made* (Cambridge, MA: Harvard University Press, 1987).

George Dangerfield, *The Awakening of American Nationalism, 1815–1828* (New York: Harper & Row, 1965).

Michael Drolet, *Tocqueville, Democracy, and Social Reform* (Basingstoke: Palgrave, 2003).

Thomas Dublin, *Women at Work: The Transformation of Work and Community in Lowell, Massachusetts, 1826–1860* (New York: Columbia University Press, 1979).

Abraham S. Eisenstadt, ed., *Reconsidering Tocqueville's* Democracy in America (New Brunswick, NJ: Rutgers University Press, 1988).

Arthur A. Ekirch Jr., *The Idea of Progress in America, 1815–1860* (New York: Columbia University Press, 1944).

Richard E. Ellis, *The Union at Risk: Jacksonian Democracy, States' Rights, and the Nullification Crisis* (New York: Oxford University Press, 1987).

Richard J. Ellis and Stephen Kirk, "Presidential Mandates in the Nineteenth Century: Conceptual Change and Institutional Development," *Studies in American Political Development*, vol. 9, no. 1 (Spring 1995), pp. 117–86.

Daniel Feller, *The Jacksonian Promise: America, 1815–1840* (Baltimore: Johns Hopkins University Press, 1995).

——, "Politics and Society: Toward a Jacksonian Synthesis," *Journal of the Early Republic*, vol. 10, no. 2 (Summer 1990), pp. 135–61.

David Hackett Fischer, *The Revolution of American Conservatism: The Federalist Party in the Era of Jeffersonian Democracy* (New York: Harper & Row, 1965).

Marvin Fisher, *Workshops in the Wilderness: The European Response to American Industrialization* (New York: Oxford University Press, 1967).

John Fitch, *Autobiography*, Frank D. Prager, ed. (Philadelphia: American Philosophical Society, 1976).

Marshall Foletta, *Coming to Terms with Democracy: Federalist Intellectuals and the Shaping of an American Culture* (Charlottesville: University Press of Virginia, 2001).

Philip S. Foner, *History of the Labor Movement in the United States* (New York: International Publishers, 1947–94), vol. 1.

Ronald P. Formisano, "Political Character, Antipartyism and the Second Party System," *American Quarterly*, vol. 21, no. 4 (Winter 1969), pp. 683–709.

Constance McLaughlin Green, *Eli Whitney and the Birth of American Technology* (Boston: Little, Brown, 1956).

M. J. Heale, *The Presidential Quest: Candidates and Images in American Political Culture, 1787–1852* (London: Longman, 1982).

Brooke Hindle, *Emulation and Invention* (New York: New York University Press, 1981), chs. 1–3.

Brooke Hindle and Steven Lubar, *Engines of Change: The American Industrial Revolution, 1790–1860* (Washington, D.C.: Smithsonian Institution Press, 1986).

Richard Hofstadter, *The American Political Tradition and the Men Who Made It* (New York: Alfred A. Knopf, 1948), chs. 1–3.

Michael F. Holt, *The Rise and Fall of the American Whig Party: Jacksonian Politics and the Onset of the Civil War* (New York: Oxford University Press, 1999).

Daniel Walker Howe, *The Political Culture of the American Whigs* (Chicago: University of Chicago Press, 1979).

———, *What Hath God Wrought: The Transformation of America, 1815–1848* (New York: Oxford University Press, 2007).

Walter Hugins, *Jeffersonian Democracy and the Working Class: A Study of the New York Workingmen's Movement, 1829–1837* (Palo Alto: Stanford University Press, 1960).

André Jardin, *Tocqueville*, Lydia Davis, trans. (New York: Farrar Straus Giroux, 1988).

Peter J. Kastor, *The Nation's Crucible: The Louisiana Purchase and the Creation of America* (New Haven: Yale University Press, 2004).

Peter J. Kastor, ed., *The Louisiana Purchase: Emergence of an American Nation* (Washington, D.C.: CQ Press, 2002).

Linda K. Kerber, *Federalists in Dissent: Imagery and Ideology in Jeffersonian America* (Ithaca, NY: Cornell University Press, 1970).

Lawrence F. Kohl, *The Politics of Individualism: Parties and the American Character in the Jacksonian Era* (New York: Oxford University Press, 1989).

Jon Kukla, *A Wilderness So Immense: The Louisiana Purchase and the Destiny of America* (New York: Alfred A. Knopf, 2003).

John Lauritz Larson, "'Bind the Republic Together': The National Union and the Struggle for a System of Internal Improvements," *Journal of American History*, vol. 74, no. 2 (September 1987), pp. 363–87.

———, "Jefferson's Union and the Problem of Internal Improvements," in Peter S. Onuf, ed., *Jeffersonian Legacies* (Charlottesville: University Press of Virginia, 1993), pp. 340–69.

Richard B. Latner, "Preserving the 'Natural Equality of Rank and Influence': Liberalism, Republicanism, and Equality of Condition in Jacksonian Politics," in Thomas L. Haskell and Richard F. Teichgraeber III, eds., *The Culture of the Market* (Cambridge: Cambridge University Press, 1993), pp. 189–230.

———, *The Presidency of Andrew Jackson: White House Politics, 1829–1837* (Athens: University of Georgia Press, 1979).

Andrew Lenner, *The Federal Principle in American Politics, 1790–1833* (Lanham, MD: Rowman & Littlefield, 2001).

Gerald Leonard, *The Invention of Party Politics: Federalism, Popular Sovereignty, and Constitutional Development in Jacksonian Illinois* (Chapel Hill: University of North Carolina Press, 2002).

Shaw Livermore Jr., *The Twilight of Federalism: The Disintegration of the Federalist Party, 1815–1830* (Princeton: Princeton University Press, 1962).

Dumas Malone, *Jefferson and His Time* (Boston: Little, Brown, 1948–81), vols. 4–5.

Matthew Mancini, *Alexis de Tocqueville* (New York: Twayne, 1994).

Lynn L. Marshall, "The Strange Stillbirth of the Whig Party," *American Historical Review*, vol. 72, no. 2 (January 1967), pp. 445–68.

Louis P. Masur, *1831: Year of Eclipse* (New York: Hill and Wang, 2001).

Richard P. McCormick, *The Second American Party System: Party Formation in the Jacksonian Era* (Chapel Hill: University of North Carolina Press, 1966).

Jane L. Mesick, *The English Traveller in America, 1785–1835* (New York: Columbia University Press, 1922).

Douglas T. Miller, *Jacksonian Aristocracy: Class and Democracy in New York, 1830–1860* (New York: Oxford University Press, 1967).

David Montgomery, *Citizen Worker: The Experience of Workers in the United States with Democracy and the Free Market during the Nineteenth Century* (Cambridge: Cambridge University Press, 1993).

———, "The Working Classes of the Pre-Industrial American City, 1780–1830," *Labor History*, vol. 9, no. 1 (Winter 1968), pp. 3–22.

James A. Morone, *The Democratic Wish: Popular Participation and the Limits of American Government* (New York: Basic Books, 1990), ch. 2.

Curtis P. Nettels, *The Emergence of a National Economy, 1775–1815* (New York: Holt, Rinehart and Winston, 1962).

Maurice F. Neufeld, "Realms of Thought and Organized Labor in the Age of Jackson," *Labor History*, vol. 10, no. 1 (Winter 1969), pp. 5–43.

Jeffrey L. Pasley et al., eds., *Beyond the Founders* (Chapel Hill: University of North Carolina Press, 2004).

Edward Pessen, *Jacksonian America: Society, Personality, and Politics*, rev. ed. (Urbana: University of Illinois Press, 1985).

——, *Most Uncommon Jacksonians: The Radical Leaders of the Early Labor Movement* (Albany: State University of New York Press, 1967).

——, *Riches, Class, and Power: America before the Civil War* (Lexington, MA: D. C. Heath, 1973).

Edward Pessen, comp., *New Perspectives on Jacksonian Parties and Politics* (Boston: Allyn and Bacon, 1969).

J. R. Pole, *The Pursuit of Equality in American History*, rev. ed. (Berkeley: University of California Press, 1993), esp. ch. 6.

Willard S. Randall, *Thomas Jefferson* (New York: Henry Holt, 1993).

Robert V. Remini, *Andrew Jackson*, 3 vols. (New York: Harper & Row, 1977–84).

——, *Henry Clay: Statesman for the Union* (New York: W. W. Norton, 1991).

——, *The Jacksonian Era* (Arlington Heights, IL: Harlan Davidson, 1989).

——, *John Quincy Adams* (New York: Times Books/Henry Holt, 2002).

——, *The Legacy of Andrew Jackson* (Baton Rouge: Louisiana State University Press, 1988).

——, *Martin Van Buren and the Making of the Democratic Party* (New York: Columbia University Press, 1959).

Stephen P. Rice, *Minding the Machine: Languages of Class in Early Industrial America* (Berkeley: University of California Press, 2004).

Norman K. Risjord, ed., *The Early American Party System* (New York: Harper & Row, 1969).

Donald L. Robinson, *Slavery in the Structure of American Politics, 1765–1820* (New York: Harcourt Brace Jovanovich, 1971).

W. J. Rorabaugh, *The Craft Apprentice: From Franklin to the Machine Age in America* (New York: Oxford University Press, 1986).

Mary P. Ryan, *Civic Wars: Democracy and Public Life in the American City During the Nineteenth Century* (Berkeley: University of California Press, 1997), part 1.

Kirkpatrick Sale, *The Fire of His Genius: Robert Fulton and the American Dream* (New York: Free Press, 2001).

Arthur M. Schlesinger Jr., *The Age of Jackson* (Boston: Little, Brown, 1946).

Arthur M. Schlesinger Jr., ed., *History of American Presidential Elections, 1789–1968* (New York: Chelsea House, 1971), vol. 1.

James T. Schliefer, *The Making of Tocqueville's Democracy in America* (Chapel Hill: University of North Carolina Press, 1980).

Michael Schudson, *The Good Citizen: A History of American Civic Life* (New York: Free Press, 1998), ch. 3.

Charles Sellers, *The Market Revolution: Jacksonian America, 1815–1846* (New York: Oxford University Press, 1991).

Larry Siedentop, *Tocqueville* (New York: Oxford University Press, 1994).

Joel H. Silbey, *The American Political Nation, 1838–1893* (Palo Alto: Stanford University Press, 1991).

C. Edward Skeen, *1816: America Rising* (Lexington: University Press of Kentucky, 2003).

Kimberly K. Smith, *The Dominion of Voice: Riot, Reason, and Romance in Antebellum Politics* (Lawrence: University Press of Kansas, 1999).

Darwin H. Stapleton, *The Transfer of Early Industrial Technologies to America* (Philadelphia: American Philosophical Society, 1987).

Patricia Sykes, "Party Constraints on Leaders in Pursuit of Change," *Studies in American Political Development*, vol. 7, no. 1 (March 1993), pp. 151–76.

Alexis de Tocqueville, *Democracy in America*, Henry Reeve and Francis Bowen, trans., and Phillips Bradley, ed., 2 vols. (New York: Alfred A. Knopf, 1945).

Robert W. Tucker and David C. Hendrickson, *Empire of Liberty: The Statecraft of Thomas Jefferson* (New York: Oxford University Press, 1990).

Glyndon G. Van Deusen, *The Jacksonian Era, 1828–1848* (New York: Harper & Brothers, 1959).

Michael Wallace, "Changing Concepts of Party in the United States: New York, 1815–1828," *American Historical Review*, vol. 74, no. 2 (December 1968), pp. 453–91.

Julie M. Walsh, *The Intellectual Origins of Mass Parties and Mass Schools in the Jacksonian Period: Creating a Conformed Citizenry* (New York: Garland, 1998).

Harry L. Watson, *Liberty and Power: The Politics of Jacksonian America* (New York: Hill and Wang, 1990).

Rush Welter, *The Mind of America, 1820–1860* (New York: Columbia University Press, 1975).

Leonard D. White, *The Jacksonians: A Study in Administrative History, 1829–1861* (New York: Macmillan, 1954).

Robert H. Wiebe, *The Opening of American Society: From the Adoption of the Constitution to the Eve of Disunion* (New York: Alfred A. Knopf, 1984).

Sean Wilentz, *Chants Democratic: New York City & the Rise of the American Working Class, 1788–1850* (New York: Oxford University Press, 1984).

——, *The Rise of American Democracy: Jefferson to Lincoln* (New York: W. W. Norton, 2005).

Garry Wills, *James Madison* (New York: Times Books/Henry Holt, 2002).

Major Wilson, "Republicanism and the Idea of Party in the Jacksonian Period," *Journal of the Early Republic,* vol. 8, no. 4 (Winter 1988), pp. 419–42.

Sheldon S. Wolin, *Tocqueville between Two Worlds: The Making of a Political and Theoretical Life* (Princeton: Princeton University Press, 2001).

David A. Zonderman, *Aspirations and Anxieties: New England Workers and the Mechanized Factory System, 1815–1850* (New York: Oxford University Press, 1992).

＊ ＊ ＊

199 ["Friends and Fellow-Citizens"]: Jefferson, "First Inaugural Address," in Jefferson, *Writings,* Merrill D. Peterson, ed. (New York: Library of America, 1984), pp. 492–96, quoted at pp. 492, 494, 495, 493, respectively. In drafting this chapter, I drew upon my *Vineyard of Liberty.*

200 ["*Rejoice!*"]: quoted in Malone, vol. 4, p. 30.

202 ["the Hudson, the Delaware"]: letter to Charles Pinckney, November 27, 1802, in Madison, *Writings,* Gaillard Hunt, ed. (New York: G. P. Putnam's Sons, 1900–10), vol. 4, pp. 461–64, quoted at p. 462.

202 ["very ominous"]: letter to James Monroe, May 26, 1801, in Jefferson, *Writings,* Paul Leicester Ford, ed. (New York: G. P. Putnam's Sons, 1892–99), vol. 8, pp. 57–58, quoted at p. 58.

202 ["moral monster":]: quoted in Randall, p. 935.

203 ["laws of necessity"]: letter to John B. Colvin, September 20, 1810, in Jefferson, *Writings* (Ford), vol. 9, pp. 279–82, quoted at p. 279.

204 ["conqueror of Europe"]: Justice Joseph Story, quoted in Brant, p. 590.

204 ["so essentially lacked"]: Louis Serurier, quoted in ibid., p. 589.

204 ["will of the majority"]: Jefferson, "First Inaugural Address," pp. 492–93.

205 ["American Tory party"]: Wilentz, *Rise of American Democracy,* p. 165.

205 ["radical reform"]: quoted in ibid.

205 [Madison's reaction to Hartford recommendations]: Irving Brant, *James Madison: Commander in Chief, 1812–1836* (Indianapolis: Bobbs-Merrill, 1961), p. 361.

206 ["good old jeffersonian"]: quoted in Remini, *Jacksonian Era,* p. 12.

206 ["people are the government"]: ibid., p. 24.

207 ["*Judas* of the West"]: letter to William B. Lewis, February 14, 1825, in Jackson, *Papers,* Sam B. Smith, Harold D. Moser et al., eds. (Knoxville: University of Tennessee Press, 1980–), vol. 6, pp. 29–30.

207 [Voter participation, 1824, 1828]: Michael J. Dubin, *United States Presidential Elections, 1788–1860* (Jefferson, NC: McFarland, 2002), pp. 31, 42.

207 ["appointed against"]: Jackson, "Outline of principles," February 23, 1829, quoted in Remini, *Andrew Jackson,* vol. 2, p. 184.

207 ["Reign of Terror"]: quoted in ibid., p. 185.

208 ["power to control"]: quoted in Robert V. Remini, *Andrew Jackson* (New York: Twayne, 1966), p. 142.

208 ["to riches"]: quoted in Feller, *Jacksonian Promise,* p. 66.

209 ["if one drop"]: quoted in Howe, *What Hath God Wrought,* p. 406.

210 [Population growth and immigration in Jacksonian era]: U.S. Bureau of the Census, *Historical Statistics of the United States, Colonial Times to 1970* (Washington, D.C.: U.S. Government Printing Office, 1975), pt. 1, pp. 8 (series A 7: total population), 22 (A 172: regional), and 106 (C 89, 91–92, 95: immigration); see also Pessen, *Jacksonian America,* ch. 3.

210 [Jefferson and Bacon]: see Hindle, p. 11.

210 ["Infinity of Utensils"]: quoted in ibid.

210 [Hindle on U.S. technological progress]: ibid., pp. 22–23, quoted at p. 23.

212 ["controlled the Bay State"]: Foner, vol. 1, p. 56.

213 ["not only excite similar"]: March 30, 1795, quoted in ibid., p. 70.

213 ["monied influence"]: quoted in Pessen, *Most Uncommon Jacksonians,* p. 123.

213 ["even the trade societies"]: Feller, *Jacksonian Promise,* p. 128.

214 ["Distinctions in society"]: Veto Message, July 10, 1832, in *A Compilation of the Messages and Papers of the Presidents* (Washington, D.C.: Bureau of National Literature, 1913), vol. 2, pp. 1139–54, quoted at p. 1153.

214 ["full and General Division"]: quoted in Wilentz, *Rise of American Democracy,* p. 353.

214 ["no lenders"]: ibid., p. 354.

215 ["sole and absolute control"]: quoted in Pole, p. 167.

215 ["legitimate object"]: Lincoln, "Fragment on Government," July 1, 1854, in Lincoln, *Collected Works,* Roy P. Basler, ed. (New Brunswick, NJ: Rutgers University Press, 1953–55), vol. 2, pp. 220–21, quoted at p. 220.

216 ["more perfect"]: quoted in Howe, pp. 112, 111, 112, respectively.

216 ["sent to make the rich"]: George H. Evans, quoted in Pessen, *Most Uncommon Jacksonians,* p. 123.

217 [Voter participation, 1840]: Silbey, p. 145 (table 8.1).

218 ["age of travel"]: May, "Tocqueville and the Enlightenment Legacy," in Eisenstadt, pp. 25–42, quoted at p. 38.

218 [Martineau on American women]: Martineau, *Society in America,* 4th ed. (London: Saunders and Otley, 1837), vol. 2, pp. 228, 227, respectively.

218 [Tocqueville on the Bourbons]: quoted in Jardin, pp. 86–87.

219 ["unlimited power"]: see Tocqueville, vol. 1, esp. ch. 15.

219 ["like an impure being"]: ibid., vol. 1, p. 264 (ch. 15).

219 ["disposes each member"]: ibid., vol. 2, p. 98 (bk. 2, ch. 2).

220 ["downright selfishness"]: ibid.

220 ["most obvious"]: ibid., vol. 2, p. 4 (bk. 1, ch. 1).

220 ["enormous pressure"]: ibid., vol. 2, p. 10 (bk. 1, ch. 2).

11. *Britain: The Fire for Reform*

A. Aspinall, "English Party Organization in the Early Nineteenth Century," *English Historical Review,* vol. 41, no. 163 (July 1926), pp. 389–411.

John Belchem, *"Orator" Hunt: Henry Hunt and English Working-Class Radicalism* (Oxford: Clarendon Press, 1985).

Asa Briggs, "The Background of the Parliamentary Reform Movement in Three English Cities, 1830–1832," in Briggs, *Collected Essays* (Urbana: University of Illinois Press, 1985), vol. 1, pp. 180–201.

Michael Brock, *The Great Reform Act* (London: Hutchinson University Library, 1973).

Anthony Brundage, *The English Poor Laws, 1700–1930* (Basingstoke: Palgrave, 2002), chs. 2–4.

———, *The Making of the New Poor Law: The Politics of Inquiry, Enactment, and Implementation, 1832–1839* (New Brunswick, NJ: Rutgers University Press, 1978).

J. H. Burns, "J. S. Mill and Democracy, 1829–61," in J. B. Schneewind, ed., *Mill* (Notre Dame, IN: University of Notre Dame Press, 1969), pp. 280–328.

John Cannon, *Parliamentary Reform, 1640–1832* (Cambridge: Cambridge University Press, 1973).

Nicholas Capaldi, *John Stuart Mill* (Cambridge: Cambridge University Press, 2004).

J. C. D. Clark, *English Society, 1660–1832: Religion, Ideology, and Politics during the Ancien Regime,* 2nd ed. (Cambridge: Cambridge University Press, 2000), ch. 6.

Linda Colley, *Britons: Forging the Nation, 1707–1837* (New Haven: Yale University Press, 1992), ch. 8.

Richard W. Davis, "Deference and Aristocracy in the Time of the Great Reform Act," *American Historical Review,* vol. 81, no. 3 (June 1976), pp. 532–39.

John W. Derry, *Politics in the Age of Fox, Pitt, and Liverpool,* rev. ed. (Basingstoke: Palgrave, 2001), ch. 4.

J. R. Dinwiddy, *From Luddism to the First Reform Bill: Reform in England, 1810–1832* (Oxford: Basil Blackwell, 1986).

Derek Fraser, "The Agitation for Parliamentary Reform," in Ward, pp. 31–53.

Peter Fraser, "Public Petitioning and Parliament before 1832," *Historian*, vol. 46 (October 1961), pp. 195–211.

W. H. Fraser, "Trade Unionism," in Ward, pp. 95–115.

Norman Gash, *Aristocracy and People: Britain, 1815–1865* (Cambridge, MA: Harvard University Press, 1979).

———, *Lord Liverpool* (Cambridge, MA: Harvard University Press, 1984).

———, *Politics in the Age of Peel: A Study in the Technique of Parliamentary Representation, 1830–1850* (London: Longmans, Green, 1953).

———, *Sir Robert Peel* (Lanham, MD: Rowman and Littlefield, 1972).

Izhak Gross, "The Abolition of Negro Slavery and British Parliamentary Politics, 1832–3," *Historical Journal*, vol. 23, no. 1 (March 1980), pp. 63–85.

Joseph Hamburger, *Intellectuals in Politics: John Stuart Mill and the Philosophic Radicals* (New Haven: Yale University Press, 1965).

———, *James Mill and the Art of Revolution* (New Haven: Yale University Press, 1963).

Philip Harling, *The Waning of "Old Corruption": The Politics of Economical Reform in Britain, 1779–1846* (Oxford: Clarendon Press, 1996), esp. ch. 5.

J. F. C. Harrison, *Quest for the New Moral World: Robert Owen and the Owenites in Britain and America* (New York: Charles Scribner's Sons, 1969).

E. J. Hobsbawm and George Rudé, *Captain Swing* (New York: Pantheon, 1968).

Robert Hole, *Pulpits, Politics, and Public Order in England, 1760–1832* (Cambridge: Cambridge University Press, 1989), esp. ch. 16.

Patricia Hollis, *The Pauper Press: A Study in Working-Class Radicalism of the 1830s* (New York: Oxford University Press, 1970).

Joanna Innes, "Central Government 'Interference': Changing Conceptions, Practices, and Concerns, c. 1700–1850," in Jose Harris, ed., *Civil Society in British History: Ideas, Identities, Institutions* (New York: Oxford University Press, 2003), pp. 39–60.

———, "The Distinctiveness of the English Poor Laws, 1750–1850," in Donald Winch and Patrick K. O'Brien, eds., *The Political Economy of British Historical Experience, 1688–1914* (New York: Oxford University Press, 2002), pp. 381–407.

T. A. Jenkins, *The Liberal Ascendancy, 1830–1886* (New York: St. Martin's Press, 1994), ch. 1.

Peter Jupp, *British Politics on the Eve of Reform: The Duke of Wellington's Administration, 1828–30* (New York: St. Martin's Press, 1998).

Abraham D. Kriegel, "Liberty and Whiggery in Early Nineteenth-Century England," *Journal of Modern History*, vol. 52, no. 2 (June 1980), pp. 253–78.

Kim Lawes, *Paternalism and Politics: The Revival of Paternalism in Early Nineteenth-Century Britain* (New York: St. Martin's Press, 2000).

Lynn Hollen Lees, *The Solidarities of Strangers: The English Poor Laws and the People, 1700–1948* (Cambridge: Cambridge University Press, 1998), parts 1–2.

Nancy D. LoPatin, *Political Unions, Popular Politics, and the Great Reform Act of 1832* (New York: St. Martin's Press, 1999).

S. Maccoby, *English Radicalism, 1832–1852* (London: George Allen & Unwin, 1935).

Ian Machin, *The Rise of Democracy in Britain, 1830–1918* (New York: St. Martin's Press, 2001), chs. 1–2.

William Henry Maehl Jr., ed., *The Reform Bill of 1832: Why Not Revolution?* (New York: Holt, Rinehart and Winston, 1967).

Peter Mandler, *Aristocratic Government in the Age of Reform: Whigs and Liberals, 1830–1852* (Oxford: Clarendon Press, 1990).

———, "The Making of the New Poor Law *Redivivus*," *Past & Present*, no. 117 (November 1987), pp. 131–57.

Bruce Mazlish, *James and John Stuart Mill: Father and Son in the Nineteenth Century* (New York: Basic Books, 1975).

John Stuart Mill, *Autobiography* (New York: Columbia University Press, 1944).

John Milton-Smith, "Earl Grey's Cabinet and the Objects of Parliamentary Reform," *Historical Journal*, vol. 15, no. 1 (March 1972), pp. 55–74.

Austin Mitchell, *The Whigs in Opposition, 1815–1830* (Oxford: Clarendon Press, 1967).

L. G. Mitchell, "Foxite Politics and the Great Reform Bill," *English Historical Review*, vol. 108, no. 427 (April 1993), pp. 338–64.

———, *Lord Melbourne, 1779–1848* (New York: Oxford University Press, 1997).

T. W. Moody et al., eds., *A New History of Ireland* (Oxford: Clarendon Press, 1976–), vol. 5.

D. C. Moore, "Concession or Cure: The Sociological Premises of the First Reform Act," *Historical Journal*, vol. 9, no. 1 (1966), pp. 39–59.

———, "The Other Face of Reform," *Victorian Studies*, vol. 5, no. 1 (September 1961), pp. 7–34.

———, *The Politics of Deference: A Study of the Mid-Nineteenth Century English Political System* (Hassocks, UK: Harvester Press, 1976).

Iris W. Mueller, *John Stuart Mill and French Thought* (1956; reprinted by Books for Libraries Press, 1968).

Ian Newbould, *Whiggery and Reform, 1830–41: The Politics of Government* (Palo Alto: Stanford University Press, 1990).

David Nicholls, "The English Middle Class and the Ideological Significance of Radicalism, 1760–1886," *Journal of British Studies,* vol. 24, no. 4 (October 1985), pp. 415–33.

Fergus O'Ferrall, *Catholic Emancipation: Daniel O'Connell and the Birth of Irish Democracy, 1820–30* (Atlantic Highlands, NJ: Humanities Press International, 1985).

Frank O'Gorman, *Voters, Patrons, and Parties: The Unreformed Electoral System of Hanoverian England, 1734–1832* (Oxford: Clarendon Press, 1989).

Frank O'Gorman and Peter Fraser, "Party Politics in the Early Nineteenth Century (1812–32)," *English Historical Review,* vol. 102, no. 402 (January 1987), pp. 63–88.

Michael St. John Packe, *The Life of John Stuart Mill* (New York: Capricorn Books, 1970).

Jonathan Parry, *The Rise and Fall of Liberal Government in Victorian Britain* (New Haven: Yale University Press, 1993).

John A. Phillips, *The Great Reform Bill in the Boroughs: English Electoral Behaviour, 1818–1841* (Oxford: Clarendon Press, 1992).

John A. Phillips and Charles Wetherell, "The Great Reform Bill of 1832 and the Rise of Partisanship," *Journal of Modern History,* vol. 63, no. 4 (December 1991), pp. 621–46.

G. Bingham Powell Jr., "Incremental Democratization: The British Reform Act of 1832," in Gabriel A. Almond et al., eds., *Crisis, Choice, and Change: Historical Studies of Political Development* (Boston: Little, Brown, 1973), pp. 103–51.

Roland Quinault, "The Industrial Revolution and Parliamentary Reform," in Patrick K. O'Brien and Quinault, eds., *The Industrial Revolution and British Society* (Cambridge: Cambridge University Press, 1993), pp. 183–202.

M. E. Rose, "The Anti-Poor Law Agitation," in Ward, pp. 78–94.

D. J. Rowe, "Class and Political Radicalism in London, 1831–2," *Historical Journal,* vol. 13, no. 1 (March 1970), pp. 31–47.

———, "London Radicalism in the Era of the Great Reform Bill," in John Stevenson, ed., *London in the Age of Reform* (Oxford: Basil Blackwell, 1977), pp. 149–76.

George Rudé, "English Rural and Urban Disturbances on the Eve of the First Reform Bill, 1830–1831," *Past & Present,* no. 37 (July 1967), pp. 87–102.

James Sambrook, *William Cobbett* (London: Routledge & Kegan Paul, 1973).

E. A. Smith, *Lord Grey, 1764–1845* (Oxford: Clarendon Press, 1990).

George Spater, *William Cobbett: The Poor Man's Friend,* 2 vols. (Cambridge: Cambridge University Press, 1982).

John Stevenson, *Popular Disturbances in England, 1700–1870* (London: Longman, 1979), chs. 10–11.

Howard Temperley, *British Antislavery, 1833–1870* (London: Longman, 1972).

William Thomas, *The Philosophic Radicals: Nine Studies in Theory and Practice, 1817–1841* (Oxford: Clarendon Press, 1979).

————, "The Philosophic Radicals," in Patricia Hollis, ed., *Pressure from Without in Early Victorian England* (London: Edward Arnold, 1974), pp. 52–79.

Malcolm I. Thomis and Peter Holt, *Threats of Revolution in Britain, 1789–1848* (London: Macmillan, 1977), ch. 4.

E. P. Thompson, *The Making of the English Working Class* (London: Victor Gollancz, 1963).

A. S. Turberville, *The House of Lords in the Age of Reform, 1784–1837* (London: Faber and Faber, 1958).

James Vernon, *Politics and the People: A Study in English Political Culture, c.1815–1867* (Cambridge: Cambridge University Press, 1993).

Dror Wahrman, *Imagining the Middle Class: The Political Representation of Class in Britain, c. 1780–1840* (Cambridge: Cambridge University Press, 1995).

J. T. Ward, ed., *Popular Movements, c. 1830–1850* (New York: St. Martin's Press, 1970).

D. G. Wright, *Popular Radicalism: The Working-Class Experience, 1780–1880* (London: Longman, 1988).

*   *   *

221 ["edgily on the right center"]: Harvie, "Revolution and the Rule of Law (1789–1851)," in Kenneth O. Morgan, ed., *The Oxford History of Britain,* rev. ed. (New York: Oxford University Press, 1999), pp. 470–517, quoted at p. 492.

222 [Population growth, United Kingdom]: ibid., p. 477 (table).

222 [Owen's profits]: see Harrison, pp. 154–55.

223 ["feeling in favour"]: Birmingham *Journal,* August 27, 1831, quoted in Fraser, "Agitation," p. 31.

224 ["Han ye done?"]: quoted in Thompson, p. 731.

225 [Circulation of radical press]: Hollis, p. 119.

225 ["worked himself furious"]: Samuel Bamford, *Passages in the Life of a Radical* (2 vols., first published 1839–41), in Bamford, *Autobiography,* W. H. Chaloner, ed. (London: Frank Cass, 1967), vol. 2, p. 16.

225 [Hunt at Spa Fields]: quoted in Thompson, pp. 603–4.

225 ["maintain *a thousand families*"]: Cobbett, "To the Journeymen and Labourers," *Political Register,* November 1816, in Cobbett, *Selections from Cobbett's Political Works,* John M. Cobbett and James P. Cobbett, eds. (London: Anne Cobbett, 1835), vol. 5, pp. 1–17, quoted at p. 9.

226 [Hazlitt on Cobbett and Paine]: Hazlitt, "Character of Cobbett," *Table-Talk* (Essay VI), in Hazlitt, *Collected Works,* A. R. Waller and Arnold Glover, eds. (London: J. M. Dent, 1902–04), vol. 6, pp. 50–59, esp. p. 51.

226 ["parallelogram of paupers"]: quoted in Thompson, p. 782.

226 ["community of slaves"]: Sherwin's *Political Register,* September 20, 1817, quoted in ibid., p. 783.

226 ["an important distinction"]: quoted in Max Lerner, *Ideas Are Weapons: The History and Uses of Ideas* (New York: Viking Press, 1939), p. 3.

227 ["Bentham needed"]: Mazlish, pp. 69–70.

228 ["the masses and millions"]: quoted in Hamburger, *Intellectuals in Politics,* p. 48.

228 [Hamburger on Mill's doctrine]: ibid., pp. 32–33.

228 ["Nothing is more important"]: Hamburger, *James Mill and the Art of Revolution,* pp. 24–25.

228 ["such a fear of it"]: ibid., p. 61 fn. 4.

229 ["Greek prose authors"]: Mill, *Autobiography,* p. 4.

229 ["unsettlingly mature"]: Mazlish, p. 170.

229 ["never was a boy"]: Caroline Fox, quoted in ibid., p. 169.

229 ["abundant evidence"]: ibid., p. 158.

229 ["slovenliness of thinking"]: Macaulay, "Mill's Essay on Government," in Macaulay, *Critical and Historical Essays* (Boston: Houghton Mifflin, 1901), vol. 1, pp. 381–422, quoted at pp. 387, 393.

230 ["much to think about"]: Mill, *Autobiography,* pp. 110, 113, 114.

230 ["I went at once"]: ibid., p. 121.

230 ["Debout!"]: quoted in Packe, p. 100.

230 ["perfect equality"]: Mill, *Autobiography,* p. 118.

231 ["examples of the other nations"]: quoted in Brock, p. 37.

231 ["agreement upon that question"]: quoted in Mitchell, *Whigs in Opposition,* p. 17.

231 [Lamb on reform]: quoted in Brock, p. 37.

232 ["the Court and the Democrats"]: quoted in Kriegel, p. 264.

232 ["pressure almost to bursting"]: quoted in Hamburger, *James Mill and the Art of Revolution,* p. 36.

232 ["real and positive"]: quoted in Kriegel, p. 276.

233 ["afford sure ground"]: quoted in Cannon, p. 204; and see ibid., p. 204 fn. 6.

233 ["stand by his order"]: ibid., p. 231.

234 ["*half a loaf*"]: Cobbett and Hunt, "To the Reformers of the Whole Kingdom," July 11, 1829, quoted in Belchem, p. 195.

234 ["all the working classes"]: quoted in Brock, pp. 259, 250, respectively.

234 ["violent revolution"]: Francis Place, reporting a discussion with Lord Grey, quoted in Hamburger, *James Mill and the Art of Revolution*, p. 126.

234 ["shall have a commotion"]: quoted in LoPatin, p. 149.

234 ["staggered the politicians"]: Brock, p. 169.

235 ["Artisans in country places"]: ibid.

235 ["with the farmers"]: quoted in Sambrook, pp. 175–76; see also Spater, vol. 2, p. 503.

235 ["most dangerous body"]: quoted in LoPatin, p. 50.

235 ["preservation of tranquillity"]: quoted in Brock, p. 253.

235 [Cobbett on "Country Labourers" securing reform]: Sambrook, p. 175.

236 ["might have talked"]: Francis Place, quoted in Hamburger, *James Mill and the Art of Revolution*, p. 265.

237 ["manly bearing"]: quoted in Parry, p. 103.

237 [Irish poverty and literacy]: see Cormac Ó Gráda, "Poverty, Population, and Agriculture, 1801–45," in Moody et al., *A New History of Ireland*, vol. 5, pp. 108–36, esp. p. 110.

238 ["in the mainstream"]: MacDonagh, "Ideas and Institutions, 1830–1845," in ibid., vol. 5, pp. 193–217, quoted at p. 197.

238 ["as like prisons"]: quoted in Thompson, p. 267.

239 ["legal and ancient title"]: George Poulett Scrope, quoted in Brundage, *English Poor Laws*, p. 68.

240 ["ultimate fact"]: Parry, p. 134.

12. *The Negative of Liberty*

Robert Anstey, *The Atlantic Slave Trade and British Abolition, 1760–1810* (Atlantic Highlands, NJ: Humanities Press, 1975).

Hannah Barker and Elaine Chalus, eds., *Women's History: Britain, 1700–1850* (London: Routledge, 2005).

Ira Berlin, *Many Thousands Gone: The First Two Centuries of Slavery in North America* (Cambridge, MA: Belknap Press, 1998).

Robin Blackburn, *The Overthrow of Colonial Slavery, 1776–1848* (London: Verso, 1988).

Arianne Chernock, "Cultivating Woman: Men's Pursuit of Intellectual Equality in the Late British Enlightenment," *Journal of British Studies*, vol. 45, no. 3 (July 2006), pp. 511–31.

Harvey Chisick, *The Limits of Reform in the Enlightenment: Attitudes Toward the Education of the Lower Classes in Eighteenth-Century France* (Princeton: Princeton University Press, 1981).

William J. Cooper Jr., *The South and the Politics of Slavery, 1828–1856* (Baton Rouge: Louisiana State University Press, 1978).

David Brion Davis, *The Problem of Slavery in the Age of Revolution, 1770–1823* (New York: Oxford University Press, 1999).

———, *The Problem of Slavery in Western Culture* (Ithaca, NY: Cornell University Press, 1966).

John P. Diggins, "Slavery, Race, and Equality: Jefferson and the Pathos of the Enlightenment," *American Quarterly,* vol. 28, no. 2 (Summer 1976), pp. 206–28.

Seymour Drescher, "Whose Abolition? Popular Pressure and the Ending of the British Slave Trade," *Past & Present,* no. 143 (May 1994), pp. 136–66.

Stanley M. Elkins, *Slavery: A Problem in American Institutional and Intellectual Life,* 3rd ed. (Chicago: University of Chicago Press, 1976).

David Eltis and James Walvin, eds., *The Abolition of the Atlantic Slave Trade: Origins and Effects in Europe, Africa, and the Americas* (Madison: University of Wisconsin Press, 1981).

Joseph V. Femia, *Against the Masses: Varieties of Anti-Democratic Thought since the French Revolution* (New York: Oxford University Press, 2001).

Louis Filler, *The Crusade Against Slavery, 1830–1860* (New York: Harper & Brothers, 1960).

Paul Finkelman, "Jefferson and Slavery: 'Treason Against the Hopes of the World,'" in Peter S. Onuf, ed., *Jeffersonian Legacies* (Charlottesville: University Press of Virginia, 1993), pp. 181–221.

Betty Fladeland, "Abolitionist Pressures on the Concert of Europe, 1814–1822," *Journal of Modern History,* vol. 38, no. 4 (December 1966), pp. 355–73.

———, *Men and Brothers: Anglo-American Antislavery Cooperation* (Urbana: University of Illinois Press, 1972).

Eleanor Flexner and Ellen Fitzpatrick, *Century of Struggle: The Woman's Rights Movement in the United States* (Cambridge, MA: Belknap Press, 1996), part 1.

Eugene D. Genovese, *The Slaveholders' Dilemma: Freedom and Progress in Southern Conservative Thought, 1820–1860* (Columbia: University of South Carolina Press, 1992).

Gretchen Gerzina, *Black London: Life Before Emancipation* (New Brunswick, NJ: Rutgers University Press, 1995).

Paul Goodman, *Of One Blood: Abolitionism and the Origins of Racial Equality* (Berkeley: University of California Press, 1998).

David Allen Harvey, *The French Enlightenment and Its Others* (New York: Palgrave Macmillan, 2012).

Claudine Hunting, "The *Philosophes* and Black Slavery: 1748–1765," *Journal of the History of Ideas,* vol. 39, no. 3 (July–September 1978), pp. 405–18.

William S. Jenkins, *Pro-Slavery Thought in the Old South* (Chapel Hill: University of North Carolina Press, 1935).

Lawrence C. Jennings, *French Anti-Slavery: The Movement for the Abolition of Slavery in France, 1802–1848* (Cambridge: Cambridge University Press, 2000), ch. 1.

Linda Kerber, "The Republican Mother: Women and the Enlightenment—An American Perspective," *American Quarterly,* vol. 28, no. 2 (Summer 1976), pp. 187–205.

Paul Michael Kielstra, *The Politics of Slave Trade Suppression in Britain and France, 1814–1848: Diplomacy, Morality and Economics* (New York: St. Martin's Press, 2000).

V. G. Kiernan, *The Lords of Human Kind: Black Man, Yellow Man, and White Man in an Age of Empire* (New York: Columbia University Press, 1986).

Daniel Kilbride, "Slavery and Utilitarianism: Thomas Cooper and the Mind of the Old South," *Journal of Southern History,* vol. 59, no. 3 (August 1993), pp. 469–86.

Sarah Knott and Barbara Taylor, eds., *Women, Gender, and Enlightenment* (Basingstoke: Palgrave, 2005).

Peter Kolchin, "In Defense of Servitude: American Proslavery and Russian Proserfdom Arguments, 1760–1860," *American Historical Review,* vol. 85, no. 4 (October 1980), pp. 809–27.

———, *Unfree Labor: American Slavery and Russian Serfdom* (Cambridge, MA: Belknap Press, 1987).

Robert J. Loewenberg, "John Locke and the Antebellum Defense of Slavery," *Political Theory,* vol. 13, no. 2 (May 1985), pp. 266–91.

Waldo E. Martin Jr., *The Mind of Frederick Douglass* (Chapel Hill: University of North Carolina Press, 1984).

Henry Mayer, *All on Fire: William Lloyd Garrison and the Abolition of Slavery* (New York: St. Martin's Press, 1998).

Daniel J. McInerney, *The Fortunate Heirs of Freedom: Abolition & Republican Thought* (Lincoln: University of Nebraska Press, 1994).

Clare Midgley, *Women Against Slavery: The British Campaigns, 1780–1870* (London: Routledge, 1992), part 1.

Sylvia Neely, *Lafayette and the Liberal Idea, 1814–1824: Politics and Conspiracy in an Age of Reaction* (Carbondale: Southern Illinois University Press, 1991).

Richard S. Newman, *The Transformation of American Abolitionism: Fighting Slavery in the Early Republic* (Chapel Hill: University of North Carolina Press, 2002).

Karen O'Brien, *Women and Enlightenment in Eighteenth-Century Britain* (Cambridge: Cambridge University Press, 2009).

Harry C. Payne, *The Philosophes and the People* (New Haven: Yale University Press, 1976).

John Pollock, *Wilberforce* (London, Constable, 1977).

Candice E. Proctor, *Women, Equality, and the French, Revolution* (New York: Greenwood, 1990).

James A. Rawley, *London, Metropolis of the Slave Trade* (Columbia: University of Missouri Press, 2003).

Jane Rendall, *The Origins of Modern Feminism: Women in Britain, France, and the United States, 1780–1860* (New York: Schocken, 1984).

———, "Women and the Enlightenment in Britain c. 1690–1800," in Barker and Chalus, pp. 9–32.

Donald L. Robinson, *Slavery in the Structure of American Politics, 1765–1820* (New York: Harcourt Brace Jovanovich, 1971).

Louis Sala-Molins, *Dark Side of the Light: Slavery and the French Enlightenment,* John Conteh-Morgan, trans. (Minneapolis: University of Minnesota Press, 2006).

Beth A. Salerno, *Sister Societies: Women's Antislavery Organizations in Antebellum America* (DeKalb: Northern Illinois University Press, 2005).

Robert E. Shalhope, *The Roots of Democracy: American Thought and Culture, 1760–1800* (New York: Twayne, 1990).

Samia I. Spencer, ed., *French Women and the Age of the Enlightenment* (Bloomington: Indiana University Press, 1984).

Robert Stein, "The Revolution of 1789 and the Abolition of Slavery," *Canadian Journal of History,* vol. 17, no. 3 (December 1982), pp. 447–67.

Lieselotte Steinbrügge, *The Moral Sex: Woman's Nature in the French Enlightenment,* Pamela E. Selwyn, trans. (New York: Oxford University Press, 1995).

Hugh Thomas, *The Slave Trade* (New York: Simon & Schuster, 1997).

Larry E. Tise, *Proslavery: A History of the Defense of Slavery in America, 1701–1840* (Athens: University of Georgia Press, 1987).

David Turley, *The Culture of English Antislavery, 1780–1860* (London: Routledge, 1991).

James Walvin, *England, Slaves, and Freedom, 1776–1838* (Jackson: University Press of Mississippi, 1986).

———, *Questioning Slavery* (London: Routledge, 1996).

———, "Slavery," in Iain McCalman, ed., *An Oxford Companion to the Romantic Age: British Culture, 1776–1832* (New York: Oxford University Press, 1999), pp. 58–65.

Chilton Williamson, *American Suffrage: From Property to Democracy, 1760–1860* (Princeton: Princeton University Press, 1960).

Jean Fagan Yellin and John C. Van Horne, eds., *The Abolitionist Sisterhood: Women's Political Culture in Antebellum America* (Ithaca, NY: Cornell University Press, 1994).

* * *

241 ["populace which has only"]: quoted in Payne, p. 96.

241 ["every citizen"]: Webster, "On the Education of Youth in America" (1788), in Webster, *A Collection of Essays and Fugitive Writings* (Boston: I. Thomas and E. T. Andrews, 1790), pp. 1–37, quoted at p. 24.

241 ["to illuminate"]: Jefferson, "A Bill for the More General Diffusion of Knowledge" (1778), in Jefferson, *Papers*, Julian P. Boyd, ed. (Princeton: Princeton University Press, 1950–), vol. 2, pp. 526–33, quoted at p. 526.

242 ["the vulgar"]: Webster, *An American Dictionary of the English Language* (1828; republished by Foundation for American Christian Education, 1967).

242 ["To be sold"]: quoted in Walvin, *England, Slaves, and Freedom*, p. 32.

243 ["proud, lazy"]: quoted in ibid., p. 79.

243 ["scandal of religion"]: letter to William Wilberforce, February 24, 1791, in Wesley, *Letters*, George Eayrs, ed. (London: Hodder and Stoughton, 1915), pp. 489–90, quoted at p. 489.

243 ["If this is not an Evil"]: Ralph Sandiford, quoted in Davis, *Problem of Slavery in Western Culture*, p. 326.

243 ["vile and miserable"]: Locke, *Two Treatises of Government*, Peter Laslett, ed. (Cambridge: Cambridge University Press, 1988), p. 141 (*First Treatise*, ch. 1, §1).

243 ["*State of War*"]: ibid., p. 284 (*Second Treatise*, ch. 4, §24).

244 ["naturally inferior"]: Hume, "Of National Character," in Hume, *Philosophical Works*, T. H. Green and T. H. Grose, eds. (1882–86; reprinted by Scientia Verlag Aalen, 1964), pp. 244–58, quoted at p. 252 fn.

244 ["acquire no property"]: Smith, *An Inquiry into the Nature and Causes of the Wealth of Nations*, Edwin Cannan, ed. (New York: Modern Library, 1944), p. 418.

244 ["Permanent power"]: Hutcheson, *A System of Moral Philosophy* (1755), in Hutcheson, *Collected Works* (Hildesheim: Georg Olms Verlag, 1990), vol. 5, p. 301 (bk. 2, ch. 5, sect. 2).

245 ["rage for emancipation"]: entry of January 26, 1833, in Charles C. F. Greville, *The Greville Memoirs: A Journal of the Reigns of King George IV and King William IV*, Henry Reeve, ed. (New York: D. Appleton, 1887), vol. 2, p. 139.

245 ["Everything concurs"]: quoted in Hunting, p. 407.

245 ["To renounce liberty"]: Rousseau, *The Social Contract*, Henry J. Tozer and Susan Dunn, trans., in Rousseau, *The Social Contract* and *The First and Second Discourses*, Susan Dunn, ed. (New Haven: Yale University Press, 2002), p. 159 (bk. 1, ch. 4).

245 ["This is the price"]: Voltaire, *Candide: Or, Optimism*, Peter Constantine, trans. (New York: Modern Library, 2005), p. 64.

246 ["repugnant to the principles"]: quoted in Thomas, p. 585.

246 ["had much difficulty"]: Jennings, p. 20.

247 [U.S. slave-owner opposition to slave trade]: see Finkelman, pp. 201–2.

247 ["violations of human rights"]: Sixth Annual Message, December 2, 1806, in *The Complete Jefferson*, Saul K. Padover, ed. (New York: Tudor Publishing, 1943), pp. 421–26, quoted at p. 424.

247 [U.S. slave population, 1800–1820s]: U.S. Bureau of the Census, *Historical Statistics of the United States: From Colonial Times to 1957* (Washington, D.C.: U.S. Department of Commerce, 1960), p. 9 (A 60, 66, and fn. 1).

248 ["True patriotism"]: quoted in Proctor, p. 164.

248 ["weakness of mind"]: Wollstonecraft, *A Vindication of the Rights of Woman*, in Wollstonecraft, *Political Writings*, Janet Todd, ed. (Toronto: University of Toronto Press, 1993), quoted at pp. 276, 77, 293, 295, respectively.

248 ["good laws"]: quoted in Rendall, *Origins*, p. 239.

248 ["woman's intellect"]: Martineau, *Society in America*, 4th ed. (London: Saunders and Otley, 1837), vol. 2, p. 226.

249 ["all men and women"]: "Declaration of Sentiments," in Elizabeth Cady Stanton and Susan B. Anthony, *Selected Papers*, Ann D. Gordon, ed. (New Brunswick, NJ: Rutgers University Press, 1997–2013), vol. 1, pp. 78–82, quoted at pp. 78, 79.

249 ["sacred right"]: quoted in Flexner and Fitzpatrick, p. 71.

249 ["same sources"]: Douglass, "I Am a Radical Woman Suffrage Man," address at Boston, May 28, 1888, in Douglass, *Papers*, John Blassingame and John R. McKivigan, eds., series 1 (New Haven: Yale University Press, 1979–), vol. 5, pp. 378–87, quoted at p. 381.

249 ["more intellectual life"]: letter to Sidney Howard Gay, September 1847, in Douglass, *Life and Writings*, Philip S. Foner, ed. (New York: International Publishers, 1950–55), vol. 1, pp. 262–65, quoted at p. 264.

249 ["heart and conscience"]: Douglass, *Life and Times*, rev. ed. (1892; reprinted by Collier, 1962), p. 469.

250 ["imperious duty"]: quoted in Goodman, p. 231.

250 [Bentham on slavery]: Bentham, *Principles of the Civil Code*, in Bentham, *Theory of Legislation* (London: Kegan Paul, Trench, Trübner, 1904), p. 202 (pt. 3, ch. 2).

250 ["careful analysis"]: quoted in Kilbride, pp. 478, 481, 478, respectively.

250 ["broadest light"]: Hammond, "Two Letters on the Subject of Slavery in the United States," January 28 and March 24, 1845, in Hammond, *Selections from the Letters and Speeches*, Clyde N. Wilson, ed. (1866; reprinted by Reprint Company, 1978), pp. 114–98, quoted at pp. 172, 183, 152, respectively.

250 ["more heartfelt"]: ibid., pp. 184, 171, respectively.

251 ["Allow our slaves"]: ibid., p. 143.

251 ["our politics"]: in Wendell P. Garrison and Francis Jackson Garrison, *William Lloyd Garrison, 1805–1879* (Boston: Houghton, Mifflin, 1894), vol. 1, pp. 127–37, quoted at pp. 127, 132.

251 ["On our estates"]: Hammond, p. 149.

252 ["power of the master"]: Judge Ruffin, quoted in Elkin, p. 57 fn. 53.

252 ["far nearer the truth"]: Fitzhugh, *Sociology for the South; or The Failure of Free Society* (Richmond: A. Morris, 1854), p. 179; see also Wilentz, pp. 725–32.

252 ["nowhere in this broad Union"]: speech in the U.S. Senate, February 24, 1854, appendix to the *Congressional Globe,* 33rd Congress, 1st session, pp. 228–32, quoted at p. 230.

252 ["stir up"]: letter to Postmaster General Amos Kendall, August 9, 1835, in Jackson, *Correspondence,* John S. Bassett, ed. (Washington, D.C.: Carnegie Institution, 1926–35), vol. 5, pp. 360–61, quoted at p. 360.

253 ["All is safe"]: quoted in Robert V. Remini, *The Legacy of Andrew Jackson* (Baton Rouge: Louisiana State University Press, 1988), p. 110.

13. *The Transformation*

Anthony Arblaster, *The Rise and Decline of Western Liberalism* (Oxford: Basil Blackwell, 1984).

C. J. Arthur, *Dialectics of Labour: Marx and His Relation to Hegel* (Oxford: Basil Blackwell, 1986).

Franklin L. Baumer, "Intellectual History and Its Problems," *Journal of Modern History,* vol. 21, no. 3 (September 1949), pp. 191–203.

Carl L. Becker, *The Heavenly City of the Eighteenth-Century Philosophers* (New Haven: Yale University Press, 1932).

James H. Billington, *Fire in the Minds of Men: Origins of the Revolutionary Faith* (New York: Basic Books, 1980).

Jerome Blum, *In the Beginning: The Advent of the Modern Age—Europe in the 1840s* (New York: Charles Scribner's Sons, 1994).

———, *Lord and Peasant in Russia: From the Ninth to the Nineteenth Century* (Princeton: Princeton University Press, 1961).

Alexander Brady, *William Huskisson and Liberal Reform,* 2nd ed. (London: Frank Cass, 1967).

Tony Burns and Ian Fraser, eds., *The Hegel-Marx Connection* (New York: St. Martin's Press, 2000).

Nicholas Capaldi, *John Stuart Mill* (Cambridge: Cambridge University Press, 2004).

Ernst Cassirer, *The Philosophy of the Enlightenment,* Fritz C. A. Koelln and James P. Pettegrove, trans. (Princeton: Princeton University Press, 1951), esp. ch. 5.

Alfred Cobban, *In Search of Humanity: The Role of the Enlightenment in Modern History* (New York: Jonathan Cape, 1960).

Boris DeWiel, *Democracy: A History of Ideas* (Vancouver: UBC Press, 2000).

Graeme Duncan, *Marx and Mill: Two Views of Social Conflict and Social Harmony* (Cambridge: Cambridge University Press, 1973).

Louis Dupré, *The Enlightenment and the Intellectual Foundations of Modern Culture* (New Haven: Yale University Press, 2004).

Arthur A. Ekirch Jr., *The Idea of Progress in America, 1815–1860* (New York: Columbia University Press, 1944).

C. Hamilton Ellis, *British Railway History, 1830–1876* (London: George Allen and Unwin, 1954).

Richard A. Epstein, ed., *Classical Foundations of Liberty and Property* (New York: Garland, 2000).

Joseph V. Femia, *Against the Masses: Varieties of Anti-Democratic Thought since the French Revolution* (New York: Oxford University Press, 2001).

John Foster, *Class Struggle and the Industrial Revolution: Early Industrial Capitalism in Three English Towns* (London: Weidenfeld and Nicolson, 1974).

Charles Frankel, *The Faith of Reason: The Idea of Progress in the French Enlightenment* (New York: King's Crown Press, 1948).

Simon Garfield, *The Last Journey of William Huskisson* (London: Faber, 2002).

Peter Gay, *The Enlightenment: An Interpretation*, 2 vols. (New York: Alfred A. Knopf, 1966–69).

——, *The Party of Humanity* (New York: Alfred A. Knopf, 1964).

James Gilreath, ed., *Thomas Jefferson and the Education of a Citizen* (Washington, D.C.: Library of Congress, 1999).

Sarah H. Gordon, *Passage to Union: How the Railroads Transformed American Life, 1829–1929* (Chicago: Ivan R. Dee, 1996).

E. J. Hobsbawm, *The Age of Revolution, 1789–1848* (Cleveland: World Publishing, 1962).

Thomas A. Horne, *Property Rights and Poverty: Political Argument in Britain, 1605–1834* (Chapel Hill: University of North Carolina Press, 1990).

John R. Kellett, *The Impact of Railways on Victorian Cities* (London: Routledge & Kegan Paul, 1969).

Carl Landauer, *European Socialism: A History of Ideas and Movements* (Berkeley: University of California Press, 1959), vol. 1, parts 1–2.

Michael Levin, *Marx, Engels, and Liberal Democracy* (New York: St. Martin's Press, 1989).

——, *The Spectre of Democracy: The Rise of Modern Democracy as Seen by Its Critics* (New York: New York University Press, 1992).

Albert S. Lindemann, *A History of European Socialism* (New Haven: Yale University Press, 1983), ch. 3.

Alan Macfarlane, *The Riddle of the Modern World: Of Liberty, Wealth, and Equality* (New York: St. Martin's Press, 2000).

Harold Mah, *The End of Philosophy, the Origin of "Ideology": Karl Marx and the Crisis of the Young Hegelians* (Berkeley: University of California Press, 1987).

Pierre Manent, *An Intellectual History of Liberalism,* Rebecca Balinski, trans. (Princeton: Princeton University Press, 1994).

David McLellan, *Karl Marx* (New York: Harper & Row, 1973).

———, *The Young Hegelians and Karl Marx* (New York: Praeger, 1969).

J. G. Merquior, *Liberalism: Old and New* (Boston: Twayne, 1991).

John M. Merriman, "Contested Freedoms in the French Revolutions, 1830–1871," in Isser Woloch, ed., *Revolution and the Meanings of Freedom in the Nineteenth Century* (Palo Alto: Stanford University Press, 1996), pp. 173–211.

John Stuart Mill, *On Liberty,* David Bromwich and George Kateb, eds. (New Haven: Yale University Press, 2003).

Jennifer Nedelsky, *Private Property and the Limits of American Constitutionalism: The Madisonian Framework and Its Legacy* (Chicago: University of Chicago Press, 1990), esp. ch. 5.

R. R. Palmer, "The World Revolution of the West: 1763–1801," *Political Science Quarterly,* vol. 69, no. 1 (March 1954), pp. 1–14.

Ellen Frankel Paul and Howard Dickman, eds., *Liberty, Property, and the Foundations of the American Constitution* (Albany: State University of New York Press, 1989).

Harry C. Payne, *The Philosophes and the People* (New Haven: Yale University Press, 1976).

Zbigniew Pelczynski and John Gray, eds., *Conceptions of Liberty in Political Philosophy* (New York: St. Martin's Press, 1984).

Joseph Persky, "On the Thinness of the Utilitarian Defense of Private Property," *Journal of the History of Economic Thought,* vol. 32, no. 1 (March 2010), pp. 63–83.

John Plamenatz, *Karl Marx's Philosophy of Man* (Oxford: Clarendon Press, 1975).

———, *Man and Society,* 2 vols. (London: Longmans, Green, 1963).

J. R. Pole, *The Pursuit of Equality in American History,* rev. ed. (Berkeley: University of California Press, 1993).

John Rees, *Equality* (New York: Praeger, 1971).

John Phillip Reid, *The Concept of Liberty in the Age of the American Revolution* (Chicago: University of Chicago Press, 1988).

Guido de Ruggiero, *The History of European Liberalism,* R. G. Collingwood, trans. (New York: Oxford University Press, 1927).

Joseph M. Schwartz, *The Future of Democratic Equality: Rebuilding Social Solidarity in a Fragmented America* (London: Routledge, 2009).

Steven Seidman, *Liberalism and the Origins of European Social Theory* (Berkeley: University of California Press, 1983).

Jack Simmons, *The Victorian Railway* (New York: Thames and Hudson, 1991).

Darren Staloff, *Hamilton, Adams, Jefferson: The Politics of Enlightenment and the American Founding* (New York: Hill and Wang, 2005).

John F. Stover, *American Railroads* (Chicago: University of Chicago Press, 1961).

Trygve R. Tholfsen, *Ideology and Revolution in Modern Europe* (New York: Columbia University Press, 1984).

Nadia Urbinati and Alex Zakaras, eds., *J. S. Mill's Political Thought* (Cambridge: Cambridge University Press, 2007).

Sidney Verba and Gary R. Orren, *Equality in America: The View from the Top* (Cambridge, MA: Harvard University Press, 1985).

Henry Vyverberg, *Historical Pessimism in the French Enlightenment* (Cambridge, MA: Harvard University Press, 1958).

Jeremy Waldron, *The Right to Private Property* (New York: Oxford University Press, 1988).

Sean Wilentz, *The Rise of American Democracy: Jefferson to Lincoln* (New York: W. W. Norton, 2005).

Allen W. Wood, *Karl Marx*, 2nd ed. (London: Routledge, 2004).

Bernard Yack, *The Longing for Total Revolution: Philosophic Sources of Social Discontent from Rousseau to Marx and Nietzsche* (Princeton: Princeton University Press, 1986).

＊　＊　＊

254 ["government and legislature"]: quoted in Brady, p. 17; for Huskisson's accident, see Cyril B. Andrews, *The Railway Age* (New York: Macmillan, 1938), pp. 118–23; Elizabeth Longford, *Wellington: Pillar of State* (New York: Harper & Row, 1972), pp. 219–21; and Ellis, pp. 17–20.

255 ["to a jelly"]: quoted in Longford, p. 221.

255 ["Is then no nook"]: Wordsworth, "Sonnet: On the Projected Kendal and Windermere Railway" (1844), in Wordsworth, *Last Poems, 1821–1850,* Jared Curtis, ed. (Ithaca, NY: Cornell University Press, 1999), pp. 389–90 (lines 1–2).

255 [Miles of rail lines, 1840]: see Blum, *In the Beginning*, p. 10; L. Girdard, "Transport," in H. J. Habakkuk and M. Postan, eds., *The Industrial Revolutions and After*, vol. 6, pt. 1 of *The Cambridge Economic History of Europe* (Cambridge: Cambridge University Press, 1965), pp. 212–73, esp. pp. 228–49; and Blum, *Lord and Peasant*, p. 284.

256 ["Nothing can be"]: Locke, *An Essay Concerning Human Understanding,* Peter H. Nidditch, ed. (New York: Oxford University Press, 1975), p. 618 (bk. 4, ch. 9, §3).

256 ["'real' or fundamental"]: Arblaster, p. 15.

256 [Hobbes on man's unsociability]: see Hobbes, *Leviathan,* C. B. Macpherson, ed. (London: Penguin, 1985), pp. 223–28 (pt. 2, ch. 17).

256 ["every man against"]: ibid., p. 185 (pt. 1, ch. 3).

257 ["rampart raised"]: quoted in Horne, p. 179.

257 ["universally described"]: Mill, *Essay on Government* (1820), Currin V. Shields, ed. (New York: Liberal Arts Press, 1955), p. 89.

257 ["necessary aim"]: Constant, *Principles of Politics Applicable to All Representative Governments* (1815), in Constant, *Political Writings,* Biancamaria Fontana, ed. and trans. (Cambridge: Cambridge University Press, 1988), p. 215.

257 ["not by mere numbers"]: Macaulay, Speech on Parliamentary Reform, March 2, 1831, in Macaulay, *Speeches* (New York: Redfield, 1853), vol. 1, pp. 75–92, quoted at p. 79.

258 ["fight between life and death"]: Félicité de Lamennais, quoted in McMahon, p. 164.

258 ["*Enrichissez-vous*"]: François Guizot, quoted in Sperber, p. 65.

260 ["Oppressor and oppressed"]: Marx and Frederick Engels, *Manifesto of the Communist Party,* in Marx, *The Revolutions of 1848,* David Fernbach, ed. (New York: Random House, 1974), pp. 67–98, quoted at p. 68.

260 ["handmill gives you"]: Marx, *The Poverty of Philosophy* (Moscow: Foreign Languages Publishing House, n.d.), p. 105 (ch. 2, sect. 1, 'Second Observation').

260 ["ideas that revolutionize"]: Marx and Engels, *Manifesto,* p. 85.

260 ["philosophers have only"]: Marx, "Theses on Feuerbach," in Marx and Frederick Engels, *Selected Works* (New York: International Publishers, 1968), pp. 28–30, quoted at p. 30 (Thesis 1).

261 ["mutilate the laborer"]: Marx, *Capital: A Critique of Political Economy,* Samuel Moore and Edward Aveling, trans. (New York: Modern Library, 1936), p. 708.

261 ["something extraneous"]: Marx and Engels, *The German Ideology,* in Marx and Engels, *Collected Works* (New York: International Publishers, 1975–), vol. 5, p. 79.

262 ["merit and demerit"]: Mill, review of Francis William Newman, *Lectures on Political Economy, Westminster Review,* vol. 56 (October 1851), pp. 83–101, in Mill, *Collected Works,* John M. Robson et al., eds. (Toronto: University of Toronto Press, 1963–91), vol. 5, pp. 439–57, quoted at p. 444.

262 ["trampling, crushing"]: Mill, *Principles of Political Economy,* in ibid., vol. 3, p. 754.

262 ["herd of vulgar"]: Marx, *Capital,* p. 669 fn. 1.

262 ["unlikeness of one man"]: Mill, review of Tocqueville's *Democracy in America, Edinburgh Review,* vol. 72 (October 1840), pp. 1–83, in Mill, *Collected Works,* vol. 18, pp. 153–204, quoted at p. 197.

262 ["combination of rich men"]: letter to Edward Herford, January 22, 1850, in ibid., vol. 14, pp. 43–45, quoted at p. 44.

262 ["individual's own energies"]: ibid., vol. 3, p. 982 fn. (Appendix A).

262 ["general practice"]: ibid., vol. 3, pp. 944–45.

262 ["exclusive & engrossing"]: letter to Gustave d'Eichtal, May 15, 1829, in ibid., vol. 12, pp. 30–34, quoted at pp. 31, 32.

262 ["brutish ignorance"]: Mill, "A Letter to the Earl of Durham on Reform in Parliament, by Paying the Elected," *London and Westminster Review,* vol. 32 (April 1839), pp. 475–508, in ibid., vol. 6, pp. 465–95, quoted at p. 488.

262 ["social tyranny"]: Mill, *On Liberty,* in ibid., vol. 18, p. 220.

263 ["What is right"]: Mill, "Pledges [2]," *Examiner,* July 15, 1832, pp. 449–51, in ibid., vol. 23, pp. 496–504, quoted at p. 502.

263 ["people ought to be"]: Mill, review of Tocqueville's *Democracy in America, London Review,* vol. 1 (October 1835), pp. 85–129, in ibid., vol. 18, pp. 47–90, quoted at p. 72.

264 ["understand his duties"]: Report of the Commissioners for the University of Virginia, August 4, 1818, in Jefferson, *Selected Writings* (New York: Library of America, 2011), pp. 131–47, quoted at p. 133.

264 ["to the rising generation"]: letter to the Marquis de Chastellux, June 7, 1785, in Jefferson, *Papers,* Julian P. Boyd, ed. (Princeton: Princeton University Press, 1950–), vol. 8, pp. 184–86, quoted at p. 184.

265 ["natural Equality"]: letter to Jefferson, July 13, 1813, in Lester J. Cappon, ed., *The Adams-Jefferson Letters* (Chapel Hill: University of North Carolina Press, 1959), vol. 2, pp. 354–56, quoted at p. 355.

265 ["have our sex"]: note to her sister, Elizabeth Shaw Peabody, July 17, 1799, quoted in Page Smith, *John Adams* (Garden City, NY: Doubleday, 1962), vol. 2, p. 1006.

265 ["source of revolution"]: letter to Thomas Adams, October 17, 1799, quoted in ibid., vol. 2, pp. 1016–17.

266 ["whether societies"]: Hamilton, Federalist No. 1, in Jacob E. Cooke, ed., *The Federalist* (Middletown, CT: Wesleyan University Press, 1961), pp. 1–7, quoted at p. 1.

266 ["collected wisdom"]: "Circular to the States," June 8, 1783, in Washington, *Writings,* John C. Fitzpatrick, ed. (Washington, D.C.: U.S. Government Printing Office, 1931–44), vol. 26, pp. 483–96, quoted at p. 485.

266 ["endless variety"]: Washington, "Farewell Address" (published September 19, 1796), in ibid., vol. 35, pp. 214–38, quoted at pp. 226, 227.

266 ["hope of civilized men"]: Gay, vol. 2, p. 567.

267 ["In proportion"]: Washington, "Farewell Address," p. 230.

267 ["Institutions for"]: ibid.

268 ["great equalizer"]: quoted in Ekirch, p. 196.

270 ["free hearts"]: Tennyson, "Ulysses," in Tennyson, *Poetry,* Robert W. Hill Jr., ed., 2nd ed. (New York: W. W. Norton, 1999), pp. 82–84, quoted at p. 83 (lines 49, 31–32, 54–61, respectively).

Acknowledgments

Fire and Light has been long in the making, and I am deeply grateful to the colleagues, friends, and family members who helped me over the years bring this project to fruition.

I owe special thanks to my agents, Ike Williams and Katherine Flynn, and their colleague Hope Denekamp, who inspired me with their enthusiasm for *Fire and Light* and whose excellent advice helped propel it toward completion.

At Thomas Dunne Books, the critical wisdom of editors Thomas Dunne and Peter Wolverton contributed to significant improvements in the book. Associate editor Anne Brewer was unfailingly helpful and patient in coaxing the manuscript through the publication process. Creative and meticulous, production editor David Stanford Burr guided the book across the finish line. Janet Byrne was a skillful copy editor, sharp-eyed and judicious.

My daughter Deborah Burns, after reading a late version of the manuscript, made many important and substantive suggestions. I am also very grateful to Jo-Ann Irace, head of Access Services, and her staff at the Williams College Library. Alison O'Grady at Interlibrary Loan reeled in the most obscure works from the remotest places. Also at Williams, faculty secretary Robin Keller cheerfully provided her useful assistance.

Finally, the dedication to *Fire and Light* reflects my deepest appreciation to Milton Djuric, whose expert research and editorial assistance from the first days of work on this project was extensive and indispensable, and to Susan Dunn, whose insightful historical and literary contributions to this study as well as the constant encouragement she warmly offered were, once again, invaluable to me.

Index